The History of
ISRAEL

THE HISTORY OF
ISRAEL

VOLUME I
From the Beginning to the Exile

GIUSEPPE RICCIOTTI

TRANSLATED BY

CLEMENT DELLA PENTA, O.P., S.T.Lr., Ph.D.
AND
RICHARD T. A. MURPHY, O.P., S.T.D., S.S.D.

SECOND EDITION

THE BRUCE PUBLISHING COMPANY
MILWAUKEE

IMPRIMI POTEST:
    EDWARD L. HUGHES, O.P., S.T.M.,
    Prior Provincialis

NIHIL OBSTAT:
    JOHN A. SCHULIEN, S.T.D.,
    Censor librorum

IMPRIMATUR:
    ✠ ALBERTUS G. MEYER,
    Archiepiscopus Milwauchiensis

Die 27a ianuarii, 1955

Library of Congress Catalog Card Number: 58–11751

© 1958, THE BRUCE PUBLISHING COMPANY
MADE IN THE UNITED STATES OF AMERICA
(Second Printing — 1958)

CORDI
IMMACULATO
BEATAE VIRGINIS MARIAE

PREFACE

Since its publication in 1933 and 1934 Ricciotti's *Storia d'Israele* has gone through four editions. The fact that it was quickly translated into French and Spanish serves to indicate the welcome that awaited it on the Continent. In America all to whom the original Italian was no obstacle used and appreciated it almost at once. Its appearance in English now makes it possible for a much larger audience to satisfy its hunger for knowledge about the history of God's dealings with the Chosen People.

This HISTORY OF ISRAEL, moreover, fills in what has been a lamentable gap in the field of Catholic scriptural literature in English. Up to the present, English-speaking Catholics have had little to appeal to in this field, aside from manuals of general or special introduction, and, more recently, the *Catholic Biblical Quarterly* and the English periodical *Scripture*.

Thus there has never been, in English, anything that quite compares with the famous histories of Wellhausen, Kittel, Renan, or Loisy, to mention only a few of the foreign authors whose works have influenced thought even in America. Most of these works were written according to principles which for Catholics were wholly or in part inadmissible, and the conclusions, naturally, were often such that Catholics could not and would not allow them.

The importance and the timeliness of this HISTORY OF ISRAEL, therefore, is easy to grasp. It was written by a Catholic priest well trained in oriental languages, familiar with the Holy Land, thoroughly acquainted with non-Catholic literature, and able to appreciate the complexities of the problems raised by the Bible and the new discoveries of historians and archaeologists. His work is somewhat unique in this latter respect, in that it so faithfully evaluates and assimilates what is good in the findings of modern archaeology.

Add to these qualifications the facts that the author writes easily and interestingly, tells the story simply, and keeps it moving. Disputed points are presented as disputed points and are discussed calmly and reasonably. A sense of proportion is one of the chief features of the book;

the author avoids pet subjects and beloved theories, whether his own or another's, and provides the reader with the facts necessary for the formation of a personal judgment in disputed cases.

To present this already famous work in English dress it was necessary, in view of recent discoveries and developments, to introduce a number of changes into the text. These for the most part had to do with archaeology, whose restless spade provides scholars with a constantly increasing amount of material to fit into their picture of history. Startling good fortune has attended the work of the investigators in the past few years, notably the discoveries at Qumran and Murabba'at. Other changes concerned dates, or the progress of excavations, but the text remains substantially that of the fourth Italian edition.

The present translation was the work of three men. Father Patrick Skehan of Catholic University had translated most of the first section, which deals with archaeology and the history of Israel's neighbors, when Father Della Penta signified his willingness to complete the laborious task. Once this was done, Father Murphy prepared the manuscript for publication.

Ricciotti's *History* was primarily intended to be a work of *haute vulgarization*. The informed reader will quickly notice that the author has more than a mere nodding acquaintance with the literature pertinent to his subject, and that his awareness of major trends and directions is such as to inspire confidence in his competence. To the author's own references to German, French, and other writings, there have now been added numerous references to more modern sources, notably to the *Revue Biblique, The Biblical Archaeologist*, Pritchard's *Ancient Near Eastern Texts*, and to other works. It is, of course, quite impossible to keep abreast of the current literature on the Dead Sea Scrolls, the definitive evaluation of which has not yet been reached, and the same may be said of the excavations at Jericho. Enough has been added, it is thought, to help the reader form a reasonably adequate picture of the present situation of Old Testament biblical studies.

The citations from Scripture which appear in the text may be mentioned here, for they are not always the familiar quotations, being direct translations from the Hebrew or Greek texts. (For *Genesis* and *Exodus* the Confraternity text has been followed.) The somewhat variant nature of these quotations as compared with the older and more familiar ones can hardly cause surprise after the publication of the *Divino afflante Spiritu*, in which the Holy Father Pope Pius XII earnestly recommended that Catholic scholars avail themselves of the conclusions of modern biblical research, and make their own the more perfected techniques governing the understanding of ancient languages and modes of composi-

tion. It is gratifying to be able to observe that Dom Ricciotti has faithfully fulfilled and, in a sense, anticipated this paternal directive.

With the publication of this HISTORY OF ISRAEL, then, English readers
now have at their disposal something to oppose to the infamous trilogy
of Renan. It is fervently hoped that Ricciotti's HISTORY OF ISRAEL will,
along with his *Life of Christ* and his *Paul the Apostle,* exercise a greater
influence for good than Renan's three works on the same topics exercised
for evil. Renan is long since dead and is in the process of being forgotten; the Ricciotti trilogy, of which the HISTORY OF ISRAEL forms an important part, will have a much longer life, for it constantly bears in mind
Him for whom that history was but the preparation.

Sincere thanks are hereby extended to all who have collaborated in
this work, first of all to that Nestor of Palestinian archaeology, Père
Vincent of the Ecole Biblique, who has graciously given permission for
the use of his excellent maps of Jerusalem, particularly the contour map
of the Holy City; to Père de Vaux, for information pertinent to Qumran
and Murabba'at; to Fathers Considine and McDonnell for their valuable
assistance in preparing the manuscript; and to the editors of The Bruce
Publishing Company for their edifying patience and co-operation.

M.

ABBREVIATIONS

ANET — Ancient Near Eastern Texts (ed. by J. B. Pritchard)

AO — Altorientalische Texte zum A. T.[2] (H. Gressmann et al.)

BA — The Biblical Archaeologist

BASOR — Bulletin of the American School of Oriental Research

CBQ — Catholic Biblical Quarterly

DBS — Dictionnaire de la Bible (Vigoroux), Supplément

JNES — Journal of Near Eastern Studies

RB — Revue Biblique

CONTENTS

LIST OF MAPS

CONTENTS

LIST OF TABLES

The History of
ISRAEL

BABYLONIA AND ASSYRIA

1. The territory held by the Babylonians and the Assyrians extended from the Persian Gulf, which in ancient times penetrated farther inland than it does today, northward toward the mountains of Armenia (Urartu). At the south it included the region from the Euphrates across and beyond the Tigris; in the north, from far to the west of the Tigris — practically from the Euphrates — through the entire drainage basins of the Great and the Little Zab. The line of demarcation between the two districts came at about the point where the Tigris and the Euphrates are closest, somewhat to the north of modern Bagdad.

Bordering this territory to the east, from south to north, were Elam (Elamtu), and then the Persian or Iranian plateau, on which dwelt the Cassites (Kasshu) and, more to the north, the Medes (Manda). On the west, the Babylonian-Assyrian territory was hemmed in again from south to north, by the Syrian Desert, then by the districts of the Amorites (Amurru: § 47 ff.) and of the Mitanni.

The south of Babylonia was called Sumer (Shumer), and its northern part Akkad (Akkadu); at a late period, after the rise to power (625 B.C.) of the Chaldean dynasty which originated from the southerly tribe of the Kaldu, both parts together were called Chaldea. Assyria was called Subartu.

2. Of the Babylonian cities whose antiquity is greatest, the following are of principal interest for the present purpose. Uru, the biblical "Ur of the Chaldees" (now Muqayyar), was near the ancient northern

1

limit of the Persian Gulf; it was a center of worship of the moon-god,
Sin, and contained a celebrated temple area (*egishshirgal*) including a
tower (§ 394). More to the north was Uruk (modern Warka), the Erech
of the Bible; the Babylonian hero Gilgamesh (§ 184) is alleged to have
been its king. Still farther to the north was Shuruppak (today Fara),
the home of Utnapishtim, the Babylonian deluge hero (§ 184). About
a hundred miles northwest of Ur, and near where the two rivers are
closest, was Babel (Bab-ili, "gate of god") or Babylon, the chief city of
the entire country, whose importance dates from approximately the time
of its king Hammurabi (§ 4). Here the principal temple, *Esagila*, "House
whose top is lofty," was dedicated to the god Marduk; a little to
the north of it was the highest tower in Babylon, called *Etemenanki*,
"House of the foundation of heaven and earth" (§ 394). Other very old
cities, of great significance in Babylonian history were, from south to

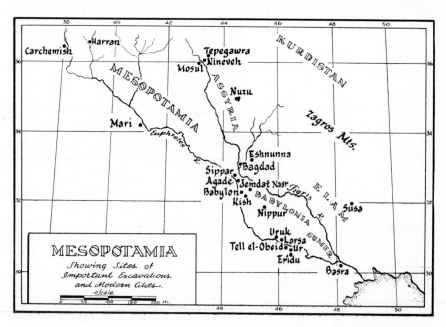

north, Eridu, Larsa, Lagash, Nippur, Kish, Borsippa, Akkad (Agade).
Of the cities of Assyria, the most important for biblical history are
Asshur, on the upper reaches of the Tigris between the confluence of
the Lower Zab and that of the Upper Zab; farther north on the Tigris,
Nineve (Ninua, now Kuyunjik), the rival metropolis of Babylon; and
much more to the west, on the Balikh, a tributary of the Euphrates,
Harran, the Charan of the Bible, another center of worship for the
moon-god, Sin (§ 123).

3. Babylonia and Assyria have separate histories, though their relations, considerable throughout the third and second millennia B.C., become extremely close from the end of the second millennium onward.

Already at the beginning of the fourth millennium B.C. there were settled in Babylonia two peoples of different race: the Sumerians to the south, the Akkadians in the north. The Sumerians, of non-Semitic stock, had migrated into Babylonia as well as into Elam and Assyria from parts unknown, perhaps during the fifth millennium. The Akkadians, on the other hand, were Semites who, in the earliest period, appear as culturally inferior to the Sumerians. As far back as one can go, the Sumero-Akkadian territory was governed by local dynasties which took their names from the cities of their origin. These ruled for varying periods but their authority fluctuated in its extent. Leaving out of account the "antediluvian" dynasties, for which the figures are fantastic, there were several dynasties at Kish and at Erech, as well as others at Ur, Lagash, and elsewhere. Outstanding was the dynasty of Agade (Akkad), founded after the middle of the third millennium by Sargon (Sharru-kin: 2360 B.C.? § 203). This marked the predominance of the Semitic element in the population; of the rulers during the two centuries or so the dynasty lasted, one was the conqueror Naram-Sin (2280 B.C.?). When later the region was overrun by the barbarian Guti, Babylonian culture found refuge in Lagash, and flourished there during the prosperous reign of Gudea. After the Guti were driven out, the Sumerian dynasty of Ur came to power, and extended its sway beyond Harran as far as the Assyrian colonies in Cappadocia (§ 45). It was followed in turn by the Semitic dynasties of Isin and of Larsa, and eventually by the likewise Semitic (Amorite) dynasty known as the First Dynasty of Babylon, founded (1830 B.C.?) by Sumu-Abum.[1]

4. The most illustrious king of this dynasty was its fifth ruler, Hammurabi, who governed from about 1728 to 1686 B.C. He managed to unite under his rule all of Babylonia; its northern part he took from the Elamite Rim-Sin of Larsa, who had previously overcome the Isin dynasty and seized its capital city. Hammurabi then directed his arms against Emutbal and against Elam, which had supported Rim-Sin, in two eastern campaigns during the eighth and thirtieth years of his reign (1721; 1699?). Other expeditions carried his authority to the northwest halfway up the Euphrates, and northward along the Tigris in the land of Subartu (Assyria) to the neighborhood of Urartu (Armenia). He was a shrewd administrator with pronounced initiative. He dug canals which were vital to the Babylonian irrigation system, built temples of renown, and caused his name to be linked to that famous collection of laws based

---

[1] For the correlations on which the dates in §§ 3–6 are based, cf. W. F. Albright, "A Third Revision of the Early Chronology of Western Asia," in BASOR, 1942, 28–36.

The temple tower of Ur of the Chaldees. (*Enciclopedia Italiana.*)

on earlier Sumerian models, which was intended to harmonize the separate legal systems of the Sumerian and the Semitic people — the Code of Hammurabi (§§ 246, 274).

5. The golden era of Hammurabi was followed by a speedy decline. Various local dynasties set up revolts against the capital. A rival regime, which was to last for some two centuries, arose in the prevailingly Sumerian district to the south along the shores of the Persian Gulf (the "Sea-land"); at the same time a first invasion of Cassites (§ 1) swept into the kingdom and laid it waste — all this scarcely ten years after Hammurabi's death. The country remained in a disturbed condition, with the Babylonian dynasty growing weaker and weaker, until an invasion of Hittites (§ 44 ff.) coming down the Euphrates from the northwest overturned it altogether (1550 B.C.?)

6. In the time of Agum II, about the year 1520 B.C., the Cassite dynasty was firmly established in Babylon; it then endured for some 350 years, and succeeded after a time (1475 B.C.?) in removing from the scene Ea-Gamil, last king of the "Sea-land" dynasty. However, the Cassite period in general was one of cultural and political decline, partly because the semibarbarian overlords came to appreciate the civilization of Babylonia only very slowly, and partly by reason of strong new nationalities that pressed threateningly against the borders. Egypt towered hugely in the west; and farther north the Mitanni and the Hittites were conducting raids. Closer to home, Assyria rudely repulsed every move of Babylon to maintain control, and was scarcely kept in check by the diplomatic marriages which linked her to the Babylonian royal house; Elam loomed as an equal menace on the east. This was the

portentous "Amarna period" (§ 43 ff.). Despite the adroitness of Babylonian policy, conflict with Assyria could not be prevented; and the Cassites, several times defeated in the fourteenth and thirteenth centuries, were finally crushed by an Elamite invasion (1150 B.C.) in the course of the war with Assyria.

7. The subsequent history of Babylonia, which comes to us in a confused and fragmentary manner, bears witness more and more to the hegemony of Assyria, with the occasional intervention of Elam. From this time until the rise of the Chaldean dynasty Babylon is overshadowed by Nineve and emerges only spasmodically from its obscurity. The Cassite dynasty was followed by that of Pashe, the fourth Babylonian dynasty, also known as the second dynasty of Isin; this lasted through one hundred thirty-two years (1170–1038) with eleven kings, of whom most noteworthy was Nabukudurri-usur I (Nabuchodonosor I), who conquered Elam only to be overcome in turn by Assyria. Then came the "Sea-land" dynasty, the second to be so named; its three (or five?) kings ruled for twenty-one years. The sixth dynasty, of Basu, similarly lasted only a score of years, with three kings. Next an Elamite, Mar-biti-apal-usur, ruled for five or six years as the sole king of the seventh dynasty. He was followed by an eighth Babylonian dynasty, under which raids by the Arameans (§ 49 ff.) afflicted the country and prepared it for complete subjection to Assyria, in spite of appeals to Elam for support.

8. In 732 Nabu-shum-ukin, last king of the eighth dynasty, was killed

Palace of Sargon. (*Enciclopedia Italiana.*)

in a revolt prompted by Ukin-zer (Nabu-mukin-zer), head of the Chaldean tribe of Bit-Ammukkani, who then mounted the throne of Babylon. With the latter the cuneiform documents begin a new dynasty, the ninth; this in fact was entirely Assyrian, for the Assyrian Tiglath-pileser III (745–727) intervened after having repelled the Arameans (§ 450), defeated the tribes which were supporting the new ruler, and seized the Babylonian scepter for himself (729). In the cuneiform texts he is called Pulu (§ 450 ff.).

His successor, Salmanassar V (727–722; § 455), called Ululai by the Babylonians, continued as king of the joint domain of Assyria and Babylonia. Scarcely had Sargon (722–705; § 455 ff.) mounted the Assyrian throne when revolt broke out in Babylonia under the captaincy of Marduk-apaliddina (the biblical Merodach-baladan), chief of the other Chaldean tribe of Bit-Yakin, who had been subject to Tiglath-pileser III, but now rose as the representative of Chaldean nationalism. With assistance from the ever warlike Elam, he seized the throne of Babylon in 721. The following year, Sargon took action, moving first against Elam, but with little success. He may even have suffered a real defeat, and in any case was obliged to withdraw. This gave rise at once to other rebellions, both in the north and in the east of his kingdom. Sargon left the Babylonian rebels in possession for the time being, and put down all the other insurgents in an uninterrupted series of campaigns among which those of 720 and of 711 merit particular mention. In the former, which ended with the battle of Raphia (§ 458), he overcame a coalition of Philistines and Syrians reinforced by Sib'e, *turtan* of Egypt (§ 37); Ezechias, king of Juda, was involved (§ 488) in the campaign of 711 against Ashdod. Finally in 710 Sargon was free to turn against Babylon, which he made subject once more, without, however, taking the title of king, for which he substituted the more ancient designation of *shakkanaku* (governor). Merodach-baladan was left in possession of his territory of Bit-Yakin, to which he had fled; and he remained there to the end of Sargon's reign.

9. He came to the fore again, however, as soon as Sennacherib (705–681) ascended the throne. The new Assyrian monarch was in fact the true ruler of Babylonia in the first two years of his reign (705–703); and he is so listed in the Babylonian annals. But since the appropriate religious ceremony of "taking the hands of Bel" was not carried out his authority was not official, and hence he is not included in the canon of Ptolemy. During this "interregnum" Merodach-baladan laid his plans and sought alliances against Assyria on all sides of that nation. From the military point of view Elam was his strongest ally; more interesting for the history of Israel was the far-off king of Juda, Ezechias (§ 489). Meanwhile it seems that the Babylonians were unsympathetic toward the Chaldean chieftain; they set on the

Excavated Babylon. (From Koldewey, *Das wiederstehende Babylon.*)

throne officially one Marduk-zakir-shum II (703), who ruled for only one month before Merodach-baladan stepped in with the help of Elam and took the scepter for himself. Sennacherib also took the field that year, defeating the Elamites, entering Babylon victoriously, and setting up Bel-ibni as its ruler. Merodach-baladan took refuge in his own territory and soon began his intrigues anew, taking advantage of the ineptitude of Bel-ibni and the absence of Sennacherib, who was engaged in his Palestinian campaign. But once more the Assyrian army, perhaps under the direction of Ashur-nadin-shum, son of Sennacherib, stemmed the tide of Babylonian revolt; it now drove Merodach-baladan out of even his own Bit-Yakin, forcing him to flee to Elam. Ashur-nadin-shum was placed on the Babylonian throne (700). Meanwhile Sennacherib himself had been victorious in Palestine, over a league encouraged by the Pharaoh Shabaka (§ 38) to rebel against Assyria; its principals were Luli, king of Sidon, and Ezechias, king of Juda. Sennacherib quickly defeated Luli and reduced Phoenicia and Philistia; then he faced the Egyptian army coming to the support of the league, and routed it completely in battle at Eltekeh, near Accaron (700). Finally he turned against Ezechias of Juda (§ 490 ff.).

10. Despite all this, Babylonia was still not pacified. Though Merodach-baladan seems not to have survived very long, since later we find his son Sam'una ruling Bit-Yakin, his intrigues and those of his party called for action on a grand scale against Elam, the main-

Towers of the Gate of Ishtar of Babel.

spring of the rebellion. This campaign began in 694, and continued over a number of years because of the wide scope of the conflict. A fleet was sent down the Euphrates and into the Persian Gulf, against the Elamite coast, to take the enemy by surprise. Hallushu, then king of Elam, counterattacked on the flank by striking against Babylon. Apparently he surprised and captured Asshur-nadin-shum, for whom he substituted Nergal-ushezib, probably a member of the Chaldean party, as king of Babylon. The new ruler was, however, in turn overcome and imprisoned after eighteen months (693) by the Assyrians striking overland. He was succeeded by Mushezib-Marduk; despite the vigilance of the Assyrian officials, this king continued the Chaldeo-Elamite policies. Hostilities soon broke out again (692); Mushezib-Marduk fled to Elam to join its then reigning king, Umman-menanu, and other peoples in a general attack on Assyria. The forces met at Halule, near Bagdad, in a clash so fierce that throughout the year 690 neither side was in a position to reap the benefits of the victory it claimed. Then in the beginning of 689 Umman-menanu was stricken with apoplexy, and his administration gave up its interest in the affairs of Babylonia. Sennacherib besieged Babylon and in a few months took it by storm. Those of its inhabitants who survived the slaughter were taken prisoner with their king, the city was razed to the ground, and to make the destruction more complete a canal was turned from its course so as to flow over the ruins. Sennacherib adopted the title of "king of Sumer and Akkad"; but as in the former instance, and for the same reason, the canon of Ptolemy treats this period (689–681) also as an "interregnum." During these years Assarhaddon acted as the vice-regent for his father, Sennacherib, until the latter's death (§ 498); he was supported by his mother Naqi'a, who was probably a Babylonian.

11. Under Assarhaddon (681–669) Babylon was rebuilt, and civic reorganization was advanced considerably, despite the constant dis-

turbances raised by the Chaldean tribes in the south and of the unremitting intrigues of Elam. The year 671 saw Assarhaddon's victorious campaign in Egypt (§ 39). Toward the end of his life he took cognizance of the differing factions at the court by appointing as hereditary prince (*marsharri*) of Assyria his son Ashurbanipal (the Sardanapalus of the Greeks) and by according to his other son, Shamash-shum-ukin, a like position for Babylonia; when he died this division was actually carried out. Ashurbanipal (669–c. 633), from whom comes much of our knowledge of Assyro-Babylonian civilization (§ 484), recognized (668) his brother Shamash-shum-ukin as king of Babylonia, but with a government kept constantly under the closest surveillance from Assyria. Matters continued thus for some years, but the latent cleavage, made increasingly more profound by the growing preponderance of the Chaldean element in Babylonia, at last issued into open revolt. About 653 Shamash-shum-ukin went over to the Chaldean cause and became the head of a huge anti-Assyrian coalition which included Babylonia, Elam, various Chaldean, Arab, and Aramean peoples to the east and north, and in the west Egypt and several principalities in Palestine. Military operations began in the following year, and met with a prompt resistance from Assyria. The Assyrian counterattack proved long and arduous; it succeeded, nevertheless, in removing from the conflict, one after another, all the members of the coalition. Against Egypt in particular there had already been two victorious campaigns, in 667 and 663 (§ 40); in 648 it was Babylon's turn, and the Chaldean metropolis fell that year after about two years of siege, more from hunger than by assault. Shamash-shum-ukin, rather than surrender, came to the end which later legend ascribed to his brother Sardanapalus, casting himself into the flames which consumed his palace. Babylon was promptly restored, and Ashurbanipal placed on its throne a certain Kandalanu (648–626), who remained completely dependent on Assyria.

12. The death of the Assyrian conqueror gave rise to renewed disorders, this time with fateful consequences.[2] Important territories, among them Media to the north and Babylonia to the south, broke loose from Assyria during the insignificant reign of Ashurbanipal's son, Ashur-etil-ilani, whose continuance was due to the intervention of Sin-shum-lishir (626–619). When Kandalanu disappeared from the scene, Nabopolassar (Nabu-apla-usur), a man of certain Chaldean origin, was already seated upon the throne of Babylon; in his inscriptions he delights to call himself "son of nobody." His kingdom in the first years of his reign (625–605) must have been quite small, for contemporary documents give evidence

---

[2] The persons and events of this period, with their dates, have been reviewed recently by W. H. Dubberstein, "Assyrian-Babylonian Chronology," 669–612 B.C., in *JNES*, 3, 1944, 38–42.

of Assyrian troops and functionaries at various points on Babylonian soil.[3]

In these years, it would seem, the enterprising Chaldean gathered forces and arranged alliances for the launching of his attack. The attack itself began in 616, and was carried out at first by Nabopolassar alone, in several campaigns from the south. In one expedition along the Euphrates he had even to deal with serious opposition on the part of an Egyptian army sent against him by the Pharaoh Psammetichus, who had become an ally of the Assyrians; but in 614, toward the close of the reign of Sin-shar-ishkun, the last king to sit on a throne at Nineve (619–612), the attacks from the south were seconded by others from the north, and Assyria was threatened on both sides at once.

13. From across the bordering mountains on the northeast, a young people of Aryan stock had for some time been casting hungry glances at the rich Mesopotamian valleys, and stood poised for invasion. These were the Medes, who had already made difficulties for Ashurbanipal and forced him to take up arms against them. United now under the energetic leadership of Cyaxares (Uvakhshatra), and reinforced by Cimmerian and Scythian hordes, they saw that the opportune time had come to swoop down upon Assyria. The similarity of their goals brought about an alliance in 615 between Nabopolassar and Cyaxares. With his hordes of the *Umman-manda*,[4] Cyaxares in 614 came under the very walls of Nineve; but the meeting with the army of his southern ally took place too late. In the following year the attack was pressed once more. The city was besieged, and it fell in the month of Ab (July-August) of the year 612. Apparently the king of Assyria perished by casting himself into the flames; the great metropolis, for a time the chief city of western Asia, was destroyed forever, so effectively that not long afterward even the recollection of where it had been faded away.

14. A nucleus of Assyrian fighting men escaped the slaughter and fled under the leadership of Ashur-uballit II, the last king of Assyria, to the fortified city of Harran (§ 2), from which the Assyrians had once ruled the Syrian west. Nabopolassar first subdued the other Assyrian cities and then, in 610, turned against Harran, once more with the assistance of the Umman-manda. In the month Ada (February-March) of the year 609 Harran fell into his hands; in the month Elul (August-September) of the same year he defeated an Egyptian army sent to the aid of Ashur-uballit by the Pharaoh Nechao II, which had combined with the remnants of the Assyrian forces a short time before (§ 519). From this last date, Assyria ceased to exist.

---

[3] For the first years of Nabopolassar's reign, cf. *RB*, 1924, 225 ff.

[4] The identification of the *Umman-manda* with the Medes stems from the document cited in *RB*, 1927, 152; cf. *ibid.*, 1930, 460.

15. With the accession of Nabopolassar to the throne of Babylon (626) began the tenth and last Babylonian dynasty, commonly spoken of as Chaldean or Neo-Babylonian. Its chief figure was Nabuchodonosor II (Nabu-kudurri-usur II), the son and successor of Nabopolassar; he was to destroy Jerusalem. He had already taken prominent part beside his father in the campaign against Harran which gave the *coup de grâce* to the Assyrian empire. Immediately afterward he was commissioned by his aging father to carry to a finish the conflict with the Pharaoh Nechao, who even after the defeat near Harran had not given up his ambitions to overlordship of Syria and Palestine. After three years of temporizing Nabuchodonosor opened the attack by striking the enemy at Carchemish, in the region which controlled the roads to Palestine and Egypt. The Egyptians were completely routed (605). With this victory, Syria and Palestine passed automatically under Babylonian control, since Nechao hurriedly drew back within his own frontiers, which he never crossed again. The heir to the Babylonian throne had for his part set out in pursuit of the Egyptian forces, but was compelled to turn aside at the news of his father Nabopolassar's death (§ 525). He returned posthaste to Babylon, where he assumed the crown which he subsequently made illustrious with the many civic and military accomplishments of his long reign (605–562).

Of Nabuchodonosor's successful campaigns in Syria, in Phoenicia, and even — as seems certain — in Egypt toward the end of his life, none has for a history of Israel the importance of his two Palestinian campaigns: the first in 597, during which he took Jerusalem, plundered the temple, and deported the king Joachin (§ 529 ff.) to Babylon; the second in 588–586, when he destroyed the city utterly and carried out a mass deportation to Babylonia of the kingdom of Juda (§ 536 ff.).

16. From this apogee under Nabuchodonosor the Babylonian empire fell into a swift decline. The reigns of his immediate successors were the gathering darkness before a complete eclipse. His son Evil-merodach (Amel-marduk) was killed after two short years (562–560) in an insurrection provoked by his kinsman Neriglissar (Nergal-shar-usur), who succeeded him on the throne (560–556); Labosordach (Labashi-marduk) came next and lasted only a few months before a new disturbance deposed him in favor of Nabonidus (Nabu-na'id). This latter, who attained the throne with the support of the priestly caste (556), was a student quite divorced from the cares of state and altogether taken up with monuments of antiquity and with archaeological matters. Hence he busied himself with the restoration of ancient buildings such as the temple of the moon-god Sin in Harran, from which district his family may have come. He waged two rather ineffectual campaigns in Syria and Arabia, but neglected to take proper account of the rise of Persia. This new power had supplanted the Medes across

the eastern border, and harbored no such sentiments toward Babylon
as her former allies may have. Thus while disorganization became widespread on the one side of the frontier, with Nabonidus leaving the
management of affairs to his son Balthasar (Belshazzar), on the other
side Cyrus the Great, ruler of Media since about 550, had welded into
a solid unity with Persia all the mountain tribes of the east and north,
and was prepared to erupt with his forces into the Mesopotamian
plain. The right moment came in 540; the campaign was short, because
the Persian ruler was generally welcomed as a liberator. In 539 Babylon
fell into his power and the Babylonian empire ceased to exist — an
event which goes beyond the limits of this first volume.

✲   ✲   ✲

17. The history of Assyria proper, insofar as it can be separated from
its Babylonian neighbor, may be divided into two periods: an Old
Assyrian period, from the beginnings to the advent of Tiglath-pileser I
in 1115; and a Neo-Assyrian period from 1115 to the fall of Nineve.[5]

Assyria, which seems to have been Sumerian in origin, was centered
in the earliest period in the prehistoric capital city of Asshur (§ 2), the
source of its name. There was an early invasion of Semites who
mingled with the Sumerian stock, and most likely Hittite and
Mitannian incursions succeeded these. Assyrian expansion, on the other
hand, dates back to the third millennium B.C. in the form of trading
colonies (§ 45). At first politically dependent on Babylonia, Assyria liberated itself with the decline of the first dynasty of Babel (1758?; § 5).
During the eighteenth century B.C., just before Hammurabi, King
Shamshi-Adad II (c. 1748-1716) extended his conquests in Syria as far as
the Mediterranean. Later, Assyria was subdued by the Hurrians of Mitanni,
who retained control of it until the Amarna period (§ 43 ff.). At this time
Ashur-uballit II (1363-1327) recovered his freedom; he maintained a close
correspondence with the Pharaoh Amenophis IV (§ 34), and extended his
influence even to the affairs of Babylonia. Adad-Nirari I (1305-1273)
did much to build up the Assyrian power, defeating the Cassites of
Babylonia and greatly extending his northern and western frontiers.
Still greater advances were made under Salmanassar I (1273-1243),
who carried on the work of conquest on practically every side of his
domain. His son Tukulti-Ninurta I (1243-1206) made Assyria definitely
superior to Babylonia, conquering the capital itself from the Cassites.
He also fought successfully against the Hittites (§ 44 ff.) and other
peoples to the northwest so that he could call himself "king of Assyria

---

[5] For the chronology of Assyrian rulers, a high degree of accuracy is now possible
as far back as the nineteenth century B.C., following the publication, by A. Poebel,
of the Assyrian King-List from Khorsabad, in *JNES*, 1, 1942, 247–306, 460–492;
2, 1943, 56–90. See also the article of Albright cited above, § 3.

and Karduniash, of Sumer and Akkad, of Sippar and Babylon, of Dilmun and Meluhha." Yet in the end he was killed by his son, and there ensued more than a century of obscurity and weakness.

18. Assyria was once more brought out of decadence by Tiglath-pileser I (1115–1076), who by his military exploits made it the chief power in western Asia. He overcame various peoples to the north, the west, and the southeast, until in the fifth year of his reign he could boast of having overcome forty-two countries from the Zab to the Euphrates. He went even beyond the Euphrates, and in a campaign along the Mediterranean collected tribute from Byblos, Sidon, and Arwad, as well as from the inland centers of Tadmor (Palmyra) and Anah. For his building activities he cut down cedars from Lebanon. About 1107 he took Babylon, in the reign of Marduk-nadin-akhe, the second successor of Nabuchodonosor I of the dynasty of Pashe (§ 7).

19. This reign likewise was followed by a period of fluctuation and decay, occasioned partly by internal disturbances, and partly by the steady infiltration of the Arameans (§ 49 ff.), who managed to establish a number of small states along the Euphrates to the northwest, but the renascence of Assyria began again with Adad-nirari II (912–891), and was completed under Ashur-nasir-pal II (884–859), who secured peace on the eastern frontier and restored the full extent, and more, of the other borders. He conquered the various Aramean principalities of the upper Euphrates region, and went on across Syria to the Mediterranean, where he exacted tribute from Tyre, Sidon, and other Phoenician cities. His son Salmanassar III (859–824) retained the great bulk of the conquered territory despite difficulties with the kingdom of Urartu (Armenia) and with several states in Syria. In this latter region, in 857 he conquered Carchemish; in 855 he conclusively defeated Ahuni, king of Bit-adini on the left bank of the Euphrates; and in 853 he waged a bitter campaign against a Syrian coalition headed by Irhuleni of Hamath and Adad-idri (the biblical Ben-Hadad II, § 435) of Damascus, which included twelve kings, among them Achab of Israel. The pitched battle took place at Karkar, and although the coalition had 63,000 foot soldiers in addition to cavalry, chariots, and camels (Achab had 10,000 foot soldiers and 2000 chariots), it turned out even more disastrously for the allies than for their Assyrian foe. Hostilities were broken off for a time, only to be resumed in 849 and 845, until, with the coalition practically dissolved, Salmanassar finally overcame Hazael, the successor of Adad-idri, in 841 (but without taking Damascus), and took tribute from Tyre and Sidon, as well as from Jehu, then king of Israel (§ 445). Ten years before his aid had been invoked by Marduk-zakir-shum, king of Babylonia, whose brother was usurping his throne, and the Assyrian had intervened as overlord.

20. Shamshi-Adad V (824–811), his son and successor, was at first concerned with suppressing an attempted usurpation by his brother, and later with the task of subduing Babylonia, which he accomplished successfully.

His son Adad-nirari III (811–783) may have been a minor when he came to the throne, and so ruled from 811 to 808 under the regency of his mother Sammu-rammat (Semiramis). In 802 he confirmed the dominance of Assyria over western Syria by the conquest of Damascus, and received the homage of the kingdom of Israel along with that of a number of Phoenician and Palestinian states (§ 446).

Then came a new period of decline, from which Assyria emerged at the advent of Tiglath-pileser III, from which time (§ 8) its history is more and more involved with that of Babylonia, outlined above.

EGYPT

21. The land in which the Egyptians lived was, in effect, coextensive with the valley of the Nile; Herodotus' familiar phrase, that Egypt is a "gift of the Nile," states the case precisely for both the geographer and the historian.

Surveying this territory from the Delta of the river toward its sources one sees that it is sharply defined by natural limits on three sides: the Mediterranean to the north, the Arabian Desert and the Red Sea on the east, and the Lybian Desert all the way along the western side. Even on the south nature has provided a boundary almost equally well marked at the latitude of Aswan (the Syene of the Greeks; 24° 5′ 30″ north latitude), where the Nile, near the island of Elephantine, forms its First Cataract (that is, the one farthest downstream). At this point the river issues from narrow mountainous confines which mark a sharp break between the region upstream from the cataract and the rest of the valley toward the sea. It is the point which through the centuries has been regarded as the real southern boundary of Egypt; beyond it is Nubia, which, however, was consistently under the influence of Egypt or politically subordinate to it except during the twenty-fifth dynasty, when the political relations were reversed.

22. From earliest historical times, Egypt was divided into two parts which again are geographically distinct from many points of view: Lower Egypt, the northern part comprising the Delta, toward Lake Moeris below Cairo; and Upper Egypt, the whole south from that point to the First Cataract.

The ancient inhabitants called Egypt as a whole *Kimet*, "the black (land)" — in contrast, apparently, with the arid, ruddy desert that surrounds it. The Bible calls it Misrayim, Masor, in accord with the cuneiform documents which named it Misri, Missari (in the el-Amarna period), Musur, Musri (at a later time). The current name, "Egypt," is of Greek origin (Αἴγυπτος), seemingly an adaptation of the Egyptian expression *ha (t)-ka-Ptah*, "abode of the *ka* of Ptah," used to designate Memphis, the city sacred to the god Ptah.

15

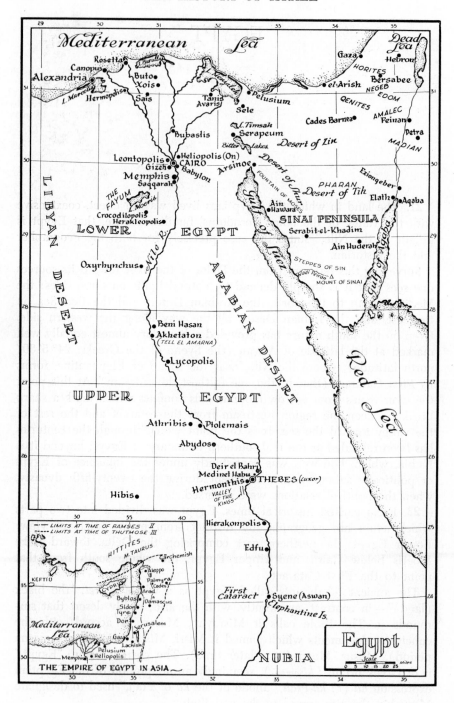

THE EMPIRE OF EGYPT IN ASIA

Egypt

View of the Nile at Assuan. (Wide World Photo.)

23. The Nile itself provides an excellent channel of communications extending the whole length of Egypt; far back in antiquity it was traversed by speedy boats of reeds and by cargo vessels. Though in Upper and Lower Nubia its course is broken by six cataracts it presents no such obstacle in Egypt proper, but is completely navigable from Aswan to the Mediterranean, varying in width from over 500 to over 900 yards. The Delta has undergone considerable changes in the course of time. In antiquity seven arms of the river are referred to as reaching the sea — the most westerly that of Canopus, and that of Pelusium the easternmost, whereas today there are only two in use, the Rosetta branch in the west and that of Damietta in the east.

These transformations are for the most part the effect of the well-known phenomenon, the annual flood of the Nile. Swollen by the torrential rains of Ethiopia, the stream rises from five to seven yards above the normal level from June to September and inundates the surrounding land. When the waters subside a blackish deposit (hence the name *Kimet*) of fertile soil remains in the wake of the flood; the floor of the river valley has been raised by this means some ten yards in the course of the centuries. The river bed itself has risen, in the course of five millennia, at the rate of about four inches every hundred years; thus changes have been brought about.

There is no need to stress the vital importance of the river to the whole countryside. In a region where rain is scarce in the north and all but unknown in the south, and which has no other watercourse, it is the Nile alone which creates a luxuriant garden in the midst of the surrounding desert.

24. Among the cities of Lower Egypt the following merit particular notice: Sais, in the western Delta; Bubaste, in the southeastern Delta; Tanis, in the northeastern Delta; Pelusium, at the Delta's eastern extremity, the key to Egypt from the side of Asia; Heliopolis, the biblical 'On, a little to the north of Cairo on the right bank of the Nile; Memphis, the biblical Noph (Moph), a little to the south of Cairo and on the left bank. The chief localities of Upper Egypt were: Abydos, about 350 miles up the Nile from Cairo on the river's left bank; and especially Thebes (Luxor), the biblical No-Amon, the Homeric city of the hundred gates, about 460 miles south of Cairo by the Nile (§ 394). Almost all of these cities were at some time capitals for ruling dynasties; others mentioned in the Bible can be identified only doubtfully.

25. The history of Egypt can be followed with assurance for some thirty centuries before the Christian era. Although there is a fairly detailed record of events for the chronological framework, certainty begins only with the founding (663 B.C.) of the twenty-sixth dynasty by the Pharaoh Psammetichus I; the preceding period is involved in uncertainties which multiply steadily the further back one goes. This is because the Egyptians, after the manner of other peoples of ancient times, dated events by the years of the reigning Pharaoh, without, however, establishing any common point of reference for the several reigns. Long lists of Pharaohs were compiled at various times in an attempt to overcome this difficulty. Fragments of such lists have come down to us (the Turin Papyrus, inscriptions at Abydos and Thebes, etc.). About 250 B.C. an Egyptian priest, Manetho, made use of similar lists to put together his own compilation, which again has reached us in fragmentary form. The patient and informed studies of modern scholars have not yet succeeded in filling all the gaps and in harmonizing the data of the different fragments in a definitive manner; so that the dates assigned to a given reign or event may vary at times by as much as several centuries.

26. Modern historians have taken over from Manetho the system of classifying into thirty-one dynasties the many Pharaohs who ruled Egypt. This is not, however, a chronological arrangement, as not all of the dynasties governed the entire country and sometimes rival dynasties flourished simultaneously. The entire series of dynasties covers the period from the dawn of Egyptian history down to the conquest of the country by Alexander the Great (332 B.C.).

Two principal tendencies have been current among students of Egyptian chronology.[1] The first, which yields a "long chronology,"

---

[1] For Egyptian chronology, cf. R. Weill, *Bases, méthodes et résultats de la chronologie égyptienne*, Paris, 1926; and *Compléments*, 1928, Borchardt, L., *Die*

fixes the beginnings of Egyptian history in the early part of the fifth millennium, in the neighborhood of 5000–4700 B.C. The "short chronology" of other students places these same beginnings in the second half of the fourth millennium, about 3500–3400 or even 3100–3000 B.C. Strong, but not compelling, arguments have been advanced on either side. Yet though the "long chronology" has been followed by distinguished Egyptologists in the past (Maspero, Flinders Petrie, etc.), it is being gradually forsaken today; it is the "short chronology" which has been followed in practice by the overwhelming majority of recent historians of Egypt (Breasted, Meyer, Hall, etc.). For this reason, though it cannot be considered beyond question,[2] the short chronology will be adopted here also, with the preliminary warning that all dates before 663 B.C. should actually be accompanied by a question mark.

27. The period before the dynasties in Egypt is shrouded in the obscurity of prehistoric times. Some little light has been shed on it by the excavations of the past forty years or more in predynastic tombs; but to the question of the place of origin of the early settlers in the Nile valley only a tentative, approximate answer can be given. The first inhabitants of Egypt seem to have been of Hamitic origin akin to the Lybian, Mediterranean, and Semitic peoples of the west, north, and east. Later a second influx of the same race, but of a group with slightly different characteristics, entered the valley most probably from the south. The two groups of this one race were at the Stone Age level (§ 69) of civilization. They formed separate kingdoms, one in the north (Lower Egypt, with Sais and Buto in the Delta as its centers), and the other in the south (with centers at Hierakonpolis and Edfu in Upper Egypt). These two kingdoms, which fought each other occasionally, were subdivided in feudal fashion into smaller principalities that may be recognized as the source of the "nomes," or districts, into which Egypt was divided at the beginning of historical times.

Somewhat later a new invasion, but of different ("Armenoid") stock, came down from Syria with a civilization of higher degree, which included the rudimentary use of metals; it is supposed that these peoples, being Asiatics, acquired their higher culture through contact with the Elamite-Mesopotamian civilization. They formed a minority which infiltrated the country from north to south, gaining control everywhere because of their physical and cultural superiority, and

---

Mittel zur zeitlichen Festlegung von Punkten der ägyptische Geschichte und ihre Anwendung, Cairo, 1935. For particular periods, H. E. Winlock, "The Eleventh Egyptian Dynasty," *JNES*, 1943, 249–283; W. F. Edgerton, "Chronology of the Twelfth Dynasty," *ibid.*, 1942, 307–314; *id.*, "On the Chronology of the Early Eighteenth Dynasty . . . " *Amer. Journ. of Semitic Lang. and Lit.*, 1937, 188–197.

[2] The evidences of Mesopotamian influence on Egypt in the late predynastic period are now sufficiently cogent to render the "long chronology," which could not be reconciled with the data from Mesopotamia, wholly inadmissible.

Step pyramid of Saqqara.

they brought about a considerable advance in the civilization of the natives. It has been maintained that during this predynastic period, in the year 4241 B.C., the first Sothic cycle, a period of 1460 years based on astronomical observations regarding the star Sirius (called *Soti* by the Egyptians), was begun in Egypt.[3] This cycle was never used as an era for the dating of events.

Egypt was united as a result of victory over the kings of Lower Egypt by those of Upper Egypt; but the remembrance of the older partition survived the union, in that the ruler of the entire country was called "king of the two lands," and from the middle of the First Dynasty onward was represented by the symbol of a double crown (*Insi-bya*) combining the white crown of Upper Egypt (*Insi*) with the red crown (*Bya*) of Lower Egypt. The first ruler of this joint domain, traditionally known as Menes, begins the period of the dynasties.

28. These dynasties are variously grouped by modern scholars for reasons of convenience, but no arrangement has won universal acceptance. Maspero grouped them into three periods, giving to each the name of the city which was the seat of the ruling dynasties for the greater part of the period in question. He therefore recognized an Archaic (Memphitic) Period, including Dynasties 1–10; a Theban Period, Dynasties 11–21, with an interruption by the Hyksos; and a Saitic Period, Dynasties 21–30 (31) with an interruption by the Persians. Egyptologists of today more commonly restrict their broad classifications to an Old Kingdom (Dynasties 1–6), a Middle Empire (Dynasties

---

[3] See, however, O. Neugebauer, "The Origin of the Egyptian Calendar," in *JNES*, 1942, 396–403, and the literature there cited, for a current tendency to exclude astronomical considerations as the basis for the Egyptian calendar.

The (second) pyramid of Chephren.

11–12), and a New Empire (Dynasties 18–20); the other dynasties either form intermediate periods or are designated by the racial origin or the capital city of the rulers.

29. The First Dynasty (3000–2900?), known as Thinite from This, near Abydos (§ 24) where its tombs are located, is that which Manetho tells us was founded by Menes. In this figure of Menes are combined more than one historical personage, among them Ip ("Scorpion"), Narmer, and Aha, who were the conquerors of the Delta and the unifiers of Egypt.

The Sphinx; to the right, the pyramid of Chephren.

The Second Dynasty (also Thinite 2900–2750) beginning with Hotepsekhemui, has its tombs at Memphis and Abydos; during its rule there are still tokens of an internal conflict between south and north. The Third (Memphitic) Dynasty had as its chief figure King Zoser, the builder of the "step pyramid" at Saqqara.

The Fourth Dynasty (2700–2563?), which ruled in a period of great splendor, included the well-known monarchs Cheops (Khufu), Chephren (Khafre), and Mycerinus (Menkaure), builders of the three pyramids at Gizeh, near Cairo to the west; these were among the greatest wonders of the ancient world (§ 399). The Fifth Dynasty was founded by Userkaf, high priest at Heliopolis (§ 24); it too belongs to a time of great prosperity. The Sixth Dynasty (2423–2280?) ruled in still flourishing times, particularly under the energetic kings Pepi (Piope) I and II; but it unexpectedly fell prey to internal dissensions and to invasions of Negro tribes which came down the Nile valley through Nubia.

The next period was one of disorder, in which the Seventh and Eighth Dynasties continued to dwell at Memphis with an authority restricted almost entirely to Lower Egypt; only a short distance away, in the northern part of Upper Egypt, the princes of Heracleopolis declared their independence and began the Ninth and Tenth Dynasties, which must have been contemporary in part with those just named, and in part with those that follow (2242–2061?).

30. The Middle Empire began with a rebellion of Thebes against Heracleopolis; the Eleventh Dynasty (2143–2000?) succeeded in supplanting the rulers of Heracleopolis after a long struggle. — The Twelfth Dynasty, at Thebes (2000–1788?), brought the country a period of political power and of flourishing arts. Among its prominent members were Amenemhet I, founder of the dynasty, who restored order to the country; Sesostris (Senusret) I, conqueror of Nubia; Sesostris III, known to Grecian legend, who fought both in Nubia and at a place in southern Palestine called Sekmem (the biblical Sichem? cf. § 88); Amenemhet III, who built the great structure at Hawara, south of Lake Moeris in the Fayum, that was regarded as another of the chief wonders of antiquity, under the name of the "Labyrinth."

The (Theban) Thirteenth Dynasty (1788–1680?) began in a very flourishing manner, but later gave way before the pressure of internal difficulties which prompted the rise of the insignificant Fourteenth Dynasty (parallel to the above, but at a period not ascertained), centered at Xois in the Delta. The subsequent Hyksos invasion overturned the entire land.

31. Hyksos, the name given by the Egyptians to the invaders, is explained by Manetho as "Shepherd Kings" (hiq-shasu), but it seems to have represented originally "Kings of the Deserts" (hiq-khasut); those so described actually entered Egypt from the Syro-Palestinian

deserts. Their mass migration was apparently a repercussion from the
arrival of the Aryans in Media (after 2000 B.C.). It is part of the same
movement that led ultimately to the establishment of a Hurrian kingdom
in the Mitanni district at the expense of Assyria, and to the Cassite
attacks against Babylon (§§ 4, 6). The advancing hordes upset the
entire region of Syria and Mesopotamia, driving crowds of fugitives
before them into the west. The Hyksos group was strong enough to
pierce the frontiers of Egypt and enter the country; its racial origins
must of course have been very mixed, as it was made up of peoples
gathered along the road — but the majority were Semites. The success
of the invaders was aided by their use of horse and chariots, unknown
in Egypt up to that time, and by their bronze scimitars, far more
powerful than the slender weapons of the Egyptians. The invasion
was disastrous for ordered life in the Nile valley; the natives retained
a horrified recollection of it down to a very late period and developed
in consequence an imperishable hatred for Asiatics in general. The
initial looting was followed by systematic oppression; the chiefs of
the invaders settled permanently in the Delta, fortifying Avaris (§ 194).
From there they extended their domination over all of Lower and
Upper Egypt, supplanting the Pharaohs and acquiring a smattering
of Egyptian culture, but looking out for their own military superiority
above all. It seems that Thebes was last to be subdued. The beginning
of the invasion can be put at about 1720 and the final expulsion of
the Hyksos came about 1570; so that between these limits should be
included the Fifteenth and Sixteenth Dynasties, which Manetho assigns
to the Hyksos.

32. But at the same time a new dynasty arose at Thebes — the native
Seventeenth Dynasty. About forty years before the expulsion of the
Hyksos, the local ruler Seqenenre I Taa threw over his vassalage, and
began the war for national independence which his dynasty (1635–
1580?) pursued with varying fortunes until the final victory. The Hyksos
made their last stands, in falling back toward their native Asia, at the
stronghold of Avaris, which was taken about 1568, and at Sharuhen,
in the extreme south of Palestine, where the Egyptian victory was
clinched about 1565. The conquerer was Ahmose, last Pharaoh of the
Seventeenth Dynasty and founder of the Eighteenth.

33. The New Empire embraces three dynasties (Eighteenth to Twentieth, all Theban) which because of their importance for the history
of Israel, must be treated more in detail.

They mark the apogee of Egypt's might: the internal administration
of the state was reorganized, the arts flourished tremendously, and
Egyptian arms were carried victoriously beyond the confines of the
nation to countries never before reached. The foreign expansion was
prompted by two considerations. First of all, the Hyksos invasion had

driven home in a painful manner the lesson that a frontier on the Isthmus, at Pelusium, was no adequate guarantee of safety for the valley of the Nile. It must be reinforced with a bridgehead to be carved out in the region beyond the Isthmus. Then too, the territory with no fixed borders that spread through Palestine and the regions to the north of it was passing through a time of upheaval, the second part of which is known to us as the "Amarna Age" (§ 43 ff.), and it had no such unity, either ethnic or political, as would enable it to resist external aggression. Thus Asia practically invited conquest; and in their enduring hatred of the Asiatics the Egyptians found incentive enough to take up the invitation.

Eighteenth Dynasty (1570–1315?)

Ahmose I	1570–1546
Amenophis (Amenhotep) I	1545–1525
Thutmose I	1524–1507
Thutmose II	
Kemare-Hatshepsut (a woman)	1507–1447
Thutmose III	
Amenophis II	1447–1420
Thutmose IV	1420–1412
Amenophis III	1412–1375
Amenophis IV (Ikhnaton)	1375–1358
——	
Tutankhamon	1358–1350
——	
Harmais (Harmhab)	1350–1315

Nineteenth Dynasty (1315–1205?)

Rameses I	1315–1314
Seti I	1314–1292
Rameses II	1292–1225
Merneptah (Amenophath)	1225–1215
Amenmose	
Siptah	1215–1205
Seti II	

(Anarchy: 1205–1200)

Twentieth Dynasty (1200–1090)

Setnakht	1200–1198
Rameses III	1198–1167
Rameses IV–XII (uninterrupted succession) . . .	1167–1090

34. Without making any attempt to describe the civic grandeur or the military exploits of these rulers,[4] their campaigns in Asia will be briefly surveyed.

Under Ahmose the last resistance of the Hyksos to the east of the Delta was overcome. The first steps toward a Syrian expansion may have occurred under his successor, Amenophis I. There is no doubt of the penetration of Thutmose I even as far as the lands of the Mitanni (§ 1), where he overcame Asiatic groups in a full-scale battle. The Egyptian hold on the conquered regions later slipped somewhat, and in 1479 Thutmose III campaigned in Palestine, routing a coalition of Asiatics at the classic battlefield of Megiddo (§ 64). The resulting conquests were consolidated and extended as far as the Euphrates

Thutmose III. (Turin Museum.)

in no less than fourteen campaigns by the same Pharaoh, and in others by Amenophis II (in 1446) and Thutmose IV. The reign of Amenophis III carries to the "Amarna Age" (§ 43 ff.).

Amenophis IV was possibly the most bizarre figure in the entire line of Pharaohs. He was by nature speculatively inclined; at the urging of the priests of Heliopolis (§ 24), center of worship of the sun-god Aton, he set himself up as a champion of Aton worship and a monotheistic reformer of Egyptian religion. The official cult of the time was that of Amon, god of Thebes; the Pharaoh's hatred for this god led him to change his name Amenophis ("Amon is satisfied") to Ikhnaton ("Splendor of Aton"), which included the name of his chosen divinity. Shortly afterward and for the same reason he left Thebes, transferring his capital to the new city which he had founded and named Akhetaton ("Horizon of Aton"), at a place now known as Tell el-Amarna, about 200 miles south of Cairo. Effective control of the affairs of the kingdom, above all in distant Asia, was naturally impossible to an enthusiast of this sort; so that the Egyptian holdings in Syria and Palestine, already partitioned among ambitious native vassals, were on the point of being overwhelmed by Hittite invaders and by roving bands of Habiri (§ 54).

---

[4] The splendors brought to light in October, 1922, from the tomb of Tutankhamon of the Eighteenth Dynasty, in the Valley of the Tombs of the Kings near Thebes, caused a furor in the world press which has hardly yet been forgotten.

Colossal statues of Memnon (Amenophis III) at Thebes.

35. Seti I retook Palestine and stemmed the Hittite flood. In 1288 Rameses II defeated a league of Asiatics headed by the Hittites at Qadesh on the Orontes, but at a terrible cost; a treaty of alliance with the Hittites followed a little later, by which Rameses kept Palestine for himself and left the more northerly regions to his new allies. In 1223 Merneptah was forced to campaign against rebellion in Palestine; in a well-known inscription he boasts of his successes in the following words:

> "The princes are prostrate and cry out: 'Shalom'!
> None of the vassal peoples raises its head!
> Tehenu is laid waste, Hatti is at peace;
> Canaan is despoiled with (?) all the wicked;
> Ascalon has been deported, Gezer vanquished, Yanu'am annihilated;
> Israel is destroyed, without progeny.
> Palestine is become like a widow for Tameri."[5]

---

[5] *Shalom* is a Canaanite-Semitic word which even in Hebrew means "peace"; it was intentionally preserved in the Egyptian document. The *Tehenu* were a Libyan people; *Hatti* is for Hittites. For Canaan, see § 58; for Ascalon, § 328; for Gezer, § 76; for *Yanu'am* and Israel, § 231. *Tameri* is a poetic term for Egypt, § 205, before whom Palestine is pictured as a widow, i.e., an abject and defenseless person. The text of the Merneptah Stele is in H. Gressman, *Altorientalische Texte zum Alten Testament*, 24 f. (hereafter referred to as *AO*), and in *Ancient Near Eastern Texts* (ed. J. B. Pritchard), Princeton, N. J., 1950, 376–378 (hereafter referred to as *ANET*).

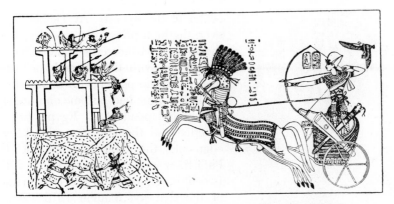

Rameses I attacking a fortress. Wall picture at Abu Simbel.

This list of places in Palestine is informative, and especially note-worthy is the mention of "Israel," which here makes its first appearance in extrabiblical sources (§§ 172, 231).

Rameses III once more saved, with great difficulty, the Egyptian bor-ders and part of the Palestinian hinterland (1190) when he repelled the "Peoples of the Sea" (Philistines, etc.) who swept down by land and sea from the Asia Minor coast for a concerted attack on the Delta (§ 328).

With the end of the New Empire the splendor of Egypt faded; dynas-tic rivalries and a series of weak rulers paved the way for foreign in-vaders, and the few forceful monarchs to sit on the Egyptian throne from this time on were of alien race.

36. The Twenty-First Dynasty (1090–947?) was founded by Nesu-benebded (Smendes), viceroy of Tanis in the Delta, which became the

Wood models of Egyptian troops of the time of the Pharaohs.
(Cairo Museum.)

Stele of Merneptah.
(Cairo Museum.)

center of the dynasty. At Thebes, however, the high priests of Amon had from
the time of Hrihor either alternated on
the throne with the Pharaohs at Tanis
or divided the power with them. Meanwhile Palestine had become almost completely independent of Egypt, first in
practice and then by general acknowl-
edgment; the predominance of the
Philistines gave place to that of the
Israelites. The next to the last Pharaoh
of the dynasty, Siamon (970–950), is
apparently the Pharaoh cited in the
Bible as the father-in-law of Solomon
(§ 383).

The Twenty-Second, Bubastite, Dynasty (947–702?) was descended from
the chieftains of Libyan mercenaries
hired and settled in the Delta by the
earlier Pharaohs as a reinforcement of
their weak military position. Its founder,
Sheshonk I, the biblical Sesac, in the
seventeenth year of his reign (c. 930)
raided Palestine (§ 416), taking Jerusalem by storm and plundering the
Temple of Solomon. The kinship which existed between Roboam, then
reigning at Jerusalem, and the Tanite dynasty overturned by Sesac can
be accepted as one of the prime motives for the Pharaoh's campaign. At
the same time, there must have been active Egyptian intervention in the
plots and disorders which broke out in Palestine after Solomon's death,
leading at last to the splitting of the nation into two kingdoms (§ 409 ff.);
even earlier, Egypt had willingly offered asylum to the fugitive Jeroboam
(§ 407). Sesac was followed on the throne by Osorkon I (925–889),
whom some would make out to be Zerah the Ethiopian (Zerah from
O[serak]hon?) who invaded Palestine in the days of Asa, king of Juda,
but was repelled with losses, according to the isolated reference preserved in 2 Paralipomenon, 14:9 ff. (§ 461).

37. While the Twenty-Second Dynasty continued at Thebes with rulers
each of whom was weaker than his predecessor, about the time of the
campaigns of Salmanassar III in Syria (§ 19) the high priest Harsiesi
made himself independent, and was succeeded by Pedubastis, whom
Manetho gives as the founder of the Twenty-Third Dynasty ([860]
838–740?). This rival dynasty also provided only shadowy rulers from
whose control the country fell away into tatters. Independent prince-

doms were formed in the Delta under the chieftains of Libyan ancestry. Also a Libyan at least in part, it would seem, was Kashta, the autonomous governor of Nubia who came down into Upper Egypt and conquered Thebes about 745 B.C. By establishing kinship with the fallen dynasty he gave some color of legality to his own claim of succession.

During this time of confusion, the Libyan Tefnakhte, prince of Sais and of Memphis, made an effort to gain control of the rest of Lower, and then of Upper, Egypt; he founded a Twenty-Fourth Dynasty (726–712?).

This southward advance was checked by Piankhi, who succeeded Kashta about 742 both in his authority and in his ambitions. In 721 Piankhi defeated Tefnakhte and his confederate princes, and conquered the Delta. Before he withdrew into Nubia he seems to have set over the vanquished chieftains, who were allowed to exercise a subordinate authority over their former territories, one whom the Assyrian documents call Sib'e and identify as the *turtan* (generalissimo) of Egypt (§§ 8, 458). This Sib'e is probably the So' (or *Seve; Vulgate, Sua*) described in the Bible as "king of Egypt," who had a secret agreement with Osee, king of Israel (2 Kings[6] 17:4). Some have supposed that he is to be identified with Shabaka, who succeeded Piankhi as Pharaoh five years later, and that the biblical passage is out of its proper chronological context.[7]

38. Thus in the south there existed a Twenty-Fifth, Ethiopian, Dynasty, which for all practical purposes had begun with Kashta ([745] 721?–663); it quickly did away with the Twenty-Fourth Dynasty, for Bokenenraf (the Bocchoris of the Greeks), who succeeded Tefnakhte in 718, was dethroned and, tradition has it, burned alive by Shabaka in 712.

---

[6] 1 Sam., 2 Sam., 1 Kings, 2 Kings correspond respectively to 1 Kings, 2 Kings, 3 Kings, 4 Kings of the Douay-Rheims version of the Bible.

[7] It should be noted that the Lucianic recension of the Septuagint and the margin of the codex *Legionensis* of the Itala read *Adramelech* the Ethiopian, and not So' or Sua in this passage.

The peoples of the sea repulsed by Rameses III.

Pharaoh Taharqa the Ethiopian.
(Cairo Museum.)

Shabaka had apparently been taken as colleague in the government of Egypt in 715 by Piankhi, who had retired to Napata, capital of his own Nubia. He ruled until 700, when he challenged the Assyrian power in Palestine by furnishing aid to the local rebel confederacy, and met defeat at Elteqeh (§ 9). His reign was followed by the unimportant one of a son, Shabataka (the Sebichos of the Greeks: 700–689), who was deposed and slain by his cousin Taharqa (689–664), the Tirhaqah (Vulgate, *Tharaca*) of the Bible. In the biblical text this ruler is called "king of Ethiopia" (2 Kings 19:9; Isa. 37:9), which is understandable in view of the origin of the dynasty. There is, however, the chronological difficulty that the expression is applied to Taharqa on the occasion of Sennacherib's campaign in Palestine, when Shabaka was Pharaoh. This and other considerations have led some to suppose that Sennacherib conducted two campaigns in Palestine, the one in 700, ending with the battle of Elteqeh, and the other about ten years later in the reign of Taharqa. Since there is not the slightest allusion to such a second, distinct, campaign in either the Bible or the cuneiform sources, others assume with greater plausibility that the title "king of Ethiopia" assigned to Taharqa is to be taken in the same broad sense as that of "king of Egypt" given to So' (Sua), and that in both cases what is meant is the office of *turtan* (§ 37); the more so as, by the time the biblical account was written, Taharqa had in fact been king both of Ethiopia and of Egypt (§ 495).

39. During Taharqa's reign the Asiatic bridgehead necessary for the protection of Egypt's northeastern frontier collapsed utterly (§ 33), and the frontier itself was invaded. Assyria had by this time become the ruling power of all western Asia as far as the Isthmus; and under Assarhaddon, either in 675 or 674, the Assyrians won a firm footing in the eastern end of the Delta, from which in 671 they rounded out a methodical conquest of the valley of the Nile. The course of events is described as follows in the laconic style of the Babylonian Chronicle: "In the year ten [*of Assarhaddon, who mounted the throne in 681*] in the month Nisan, the Assyrian army reached Egypt. On the third, sixteenth, and

eighteenth of the same month Tammuz, three times, battles were fought
in Egypt. On the twenty-second, Mimpi [*Memphis*], its royal city, was
taken; its king fled; his son and his brother were taken alive. Its booty
was taken, its people were plundered, their goods were carried off."[8]
Taharqa fled to Napata in Nubia. Assarhaddon subdued the land beyond
Thebes to the south; his generals continued beyond the First Cataract.
In stabilizing his conquests Assarhaddon left at their posts, subordinate
to his own authority, a number of the local rulers, especially in the Delta;
most prominent among them was Nechao (Niku) of Sais, who before
long entered into friendly relations with Taharqa (§ 503).

40. Hardly had Assarhaddon died (669) when Taharqa returned from
Nubia to win back his domain. With ease he recovered Thebes and
Memphis and wiped out the Assyrian garrisons in the Delta. Ashurbanipal, who succeeded Assarhaddon, was unable to take up the conflict
until 667; in that year he routed Taharqa at Karbanibi in the Delta,
near Memphis. The Pharaoh fled again to Napata. The land was regained for Assyria with the same ease with which it had been reoccupied
by the Ethiopian; a Phoenician fleet sent up the Nile for the purpose
carried the Assyrian king and his army from Memphis to Thebes, which
saved itself by surrendering. Over the princes of the Delta, who rebelled
again shortly afterward, Ashurbanipal set Nechao, forgiven after punishment for his disloyalty. His son, Psammetichus, became prince at Athribis.

Taharqa never again left Napata, but at his death (664) his son, Tanutamon, attempted to recoup; he took Upper Egypt, stormed Memphis,
and slew Nechao; Psammetichus fled to the Assyrians.

Ashurbanipal then returned a second time (663). Tanutamon quickly
withdrew and the Assyrian ruler recovered Thebes, which this time he
plundered of its immense riches. "The entire city," boasts Ashurbanipal,
"I conquered with the aid of Asshur and of Ishtar. Silver, gold, precious
stones, all the possessions in its palace, varicolored garments, linens,
large horses, male and female slaves, two huge obelisks of shining elec-
trum weighing 2500 talents, and the doorposts of the temple which I
took from their bases I sent to Assyria. An immense booty beyond all
counting I took from Thebes."[9] The fame of this pillage reverberated
throughout the ancient world (cf. Nahum 3:8 ff.); recent excavations at
Karnak have proved the seriousness of the destruction, and the Upper
Egyptian metropolis never completely recovered from it.

41. The Twenty-Sixth Dynasty (663–525) was founded by Psammetichus I (663–609), son of Nechao, already mentioned above. The
Assyrians left him as viceroy of Egypt; by diplomacy and by family ties

---

[8] For the text of Ashurbanipal, from the "Rassam Cylinder," cf. *ANET*, 295;
AO, 359–361. Cf. also J. M. A. Janssen, "Que sait-on actuellement du pharaon
Taharqa," in *Biblica*, 1953, 23–43, esp. 38 f.

[9] For the text of Ashurbanipal, from the "Rassam Cylinder," cf. *ANET*, 295.

with the descendants of the earlier Pharaohs he solidified his grasp on Upper and Lower Egypt. During his first years he admitted the suzerainty of the Assyrians; but this was given up about 650, when the Assyrian garrisons were withdrawn from the Delta in view of the war against Babylonia (§ 11). The aid furnished to Egypt by Gyges, king of Lydia, had also an influence on the new state of affairs. Free though he was in his own territory, Psammetichus remained always the friend of the Assyrians (§ 12). His rule was a time of renascence for Egypt. Nubia to the south was definitely detached from Egypt, but there was peace between them; the existing contacts with Greek merchants in the Delta were developed; the great Scythian invasion which overwhelmed western Asia between about 632 and 622 (§ 508) was astutely checked by Psammetichus at the approaches to the Delta. When the Scyths had withdrawn he set up anew the Asiatic bridgehead beyond his frontiers, with the conquest after a prolonged siege of the Philistine city of Ashdod.

42. His son Nechao II (609–593) fell heir, when he ascended the throne, to the project of recovering territory in Asia. His attempts to carry out the plan are merged in the chain of events which involved the last days of the Assyrian empire (§14 ff.) and the last kings of Juda (§ 519 ff.). There is no notice of his son and successor Psammetichus II (593–588) except that of a victorious expedition into Nubia. He was followed by the Pharaoh Hophra (Apries, Uaphris: 588–586), apparently his son. This ruler renounced the policy of noninterference in Asia that had been maintained consistently since the defeat of Nechao II at Carchemish (§ 15). He at once entered into an agreement with the powerful anti-Babylonian faction in Jerusalem, aroused them to open revolt against Nabuchodonosor with the promise of military aid, and occupied Phoenicia with an army made up in large part of Greek mercenaries (§ 535 ff.). Any hopes of Asiatic dominion he may have had, however, were blasted once and for all by Nabuchodonosor's destruction of the kingdom of Juda (586). The only actual help he gave the Jews in these circumstances, for all their vain confidence in him, was to admit the fugitives who came to Egypt after the slaying of Godolias (§ 545), and to settle them at Taphnes (modern Tell el-Defenneh) in the eastern Delta, which was a military and commercial post for the Greeks. The failure of Hophra in his military undertakings, and the favoritism he showed to foreigners, led to a military revolt by which the Egyptian general Amasis (I'ahmases) was set up as Pharaoh in fact if not in name (569); somewhat later (566) Hophra called on his mercenaries to quit him of this rival, but was himself defeated and killed.

The last two Pharaohs of this dynasty are beyond the period treated in the present volume. It may suffice to say that under Amasis (569–526) there occurred in all likelihood an invasion of Egypt by Nabuchodonosor in the thirty-seventh year of his reign (567); and that in the short reign of Psammetichus III (526–525) Cambyses the Persian conquered Egypt and made of it a simple province of his world-wide empire.

The Twenty-Seventh Dynasty of Egypt was composed of the Persian successors of Cambyses.

THE AMARNA AGE

43. Toward the close of the year 1887, a chance discovery shed new and surprising light on one of the most critical periods in the history of western Asia. Egyptian Bedouin, rummaging in the ruins of Akhetaton, the capital city of Amenophis IV (§ 34), turned up a buried deposit of inscribed clay tablets of ancient date. After the usual concealment and piecemeal distribution of the find for the sake of profit, the tablets came to rest for the most part (more than 200) in the Berlin Museum, with smaller hoards in the British Museum, at Cairo, at Oxford, and even in private hands. The total number of these el-Amarna tablets, so called from the modern name of the site where they were found, exceeds 500. Scholars have extended the term used for identifying the tablets to the period of history from which they come, so that the first half of the fourteenth century B.C., the time of the Pharaohs Amenophis III and IV, is known as the "Amarna Age."

The documents brought to light in this way proved to be what we would call the archives of the Foreign Office of the two Pharaohs; they had been assembled in the place of their discovery as a record of the letters received from, and sometimes of those dispatched to, the various prominent rulers of Asia and the petty vassals and Egyptian governors in Palestine. Babylonian was at the time the language of state for international correspondence in the Orient, and all but three of the tablets are written in that tongue, but the very nature of the documents made it a matter of course that fascinating dialectal peculiarities and non-Babylonian glosses should be included.

Of the nations taking part in this correspondence, Egypt, Babylonia, and Assyria have already been spoken of; there are others which also merit our attention.

44. First of all there were the Hittites[1] (*Hatti*), the *Hethaei* of the Vulgate Bible. Not so long ago our knowledge of this people depended

---

[1] For the Hittites in general, cf. Garstang, John, *The Hittite Empire*, London, 1929; L. Delaporte, *Les Hittites*, Paris, 1936; A. Götze, *Hethiter, Cherriter und Assyrer*, Oslo, 1936; O. R. Gurney, *The Hittites*, London, 1951.

Hittite types.

on stray notices and scattered monuments, but much clearer information
in their regard has been obtained since a discovery in 1907 which parallels that at el-Amarna — the finding of the archives of Boghazkoi. At this
spot in Asia Minor, about a hundred miles east of Ankara, in northern
Cappadocia, there once rose the city of Hattush, capital of the Hittite
empire in the fourteenth and thirteenth centuries B.C.; the place has
yielded some hundreds of clay tablets, of which only a minority are in
Babylonian (§ 43), while the rest are inscribed in six or seven different
languages that are still the subject of scholarly analysis. The archive
seems to have been built up about 1300 B.C., but contains copies of
earlier documents.

45. From these texts as a whole it is clear that the region under direct
Hittite control included eastern Asia Minor and northern Syria: approximately from the east bank of the Halys at mid-course to the west bank
of the upper Euphrates, with the Taurus, the Orontes, and the Mitanni

Typical Hittite. (Zenjirli.)　　　　Hittite God of War. (Puchstein,
　　　　　　　　　　　　　　　　　　　　　　　Boghazkoi.)

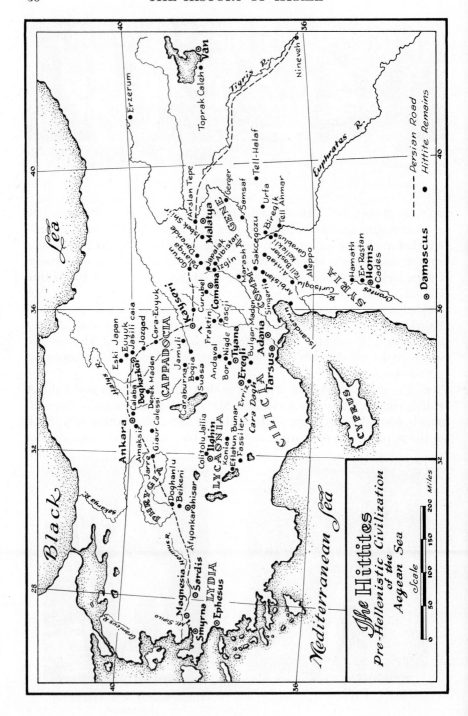

The Hittites
Pre-Hellenistic Civilization
of the
Aegean Sea

territory (§ 1) at its southern boundary. Just when the Hittites settled in this area is still a matter of dispute. What is certain, at any rate, is that the Hittites proper were not a Semitic but an Indo-European people, as has become patent from the analysis of their language. There is evidence of Assyrian merchant colonies in the same region from about the nineteenth century B.C.; their cuneiform tablets have been found especially at Kül-tepe, near Caesarea in Cappadocia. After the disappearance of these Assyrian settlements, the Hittites during several centuries welded into some sort of unity the indigenous (proto-Hattite) population and the various other racial stocks that had grafted themselves upon it at different times. It is certain, too, that brief raids and more lasting settlements carried the Hittites far beyond their customary boundaries: thus we have seen that about 1550 the First Dynasty of Babylon was overturned by a Hittite invasion (§ 5), and even before this Abraham bought land from its Hittite owners in southern Palestine (Gen. 23).

46. There was a revival of the Hittite empire in the fifteenth century under two of its rulers, Tudhalia II and Hattushil II. This was followed by a new period inaugurated by the king, Shubbiluliuma, who ruled for about forty years, beginning c. 1400 B.C., extending his domain southward as far as Aleppo, and also to the east at the expense of the Hurrian kingdom of Mitanni, then ruled over by Tushratta, brother-in-law of Amenophis III (§ 33). He came at length to agreements with both Egypt and the Mitanni, by which he retained the territory he had conquered. His son, Murshil, continued to strengthen the empire and to advance its borders southward into Amorite territory (§ 47 ff.). As the continuance of this movement ultimately became a threat to Egypt, it was resisted, and the two powers remained hostile until after the battle of Qadesh, when Hattushil, third successor of Murshil, made a treaty of peace (§ 35) with Rameses II, who later became his son-in-law (1259). The long reign of this Hattushil (1289–1255?) was the highwater mark of Hittite power; not only Syria, but the Amorite district to the south and its several ramifications were under Hittite dominion during this reign. From this or a slightly earlier period comes the basic collection of Hittite laws (§ 248) which is analogous in some respects to the Code of Hammurabi (§ 4). Evidence for later periods is scanty, partly owing to the difficulties of deciphering the texts, but it is certain that there was a period of decline, followed by swift disintegration, occasioned most likely by the invasions of new Indo-European peoples (Phrygians, Armenians, etc.) which took place about the twelfth century B.C.

47. Another people to be noticed are the Amorites,[2] the *Amorrhaei* of

---

[2] In the writings of A. T. Clay, *Amurru, the Home of the Northern Semites,*

the Vulgate. In the Old Testament the pre-Israelite inhabitants of Palestine are called sometimes Amorites, sometimes Canaanites (§ 52); from some contexts, however, it would seem as though the former were in one way or another subsequent to the latter (there are scholars who prefer the reverse order). Certain passages show clearly that the Amorites lived also beyond the borders of Palestine proper, to the east of the Jordan for example (Num. 21:23 ff.). These biblical indications are completed and clarified by other ancient sources. Egyptian texts prove that Syria was occupied at least in part by the *Amar* people, who are represented on the Pharaonic monuments as bearded individuals with yellowish skin and blue eyes. To the Babylonians, Syria and occasionally the entire district to the west of the Euphrates were known as *Amurru* (which they wrote with the ideogram MAR-TU). From early in the second millennium, the Amorites spread beyond this region into the more southerly and easterly lands by military raids. It has already been noted that the distinguished First Dynasty of Babylon (§ 4) originated in such an Amorite movement of expansion.

There have been scholars in modern times who have maintained that the very origins of Babylonian civilization were derived from an Amorite culture, which they would then date back to the fourth millennium B.C.; going further to the logical consequence, by way of an offset to the pan-Babylonian theories which would make of Babylonia the cradle of all Semitic peoples and culture, they would place rather in Amorite territory the original home of at least the northern Semites. No theory of the kind has met with a favorable reception, and such speculations are generally looked upon as unwarranted enlargements upon the facts of history as we know them.

48. About the middle of the second millennium B.C. an influx of peoples from Asia Minor into Syria, and notably the expansion of the Hittites, forced the Amorites to shift their holdings in Syria more and more to the south; so in the course of the fifteenth and fourteenth centuries they are firmly settled along the Phoenician coast, in the Lebanon region to the south of Qadesh on the Orontes, and along the east bank of the Jordan. In these districts the Amorites were open to influences alike from Egypt and from Babylonia, but perhaps rather more from the former; it was to Egypt in particular that they appealed for protection both in the continual struggles between their own small states and in the face of Bedouin attacks. Yet they were without doubt Semites, which their Hittite neighbors were not.

Philadelphia, 1909; *The Empire of the Amorites*, New Haven, 1919; and *The Antiquity of Amorite Civilization*, New Haven, 1924, may be found a sort of "pan-Amorite" construction. An opposing stand is taken by Theo. Bauer, *Die Ostkanaanaer*, Leipzig, 1926. For a general survey, cf. P. Dhorme, "Les Amorrhéens," in *RB*, 1928, 63 ff. (and later articles in continuation).

49. The Arameans[3] also are important both for the Amarna period in particular and for the later history of the chosen people as well. When at the offerings of the first fruits the Israelite repeated the prescribed words: "A wandering Aramean was my father, and he went down into Egypt, etc." (Deut. 26:5), he was referring to concrete historical fact — the long residence of Jacob in Aramean Harran (§ 2), and his multiple family ties with the Aramean Laban (§ 142 ff.). Jacob's relations with the Aramean lands and people were merely the strengthening of ancestral bonds of racial descent (Gen. 25:20; 28:2), reflected once again in the traditional genealogies (Gen. [10:22–23]; 22:20–23).

50. It has been said with some justice that in the history of the Semitic countries the Arameans give the impression of being able to be everywhere at once. Yet notwithstanding their widespread diffusion, another prominent characteristic, that of being more attached than other Semites to the nomadic life and to the scattered existence of their various tribes, kept them from setting up any sizable kingdom. If one leaves out of account a disputed mention of *A-ra-am* in an inscription of Naram-Sin (§ 3) in the third millennium,[4] the evidence for the Arameans from contemporary sources comes from the fourteenth and following centuries. At first, in a poorly preserved passage in the Amarna correspondence, they are called *Ahlamu* (which probably means "confederates," "associates"); later they are explicitly named by the compound term *Ahlamu-Arameans*. In the thirteenth century they are allied to the Hittites, who used them as a barrier against Assyria. Their persistent invasions, which took place for the most part in periods of Assyrian decadence, caused the enemy kingdom endless difficulties. But a whole series of kings beginning with Adad-nirari I (§ 17) boast of having subdued or repelled them. These hostilities flared up especially under Tiglath-pileser I (§ 18) and III (§ 8) and lasted until the reign of Sennacherib. Aramean penetration of Babylonia dates from the Eighth Dynasty of Babylon (§ 7) or earlier.

51. These Aramean onslaughts stemmed from Syria, mainly from its eastern part. Different Aramean groups established themselves at various points in both Upper and Lower Mesopotamia (the Upper Mesopotamian settlements being known as *Aram-Naharayim*, "Aram of the Two Rivers"). Still others, moving down toward the Mediterranean, found themselves in a position to build up the only Aramean states of any

---

[3] Cf. E. G. Kraeling, *Aram and Israel*, N. Y., 1918; A. Cowley, *Aramaic Papyri*, Oxford, 1923; Dhorme, "Abraham dans le cadre de l'histoire," *RB*, 1928, 367 ff.; "Arameens et Chaldeens," *ib.*, 484 ff.; F. Rosenthal, *Die aramaistische Forschung*, Leyde, 1939, 3–23; A. Dupont-Sommer, *Les Araméens*, Paris, 1949; R. O'Callaghan, *Aram-Naharaim*, Rome, 1948.

[4] For this inscription cf. P. Dhorme, *loc. cit.*, pp. 487–488.

prominence known to us. The generic name for all of them, as the Bible states, was *Aram* (in the Vulgate, *Syria*); this was followed by the specific name of the region or city on which they were hinged, so that there is an *Aram-Soba,* an *Aram-Maacha,* and an *Aram-Rohob,* all surrounding the chief center known as *Aram of Damascus,* or simply as *Aram.* Even these states were overcome by Tiglath-pileser III, who, in 732, in response to an appeal for help by Achaz, king of Juda, took Damascus, put Rasin, the last Aramean king, to death, and reduced Syria to an Assyrian province.

Yet the disappearance of these autonomous princedoms failed to check the ethnic and linguistic diffusion of Aramean influence. The ubiquitous tendencies of the Arameans, already noted, made their language, in the period after the eighth century B.C., a *lingua franca* for commercial and diplomatic purposes in international affairs (a typical example of this is contained in 2 Kings, 18:26; cf. § 494).

52. The Amarna correspondence deals with a number of states and regions (Babylonia, the Hittites, the Mitanni, Cyprus, etc.), but in a special way with Phoenicia and Palestine; and to these latter the present treatment will be restricted.[5]

The territory reaching from the ancient borders of Egypt to Qadesh on the Orontes, north of the Lebanon range, appears in the Amarna letters as divided into two parts: one from Qadesh southward as far as the port of Akka (Acre, Ptolemais, just above Carmel) and the lake of Tiberias, which was the country of the *Amurru* or Amorites; the other, southward to Egypt, was the district of the *Kinahni* or *Kinahhi,* that is, the Canaanites. These are the two names already familiar to us from biblical usage (§ 47).

The Amorites were settled along the Mediterranean coast in particular. If the cities there (Byblos, Beyrouth, Sidon, Tyre, etc.) had not yet attained the prominence they were later to enjoy under the Phoenicians, they nonetheless served as commercial outlets for the Arabs and Arameans of the interior even in the Amorite period. The Canaanites to the south were less enterprising; the coastal cities in this area (Jaffa, Ascalon, etc.) had in the Amarna Age nothing like the importance that the Philistines brought to them afterward.

---

[5] The text of the Amarna letters is given in I. A. Knudtzon (O. Weber, E. Ebeling), *Die El-Amarna Tafeln,* 2 vols., Leipzig, 1915 (still the best edition); a few texts were published later, by F. Thureau-Dangin in *Revue d'Assyriologie,* 1922, 91 ff. Cf. H. Gressman, *AO,* 371 ff. and *ANET,* 483–490. For discussions of their content and import, cf. P. Dhorme, "Les pays bibliques au temps d'El-Amarna," in *RB,* 1908, 500 ff.; *id.,* "La langue de Canaan," *ibid.,* 1913, 569 ff.; *id.,* "Les nouvelles tablettes d'El-Amarna," *ibid.,* 1924, 5–32; *id.,* s.v., "Amarna," in *DBS,* I; 207–225; also E. A. Speiser, "Ethnic Movements in the Near East in the Second Millennium B.C.," in the *Annual of the American Schools of Oriental Research,* 13 (1933), 13 ff.

53. Over both sections of this country Egypt had re-established her suzerainty under Thutmose III (§ 34); but it was a rule in name rather than in fact. The Pharaoh was served on the spot by a representative (*rabiṣu*), who had fluttering about him, however, a horde of local rulers either retained as vassals after the conquest (*sharrani*) or imposed by the overlord (*hazanu*). Every city or military post of any prominence had a local ruler of its own, so that the region was broken up into a veritable mosaic. Nor was there any real common bond; each chieftain fought his neighbors with a most bitter rivalry, and every so often a disposition to revolt would stir the common people of one locality or another to throw off the foreign yoke. The dealings of the local rulers with the Egyptian authority, whether in the person of the Pharaoh himself or through his regional representative, were utterly cynical and Machiavellian. Their letters were full of florid protestations of loyalty, using language that was servile and groveling, while at the same time they deftly drew the veil over treason and intrigue which were made to look like zeal for the interests of Pharaoh. Yet Egyptian officials and local chiefs alike were in fact very secondary figures in the sweep of forces which were upsetting the whole region. The local rulers show up clearly as timeservers (except for a few "loyalists" still faithful to Egypt) and the Egyptian officials were ready to swim with the current and to join in at any moment with the stronger party. The force with real vitality behind it was that of the nationalist revolution, with the *Habiri* as its champions.

54. Who were these people? Most of the letters represent them in cuneiform characters by means of an ideogram (SA-GAZ), but the small docket of messages from Abdi-Hipa of Jerusalem (§ 57) gives the phonetic spelling *Habiri* (Hapiri). That the reality underlying both designations is one and the same is put beyond all doubt both by the general tenor of the Amarna correspondence and by texts from Boghazkoi which use the two modes of writing indiscriminately to represent the eponymous deity of the group. The spelling in the Abdi-Hipa letters is made precise by a contemporary transcription in alphabetic characters as *'-p-r-m*, beginning with a sound for which the syllabic script does not provide. Outside of Palestine the name is to be found in Mesopotamia as well as Syria; it is documented for the eighteenth century as well as the Amarna period; and it has been found in Egyptian transcription also, on a stele of Seti I (§ 35) at Bethshan. The similarity of the name to "Hebrews" (*'ibrīm*), and the possibility on other grounds that there is some connection between the Habiri and the Israelites have provoked a number of discussions, somewhat inconclusive thus far.[6] In

---

[6] See, in particular, E. G. Kraeling, "The Origin of the Name 'Hebrews,'" *Amer. Journal of Semitic Lang. and Lit.*, 58, 1941, 237–253; *id.*, "Light from Ugarit on the

any case, the Amarna letters are full of cries of alarm, both real and pretended, at the conduct of the Habiri. In pursuit of what were evidently systematic plans of attack they struck at various localities, killing, destroying, plundering: seemingly not so much out of love for booty as to batter down everyone not on their side, whether it were an official from Egypt proper, or a local chief loyal to the Egyptians. To carry out such methodical and widespread plans, they had to be "leagued together," and this in itself must have made a deep impression on the tiny Semitic groups whose passionate attachment to individual liberty held many of them from entering into any kind of "league." This may well explain the fortunes of the word (cf. § 174).

55. For all their vagueness, their lacunae, and the direct contradictions caused by the studied duplicity of the local chiefs, the Amarna letters afford the following general view of affairs.

In the Amurru region two chieftains in particular are in conflict: Abdi-Ashirta ("Servant of Asherah," cf. § 105), along with his sons, and Rib-Addi of Byblos. It is important to note that both names are Semitic (Amorite). Abdi-Ashirta is altogether on the side of the Habiri, however much he may profess to be the "house dog" of Pharaoh. The prince of Byblos is a sincere partisan of the Egyptians, and in his more than fifty letters never stops denouncing others of the Amorite leaders as traitors, and describing the harm their undertakings are doing to the territories of Pharaoh. The Hittites to the north are undoubtedly fanning the flames and helping the revolution in an underhanded way; a number of the most prominent rebels have Hittite names. Pahnate, the Egyptian representative, is vacillating; perhaps because he has not succeeded in recognizing which party is the stronger, but also very likely for the sake of appearances, while in fact he secretly favors the rebels. And so Rib-Addi and his loyalist following steadily lose lands and cities, which pass to the control of the Habiri. After being deaf to the appeals of Rib-Addi for a long time, the Egyptian court finally sends a small reinforcement, and it suffices to transform the situation: Abdi-Ashirta is defeated and killed. His son Aziru falls heir to his aspirations, however, and with such zeal that the old state of affairs begins again. Rib-Addi sends advices and denunciations to the court, but without success, partly because in the court itself there are powerful individuals (with Semitic names!) who seem to regard the Amorite movement with favor. That movement spreads constantly. First the lands north of Byblos are lost to it; then the rebels, strengthened by aid from Sidon, move against Byblos itself. Even this city is insecure: nationalists within it, headed by the younger brother of Rib-Addi himself, grow more and more out

Khabiru," in BASOR, 1940, 32–33; W. F. Albright, FSAC, 182–183, 211, 326, 330; P. de Vaux, "Les patriarches Hébreux et les découvertes modernes" in RB, 1948, 337 ff.

of hand the closer the rebels come. Finally Rib-Addi, old and ailing, is forced to flee, while his intimates are given into the power of the insurgents. He first takes refuge in Beyrouth, then goes to Sidon, and there he, too, ends up in the hands of his enemies.

56. When faced with these conditions, the Pharaoh temporizes. He knows Aziru and his Habiri are too strong to be put down by direct action, so he appeals to what shadowy authority he has left, and scolds Aziru for his acts of rebellion, while at the same time he tries to win him over to his own side with exhortations, even addressing him as "chief of Amurru." The acts with which he charges him are matters of some concern: Aziru has received an envoy of Pharaoh badly, while on the other hand he has welcomed a Hittite ambassador with an enthusiasm altogether suspect; besides, it has been found out that he has an understanding with Itaqqamma of Qadesh, the declared enemy of Egypt. Aziru for his part is not quite so sure of himself as to throw over altogether his nominal subservience toward Egypt. When he is summoned to court *ad audiendum verbum*, first he temporizes, but in the end he goes. There ensue long discussions, but apparently he has the poise to give an adequate account of himself. On his return to his own dominions, either the growing Hittite pressure from the north has become too strong, or he has drawn his own conclusions from a firsthand inspection of the impotence of the Egyptian court. In any case he breaks off with Egypt and goes over to the Hittites. The Boghazkoi documents have preserved in part for us the treaty of alliance which he concludes with Shubbiluliuma (§ 46). The latter, as well as Itaqqamma of Qadesh, takes a hand, and combined Hittite-Amorite forces scatter the petty local chieftains who oppose them, and move on Canaan.

57. In Canaan, the chief of the insurgents is Labaya; and it is not for nothing that he too comes from the north, from Hittite territory, being originally from Arzawa in Cilicia. His active partner is one Tagi. Labaya too abases himself in words of submission to Pharaoh, but his actions show him as the ruling power in

A letter of Abdi-Hipa.

central Palestine, near the boundary between the Amurru and Canaan. With his Habiri he seizes control of several cities, among them Sichem (§ 88) and Gezer (§ 76 ff.). He is captured, however, by a faithful vassal of Egypt, Biridaia of Megiddo (§ 79); and though he manages to escape, he is killed shortly afterward. His sons continue his work, and the disturbance spreads southward. The rebels dominate the caravan roads, carrying out slaughter and pillage; but the actual perpetrators are never found out, because all the local chiefs accuse one another, and all together plead — with or without sincerity — for Egyptian intervention. A feeble effort at such intervention serves no particular purpose. The local chiefs then form an alliance among themselves to defend their own holdings. Among others who take part may be named Shuwardata of Qeila, Zurata of Akka, Milki-ili, and in particular the ruler of Jerusalem (*Uru-salim*), Abdi-Hipa ("Servant of Hipa," a goddess of the Hittites and of the Mitanni).

It is noteworthy that even at this period Jerusalem (§ 97) enjoys preeminence; its chieftain seems to be the most authoritative in the league, and never ceases denouncing in his letters the other chieftains who have rebelled. The league is disrupted by internal rivalries however and by the passage of some of its members to the rebel cause. Of those named above, the first three go over to the Habiri, and Abdi-Hipa is left alone, with the insurgents struggling to secure his important city. His appeals to Egypt remain without effect; he is himself denounced by his former ally, Shuwardata, and compared to a new Labaya. The circle about Jerusalem grows tighter: Gezer, Ascalon, Lachish go over to the enemy. The troops finally sent by the Pharaoh are betrayed en route by disloyal subalterns and the faithful Abdi-Hipa is constrained to express his doubts of the loyalty even of Janhamu, the all-powerful vizier at the court (with a Semitic name!) who disposes of the affairs of Palestine in autocratic fashion (§ 163). His last appeal is a despairing one: from Seir (Edom) to Gath of Carmel the lands have rebelled and are inimical to him; Pharaoh has no longer any representatives — "all are lost."

With this dramatic plea the documents come to an end. It is not baseless to assume that the Egyptian court, under the mad and impractical Amenophis IV (§ 34), and with such doubtful intermediaries as the officials described above, undertook to arrange a *modus vivendi* that recognized at least in practice the triumph of the Habiri, and that this lasted until the days of Seti I (§ 35).

THE LAND OF ISRAEL

58. The land in which the people of Israel settled[1] was, in the course of its history, known by many names. The territory corresponding to these names, however, was not always the same. For example, the current name *Palestine* was that used already by Herodotus (*Syria Palestina*) and by the Romans. Yet the term is of rather late origin, especially in the extended meaning which applies it to the whole country. At first it referred only to the region occupied by the Philistines (*Pelishtim*), the southern part of the coastal area of Canaan on which they settled as invaders during the twelfth century B.C., after having been repelled from the Egyptian frontier along with the other "Peoples of the Sea" by Rameses III (§§ 35, 328). It has been noted that the Amarna letters agree with the Bible in designating the country, according to its population, as the land of the Amurru or the land of the Canaanites (§§ 47, 52).

The term Canaan (in Hebrew, *Kena'an*), which appears also on the Egyptian monuments (as *K-in-'-n*), is usually in the Old Testament to indicate the territory conquered by the Israelites. Its meaning is unknown. For a long time it was supposed that the root must be *k n '*, "to make low, abase [oneself]" and that it must denote primarily the "low" land (in opposition to Aram [§ 51], which would denote the "high" country). Today, however, this interpretation is generally abandoned for both philological and geographic reasons.

The Egyptian documents of the Middle Kingdom and of the New Empire also furnish for northern Palestine the name *Retenu* (R-t-n-u), and for the southern part, where Hurrians (the biblical Horites) (Gen. 14:6; 36:20 ff.; Deut. 2:12 ff.) were to be found, the name *Haru*.

59. Palestine is in fact only the southernmost extension of the land of Syria; a strip of land marked off sharply by the Mediterranean to the west and by the Syro-Arabian Desert (*el-Hamad*) on the east. Its north-

---

[1] For the geography of Palestine, cf. F. M. Abel, *Géographie de la Palestine: I. Géographie physique et historique; II. Géographie politique; les villes*, 2 vols., Paris, 1933–1938; L. H. Grollenberg, O.P., *Atlas of the Bible*, New York, 1956.

Beersheba. (Vester, Amer. Colony.)

ern and southern boundaries are much more vague. To the north, the Lebanon range sweeps down the Mediterranean coast, paralleled inland by the Anti-Lebanon chain; Mt. Hermon forms a detached outpost of this latter chain, and the northern limit of Palestine may be placed in the gap that divides Mt. Hermon from the Lebanon. On the south, the desert lands stretching from below Beersheba (*Be'er-sheba'*) and the southern end of the Dead Sea down into the Sinai peninsula take the place of any more definite geographical boundary.

60. An expression that occurs often in the Bible to denote the length of the land of Israel from north to south is "from Dan to Bersabee" (Judg. 20:1; 1 Sam. 3:20; 2 Sam. 3:10; 17:11; etc.). A second expression, the practical equivalent of the first, is "from the entrance of Hamath to the River of Egypt" (1 Kings 8:65; etc.). The narrow stretch between Hermon and the Lebanon form a valley (el-Beqa'a: Coelesyria) which apparently was the "entrance to Hamath" (*introitus* Emath) because it extended northward toward the city of that name. The city of Dan (or: *Lais,* Judg. 18:29; modern *Tell el-Qadi*) was located at the foot of Hermon, just below the mouth of the valley. From this same valley issues the Leontes (*Litani*) river which, once free of the mountains, turns sharply toward the Mediterranean, taking the name of *Nahr el-Qasimiye,* and plunges into the sea just to the north of Tyre. It is this river, therefore, which most nearly corresponds to a precise northern boundary for Palestine. "Bersabee" at the other end of the land is well known; the "River of Egypt" must have been somewhere in its vicinity. Since here, however, the country is desert, the vicinity of Beersheba for political purposes can be but vaguely determined. Some have thought that the "river of Egypt" is to be identified with the *Wadi el-'Arish,* which cuts more or less in two the upper part of the peninsula of Sinai; others would place it at *Wadi Ghazze,* which runs quite close to Beersheba before reaching the sea just below Gaza.

Thus the country extends from 31° to 33° 20′ north latitude, between 34° 20′ and 36° longitude east of Greenwich. From the Nahr el-Qasimiye to Beersheba it is under 150 miles long. From the sea to the Jordan, the width of the country increases from less than 25 miles in the north to some 90 miles, at the south end of the Dead Sea. The area of Palestine west of the Jordan is some 6040 square miles; that of Transjordan is about 3660 square miles. Thus the combined area (9700 square miles) is about the equivalent of the state of Vermont, and is smaller than Belgium. But even of this territory the Israelites were not at any time the exclusive owners. Their secure holdings were in the middle; on the edges, both inland and along the sea, their control was either purely nominal or alto-

Lake el-Hule; Mt. Hermon in background.

gether nonexistent in many places at different times.

61. The surface of the land is split into separate regions by the deep rift through which the Jordan flows, so that besides the rift itself there are a Cisjordan country to the west, and Transjordan to the east.

The Syro-Palestinian rift is a geological phenomenon that has no

Panorama of Tiberias taken from Fortress.

End of Lake Tiberias and resumption of Jordan River.

counterpart anywhere else on the globe. It reaches down from the Taurus through Coelesyria, becomes steadily deeper as it cuts through Palestine until it reaches its greatest depth at the bottom of the Dead Sea, and continues on as an eastern boundary for the Sinai peninsula until it meets the Elanitic Gulf, the eastern arm of the Red Sea. Just above Dan (§ 60) its floor is some 1800 feet above the level of the Mediterranean; less than ten miles away, at Lake el-Hule (also Huleh), it is a bare seven feet above sea level. Less than ten miles farther on, at the Lake of Tiberias, it is some 680 feet below sea level; at the entrance to the Dead Sea it is about 1290 feet below the level of the Mediterranean, and at one point the bottom of the Dead Sea itself is as much as 2600 feet below sea level. Farther south is a rise which brings the general level of the

Scene on the Jordan along its central portion.

Dead Sea.

rift in the area toward the Red Sea back above the level of that body
of water. Modern Arabs call this stretch between the Lake of Tiberias
and the Dead Sea, in which the width of the gorge varies from just over

Banias (Caesarea-Philippi). Sources of the Jordan.

A *column of salt* on Jebel Usdum (Mount of Sodom) on the southwest bank of the Dead Sea. (Vester, Amer. Colony.)

a mile to about 14 miles, *el-Ghor;* the part from the Dead Sea (from 6 to 12 miles across) is known as *el-ʿAraba.*

Through this rift flows the only considerable stream in Palestine, the Jordan, which rises on Mt. Hermon and flows into the Dead Sea, after forming along the way the two lakes referred to above. Between the Lake of Tiberias and the Dead Sea its course is run between banks covered with a luxuriant jungle growth; several miles above the Dead Sea, however, this thins out because the water becomes saline, and at the same time the stream becomes broader (some 250 feet) and shallower.

62. The Dead Sea (*Bahr Lut,* the "Sea of Lot") is the most remarkable part of the rift. It is 48 miles long and 10 wide; two thirds of its waters come from the Jordan and the other third from lesser streams almost all on its eastern side. It has no outlet; but its great depth below sea level, combined with the heat which settles over it because of the surrounding peaks, occasions an evaporation which makes any other escape for the waters unnecessary. The daily evaporation from the sea is estimated at over two billion gallons. This results in a tremendous residue of salt; the water is so dense (holding in solution some 25 per cent of solids, by weight) that a human body floats in it when absolutely inert (cf. the story told of Vespasian by Josephus, *War of the Jews,* IV, 8, 4) and lower forms of life cannot maintain themselves there. The surrounding banks also are devoid of vegetation and are squalid and death-like to the view — hence the common name for the Sea. The rock surfaces are encrusted with salt (cf. the narrative in *Genesis,* 19:26; § 136). Besides other noxious fumes the water gives off that of petroleum, and large gobs of pitch and of asphalt are to be found floating upon its surface (for this reason Josephus called it the Asphalt Lake).

63. The Cisjordan land comprises the Mediterranean coastal strip and a much higher inland area. The coast from the mouth of the Nahr

General view of Haifa.

el-Qasimiye to the promontory of Carmel is only one to four miles in width; beyond this the heights rise abruptly. To the north is the port of Tyre, in ancient times an island; and as harbors rather inferior ones, Akka and Haifa, both lying at the foot of Carmel. From Carmel to below Gaza the coastal plain is straight and unbroken; toward the south it is as much as 13 miles wide, but, covered with the sands it has no harbor except the inadequate port of Jaffa. Between Carmel and Jaffa stretches the plain of Sharon, praised in the Bible for its beauty. The region south of Jaffa was Philistia proper (§ 58); it is joined to the Judean hill country by a district of lower hills, the *Shephelah* of the Bible.

64. The land between the coast and the Jordan is cleft in two geologically by the valley of Esdraelon, which forms a wedge extending from above Carmel obliquely to the southeast. North of this valley is the region that came to be known as Galilee; in its northern part it is mountainous, but the country becomes more open farther south. In the history of ancient Israel it was of but slight importance, both because the Hebrew infiltration there was rather scant and because the Esdraelon valley served to cut off this area from the national life as it developed in southern Palestine. The valley itself, however, was and still is of the greatest moment for the history of the country. Through it run a number

of prominent caravan routes, notably that which connected Egypt with Syria and Mesopotamia. Megiddo (§ 79), overlooking the valley, is a historic battleground (§§ 34, 311, 519).

65. South of the valley of Esdraelon come the districts of Samaria and of Judea. Both are hilly (with the highest point at *Sirat el-Bella'*, south of Jerusalem, 3370 feet), unvarying in character and poorly supplied with water. Samaria is the less fertile region, except for Mt. Carmel. Toward the Jordan valley the hills of southern Samaria and of Judea fall away sharply through the barren uncultivable tracts of the "desert of Juda," which in different sectors goes also by the local names of "desert of Ziph," "desert of Tekoa," etc. The southern slope is much more gradual, forming an inclined plateau that begins above Beersheba and drops down, as the *Negeb* district, to lose itself in the desert. The mountainous districts of Judea and Samaria were the core of the national life of Israel; and when the nation split up politically, became the separate kingdoms of Israel, with its capital at Samaria, and of Juda, governed from Jerusalem.

66. Transjordan is divided into three parts — northern, central, and southern.

The northern part, from Hermon to the Yarmuk gorge just below Lake Tiberias, is modern *Gaulan*. The ancient territory of Bashan included this district and also the *Hauran* region to the east of it. Gaulan

Valley of the Jordan near Jericho. (Koeppel, Palästina.)

The "desert of Juda."

is a volcanic plateau, sloping toward the south; its northern part is
rather dry and barren, but farther south it yields good crops of grain.
This plateau was another district in which the Hebrews found themselves in a minority; Aramean elements predominated there (§ 51).

Central Transjordan, from the Yarmuk to Wadi Hesban a little north
of the Dead Sea, is approximately ancient Galaad; its two sections, modern 'Ajlun and the greater part of the Belqa district, are separated by
the course of the Jabbok. This was at one time forest land; a well-watered
section, with scattered hills of moderate height. Even today it is pleasant
country, generously supplied with trees and pasture land.

Lower Transjordan is the land of Moab, running the length of the
Dead Sea on its eastern side and ending at the Wadi el-Hesa at the
sea's southern end. This again is a plateau, cut in two by the Arnon,
which enters the Dead Sea about midway of the eastern side. Below
the Arnon the country is higher; but the drop to the Dead Sea is steep
everywhere. There must have been thick woods here, too, in ancient
times, but now they are entirely lacking. The land is still fertile, however, and provides good pasturage. North of the Arnon the Israelite
population in ancient times was rather scanty; there was practically no
Israelite element in the south.[2]

67. Palestine is a subtropical region which has two seasons, the winter
or rainy season from November to April, and the dry, summer season
from May to October. Rain in summer is extremely rare; the winter
rainfall amounts to over 23 inches.

---

[2] Cf. N. Glueck, *Explorations in Eastern Palestine*, New Haven, 1934–1939; *The
Other Side of the Jordan*, 1940; and "Transjordan," in *BA*, 1946, 45–61.

The temperature varies from place to place. In the Jordan valley it is always comparatively high, reaching 120 degrees in the shade in August in the south. Along the Mediterranean coast the average temperature is 60 degrees in February, 85 degrees in August; the figures are higher in the south. In the hill country west of Jordan it is somewhat cooler: 46 degrees at Jerusalem in February, 77 degrees in August. The lowest recorded temperature, in January, 1864, was 25 degrees above zero. The change in temperature between day and night is very noticeable, and can be harmful to one living in the open. Snow is rare, and the fall is always light; frosty nights are also a rarity. Of the customary winds, those from the south and the southeast (*sherqiyyeh,* sirocco; *samum,* simoon) are oppressive and harmful (§ 214).

It does not seem that the climate of Palestine in ancient times was notably different from what it is today.

ARCHAEOLOGICAL EXCAVATIONS
AND SURVEYS

68. The soil of Israel, trodden from the earliest Christian centuries by the feet of devout pilgrims, is a remarkable book, containing within itself the story of its past. Of recent years this book has been opened by archaeological excavations, and although only the first chapters of that book have thus far been read, much light has already been shed upon the text of the Bible. Discoveries made in Palestinian archaeology also fill in, in an unlooked-for but welcome way, information left us in the Amarna letters and in Assyro-Babylonian and Egyptian sources.

The beginnings of this archaeological research can be placed in the final decade of the nineteenth century. The major part of the excavations, carried on in the face of obstacles and restrictions constantly imposed by the old imperial government of Turkey, were the work of the *Palestine Exploration Fund,* established in London in 1865; American, German, Austrian, Danish, and other archaeological societies made lesser contributions. A type of research which has sprung up in more recent years to supplement the excavation of limited sites is that of surface exploration of the country, with the prehistoric period and its remains especially in view. By harmonizing the various data that can be assembled for both historic and prehistoric times, it is proposed to build up as far as possible a complete and documented outline of the various stages of human history in the region.

69. As a reference framework for the detailed findings to be described in what follows, two tables are here offered; the one, *Prehistoric;* the other, *Historic.* The first is a general one, which is applicable within limits to many parts of the world; the second refers to Palestine alone, and represents the consensus of modern scholarly judgment, though on individual points there will often be variations of opinion which do not affect the usefulness of the outline as a whole.[1]

---

[1] For the *historic* periods, cf. *RB*, 1923, 275; and "Canaan" in *DBS*, I, 1009. For a bird's-eye view of the archaeological exploration in Palestine, cf. L. Hennequin, "Fouilles en Palestine . . . " in *DBS*, III, 1938, 318–524; G. Barrois, *Manuel d'Archéologie Biblique*, Paris, 1939–1953, I, 35–73; II, 469–470; J. Finegan, *Light From the Ancient Past*, Princeton, 1947, 122–163.

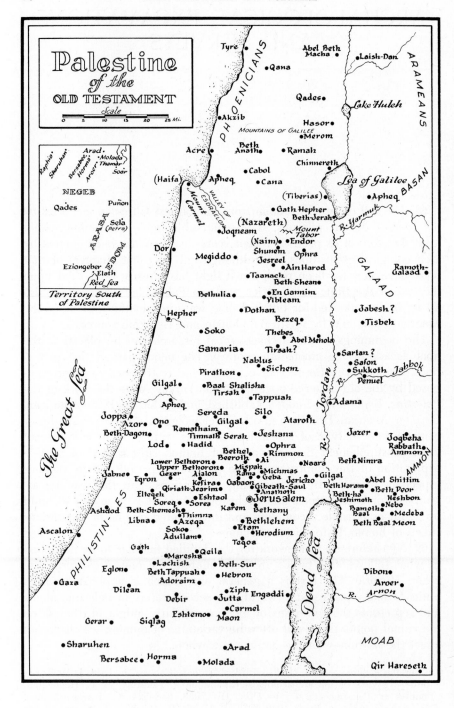

Palestine of the OLD TESTAMENT

Scale
0   5   10   15   20   25 Mi.

Territory South of Palestine

NEGEB

ARABA

EDOM

Rephia
Sheruhen
Bersabee
Horma
Arad
Molada
Thamar
Aroer
Soor

Qades   Punon

Eziongeber
Elath
Red Sea

Sela
(Petra)

Tyre
Qana
Abel Beth Macha
Laish-Dan

ARAMEANS

PHOENICIANS

Qades
Lake Huleh

Akzib
Hasor

MOUNTAINS OF GALILEE
Merom

Acre
Beth Anath
Ramah
Chinnereth

Cabol

(Haifa)
Apheq
Cana

Sea of Galilee
Apheq

BASAN

R. Yarmuk

(Tiberias)
Gath Hepher
Beth-Jerah

Mount Carmel

VALLEY OF ESDRAELON

(Nazareth)
Joqneam

(Naim)
Mount Tabor
Endor

Dor
Shunem
Jesreel
Ophra
Ain Harod

Megiddo

Taanach
Beth-Shean

GALAAD

Ramoth-Galaad

Bethulia
En Gannim
Yibleam

Hepher
Dothan
Bezeq

Jabesh?
Tisbeh

Soko
Thebes
Abel Mehola

Samaria
Tirsah?

Nablus
Sichem

Sartan?
Safon
Sukkoth
Penuel

Jabbok

R. Jordan

Pirathon

Gilgal
Baal Shalisha
Tirsah
Tappuah

Adama

Apheq
Sereda
Silo

Joppa
Azor
Ono
Gilgal
Ataroth

Jazer
Joqbeha
Rabbath-Ammon

Beth-Dagon
Ramathaim
Timnath Serah
Jeshana

The Great Sea

Lod
Hadid

Ophra
Rimmon

Beth Nimra

Jabne
Eqron

Lower Bethoron
Upper Bethoron
Gezer
Aialon
Kesira
Qiriath-Jearim

Bethel
Beeroth
Ai
Mispah
Rama
Michmas
Gabaon
Geba
Jericho
Gibeath-Saul
Anatoth

Naara

Gilgal
Abel Shittim
Beth Peor

AMMON

Eltoqeh
Soreq
Sorea
Esthaol

Jerusalem

Anatoth

Beth Harem
Beth-ha-Jeshimoth
Heshbon

Ashdod
Beth-Shemesh
Thimna
Azeqa
Soko
Adullam

Karem
Bethany

Bethlehem
Etam
Herodium

Ramoth Baal
Nebo
Medeba

Beth Baal Meon

PHILISTINES

Libna

Gath

Maresha
Lachish

Qaila

Teqoa

Dead Sea

Ascalon

Eglon
Beth Tappuah
Adoraim

Beth-Sur
Hebron

Dibon
Aroer
R. Arnon

Gaza

Dilean
Debir
Jutta
Ziph
Engaddi
Carmel
Maon

Gerar
Siqlag
Eshtemo

Sharuhen

Bersabee
Horma
Arad

Molada

MOAB

Qir Hareseth

Prehistoric Periods

Geological Period	Stone Age	Type of Industry
Quaternary	Old Stone Age (Paleolithic: chipped stone artifacts)	} Chellean Acheulian [Tayacian { Levalloisian [Mousterian
		[Aurignacian { Solutrian [Magdalenian
	Mesolithic Period (transition; microlithic industry)	[Azilian { Campignian [Natufian (Palestine)
	Neolithic Period (polished stone artifacts)	} Tahunian Ghassulian } Palestine

Historic Times

Periods	Phases	Approximate Dates
Bronze Age	I. Early Canaanite	3000–2000 B.C.
	II. Middle Canaanite	2000–1500 B.C.
	III. Late Canaanite	1500–1200 B.C.
Iron Age	I. Early Palestinian 1. Philistine 2. Early Israelite	1200– 600 B.C.
	II. Middle Palestinian: Middle Israelite	600– 300 B.C.
	III. Late Palestinian 1. Late Israelite 2. Hellenistic	300– 50 B.C.
Imperial Periods	I. Roman	B.C. 50– 350 A.D.
	II. Byzantine	A.D. 350– 636 A.D.
Modern Times	I. Early Arab	636–1100 A.D.
	II. Medieval (Crusades)	1100–1200 A.D.
	III. Recent Arab	1200– A.D.

Cave where *Homo galilaeensis* was discovered. (Vester, Amer. Colony.)

A settled chronology for the prehistoric periods is beyond reach at the present. As far as Palestine is concerned, it may be remarked that the Neolithic period (which may have begun in the sixth or fifth millennium B.C.) does not end abruptly, but is found intertwined with the first traces of the historic cultures; for many centuries its stone products remain in evidence side by side with those of copper or bronze. This period of mixed culture is called by many the Chalcolithic period, and comes to a close about 3000 B.C. with the beginning of historic times.

70. Man's presence in Palestine from the earliest times is amply demonstrated by the remains of his paleolithic workmanship. A discovery made in 1925 in a cave on the plain of Ghuweir, in Galilee, to the northwest of the Lake of Tiberias, added the evidence of a human skull of Neanderthal type. This early skull belongs to the Mousterian epoch of the Old Stone Age, and was the first of its kind to be found outside of Europe. It is commonly referred to as the *Homo galilaeensis;* naturally no absolute dating for it is possible, but it must certainly go back to a time thousands of years before Christ.

This first discovery of early man in Palestine has been followed by an even more remarkable find in a series of caves in the Wadi el-Mugharah, at the foot of the Carmel range, on its western side, southeast of the Crusaders' castle of Athlit. Here portions of ten skeletons, two of them quite complete, were brought to light in 1932; they represent evidently careful burials of early Paleolithic man. The surrounding caves provided one other skeleton and an interlocking series of strata with evidences of human occupancy ranging through the Old Stone Age and into Mesolithic times. Further excavations yielding significant material, including skeletal remains of a very early date, have been conducted at Jebel Qafseh, near Nazareth; nor does this exhaust the recent discoveries.[2]

---

[2] For the Old Stone Age in Palestine, see F. Turville-Petre, *Researches in Pre-*

Almost all of Palestine is strewn with the stone artifacts of prehistoric man. They are to be found in the different levels of the various natural caves that open out into the valleys, on the surface of the open ground in a number of "lithic stations" and in the lowest levels of the mounds selected for systematic excavation. They range from crude specimens of hand axes very imperfectly formed by a chipping process to fine, carefully polished knives; between the two extremes there are included fist hatchets, amygdaloids (almond-shaped cutting tools), axes, maces, scrapers, spear points, arrowheads, etc. They are grouped, according to such refinement of workmanship as they exhibit, into specimens from the early Paleolithic (Chellean to Mousterian), the late Paleolithic (Aurignacian to Magdalenian), and the later periods of the above table.

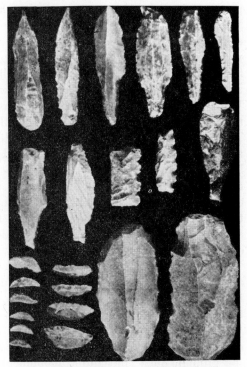

Palestinian stone instruments. (*Revue Biblique*, 1928.)

71. Early Paleolithic accumulations have been found in the neighborhood of Jerusalem, both to the south of it (the valley of Rephaim, el-Buqeïʿa; Beth-Sahur; the Herodium, etc.) and to the north (on Mt. Scopus); also in the region of Gaza, at ʿAin Qeseimeh in the Negeb, at ʿAin Musa near Bethlehem in Galilee, etc.; and in several places in Transjordan. Late Paleolithic sites include Mugharet el-Wad, the Wadi Rubin, Jebel Qafset, ʿErq el-Ahmar, ʿAin el-Qedeirat near Qades, etc. Mesolithic layers appear at Tantur; Beit Taʿamir; Tahuneh; Tell el-Ful; Ras Qerameh, and elsewhere.

During comparatively recent years, abundant evidences of man's

historic Galilee, 1925–1926, and A Report on the Galilee Skull (by Sir A. Keith), London, 1927; D. A. E. Garrod and D. M. A. Bate, The Stone Age of Mt. Carmel, I: Excavations at Wadi el-Mughara, Vol. I, Oxford, 1937; T. D. McCown and Sir Arthur Keith, The Stone Age of Mt. Carmel, II: The Fossil Human Remains from the Levalloiso-Mousterian, Oxford, 1939; R. Neuville, "Le préhistorique de Palestine," in RB, 1934, 237–259; and the pertinent chapters in C. C. McCown, The Ladder of Progress in Palestine, New York, 1943.

presence in Palestine as an agriculturalist and even an artist in the Mesolithic period have been discovered. The typical industry is known as Natufian, from the Wadi en-Natuf, in the Judean hill country northwest of Jerusalem, where it was first found. Later stages toward the final coming of the age of bronze and the beginnings of historic times are represented by culture complexes known as Tahunian (from the Wadi Tahuneh, below Bethlehem), Ghassulian (from a series of little mounds east of the Jordan not far above the Dead Sea), and Canaanean. The lower strata at Jericho and at Megiddo, as well as caves at Carmel, at Shuqbah in the Wadi en-Natuf and elsewhere, and the site just below the surface at Teleilat Ghassul (§ 94) which was never built over in later times, combine to give us a consecutive picture of agricultural civilizations succeeding one another in the country, with various techniques in the preparation of stone tools and pottery, with some artistic attainments and with early evidences of town life in houses of mud brick.[3]

Neolithic implements have turned up in almost every place where archaeological excavations have been made; usually they have been intermingled with products of the Bronze Age, and often, too, with those of the Paleolithic or Mesolithic.

72. To these traces of human life and enterprise in prehistoric times must be added evidence of gigantic size, found above the surface of the ground. Such "megalithic monuments," formed of huge blocks of rough or lightly trimmed stone, occur in various arrangements and combinations. They are normally called by the Breton names used to describe similar monuments in Europe: *dolmens*, single blocks of stone placed after the manner of a roof over two others set as upright supports (there are "double dolmens," with three supports); *menhirs*, monoliths set upright in the earth, and ordinarily pointed at the top; *cromlechs*, circles of upright blocks; haphazard masses of stone piled into *cairns* or mounds; "Cyclopic walls," and other less common groupings. For the dolmens and menhirs in particular it is not uncommon to find stones employed whose bulk exceeds five cubic yards.

The distribution of these monuments throughout Palestine has not as yet been determined precisely. In Transjordan they are very common, and are found clustered together in well-defined areas (in the 'Ajlun [§ 66], the dolmens alone number well over a thousand). West of the Jordan they are quite rare and have generally been disturbed or overturned; some have been found in the south around Hebron, Tell

---

[3] Besides the references given in the preceding note (McCown, Neuville, Garrod, and Bate), see D. Buzy, "Une industrie mésolithique in Palestine" (Ouady Tahouneh), in *RB*, 1928, 558–578; D. A. E. Garrod, "The Stone Age of Palestine," in *Antiquity*, 8, 1934, 133–150; and the excavation reports on Jericho, Megiddo, and Teleilat Ghassul (see below, §§ 79, 80 ff., 94).

Sandahannah, etc., in the Jerusalem district at Beitin, Deir Sa'ideh, Abu Dis, and other places north of the city, and still farther north at Deir Ghuzzaleh, Ta'annak, and elsewhere.

73. The period during which these megaliths were erected has been the subject of varied speculations — some have thought it the beginning of the third millennium B.C.; many now suppose it may be even later than the beginnings of the Bronze Age. It seems now an established fact that the main purpose of the dolmens was to serve as sepulchral monuments. It is possible that the roof served also as a sacrificial altar. The object of monuments of other types is quite uncertain: the cromlechs may also have been burial monuments (miniature cromlechs of small stones have been found in the course of excavations, in connection with burial deposits: § 77), but they may also have been used at times to mark sacred enclosures, or simply as commemorative monuments — a hypothesis which applies equally well to the menhirs and to the cairns or tumuli. This would establish a connection between the menhirs and the sacred steles (*masseboth*) which were so prominent a feature of the religion of the Canaanites (§ 104).

Of what race the people were who set up the megaliths of Palestine, no one knows. To ascribe to them Indo-European origin merely because of the similarity of the constructions to the megalithic remains in Europe is quite arbitrary. On the other hand, their custom of burying their dead seems to show that this early race was different from that of the earliest inhabitants of Palestine known to us from the excavations, for these practiced cremation (§ 76).

At this point it will be useful to undertake a cursory survey of the excavations conducted in Palestine, with particular reference to their bearing on the history of ancient Israel.[4]

74. **Tell el-Hesy and Tell ed-Duweir.** The former of these two sites, eighteen miles northeast of Gaza, was at one time identified with biblical Lachish; more recently it has become all but certain that

---

[4] For archaeological work in Palestine, the following general references may be used: H. Vincent, *Canaan d'après l'exploration récente*, Paris, 1907 (very complete to the date of publication); L. Speleers, *Les fouilles en Asie anterieure a partir de 1843*, Liège, 1928; Millar Burrows, *What Mean These Stones?*, New Haven, 1941; W. F. Albright, *From the Stone Age to Christianity*, Baltimore, 1940 and *Archaeology and the Religion of Israel*, Baltimore, 1942; C. Watzinger, *Denkmäler Palästinas. Eine Einführung in die Archäologie des hl. Landes, I: Von den Anfängen bis zum Ende der israel. Königszeit; II: Von der Herrschaft der Assyrer bis zur arabischen Eroberung*, Leipzig, 1933–1935; L. Hennequin, "Fouilles et champs de fouilles en Palestine et Phénicie," in DBS, 3, 318–524; D. Diringer, *Le iscrizioni antico-ebraiche raccolte e illustrate*, Firenze, 1934; S. Moscati, *L'Epigrafia Ebraica Antica*, Rome, 1951; R. A. S. Macalister, *A Century of Excavation in Palestine*, London, 1930; I. G. Duncan, *Digging up Biblical History*, London, 1931. For lesser finds and for descriptions of excavations in progress the Palestine Exploration Society publications, those of the American Schools of Oriental Research, the *Journal of Near Eastern Studies* and the *Revue Biblique* are indispensable.

Lachish was at Tell ed-Duweir, and Tell el-Hesy is supposed rather to be Eglon or Saruhen. At the last-named site there were excavations under English auspices in 1890, by Flinders Petrie, and in 1891–1893, by Bliss.[5] Eleven superimposed strata were uncovered; these were referred by Bliss to a series of eight successive occupations of the site. Between several of the levels there were evidences of destruction and fire; the third city on the site, in particular, finished in a thick layer of ashes. Later studies, with the benefit of data from other sites, have raised the chronology proposed by Bliss, so that the beginnings of the settlement should be dated in the third millennium (Bliss had supposed c. 1700 B.C.); the third city would be just prior to, or at the beginning of, the Amarna age (§ 43 ff.); the fourth is an Iron Age city; the fifth, from the time of King Roboam; the sixth appears to have been destroyed by Sennacherib (§ 491); the seventh was destroyed by Nabuchodonosor (about 590 B.C.; § 536 ff.). In the ruins of the third city was found a clay tablet quite like the letters from el-Amarna, and mentioning personages known from those letters.[6]

Tell ed-Duweir is a mound in this same region, near the road that links Gaza and Hebron. Excavations there since 1933, also under English auspices, and directed by J. L. Starkey, have disclosed a number of occupations extending from the predynastic times of Egypt down to the Arab period.[7] The arrangement of the defenses at Tell ed-Duweir shows striking resemblances to the fortifications of Lachish at the time of its siege by Sennacherib, as depicted on the Assyrian monuments (compare the illustration at § 494). Besides seals and other objects, this site has yielded a valuable series of inscribed ostraca from Israelite times.[8]

75. Sites in the Shephelah. These include (cf. § 63) *Tell es-Safy* (the biblical Gath?), *Tell Zakariyeh* (Azeka?), *Tell Sandahannah* (Maresa, Moresheth), and *Tell Judeideh* (?), the first to the north, the others to the northeast of Lachish. The places named were probed by

---

[5] W. M. Flinders Petrie, *Tell el-Hesy* (*Lachish*), London, 1891; F. J. Bliss, *A Mound of Many Cities*, London, 1898; and *AO*, 370.

[6] The latest treatment of this tablet is that of W. F. Albright, in *BASOR*, 1943, 28–30.

[7] J. L. Starkey, *Excavations at Tell ed-Duweir*, 1932–1933, 1933–1934, 1934–1935, 1935–1936; *Palestine Exploration Fund, Quarterly Statement*, 1933, 190–199; 1934, 164–175; 1935, 198–207; 1936, 178–189; id. (fifth campaign, 1936–1937), *Palestine Exploration Quarterly*, 1937, 228–241; C. H. Inge (sixth campaign, 1937–1938), *ibid.*, 1938, 240–256; O. Tufnell, C. H. Inge, L. Harding, *Lachish II: The Fosse Temple*, Oxford, 1940; P. Vincent, "Les fouilles de Tell ed-Douweir — Lachis," in *RB*, 1939, 250–277, 406–433, 565–583.

[8] H. Torczyner, *Lachish I: The Lachish Letters*, London, 1938; R. de Vaux, "Les ostraca de Lachish," in *RB*, 1939, 181–206; W. F. Albright, "The Lachish Letters after Five Years," in *BASOR*, 1941, 18–24; H. G. May, Lachish Letter IV: 7–10, *ibid.*, 1945, 22–26; D. W. Thomas in *Palestine Exploration Quarterly*, 1946, 38–42.

the English in 1898–1900.[9] Two levels from the second millennium B.C. and one from the first millennium were found at Tell es-Safy; the intermediate level contained Philistine pottery. At Tell Zakariyeh the first period represented is the Late Bronze; there were underground cavities, both natural and artificial, antedating the Israelite period, and jars with Israelite seal impressions were found. There were many underground caves at Tell Sandahannah also, some of them possibly pre-Israelite. Of the four strata at Tell Judeideh, the first is from the middle of the second millennium, the next is Philistine, the third Israelite (with Jewish names on the pottery).

76. Gezer. This city was an important center and a military strong point from remote antiquity; it stood at the edge of the Shephelah on the road from Jerusalem to the port of Jaffa. For a time it was under the overlordship of Egypt (being referred to in the Amarna letters as *Alu Gazzi*). After the Israelite invasion it remained as an isolated holding of the Canaanites (cf. Josue 16:10; Judg. 1:29); but in Solomon's time it was captured and destroyed by a Pharaoh (§ 383) who gave it to Solomon as dowry when that king became his son-in-law. It was immediately rebuilt (1 Kings 9:16–17). The excavations under Macalister in 1902–1905 and 1907–1909 yielded such abundant results that Gezer has become the chief source of archaeological information on ancient Canaan.[10] Macalister distinguishes these periods in its history: Pre-Semitic, up to about 2500 B.C.; First Semitic, to about the end of the Egyptian Twelfth Dynasty (§ 30); Second Semitic, until near the end of the Eighteenth Dynasty (§ 33); Third Semitic, until about 1000 B.C.; Fourth Semitic, until about 550 B.C.; and then the usual Persian, Hellenistic, and Roman periods, etc. But neither the nomenclature nor the chronology of Macalister (the chronology is governed by general considerations not limited to Gezer) gives complete satisfaction to more recent students of the question. The approximate limits usually assigned for the four Semitic strata at the present time are: 2500–1600; 1600–1200; 1200–950; 950–550.

The first traces of occupation at Gezer go back to about 3000 B.C., and are troglodytic. A crematorium unique in Palestine dates from this period; it is a cave whose lowest level is made up of ashes mixed with fragments of charred bones, in a stratum about one foot deep in the middle, directly below an air vent in the roof of the cave, where traces of smoke are still visible. The only artifacts are neolithic in

---

[9] F. I. Bliss, R. A. S. Macalister, *Excavations in Palestine during 1898–1900*, London, 1902.

[10] R. A. S. Macalister, *The Excavation of Gezer, 1902–1905 and 1907–1909*, 3 vols., London, 1912. For analogies elsewhere, cf. L. H. Vincent, "Le nouvelle hypogée de Byblos et l'hypogée royal de Gezer," in *RB*, 1923, 552 ff.; *id.*, "Un calendrier agricole israélite," *ibid.*, 1909, 243–269; and *AO*, 444.

The Canaanite sanctuary of Gezer. (Macalister, *Excavation of Gezer.*)

character; thus the neolithic inhabitants of Gezer burned their dead. For a place of worship they used a flat, rocky surface pierced by cup holes and channels which communicated with a nearby cave.

77. The practice of cremation was discontinued, however, with the coming of the first Semites (c. 2500 B.C.). From this time on, the same cave, now enlarged, served for ordinary burials in which the bodies were interred haphazardly — often lying on their sides and in a contracted position, sometimes surrounded by small-scale cromlechs (§ 73). The newcomers also built houses and raised walls for fortification. To facilitate resistance against prolonged attacks, access to a nearby underground spring was effected by means of a tunnel 23 feet high, 13 feet wide, and 200 feet long, which they hacked out with stone implements, and which reached the water level, by means of steps, some 94 feet below the surface of the ground (cf. § 98). These new inhabitants had religious customs of their own, for which they built a sacred "high place." Eight steles for cult purposes (*masseboth,* § 104) still remain standing — varying in height from five to ten feet, except for two which are broken off. The second in the row, the lowest and of a distinctive shape, is quite smooth and polished, probably from being anointed and kissed repeatedly over the course of centuries; the eighth is usually regarded as phallic in design (§ 104). In front of the stele there is a cube of stone which is variously conjectured to be either the base for another *massebah* which is missing, or for an *'asherah* (§ 105) or a primitive altar. A cistern and a double cave located near the stele must have been used for ritual purposes; in and about the cave many infants are buried enclosed in jars.

Gezer was destroyed, perhaps by the Egyptians, about the middle of the second millennium, but was rebuilt shortly thereafter with more extensive walls, remaining thus until Israelite times, when the destruction in Solomon's reign, already spoken of, took place. Little that is noteworthy remains to mark the Israelite occupation here. The principal find was the so-called "Agricultural Calendar," a small slab of stone which bears, in old style Hebrew letters, a terse list of the year's chief farming activities in relation to the seasons. This slab turned up in a stratum of the sixth century B.C., but it is no doubt considerably older.[11]

78. Ta'annak. This is the biblical city of the same name (Ta'anakh; Vulgate: *Thanach, Thenach*), situated on the southern edge of the valley of Esdraelon near Megiddo (§ 79). It was excavated by Austrians, under Sellin, in 1902–1904.[12] The beginnings of the city were prior to 2000 B.C.; the wall which surrounds the center of the *tell* is from about that date, with bastions of somewhat later construction to the north and west. Among the many objects recovered may be mentioned a

---

[11] The text of the "Agricultural Calendar" has been fully discussed recently by W. F. Albright, in *BASOR*, 1943, 16–26; cf. Vincent, *loc. cit.*

[12] E. Sellin, *Tell Ta'annak*, in the *Denkschriften* of the Vienna Academy, *phil.-hist. Kl.*, 50, 4, Vienna, 1904; and *Eine Nachlese aus dem Tell Ta'annek*, *ibid.*, 52, 3, Vienna, 1905; cf. also *AO*, 371.

The "masseboth" of Gezer; presumably the altar is the object in the foreground. (Macalister, *Excavation of Gezer.*)

The site of Megiddo. (Vester, Amer. Colony.)

cylinder seal of Babylonian design from about the fifteenth century B.C. bearing in cuneiform "Atanahili, son of Habsim, servant of Nergal." More important still are twelve clay tablets, five of them fragmentary, written in cuneiform, found inside or near a clay container. These are surely contemporary with the Amarna correspondence, which they resemble in every respect. They yield the name of one Ashirat-yashur (cf. § 105), possibly the local chieftain.[13] For the composite nature of the local culture it is worthy of note that along with this material with Babylonian characteristics, other remains are found to be Egyptian in style (a scarab of Thutmose III: § 33), or Cypriote (pottery), or from elsewhere.

79. Tell el-Mutesellim. This is the biblical Megiddo (Vulgate: *Mageddo*), strategically very important because of the geographical site which it occupies (§ 34). It was excavated by Germans, under Schumacher, in 1903–1905, and by the Oriental Institute of the University of Chicago in a series of campaigns beginning in 1925.[14] Schumacher distinguished seven strata, to which he assigned as approximately their earliest dates, 3000, 2000, 1500, 1200, 1000, 700, and finally 500 B.C. Later study has brought about abandonment of this classification, even by Watzinger. Evidences have been found of human habitation on the site from remote antiquity. The city walls, and two groups of buildings in the north and center have been ascribed to the Middle Bronze period; two underground burial chambers seem to be slightly older, and in one of them there was recovered a scarab with the name of Sesostris I (§ 30). The level dating from the end of the Bronze Age and that of Early Iron are separated by a deep layer of

---

[13] A recent study is that of W. F. Albright, "A Prince of Taanach in the 15th Century B.C.," in *BASOR*, 1944, 13–27.

[14] G. Schumacher, *Tell el-Mutesellim, I: Fundbericht*, Leipzig, 1908; C. Watzinger, *Tell el-Mutesellim, II: Die Funde*, Leipzig, 1929; P. L. Guy, *New Light from Armageddon*, Chicago, 1931; id., *Megiddo Tombs*, Chicago, 1939. L. H. Vincent, "Vers l'aube de l'histoire en Palestine . . . " *RB*, 1934, 403–431; 1935, 416–437; H. G. May, *Material Remains of the Megiddo Cult*, Chicago, 1935; R. S. Lamon, *The Megiddo Water System*, 1935; P. L. O. Guy, and R. M. Engberg, *Megiddo Tombs*, 1938; R. S. Lamon and G. M. Shipton, *Megiddo I*, Chicago, 1939; G. Loud, *The Megiddo Ivories*, Chicago, 1939.

ashes which can only have been produced by a fiery destruction. Some
have seen a connection between this and the Israelite conquest of
the city during the occupation of Canaan. A stone with the name of
Sheshonk, found by the American excavators, shows that the Palestinian
invasion by that Pharaoh (§§ 36, 416) reached as far as Megiddo. Among
other objects recovered are a quantity of carved ivory and two seals
with inscriptions in archaic Hebrew lettering. Both of these are from
about the eighth century B.C.; one reads "Of Asaph," along with a
number of symbolic hieroglyphs, while the other is inscribed as belonging to "Shema', steward of Jeroboam." From the period of the Hebrew
monarchy, and perhaps from Solomon's time, are an elaborate city
gate and extensive stables. There is also an elaborate shaft and tunnel
dating to about the twelfth century B.C.; it was intended to make
a supply of spring water available within the city which was invulnerable
to enemy attack.

80. Jericho. The old city of Jericho lies slightly more than a mile
north of modern Jericho, at Tell es-Sultan. It was the first city conquered by the Israelites west of the Jordan, and they destroyed it
(Josue 6). In the time of David it was mentioned as a place which
was rather out of the way, and unfrequented (2 Sam. 10:5); it was
rebuilt by a certain Hiel during the reign of Achab (1 Kings 16:34).
It was excavated under Austrian and German auspices by Sellin and
Watzinger (1907–1909), and by an English expedition under Garstang
(1929–1936).[15] Remains of human habitation from Mesolithic, Neolithic, and Chalcolithic times were brought to light. At a later date
two concentric lines of fortification ringed the city; the inner one
followed the crest of the hill, and was a masterpiece of military engin-
eering, being made up of two parallel walls, of which the inner wall,
about twelve feet thick, was the stronger. Ten or twelve feet away
arose an outer wall about six feet thick, and between the two are
traces of casemates, possibly the lower courses of towers for added
strength. The outer more extensive fortification, following the base
of the slope, whose wall was about six feet thick, was originally perhaps
twenty-five feet high, with carefully laid foundations, and further boasted
a glacis. To the east, where the spring (Ain es-Sultan) is located, this
line of fortification seems to include also the indispensable provision
for a water supply, but investigations here are hampered by the
modern post road, and have not as yet recovered the traces of
either fortification.

---

[15] E. Sellin and C. Watzinger, *Jericho*, Leipzig, 1913; John Garstang, *Annals of
Archaeology and Anthropology* (U. of Liverpool), 1932–1936; John and J. B. E.
Garstang, *The Story of Jericho*, London, 1940; L. H. Vincent, "L'aube de l'histoire a
Jericho," in *RB*, 1938, 561–589; 1939, 91–107; cf. *BA*, 1930, 32–36; 1953, 46–67;
Natl. Geographic, 1953, 853–870 (Kathleen Kenyon).

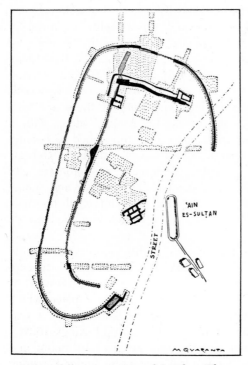

Map of the excavations of Jericho. (The dotted areas indicate recent excavations.) (*Revue Biblique*, 1930.)

81. The chronology of the remains of Jericho, and especially of the fortifications mentioned, has been the subject of so prolonged a debate, that the following summary will help one appreciate the difficulties encountered in this type of work even when it is done by experts.[16] The first excavators, once their field work was ended, changed their opinions several times. In the final report Sellin (not altogether in agreement with Watzinger) proposed the following periods for the site: Prehistoric (from the fourth millennium B.C.); Canaanite (2500–1600 B.C.); late Canaanite (1600–1200), followed by a period of abandonment; Israelite (870 –), and then Postexilic, Machabean, etc. He assigned the inner line of fortification, with its two parallel walls, to the Canaanite period, about 2000 B.C. The outer fortification which in the preliminary reports he had considered contemporary with the inner one he assigned to the Israelite period, and attributed it to Hiel. The inner fortification was, it is supposed, destroyed along with the city as a whole, by the Habiri (§§ 54, 174), whom Sellin identified with the Hebrews.

Although this chronology found favor with many students of the question, others greeted it with extensive reservations. The most delicate point was in the dating of the outermost fortifications, because on it was thought to hinge the dating of the Israelite conquest. A number of scholars (Gressman, Albright, Thomsen) refused to attribute this wall to Hiel, holding it to be a number of centuries earlier. Somewhat later, the excavators themselves reversed their judgment on the point, as the following quotation shows: "The judgment on the fall

---

[16] For the question of chronology, we may confine our references to the writings of Garstang, including his article on "The Story of Jericho . . . " in *American Journal of Semitic Languages and Literature*, 1941, 366–372; of L. H. Vincent in *RB*, 1930, 403–433; 1932, 266–276; 1935, 583–605; and of W. F. Albright in *BASOR*, 1935, 10–18; 74, 1939, 11–23.

of the outer wall of Jericho, on which Watzinger and I formerly concurred (*Jericho*, p. 181 ff.) calls for a considerable correction. On totally independent grounds — he because of the pottery of Gezer and Ain Shems, and I because of that from Sichem — we have since come to the conclusion that about 1500 B.C. only the inner city, of more ancient date [the one within the inner fortifications], must have fallen; and that it was soon rebuilt and surrounded by the outer wall with its glacis, which in its turn fell about 1200 B.C., and thus represents the wall overthrown by Josue."[17] This repeated change of opinion, which is to the credit of those who so change, is readily explained when one considers the slender, fugitive character of the indications on which the chronology depends. One of the most decisive of these is the pottery unearthed during the course of the excavations. Père Vincent, therefore, a thorough connoisseur of Canaanite pottery, putting the whole question once more under review and, basing his interpretation solely on what he called *le langage des faits*, proposed the following chronology for the ruins of Jericho: 3000–2500 B.C., Eneolithic (?); 2500–2100 B.C., traces of fortification in brickwork; 2100–1900 B.C., fortification with the double wall on the crest of the hill, with pottery from Early and Middle Bronze;

1900–c. 1250 B.C., outer fortifications, pottery from Middle and Late Bronze, destruction of the city by the Israelites under Josue; 1250–870 B.C., a gap of some four centuries; 870–c. 600 B.C., restoration effected by Hiel.

82. But even P. Vincent's careful study did not settle the question, so in the hope of throwing further light on this obscure problem, new excavations were undertaken under English auspices. Garstang, the director, thought it unlikely *a priori* that the earlier fortification should be the one on the crest of the hill, since comparable instances tended

Jericho: Canaanite wall of external enclosure. (Vester, Amer. Colony.)

[17] Ernst Sellen, *Gesch. des isr.–jüd. Volkes*, I, Leipzig, 1924, 97; P. Vincent, "La chronologie des ruines de Jericho," *RB* 1930, 403 ff.; G. E. Wright, *BA* 1940, 32 ff.; 1953, 14 ff.; 1955, 107 f.; A. D. Tushringham, "Excavations at OT Jericho," *BA* 1953, 46 ff. (Kenyon Expedition).

to show that as a rule the first step was to gird the lower slopes of any lofty site. Coming to the actual excavations, he widened their scope, recorded tens of thousands of shards in minute detail, consulted with recognized experts, and concluded that the relative order of the two fortifications simply had to be inverted: the outer wall was the older, the inner one more recent. The outer fortification, in Garstang's judgment, must have been built about 1800 B.C. and destroyed about 1600 B.C.; the outside wall of the inner ring of fortifications, on the other hand, would date from about 1600 B.C., while its inner wall would be of the same period, but built on the remains of another wall from earlier times.

Coming to the question of the destruction of this double inner fortified wall, Garstang, Fisher, and Vincent agreed to the following signed statement: "The main defenses of Jericho in the Late Bronze Age followed the upper brink of the city mound, and comprised two parallel walls, the outer six feet, the inner twelve feet thick. Investigations along the west side show continuous signs of destruction and conflagration. The outer wall suffered most, its remains falling outside down the slope. The inner wall is preserved only where it abuts upon the citadel to a height of twenty feet; elsewhere large sections of it have fallen, along with the buildings raised upon it, into the space between the walls, which was filled up with ruins and debris. Traces of intense fire are plain to see, including reddened masses of brick, cracked stones, charred timbers and ashes. Houses alongside the wall were found burned to the ground, their roofs fallen upon the domestic pottery. The date of destruction was ascertained to fall before the close of the Late Bronze Age, but the precise date and the solution of numerous other questions can only be determined by more complete and methodical excavation."[18] On the basis of these conclusions, and in view of the fact that but a single specimen of Mycenean ware (1350–1200 B.C.) was found in situ, and that not within, but outside, the ancient city, Garstang further concluded that the inner fortification was destroyed about 1400 B.C., before the importation of Mycenean pottery into the region.

This date, however, led to renewed disagreement. Père Vincent, a cosigner of the statement just given, refused to accept the dating, and maintained that the inner fortification at Jericho fell toward the end of the Late Bronze. Clarifying his previous opinion, he maintained that the outer fortification was built about 1900 B.C., and destroyed about

---

[18] J. Garstang, "Jericho," in *Palest. Explor. Fund, Quarterly Statement,* July, 1930, 123–132. Père Vincent's criticism and Garstang's rebuttal, *ibid.,* April, 1931, 104–107, and October, 186–196.

1500 B.C. Concerning the two walls of the inner fortification, he held that the older was destroyed during the Middle Bronze (when the outer fortification served to replace it), and that the later, parallel wall was destroyed in the period about 1250–1200 B.C.

Replying to this modified view of Père Vincent, Garstang maintained his own date for the overthrow of the inner fortification, basing his argument on the absence of Mycenean ware in the older strata of the fortified enclosure, conceding however that his opinion was not decisive. The finding of a Bronze Age necropolis at Jericho during the 1931 season yielded new material for the discussion without altering its basic outlines. The excavations led to the recognition of four successive cities built on the site of Jericho in the Bronze Age. City A, a seemingly peaceful settlement with brick walls, was thoroughly destroyed sometime before 2500 B.C. City B, with its thick walls and strong tower, was also an Early Bronze settlement, but at the end of that period the site was apparently abandoned for some time. City C was of the Hyksos period and spread over a wider area, necessitating the outer fortification with its glacis. City D, restricted in area as cities A and B, was occupied during the Late Bronze Age and was the city which fell before the invading Israelites. The date of the destruction — the crux of the whole question — varies between Garstang's 1400 B.C. and P. Vincent's c. 1250 B.C.; Albright holds an intermediate date, c. 1375–1300 B.C. The problem obviously awaits its final solution.

83. The period in Jericho's history which is certainly Israelite is reflected on the site itself in the extreme paucity of archaeological materials. Even this negative indication is not without value, for it may be attributed to the somewhat isolated location of the city — it was not on the main international trade routes — and also to the zealous acceptance there of the worship of Yahweh. Shortly after being rebuilt by Hiel, Jericho became a center of prophetism in the name of Yahweh (2 Kings 2:4 ff.), and again, in postexilic times, its inhabitants are among the first to be mentioned (Neh. 3:2) in the work of religious restoration. This seems to explain why no traces of idolatrous worship appear in Israelite Jericho such as were found in other Israelite settlements. The orthodox worship of Yahweh not only prevented infiltrations from Canaanite idolatry, but tended to favor the simple austere life which is witnessed to in the excavations of this city.

84. **Samaria.** This site, known today as Sebastiyeh, was excavated by the Harvard University expedition under Reisner (1908–1910) and again (1931–1935) by a group of archaeologists under the leadership of J. W. Crowfoot; this latter undertaking was supported by English, American, and Jewish funds.[19] Important remains extending into Byzan-

---

[19] G. A. Reisner, C. S. Fisher, D. G. Lyon, *Harvard Excavations at Samaria*

tine and Crusader times mark the successive periods here beginning with Omri, king of Israel and builder of Samaria (1 Kings 16:24). The palace of Omri and the additions of Achab and of Jeroboam II were brought to light. Inscribed shards, or ostraca, were recovered in the course of the two expeditions; these were at first ascribed to the middle of the ninth century B.C., but there is some likelihood that they belong rather to the days of Jeroboam II, i.e., about a century later. Others are clearly of postexilic origin. A collection of magnificent ivories compares favorably to similar finds at Megiddo, at Arslan Tash in Syria, and at Nineve (where the ivories were part of the booty taken from Damascus) and makes one think of the burning words of Amos (3:15; 5:4) and of 1 Kings (22:39) apropos of this luxurious northern capital. The period of Assyrian domination, after the fall of the city in 722 B.C., remains obscure. Also discovered were impressive remains from Hellenistic and Roman times, and a Christian shrine dedicated to St. John the Baptist.

84a. At this point a word should be said about another Tell el-Far'ah, which is located about seven miles northeast of Nablus. Since 1946 the Dominican *Ecole Biblique* of Jerusalem has conducted the excavations at this large and inviting *tell*, the site of an important city in the fourth millennium B.C. Reaching a peak of importance at the beginning of the Early Bronze period (c. 3000 B.C.), the city was abandoned some time thereafter, to be occupied later during early Israelite times. It was finally abandoned in the ninth century B.C. Thus far nothing discovered has discredited the view that the site may be ancient Tirzah (1 Kings 14:17); if so, the second palace unearthed there may well be the palace of Omri, built before he moved the capital to Samaria.[20]

85. **Tell el-Ful.** Biblical Gibe'a (Vulgate: *Gabaa*) was the home of Saul, first king of Israel (1 Sam. 10:26; 11:4 f.), and is about three miles north of Jerusalem. Two short campaigns under the direction of W. F. Albright (1922–1923 and 1933) were undertaken here, the second of which establishing the following possible history of the site: first, it was a village during the period of the Judges; then, after 1050, a fortress connected with the reign of Saul; next came the careful rebuilding of the fortress after a destruction which took place either during or just after the reign of Saul. After this a period of neglect ensued; the fortress was reduced, during the divided monarchy, to a

---

(1908–1910), Cambridge, 1924; J. W. and G. M. Crowfoot, *Early Ivories from Samaria*, 1938; J. W. Crowfoot *et al.*, *The Buildings at Samaria*, London, 1942; cf. also reports in *Palestine Exploration Fund, Quarterly Statement*, 1931–1935, and P. Vincent in *RB*, 1936, 221–232.

[20] Cf. the annual reports published in the *RB* since 1947, and in *BA*, 1949, 66–68; *ibid.*, 1953, 11–13.

Present-day Jericho. In the left background the ancient site.

simple watchtower. The village continued to be occupied all this time, reaching its widest expansion in the Persian-Hellenistic period. The final page of its history was written by Titus, who destroyed it in his march on Jerusalem.[21]

86. Beisan. Named Beth-she'an or Beth-shan in biblical times, and later known as Scythopolis, this fortress controlled the approach to the plain of Esdraelon from the Jordan valley. Ten campaigns were conducted on this site between 1921 and 1933 on behalf of the University of Pennsylvania Museum.[22] Of the eighteen numbered strata distinguished by the excavators, the oldest, resting on virgin soil which may have been artificially leveled, is contemporary in a general way with the earliest settlement at Megiddo, but much later than the beginnings at Jericho. The tenth level of occupation below the modern surface of the ground is attributed to the Middle Bronze period, and gives abundant evidences of "Hyksos" occupation. The ninth such level corresponds to the period of Egyptian reconquest and its remains date apparently from about 1350 B.C. From this time on, successive periods

---

[21] Reports by the excavators in *Annual of the American Schools of Oriental Research*, 4, 1924, 1–89; and *BASOR*, 1933, 6–12; *BA*, 1953, 7.

[22] The final reports by A. Rowe and G. M. Fitzgerald are the four volumes (in five) of the *Publications of the Palestine Section of the Museum of the University of Pennsylvania*, Philadelphia, 1930–1940. Running accounts are given in the *Museum Journal* of the same institution, in the *Palestine Exploration Fund, Quarterly Statement* and in the *Revue Biblique*.

Beisan.

of rebuilding, at least for the remarkable group of temple buildings identified on the site, follow in quick succession. In the ninth stratum were two adjoining temples, a larger one dedicated to the god Mekal, lord of Beth-shan, and to the north of this a smaller one dedicated to the goddess Anat, or Astarte, as she is variously known. At least the Mekal temple was constantly renewed during the following periods, and in the fifth period, which begins no earlier than the twelfth century, and finishes, at the latest, in the tenth, both temples exist again, considerably enlarged, and reoriented to face the east. This circumstance has naturally led to an association between the excavated remains and the temple known from the biblical text in connection with the story of Saul (1 Para. 10:10; 1 Sam. 31:10). These latter are described as dedicated to Dagon and Astarte, respectively (§ 365). What is certain is that people of varied racial and religious origins identified the god and the serpent goddess worshiped in these two temples of Beth-shan by divergent attributes, and presumably worshiped them under divergent names.

During its long history Beth-shan has been subject to an even more than usually complex series of conquests and foreign influences — having been a fortress for Canaanites, Egyptians, Hittites, Philistines, and Scythians, to mention only a few. The Egyptian domination is quite prominent in the recovered monuments. There are two steles of Seti I, and one of Rameses II, a statue of Rameses III, and other remains. Unwarranted excitement in the public press greeted the discovery of the Rameses II stele, which was misconstrued by inaccurate news reports as shedding direct light on the Hebrew Exodus. On the other hand, it seems reasonably certain that one of the steles of Seti II directly mentions Hebrews, or Habiri ('py rw) as occupying some mountainous district whose Semitic name is no longer legible on the worn surface. The period of actual Israelite control of Beth-shan, known from the time of Solomon (1 Kings 4:12 — for the period of the Judges cf. Josue 17:11–16) is very poorly attested on the site; nor is the presumed Philistine occupation after the decline of Egyptian control demonstrable in the results of the excavations.

87. Silo. Undoubtedly the ancient city is represented by present-day Khirbet Seilun, located between Nablus (§ 88) and Jerusalem, on the boundary between Samaria and Judea. Three campaigns of a Danish expedition, in 1926, 1929, and 1932, disclosed settlements on the spot in both the Early and the Middle Bronze periods. The Early Iron period, which would correspond to the beginnings of Israelite occupation, was the most flourishing in the history of the settlement, judging from the limited excavation thus far carried out. A decline in the importance of the site, which would coincide with its capture by the Philistines, about 1050 B.C., was reflected in the presence of remains just prior to that time, but nothing later, at one side of the tell. At this time it ceased to be the religious center of the Israelite nation, following on the capture of the Ark by the Philistines (§ 342).

88. Sichem. This settlement, well known from the patriarchal narratives, was at Balata, a little to the east of Nablus. Excavations here, mainly directed by E. Sellin, and in two seasons by G. Welter, were carried on at various times between 1913 and 1934. The chronology of the site is subject to some doubt. Apparently no settlement earlier than the Middle Bronze period is clearly represented in the known evidence. There is then, for about the seventeenth century B.C., a very strong fortification with walls and gates in "Cyclopean" masonry that includes enormous limestone blocks. A typical Hyksos fortification has also been found. The Late Bronze period is the most noteworthy in the remains as far as they are known. It had an acropolis constructed

Silo (central background).

Nablus. (Vester, Amer. Colony.)

by artificially raising the level of the northwestern section of the mound; materials for this were drawn in part from the Hyksos wall. A retaining wall for this acropolis on the side of the lower settlement has been uncovered. In this sector of the ancient city was an extraordinary structure — temple, or tower, or both — measuring some seventy by eighty-five feet, and with walls so thick (seventeen to eighteen feet) that the interior measurement is of a room thirty-three by forty-five feet. This acropolis and its buildings apparently persisted into the Early Iron period, with some reinforcements and modifications. It seems that here, as in other Canaanite cities, a combined temple and palace area could be transformed at will into a last-ditch stronghold for such desperate situations as that outlined for Sichem itself in the Abimelech narrative in *Judges*. The attempt to integrate the known remains at Sichem with data from *Judges* encounters serious difficulties. The excavators were inclined to identify the acropolis with the "Tower (*migdal*) of Sichem" (Judg. 9:46 ff.), and the Canaanite shrine with its fortified building with the stronghold-sanctuary of El-Berith. The narrative in *Judges*, however, puts the tower of Sichem on Mt. Salmon (Judg. 9:48) and makes it quite distinct from the city itself; and there is a separate mention in it of the temple of Baal-berith (§§ 107, 319), which is another possible identification (cf. Judg. 8:33; 9:4). Some have seen in the acropolis the *Millo* (§ 398) attested for Sichem by *Judges* 9:6, 20; and in the quest for a plausible site outside the tell for the "Tower of Sichem," appeal has been made to a level spot halfway up nearby Mt. Gerizim, where in 1931 a structure with objects suggestive of Canaanite worship was uncovered. Of the activities of Jeroboam in this locality (1 Kings 12:25) no verifiable trace has been found. By way of inscribed remains, usually rare in Palestinian excavations, Sichem has yielded a limestone plaque from the close of the Middle Bronze period which is of interest for the history of alphabetic writing, as well as two cuneiform tablets of the Amarna period.[23] The site was destroyed by fire, and this, too, has been linked with its destruction by Abimelech (§ 320).

89. Tell en-Nasbeh. This site, about eight miles north of Jerusalem, was completely excavated by W. F. Badés of the Pacific School of Religion in five seasons between 1926 and 1935.[24] Whether this or the site known as Nebi Samwil, four miles to the southwest, is biblical Mispah is as yet an unsettled question. Important settlement of Tell en-Nasbeh came apparently quite late, for the strong city walls, enclosing an area of some seven acres, date from about 900 B.C. Their thickness was from fifteen to twenty feet, their probable height between thirty-five and forty feet. The city gate had the customary guard rooms; a prolongation of the southern wall beyond this gate, to parallel the northern wall at an interval of about thirty feet, produced a square external court, overlooked by a tower at the northern end. In general, the site offers a good illustration of conditions in a town of the royal period: little distinction is traceable, until almost the Hellenistic period; and from that time on there seems to have been no noteworthy settle-

---

[23] For the former, see W. F. Albright in *BASOR*, 1936, 8–12; for the latter, the same writer, *ibid.*, 86, 1942, 28–32.

[24] Final report, delayed by the death of the director after the last season of excavation, and then by the war, C. C. McCown, ed., *Tell en-Nasbeh*, Berkeley, Calif., 1947.

Sichem. Ruins of the Acropolis. (*Zeitsch Deutsch. Morgenl. Gesellsch.*, 1928).

Tell en-Nasbeh. Canaanite wall about
16 feet wide.

ment on the tell. Images of Astarte (§ 107) which attest idolatrous practices on the part of the inhabitants, are to be found from the Israelite period; that all of them were in fact broken can perhaps be associated with the activity in Mispah of the prophet Jeremias (§ 543).

90. Tell Beit Mirsim. About thirteen miles southwest of Hebron, this settlement seems to fit the requirements for the Israelite town of Kiriath-sepher, also known as Debir — although the identification cannot be considered certain. In any case, it overlooks the Negeb (§ 65) in such a way as to control an important route from the side of Egypt into the Judean hill country. It was excavated over four seasons between 1926 and 1932, under the direction of W. F. Albright.[25] Ten periods of occupation are distinguished; fire was a frequent cause of destruction and the successive levels are rather well marked off by the resulting layer of ashes. The first distinctive city wall and palace structure dates from the Middle Bronze period. A succeeding settlement testifies to Hyksos occupation; and a new and destructive wave of Egyptian conquest was a prelude to the abandonment of the site. The city was weak and none too prosperous in the Late Bronze period, and its conquest by the Israelites, roughly about 1250 B.C., led to another abrupt change and to still further decline. The period of the divided monarchy in Israel was one of renewed prosperity, with the population overflowing the walls, and with a dyeing industry to accompany the customary agricultural activity of the inhabitants. Figurines of a goddess, usually Astarte, of the type mentioned above (§ 89) were quite common in the last period of Canaanite control, scarce in the early Israelite period, and abundant in the latter days of the monarchy at the time when the prophets were inveighing vigorously against idolatry. The city was destroyed in Nabuchodonosor's invasion of Juda in the early sixth century B.C., and was never reoccupied thereafter.

91. Mambre. This is the place often mentioned in the story of Abraham (Gen. 13:18; 14:13; 18:1; 23:17, 19; 25:9; 35:27; 49:30; 50:13),

---

[25] Final reports: W. F. Albright, *The Excavation of Tell Beit Mirsim*, I–III, New Haven, 1932–1943.

as the place where terebinths grew and Abraham built an altar. The modern name is *Haram Ramet el-Khalil*, "sanctuary of the height of the friend of God," that is to say, of Abraham. It is slightly more than a mile north of Hebron, to the east of the Jerusalem road. Excavations there were conducted by A. E. Mader in 1926–1928, for the purpose of checking the antiquity and plausibility of the tradition which associates the modern site with Abraham. A Christian basilica here goes back to Constantine, and was found to have supplanted a pagan market place and temple from the time of Hadrian, which had been built on a construction of Herod the Great. The latter had evidently indulged his taste for elaborate architectural enterprise on a spot already venerable in the estimation of earlier generations. The literary tradition — biblical, rabbinic, and Christian — associates the memory of Abraham with three things: a terebinth (or an "oak"), a well, and an altar. Study of the site has verified the well, and near it a round opening which is the presumptive location for the terebinth (cf. § 105). The Christian altar of the basilica presumably replaced the pagan one of Hadrian, which in turn took the place of a still earlier one on the same spot. The persistent tradition which holds the place to be sacred, through all the changes it has undergone at the hands of Constantine, of Hadrian, of Herod — and of how many others? — is not of a kind unfamiliar in the Orient. A pavement earlier than Herod's time seems clearly to date from the days of the Hebrew monarchy; it evidently covered a great part of the present site. Beneath this pavement were pottery remains of the beginnings of the Iron Age, and also of Early Bronze. Thus the presumption is that there was at Mambre already a Canaanite sanctuary before Abraham; and that his dwelling there, his use of the

Tell en-Nasbeh. (Vester, Amer. Colony.)

Beit Mirsim: Canaanite sanctuary. (Vester, Amer. Colony.)

place for worship of God, and his burial nearby made it a place of veneration also for the Israelites. Thus as it had been in some sense the cradle of Israel's national life, it remained, together with Hebron, a sacred spot carefully remembered throughout the centuries, in the tenacious tradition of the Orient.

92. Gerar. The identity of Gerar, where in the days of Abraham there was a King Abimelech (§§ 137, 141), with modern Tell Jemmeh, eight miles southeast of Gaza, is widely accepted. It was excavated by Flinders Petrie in a campaign begun in 1926. Satisfactory evidence for a settlement earlier than the Late Bronze period was not found in Petrie's cursory examination of the tell. Among an abundance of small objects, a considerable number of weights were found; this has suggested that Gerar was a grain market for the Negeb district (§ 65).

Tell el-Far'ah. This site, some ten miles to the southeast from Tell Jemmeh, was also excavated by Petrie, who, on utterly fantastic philological grounds identified it with the biblical Beth-Pelet (Josue 15:27; Neh. 11:26). It was fortified in a striking way by people of the Hyksos period, who made it quite impervious to attack by combining the wadi and two gullies at its sides with an enormous artificial trench eighty feet wide at the rear. Later Egyptian garrisons added mud-brick walls to a ramp thrown up in the Hyksos period. The tombs from this site have yielded museum material attesting to the presence here of peoples of various races and cultures. The site is thought to be Sharuhen (Josue 19:6; cp. § 84a).

Tell el-'Ajjul. Some five miles south of modern Gaza lies Tell el-'Ajjul, for which no satisfactory identification has yet been offered, although Petrie thought it was the original Gaza. The site was chiefly occupied during the Middle and Late Bronze. Five strata of large, well-built structures were found at the northwest corner of the tell. The finds seem to point to the sacrifice of horses, to the eating of horseflesh, and to the burial in common graves — for some reason or other — of men and horses. Smaller objects recovered at the site are Aegean in style or origin.[26]

Tell Jerisheh, five miles north of Jaffa, was excavated in part by Sukenik for the Hebrew University of Jerusalem, 1927–1928 and 1934. The site had been occupied during the Middle Bronze and Early Iron periods. A thick layer of ashes in the Bronze Age period may betoken the Philistine conquest.

93. 'Ain Shems. This is the biblical Beth Shemesh (Vulgate: *Bethsames*) some seventeen miles southwest of Jerusalem in the direction of Ascalon. It is also known in modern times as Tell er-Rumeileh. In 1911–1913 it was explored by D. Mackenzie for the Palestine Exploration Fund, and in 1928–1933 by E. Grant for Haverford College.[27] Five strata are identifiable here, ranging from Early Bronze to the period of the Hebrew exile. At least three times the city was destroyed by fire. Distinctive material from the Israelite period is scarce; but the existence of idolatry there in Israelite times is demonstrable (Astarte figurines, etc.). In the late Bronze Age much pottery of artistic worth was imported from the Aegean region; in the Early Iron Age, an abundance of what is known as "Philistine ware" is found on the site. An early fragment with characters in the linear alphabet,

'Ain Shems. (Vester, Amer. Colony.)

---

[26] For these three sites, and another across the border of Egypt, cf. F. Petrie, *Ancient Gaza*, London, 1931–1934; *Beth-Pelet*, 1930; *Gerar*, 1928; *Seventy Years in Archaeology*, 1931; also E. Macdonald, *et al.*, *Beth-Pelet II*, 1932; W. F. Albright, *Archaeology of Palestine and the Bible*, 1933, 53.

[27] D. Mackenzie, in *Annual* of the *Palestine Exploration Fund*, I–II, 1911–1913. Elihu Grant, *Beth-Shemesh*, Haverford, Pa., 1929; *'Ain Shems Excavations*, 1–5, Haverford, 1931–1939.

Teleilat Ghassul seen from the northwest.

and a clay tablet inscribed in a cuneiform alphabet, were among the smaller objects found.

94. Teleilat Ghassul. This series of low mounds was found on the edge of a plain that reaches out from the mountains of Moab to a point some four miles from the northeastern extremity of the Dead Sea. Excavations were conducted here by the Pontifical Biblical Institute, from 1929 to 1938.[28] Père Mallon described the results of the first campaign by stating that the site had held "a very ancient city, older perhaps than Jericho or Gezer; a city with a high degree of civilization, which was destroyed in the beginnings of the Age of Bronze by a huge conflagration that reduced it to ashes. It was never rebuilt, and time levelled off the ruins." This was reaffirmed as a result of the second campaign, which was said to "confirm the great antiquity of the city (third millennium) and the advanced character of its civilization. . . . The history of this large city comes to an abrupt close towards the twentieth century B.C." At about this time, a study published by Power, also under the auspices of the Biblical Institute, recalled an ancient tradition according to which the cities of the Pentapolis (Sodom, Gomorrha, etc., §§ 128, 136; Gen. 19:24 ff.) were located to the north of the Dead Sea, rather than to the south of it, where most

---

[28] A. Mallon, R. Köppel, *et al.*, *Teleilat Ghassul, I–II*, Rome, 1934–1940.

modern scholars locate the traditional site. This possibility, combined with the tentative results of the excavation under discussion, led to excesses of speculation in the popular press which can be readily imagined even by those who had not the misfortune to read them. In fact, the first statements of Père Mallon, as quoted above, are ideally descriptive of the situation except in one important respect. It is now certain that the end of the city's history, after two distinct periods of settlement over a period of centuries, and with a gradual enrichment, but no abrupt change, of cultural attainments, came actually *before 3500* B.C. This dating is possible because of the integration of the Ghassulian finds with what is known now of the early settlements at Jericho and elsewhere (cf. §§ 71, 80). At this early period, certain rooms were decorated with remarkable frescoes, for which remote parallels can be found much farther east (Persepolis, Tepe Gawra, Tell 'Uqair), but nothing in Egypt, Palestine, or farther west until perhaps a millennium later.

94a. **Qumran.**[29] In 1947, the scientific world was electrified by the discovery of several Hebrew leather rolls in a cave not far from the northwestern shore of the Dead Sea. Now famous as the *Dead Sea Scrolls* (*DSS*), the first find yielded a complete book of Isaias, a commentary on Habacuc, a religious rule of a Jewish community, and an apocryphal Aramaic Document (the Apocalypse of Lamech) which has not yet been published; these items came into the possession of the Syriac Bishop of Jerusalem, and are now in America. Another group of manuscripts was acquired by the Hebrew University of Jerusalem: one roll of Isaias (incomplete), a collection of hymns, and a writing described as "The War of the Sons of Light against the Sons of Darkness." The cave was examined anew in 1949 by the Jordan Department of Antiquities and P. de Vaux of the *Ecole Biblique;* fragments af many biblical books, especially of Leviticus (in Phoenician script), and of other nonbiblical works, were found.

A nearby ruin called Khirbet Qumran was carefully investigated in 1951 and 1953 and proved to be related to the same community responsible for hiding the rolls in the cave. In 1952 the neighboring cliff was explored, this time the American School of Oriental Research (Jerusalem) assisting in the search. Of the many caves explored, two yielded manuscript fragments and a long copper band bearing an inscription. An exploration by unauthorized persons in 1952 disclosed three other caves, one of which was especially rich in manuscript finds, providing material of great importance.

---

[29] Many articles have now been written about the *DSS.* Cf. the reports in *RB,* 1949 and after; for an excellent survey of the Qumran-Murabba'at literature, cf. *CBQ,* 1956, 62–70; and also R. E. Murphy, *The DSS and the Bible,* Westminster (Md.), 1956.

The new finds all come from the same religious sect or community which used the caves of this region as dwellings, storehouses, and hiding places. The central meeting place was Khirbet Qumran; coins found in the ruins show that it was occupied from early in the first century A.D., and was abandoned during the Jewish Revolt of 66–70, at which time the manuscripts were either hidden or abandoned in the neighboring caves. The manuscripts themselves may be considerably older than this; they are particularly important in that they provide us with an example of the Hebrew text as it existed long before its final fixation in the Masoretic Text.

However precious these finds are for the history of the Old Testament text, more interesting is the discovery of so much apocryphal literature, whose very existence was, until now, either unknown or known only in translation or thought to have been irretrievably lost.

The Rule of the community, commentary on Habacuc, and the rest throw much light on the organization and tendencies of a Jewish community which was contemporary with Jesus Christ. Everything points to the fact that the people who lived here at that period were Essenes, concerning whom the only sources of our slender information have been the writings of Pliny, Josephus, and Philo. Properly edited and studied, these manuscripts will yield information of exceptional importance concerning the religious background of the New Testament.

94b. Murabba'at. Recent finds in the desert of Juda now provide historians of the Second Jewish Revolt (A.D. 132–135) with something more substantial than the meager fare until now provided for them by Dio Cassius, the Fathers, and the rabbinical writings. The first discovery was made by the Bedouin during the summer of 1951 in Wadi Murabba'at, 15 miles SE of Jerusalem and not far from the Dead Sea. Since that date, careful investigations have been carried out by L. Harding and P. de Vaux of the Jordan Department of Antiquities and the *Ecole Biblique* respectively.

Discovered were two letters from the leader of the revolt, who calls himself Shime'on ben Kosebah. All doubt concerning his identity vanishes in the face of further finds: documents dating from the "liberation of Israel by Shime'on ben Kosebah," and coins dating from the Second Revolt. Both letters were directed to a certain Yeshua' ben Gilgolah, "chief of the camp" at Murabba'at; the second of these alludes to the approach of the Romans, which means that the operations of the war carried even into this forbidding region where the insurgents had established themselves. The Romans upon their arrival gave full vent to their fury, destroying all that they could lay their hands on, preferably the rolls of the Scriptures so sacred to the rebel Jews. Found here were fragments of violently torn rolls, i.e., sections from the Law and the

Airplane view of Jerusalem and environs. Below the city, in the center, the square of the Temple. Below the Temple the Valley of Cedron descends on both sides. To the left, from top to bottom, the Valley of Hinnom. (Dalman, *Fliegerbilder aus Paläst.*)

beginning of a roll of Isaias, as well as an undamaged phylactery. The text of the fragments is the same as that of the Masoretic Text.

95. Jerusalem. The famous city whose history sums up within itself the glories and sorrows of Israel could hardly have been overlooked by the ever zealous archaeologists. Before the turn of the past century, investigations were carried out in the Holy City by Warren, Gunther, Schick, and Bliss, and these were but the beginning. Since then the following may be mentioned: the Parker expedition (1909–1911), which yielded valuable results, thanks to the timely and generous intervention of P. Vincent and despite the extraordinary purpose of the mission itself; it was, in truth, nothing but a hunt for Solomon's "buried" treasure. The Welsh miners imported to do the digging found no treasure, of course, but they did clean out the tunnel of Ezechias. R. Weill undertook excavations here in 1913–1914, and again in 1923–1924, and was followed by Macalister and J. D. Duncan in 1923–1925, by Sukenik of the Hebrew University of Jerusalem from 1925 on, and by Hamilton and others of the Palestine Department of Antiquities within more recent years. Besides results won by these investigators, a never ending series of small finds and isolated studies of details have

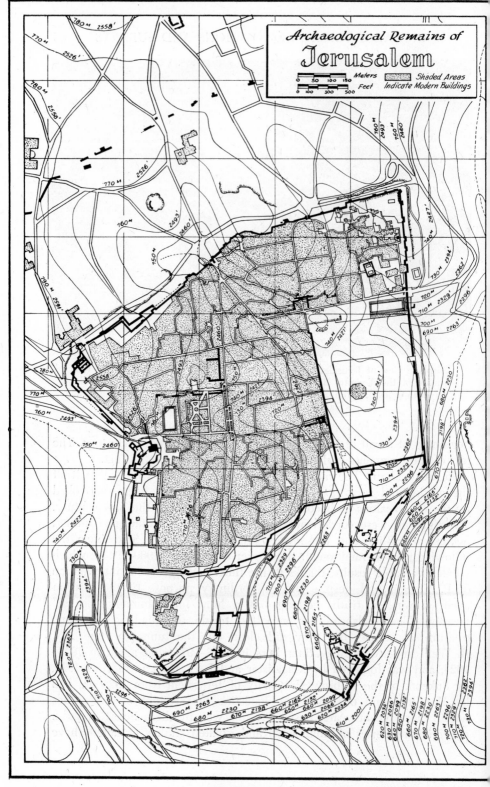

Courtesy of P. Vincent, from his *Jérusalem de l'A. T.*

contributed to our growing understanding of this most inviting, but very perplexing, site.[30]

The main features of the topography of ancient Jerusalem may be set forth here, beginning with the excellent description found in Tasso's *Jerusalem Liberated* (III, 55).

> "Upon two bold hills Jerusalem is seen
> Of size unequal, face to face opposed;
> A wide and pleasant valley lies between,
> Dividing hill from hill; three sides the coast
> Lies craggy, difficult, and high, disposed
> In steep acclivities; the fourth is cast
> In gentlest undulations, and enclosed
> By walls of height insuperable, and vast,
> That seem to brave the sky, and face the arctic blast."

The two hills, today almost entirely outside the southern walls of the city, lie side by side, running from north to south. The western hill is the more elevated (c. 2550 feet) and extensive; the hill to the east is about 2280 feet at its highest point, and is comparatively narrow and eloquent of ruins. The valley between the hills is pretty well filled in at the present time. Josephus gave it the name of the Tyropoeon Valley (i.e., "of the cheesemakers"), and modern scholars still refer to it by this name. The western hill is protected by a valley (Wadi Rababy) isolating it on the west and south; the southern section of this valley is called the *valley of* (the son of) *Hinnom* (or Gehenna)." The eastern hill is isolated to the east by the *Cedron valley* which bending slightly westward joins with the Tyropoeon, the resulting valley then flowing into the valley of Hinnom. On these three sides, then, the isolation provided by the valleys left nothing to be desired, strategically speaking. Only the north was vulnerable; but it seems that here too both hills (especially the western hill, along the *Suweiqat 'Allun*) were separated by a slight depression from the ridge rising to the north.

96. The eastern hill is usually referred to by the name *Ophel* or "hillock." In ancient times this name referred more especially to its northern section, where it joined with the Temple area (to which the

---

[30] L. H. Vincent, *Jérusalem sous terre* (tr. as *Underground Jerusalem*, London, 1911); *Jérusalem antique*, Paris, 1912; R. Weill, *La cité de David*, Paris, 1920, and article in the *Revue des études juives*, 1926, 8–22; for a bibliography cf. (up to 1932) the *Quarterly of the Department of Antiquities in Palestine*, I, 1932, 163–188; Macalister, Crowfoot, *et al.*, in *Annual of the Palestine Exploration Fund*, IV–V, 1926–1929; Sukenik and Mayer, *The Third Wall of Jerusalem*, Jerusalem, 1930; besides numerous articles in the *Quarterly of the Department of Antiquities*, in *BASOR*, in the *Palestine Exploration Quarterly* since then, and especially the *Revue Biblique*. To bring these studies up to date, and for further bibliography, confer P. Vincent's article "Jérusalem" in *DBS*, 4, 897–966, and his *Jérusalem de l'A.T.*, 2 volumes, Paris, 1953–56, 149 plates.

Valley of the Cheesemakers. (Vester, Amer. Colony.)

disputed term *Moriah* may be given, cf. § 138) which rises above it, but the western hill bore no distinctive name. The stronghold of *Sion*, occupied by the Jebusites who were there at the time of the Hebrew conquest, must of course have been on one of these two hills. Thanks to their fortified position the Jebusites easily retained possession of the city when it was attacked by the Benjamites (Judges 1:21; cf. 1:8 which is the other side of the story; Josue 16:63 is not in a suitable context; see § 305).

Indeed, the city was not successfully attacked until the time of David, when it received the name of *City of David* (2 Sam. 5:6 f.), which name has been given to both hills at different times. Until comparatively recent times the western hill was looked upon as the ancient capital, but a careful sifting of pertinent literary and archaeological data, this latter by a partial excavation of the site, has settled the question beyond all

Jerusalem seen from the Mount of Olives. Bottom, the Valley of Cedron; higher up, the walls and esplanade of the Temple.

reasonable doubt in favor of the eastern hill. It was only by extension that the terms "Sion" and "City of David" came, in time, to include the whole of Jerusalem.

It should be noted that for this particular region there are only two sources of water, both in the neighborhood of the eastern hill. One, the biblical *Rogel*, today known as "Job's Well" (or *Bir Ayyub*), lies a little to the south of the juncture of the Cedron, Tyropoeon, and Hinnom valleys. The other spring lies at the foot of the eastern flank (toward its northern end), and bears the name Gihon ("gushing") in the Bible; it is known to Christians as Ain Sitti Mariam, or the "Fountain of the Lady Mary."

97. As the western hill promised little in the way of very ancient remains, recent investigations have centered around Ophel, the oldest part of the city. The proximity of a water supply is an indication that this was in fact the earlier settlement, and the very contours lend strength to such an hypothesis. Although somewhat lower than the hill to the west (§ 95), Ophel is steeper and in greater ruin. Excavations have shown that in ancient times the bottom of the Cedron valley lay more to the west, and that on the Cedron (i.e., eastern) side, the hill was much more precipitous than it is today. The northern and vulnerable side was strengthened with a skill in fortification earlier noted as characteristic of the Canaanites elsewhere. At this northern end, Macalister in 1924 found a lateral trench or moat which proved to be of the late third millennium B.C.; it effectively barred all approach from the north, as it extended from the Tyropoeon to the Cedron. It seems to have been an adaptation and prolongation of a slight natural depression that sloped toward the Tyropoeon valley, and was called the "Valley of Sedeq" by Macalister (§ 130). For reinforcement the original (?) inhabitants had thrown up a medium-sized wall. About the middle of the second millennium, perhaps at the

The hillock of Ophel on the slope leading to the Valley of Cedron. (Vester, Amer. Colony.)

Jerusalem seen from the west. Top background, the Mount of Olives; lower down, the esplanade of the Temple.

time of Abdi-Hipa (§ 57), the early settlement spread northward. The moat was therefore filled, but another network of defenses was gradually built up, among which a strong wall, reinforced with towers, deserves attention; it protected the city on the side toward the fountain of Gihon (i.e., the eastern side).

98. This precious spring received much attention, being the city's main water supply. To facilitate its use in time of peace, and to guarantee it in time of war — the spring, located in the valley at the foot of the hill, lay outside the walls that guarded the hilltop — the inhabitants dug a tunnel approach similar to those at Gezer (§ 77), Megiddo, and elsewhere, toward it. Less elaborate than Gezer's, the Ophel construction was in three sections which formed a kind of descending zigzag. The lowest section channeled the water of the spring toward the interior of the hill, to a kind of reservoir beneath the city itself. At the back of this pool a vertical shaft some forty feet in height enabled those above to draw up the water. The upper section was an inclined tunnel whose entrance must have been

Jebusite wall on Ophel. (Lemaire.)

concealed in some way by the wall of the city. The approach to the lower shaft and to the spring itself must have been hidden — possibly by a false barricade or superstructure of some sort — so that the secret might be preserved, and in time of siege, the enemy might not learn how to cut off the city's supply of water. This construction dates back to the second millennium B.C. In addition to a number of later tunnels around the spring, there is another in the form of an uncompleted well; this too dates back to the second millennium, and its failure illus-

Ruins of the Jebusite enclosure near the pool of Siloe. (Vester, Amer. Colony.)

trates clearly the difficulties involved in such an undertaking. Later still there came the tunnel of Ezechias (§ 486 ff.), winding underground for 1777 feet, and bringing the waters of Gihon to the upper pool of Siloe in the Tyropoeon valley.

Some modern scholars hold that the Canaanite tunnel described above was the *sinnor* (water shaft) mentioned in 2 Samuel 5:8. So well-nigh impregnable was the Jebusite citadel that the inhabitants jeered at David as he prepared to invest the city (2 Sam. 5:6). David, however, somehow learned of the existence of the *sinnor*, whether by treachery or lucky discovery is not known. He then offered a great reward to the first man who would use it to gain entry into the city (1 Para. 11:16). The audacious deed was accomplished by Joab, who entered the lower tunnel, climbed up the vertical shaft, and so got into the city, for the defenders had carelessly neglected this approach, doubtless thinking it too impracticable for the enemy. During the Parker excavations an English official clambered up this same shaft, which up to then had not yet been explored, thus proving that Joab's feat could be executed without any extraordinary difficulty. It should be pointed out, however, that this reconstruction of the events is not accepted by all scholars.

99. Certain other excavations beyond the confines of Palestine proper must at least be touched upon, because they are, indirectly, of tremendous significance for our present study.

Excavations at Byblos (§ 55) under Montet and Dunand (from 1921

The pool of Siloe in the Tyropoeon. To the right, above, the slopes of Ophel. (Vester, Amer. Colony.)

on) have yielded an abundance of early epigraphic material whose full meaning has not yet been thoroughly explored.[31] Many of the easily legible inscriptions, written in a fully developed Phoenician alphabetic writing which antedates the Mesha stone (§ 439) by centuries, have been published. Especially noteworthy are the forty words inscribed on the ornate sarcophagus of a king *Ahiram* (Hiram), once customarily dated as a contemporary of Rameses II (§ 33), but now placed toward the end of the eleventh century B.C. Byblos has also yielded a group of texts inscribed apparently in syllabic characters, a sort of pseudo-hieroglyphic, dating from the end of

the third and the beginning of the second millenium B.C. Though these have not yet been deciphered (the characters thus far known from a limited amount of text are about 114 in number), there can be little doubt that they are written in a form of Old Canaanite, a language which in a general way is in the direct line of ancestry of biblical Hebrew.

100. The quest for the beginnings of the alphabet have been stimulated not only by these finds at Byblos, but also by others elsewhere.

Mouth of the tunnel of Ezechias in the spring of Gihon. (Vester, Amer. Colony.)

---

[31] P. Montet, *Byblos et l'Egypte* (Paris, 1929); M. Dunand, *Fouilles de Byblos I* (Paris, 1937–1939); *idem, Byblia grammata* (Beyrouth, 1945); and reports in the periodical *Syria* (Paris).

At Serabit el-Khadim (§§ 235, 277), located in the mountains of the Sinai Peninsula where the ancient Egyptians once mined their turquoise, Flinders Petrie in 1905 discovered a number of inscriptions written in unknown characters, together with a quantity of Egyptian material. When publishing this material in 1916, A. Gardiner advanced the suggestion that the unfamiliar characters were actually an archaic form of the regular alphabet and that the language was Semitic. As the supposition helped read an oft-repeated phrase "to the lady" (*l b ' l t*), (votive offerings to the goddess Hathor, to whom there was a sanctuary on the site), and since the Egyptians are known to have employed Semitic workmen at Sinai, the conclusion reached is reasonable. The number of inscriptions has since been enlarged by renewed finds in 1927, 1930, and 1932. Like many an obscure discovery from ancient times, these poor scribblings have been subjected to outlandish speculations some of

which went so far as to involve in them Moses, Pharaoh's daughter, and the Exodus! Actually they yield little that makes connected sense; but taken with what we know from Byblos, and from Middle and late Bronze levels of various Palestinian sites, they give Semitic alphabetic writings a history that goes back a thousand years before the adoption of the alphabet by the Greeks c. 900 B.C.[32]

100a. Ugarit — Ras Shamra.

Finally, for its bearing on the history of Canaanite culture, religion, and letters, and the indirect light it sheds on the poetic forms and imagery in the Bible itself, no site has

Entrance to the spring of Gihon. (Vester, Amer. Colony.)

---

[32] Cf. R. Butin, in *Harvard Theological Review*, 1932, 132–203; also earlier, *ibid.*, 1930, 9–67; and a supplement in *Studies and Documents*, VI, London, 1937, 31–42; W. F. Albright, in *Journal of the Palestine Oriental Society*, 1935, 334–340; A. H. Gardiner, in *The Legacy of Egypt*, ed. S. R. K. Glanville, London, 1942; for the epigraphical facts, J. Lebovitch, *Les inscriptions protosinaitiques*, Cairo, 1934. See also D. Diringer, "The Palestinian Inscriptions and the Origin of the Alphabet," *Journal of the American Oriental Society*, 1943, 24–30, for an extremely conservative approach to the problem.

so repaid its excavators as has ancient Ugarit = Ras Shamra, situated on the Syrian coast a few miles north of modern Lattaquia.[33] The discovery there of clay tablets inscribed with cuneiform writing clearly unrelated to that of the Assyro-Babylonian world, and alphabetic in character, dates from 1929. The decipherment was accomplished rather quickly by two scholars, Dhorme and Bauer, who worked as cipher experts during World War I. The language of the great majority of the texts is Semitic, and nearly akin to Hebrew. The separate efforts of Dhorme and Bauer were perfected by C. Virolleaud, who was charged with the editing of most of the succeeding discoveries. Lengthy fragments of a number of epic poems, as well as an assortment of letters and business documents, even a veterinarian manual for the treatment of horses, have been found. All are dated approximately before 1375 B.C.; two isolated parallels to their script are thus far known from Palestine itself. Like other discoveries which have a real, though not necessarily a direct relationship to biblical studies, these texts were subjected to a certain amount of overhasty exploitation, this time on behalf of unusual theories in comparative religion. The careful and diligent work of a remarkable galaxy of scholars throughout the world, not a few of them Americans, has, however, brought the entire material beyond the reach of idle speculation.[34] One of the interesting results of the study of the mythological material has been to confirm the accuracy of a description of Phoenician religion preserved for us by Eusebius from the writings of Philo of Byblos, who in turn was reporting the native tradition in the name of one Sanchuniathon, otherwise unknown. This written material by no means exhausts the interests of the discoveries from Ugarit, where excavations have been carried on since 1939; but for the student of Israelite history it does overshadow anything else found on the site, which was last occupied somewhere in the neighborhood of 1200 B.C.

101. Canaanite Civilization.[35] From the results of the excavations and other information the following summary of Canaanite civilization may be given.

---

[33] For the profuse writings on these discoveries there can now serve as an excellent index, for the present purpose, R. de Langhe's *Les textes de Ras Shamra — Ugarit et leurs rapports avec le milieu biblique de l'Ancien Testament*, Paris, 2 vols., 1945. Texts edited in the periodical *Syria*, and in the serial publication *Mission de Ras Shamra*, Paris, ed. F. A. Schaeffer. Excellent sketch by H. L. Ginsberg, "Ugaritic Studies and the Bible," in *BA*, 1945, 41–58; C. H. Gordon, *Ugaritic Literature*, Rome, 1949.

[34] The *Biblical Archaeologist* for 1945–1946 ran a series of highly successful classifications of separate archaeological finds (for Ras Shamra, however, see De Langhe, *op. cit.*) which for one reason or another have been placed in a false light in the public press reports.

[35] For Canaanite civilization in general, confer, besides those works cited in §§ 74 ff. (especially Vincent, *Canaan*), F. M. T. Böhl, *Kananäer und Hebräer*, Leipzig,

Rameses II attacking a fortified city of Syria.

The Canaanite cities whose fortifications inspired such an extraordinary respect in the Israelites (Num. 13:29 ff.; Deut. 1:28; 9:1, etc.), were certainly very skillfully fortified for those times, but which now impress as being quite unimposing. Some of them, in fact, would fit into the area of the Colosseum (about six acres) or the piazza of St. Peter's in Rome; others did not exceed this area by much. For example at Tell el-Hesy (§ 74) the original acropolis occupied about one acre; at Tell es-Safy (§ 75) the city occupied about twelve, almost as much as Tell el-Mutesellim (§ 79); at Tell Zakariyeh (§ 75) less than ten; at Tell Judeideh (§ 75) a little more than four; fortified Jericho itself (internal enclosure: § 80) occupied only about six acres. The greatest area is that of Gezer (§ 76) which covered twenty-two. Canaanite Sion (§ 95 ff.) was about twelve acres.

However carefully constructed the fortifications, or elaborate the water-works, the houses were very simple. They were generally built without plan on a level portion of a raised piece of ground or on the spur of a hill. They were in reality merely huts, with the one opening for the door. The corners were sometimes built of rough pilasters in the form of steles (in the early days of excavations these were often confused with *masseboth* by archaeologists; § 104).

102. The Canaanites took much more care of their dead than of the living. One case of cremation is known (§ 76), but from the time of the Semites onward this was everywhere replaced in Canaan by burial.

1911; in particular, W. Robertson Smith, *Lectures on the Religion of the Semites,* 2 ed., London, 1894; M. J. Lagrange, *Etudes sur les religions sémitiques,* 2 ed., Paris, 1905; S. A. Cook, *The Religion of Ancient Palestine in the Light of Archaeology* (Schweich Lectures, 1925), London, 1930; W. F. Albright, *From the Stone Age to Christianity,* Baltimore, 1940; *id., Archaeology and the Religion of Israel,* Baltimore, 1942; Barrois, *Manuel d'archéologie biblique,* Paris, 1938, 15–21.

Natural grottoes were used as burial places, or even artificial sepulchers excavated in the form of wells, which were always covered. Those who could not afford such tombs buried their dead in the open, in the "graves of the common people" (Jer. 26:23). The corpse was often arranged in a contracted position with the knees bent up under the chin;

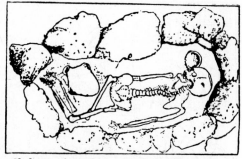

Skeleton of an old woman buried in a house. (Macalister, *Excavation of Gezer.*)

probably to remind one of the position of the child in its mother's womb, reassumed by men as they re-entered the womb of mother earth (cf. the allusion [?] to this in Job 1:21). Sometimes the tomb was surrounded by small cromlechs (§§ 73, 77), and always contained funereal objects: weapons, amulets, knives (of stone or metal), lamps, various kinds of pottery, ornaments, etc.; some tombs were provided with food for the deceased. Bodies of infants were often placed in earthen jars which were filled with fine sand and closed by a disk. At Beisan (§ 86) sarcophagi were found half the size of a man; the opening through which the corpse was inserted was closed by a cover in the form of a human face with small arms (epoch of Rameses II–III: § 33; Egyptian type).

Bodies of babies or adults were also found buried in houses. It is difficult to interpret these cases as "foundation sacrifices" (§ 103). The Bible seems to indicate the custom of burying in the house (1 Sam. 25:1; 1 Kings 2:34?; cf. Isa. 14:18); whether it does or not, the old woman of Gezer suffering from rheumatism (as far as modern examinations can ascertain) need not be interpreted as a sacrificial "offering"; the explanation may very likely be sought and found in her poverty, or some such reason which eludes us. On the other hand, the usage still persists among Egyptian peasants today — according to Macalister — of burying stillborn babies in the floor of the house (thus affording their spirit a chance to re-enter the womb of the mother). The Canaanites probably had the same custom.

Anthropomorphic sarcophagus of Beisan. (Rowe, *Topography and Hist. of Beth-Shan.*)

Infant foundation sacrifice. (Macalister, *Excavation of Gezer.*)

In fact, some immature foetuses are found among the tiny skeletons discovered in the houses. This pitiable belief may also explain the little tomb at Ta'annak (§ 78), where almost all the bodies were those of infants. Some twenty tombs were investigated in which the infants were all two years old and under; only one adult was found. Sellin was unable to decide whether he had discovered a sacrificial tomb, or a special type for babies; scholars today incline toward the second hypothesis.

103. This does not rule out, but clarifies "foundation sacrifices." That the Canaanites generally sacrificed human beings has already been attested by many biblical passages forbidding the practice for the Israelites,

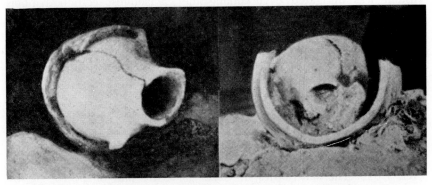

Vase found at Teleilat Ghassul at the foot of a wall containing the cranium of an infant. Left, the vase as it was found; right, after it was opened.
(*L'Illustration*, 1931.)

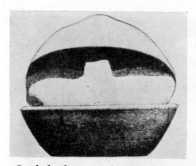

Symbolic lamp in the foundation of buildings. (Macalister, *Excavation of Gezer*.)

or which show some Canaanite infiltration into genuine Yahwism (Lev. 18:21; 20:2; Deut. 12:31; 18:10; 2 Kings 16:3; 21:6; 23:10; Jer. 7:31; 19:5; Ezech. 20:31; 23:37–39; Mich. 6:7, etc.). Moreover, besides the human sacrifice performed "in the sight of Yahweh" for religious motives (2 Sam. 21:9; cf. the case of Jephte, § 325), a "foundation sacrifice" was proposed by that very Hiel who rebuilt the walls of Jericho (1 Kings 16:34; cf. Josue 6:26). Excavations have clarified and confirmed the data of the Bible. The bodies of children found on the sacred high place of Gezer (§ 77) have been recognized generally as sacrificial victims; none are aborted foetuses, none were more than a week old, and they are of both sexes. None show any traces of mutilation; two only show signs of fire. They must have been put into the jars while still alive, their heads oftener than not at the bottom; they were buried in this manner in a sacred place for a sacred reason. They were perhaps the first-born, immolated for that very reason to the divinity. Other examples have come to confirm the finds of Gezer.

The "foundation sacrifice" was offered when a construction was begun or a given place inaugurated. The victim was thought to guarantee a perpetual protection for the building and was therefore buried near the foundations. At Megiddo (§ 79) a fifteen-year-old girl was found walled up in the foot of a fortress wall; another jar contained the body of an infant crushed between the foundations of another wall. Many other cases have been discovered by excavations. Later, however, the horrible custom was mitigated even among the Canaanites; certain symbols (usually a lamp enclosed between two lids) were substituted for the human victim, and were deposited near the foundations of the new building. Eventually but much later total substitution became the rule, as excavations have shown (cf. also the case of Hiel [ninth century] cited in the Bible). Many Syrians will even today kill an animal when they begin to build a house, or a tent, or boat, and the like.

104. The religious sentiment which forms the basis for such degenerate practices finds its explanation chiefly in the sanctuary where divinity dwelt. This was usually a high place, called *bamah* (plural, *bamoth*) in the Bible, although later on there were sanctuaries in the valleys also (Jer. 7:31). The sanctuaries of Gezer (§ 76 ff.) and of Beisan (§ 86) are the most typical examples. Liturgical objects must have been few other than the altar (Deut. 12:3) near which the animal's throat was

Sanctuary of Astarte at Idalion (Cyprus). (Hunger, Lamer, *Altorient. Kultur im Bilde.*)

cut and upon which the animal was burned. No satisfactory explanation of the liturgical use of the small canals and basins found in several Canaanite sanctuaries (§ 76) has yet been put forward. The libations were of course poured out, and foodstuffs offered.

An important element of the Canaanite sanctuary were the sacred steles of stone fixed in the ground (Hebrew, *massebah;* plural *masseboth*), as at Gezer (§ 77), sometimes arranged in a row, sometimes in pairs, or standing alone. The cruder forms resemble *menhirs* (§ 72); others were roughly quadrangular, round, or pyramidal in shape and gave some evidence of skill. The original meaning of these steles escapes us; two different concepts may have their point of union in them. One, the Semites generally considered certain stones as the dwelling place of the divinity (cf. Isa. 57:6). The black stone in the Ka'aba of Mecca is the classic example of such a concept (". . . in ancient times . . . the Arabs venerated the stone," Clement of Alexandria informs us, *Protrept.,* IV; in Migne, *P.G.,* 8, 133); another is the term *beth-el,* "house of God," given by the Semites to these stones (often meteorites) and preserved for us by the Greek historians under the form of βαίτυλος equivalent for them to λίθος ἔμψυχος, "animated stone." The other concept was of a symbolical nature, an attempt to portray the deity in some manner as the principle of being; hence the stone, the divine dwelling place, was sometimes roughly fashioned in the form of the "phallus" (§ 77; Jer. 2:27?). Originally this may have been due to a crude naïveté which quickly degenerated into licentiousness. In objects of worship, it is further believed that the *pudendum muliebre,* feminine counterparts of the symbol of the steles, is to be seen (Isa. 51:1?; cf. Herodotus, II, 106 [102]; Luciano, *De Dea Syria,* 16, 28?).

105. Another important item of the Canaanite sanctuary was the *asherah,* "trunk" or "sacred stake" (the Vulgate, following the Septuagint for the most part renders this by *lucus:* probably under the influence of the original designation of the term). This sacred object was connected

Idol with head of a bull. Phallic emblem on the forehead. (Ustinow Collection.)

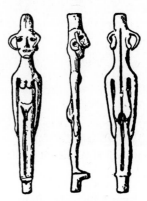

Idol of Astarte with horns (Gezer). (Macalister, *Excavation of Gezer.*)

with a widespread religious idea of the ancient Semites and one attested to also by modern Semites: that certain *trees,* especially of the more leafy and majestic variety, were the dwelling place of the divinity. Some were associated with famous personages or theophanies (§ 136); under others which were considered as it were invested with divine power, soothsayers (Judg. 9:37), the judges of the people (Judg. 4:5), and kings (1 Sam. 14:2; 22:6) consorted. But this idea, too, degenerated, and the mysterious and secret shade was later to hide obscene cults (Osee 4:13; Isa. 1:29; 57:5 ff.; Jer. 2:20, 27; 3:6; Ezech. 6:13; 20:28, etc.). From the Bible we learn that such cults were practiced in artificial(?) forests, situated for the most part on high places, at least on the sacred ones. The *asherah,* erected in the enclosure of the sanctuary itself, was a memorial or representation of these forests, but at the same time was a symbol or idol of the goddess who was worshiped in them. This goddess bore the same name, *Asherah,* but she was later confused with Astarte, the Semitic Venus (§ 107; cf. the theophoric names of Abdi-Ashirta, § 55, and of Ashirat-yashur, § 78).

106. The older Canaanite sanctuaries are hardly the place to look for sculptured figures of the divinity. At a later epoch many of these appear, fashioned of stone, clay, or metal. All of these, however, are small, and many of them were probably objects not for public but for private veneration, or were even used as charms. The first attempts were quite primitive in form, going back beyond the fourteenth century B.C., and have been interpreted as *teraphim*, "winged Gods?" (§ 144; Gen. 31:19, 34 ff.; 1 Sam. 19:13–16; etc.: they seem to be objects of public veneration according to Judg. 17:5 ff.; Osee 3:4, etc.). The preferred form for representing the divinity was that of a serpent, an example of which is the bronze found at Gezer (§ 76 ff.), other attempts at Beisan (§ 86; cf. 2 Kings 18:4; Num. 21:9), and that of a bull (cf. Exod. 32:4 ff.; 1 Kings 12:28 ff.). The majority of the small idols preserved for us

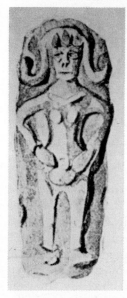

are reducible to the above-mentioned type of Astarte (§ 107): the goddess is represented in various forms and fashions and — often as befitted her purpose — completely nude with grossly exaggerated sexual characteristics.

107. The Canaanite pantheon revolved about Baal and Astarte (Judg. 2:12; 10:6; 1 Sam. 7:4; 12:10, etc.). In ancient times *ba'al* was a common noun, "owner," "master," and could be applied either to men (the *ba'al* of a woman was her husband; of a house, its proprietor; etc.) or to the divinity in relation to a given place or fact. In that sense even the Israelites applied it to God in the time of David (2 Sam. 5:20), using it even in composite theophoric personal names (1 Para. 8:33; 12:5);

Astarte of Ta'annak. (Sellin, *Tell Ta'annak*.)

Astarte of Ta'annak. (Sellin, *Tell Ta'annak*.)

when later on the term assumed a clearly idolatrous signification, a substitute was sought in the term *bosheth*, "shame" (cf. the passage cited in 1 Para. 8:33, with 2 Sam. 2:8 ff.; 'Ish-ba'al = 'Ish-bosheth).

Among the Canaanites, Baal was the god who owned and protected a particular place, the god of a given incident or of some special quality. Thus there was a Baal of Tyre, of Hermon, of Phegor (§ 270), the Baal-berith or "of the pact" (Judg. 8:33; 9:4; the equivalent of the "God of the Pact," is seen in 9:46: cf. §§ 88, 319), Baal-zebub ("of the flies?" 2 Kings 1:2 ff.), Baal 'Adon ("Lord") and the theophoric names Hanniba'al (Hannibal, "grace of Baal"; cf. Gen. 36:38), etc.

Akin to and often interchanged with Adad, god of the storm, Baal was the god of irrigation and hence of the fertility of the fields. Later on, when small ethnic communities were incorporated in monarchical political organization, even monarchical names were given to this multi-local deity, as 'Adon, "lord," "his majesty" (the Adonis of the Greeks), and Melek, "king" (changed deliberately by the Israelites to Molek, Moloch, applying to Melek the vocalization of bosheth, i.e., shame).

Baal's consort was a feminine divinity bearing the feminine form of the name of the god, i.e., ba'alah (-lath), "mistress," "lady," which crops up in geographical names. The concept of these various local "mistresses" is, at any rate, practically one with that of Astarte. In the Hebrew text the name of this goddess is vocalized 'Ashtoreth (Bosheth, again) but the Septuagint has 'Αστάρτη, as the Babylonian Ishtar (Ashtartu). For the Canaanites she was the goddess of love and of fertility, whether agricultural or human, having lost that chaste and warlike character which she often had in Babylonia. Numerous small idols of Astarte, especially those of a later date, generally assume, under various influences (Babylonian, Egyptian, etc.), more licentious forms.

108. The cult offered to these and other divinities was not preserved for us in ancient descriptions, but judging from the results of the excavations (which agree with the indications in the Bible), and from what the writers of the Greco-Roman era have to say concerning Phoenician and Syrian rites (of a later date but directly descended from the Canaanite rites), it may be assumed that they were of an orgiastic and corybantic character, almost always accompanied by wild dances and cries induced by inebriating drink (Judg. 9:27; 1 Kings 18:26–28; Isa. 28:7 ff.) — all of which produced a psychic exaltation in which spectators and participants alike were driven to human sacrifices, self-mutilation, or license and obscenity. In later times these practices were organized on a stable basis, and the enclosures or surroundings adjacent to the temples housed the qedheshoth, "sacred [women]," and qedheshim, "sacred [men]," disdainfully also called kelabhim, "dogs," "male prostitutes" (Deut. 23:17–18; Osee 4:14; 1 Kings 14:24; 22:47; 2 Kings 23:7; Ezech. 16:16, etc.; cf. also Apoc. 22:15). Many details of this subject have come down to us from Assyrian and Phoenician inscriptions; if anyone thinks that Herodotus, I, 199 (cf. Bar. 6:42–43), is guilty of exaggeration where Babylon is concerned, for Syria there is the no less significant account of Lucian (De dea Syria), of Eusebius (Vita Constantini, III, 55, in Migne, P.G., 20, 1120–1121), and others. The fascination which the Canaanite cults always exercised especially on the Israelites was due in great measure to their refined lasciviousness, joined with the contagious frenzy of these "sacred" persons.

THE HISTORICAL SOURCE

109. Whatever the importance of the materials thus far considered may be, the Bible is itself the historical source *par excellence* for matters concerning the people of Israel. A cursory glance at it is therefore now in order.

In the Hebrew Bible the Canon, or series of books which make it up, is divided into three parts; first, the *Torah* ("Law," today usually called "Pentateuch"); second, the *Nebhi'im* ("Prophets"); and third, the *Kethubhim* ("Writings" or "Sacred Writings"). Each one of these parts is a collection of various books independent of one another, yet mutually connected in many ways. Most important for our present purpose is their chronological connection. It is beyond dispute that the chronology of the content was one of the principal criteria to determine the disposition of the Canon; the period to which the content of each book is ascribed has been the general criterion according to which the editors of the Canon have set the books in order, beginning with those which have the oldest content and following step by step to the most recent. The great canonical series — with certain variations due to different causes — is uniform in the more important features.

The threefold division of the Old Testament was attested as far back as the second century B.C. by the translator of *Ecclesiasticus*. The first part, the Pentateuch, always comes first, and the five books of which it is composed are always listed in the same order. The second part (the Prophets) was subdivided into the "Early" and "Later Prophets"; the books of the first section appear consistently in the same order (*Josue, Judges, Samuel,* and *Kings*), but differences begin with the second section which contains the strictly prophetical works, and extends through the whole of the third part, the Writings. These appear in the Canon in an order that varies according to the documents which transmitted them. This indicates that for the predominantly historical books, concerning which there could be no uncertainty, the chronological disposition prevailed; but for those books which contained more doctrine than history other criteria outweighed the chronological arrangement; but these other criteria do not concern us here.

110. The book of *Ruth,* of historical content, is outside the chronological ordering because it forms a part of the "Five Rolls," assembled for the liturgy of the synagogue as a special section of the Writings. At the end of the Hebrew Canon stand the two books of *Paralipomenon,* despite the fact that they contain genealogies extending back to Adam; they seem to be an exception in the chronological pattern. But the exception is more apparent than real. It is generally admitted today that these two books were in origin part of the single historical work which included also *Esdras* and *Nehemias.* Only the second part of this historical work (*Esdras-Nehemias*) treated of an historical era which had not been described in the preceding book of the Canon; the first part (*1–2 Paralipomenon*) was only a new presentation of matter already described in the preceding *Samuel-Kings.* Hence it came about that in the ultimate arrangement of the Canon, the newer part of the work (*Esdras-Nehemias*) found a place next to the other Writings; while the two books which formed its first part were placed at the end of the Canon, a recapitulation, as it were, of the whole. This artificial dismembering of a well-knit work is a confirmation of (rather than an exception to) the chronological standard according to which the books were arranged in the Canon.

111. To follow the disposition of the Hebrew Canon, therefore, is to find in the Bible, in chronological order, the entire history of Israel, beginning with its origins (*Genesis*) right on up to the national restoration which succeeded the Babylonian Exile (*Esdras* and *Nehemias*), due abstraction being made for the two books of *Paralipomenon,* which have been relegated to the appendix position because they recapitulated so much of the story.

Genesis tells of the very origins of the world and of the human race; in considering this matter, it restricts itself with admirable singleness of purpose to the treatment of the direct progenitors of the people of Israel. Through Abraham and Isaac it comes down to Jacob, or Israel, the progenitor through his twelve sons of the twelve tribes who constitute the people; concerning these *Genesis* gives an account of their nomadic life in Canaan and finally their descent into Egypt.

Exodus tells the story of the exodus of the descendants of the twelve from Egypt, where in the interim they had become a strong people. It describes their wanderings in the steppes of Sinai and their first organization under the leadership of Moses.

Leviticus, as if to present immediately the effect of that organization, offers a collection of ritual prescriptions regarding, above all, the tribe of Levi, which was given charge of the cult.

Numbers, describing the census of the new people again takes up the account of the wanderings in the steppes; legal prescriptions and documents of other kinds are woven together and this book brings the people to the eastern bank of the Jordan opposite Canaan.

Deuteronomy, in the form of discourses of Moses, in part confirms, and in part completes, the preceding prescriptions. It tells finally of his death, overlooking the Promised Land.

112. In *Josue,* the Jordan is crossed, Canaan is conquered and, more in theory than in fact, divided among the conquering tribes.

The book of *Judges* describes rather sketchily the uncertain period which followed the entry into Canaan; the conquest was in general consolidated but during this time the material and moral reaction of the Canaanites had to be reckoned with.

In the two books of *Samuel* the transition from the patriarchal regime of the "judges" to the monarchical is described. Samuel himself was also a "judge," but the last of the series, since it was he who established the monarchy, first a transitional one with Saul, then a more durable one, David's.

The two books of *Kings* recount, often in schematic fashion, the religious and political history of the kings who governed the two kingdoms (into which the people of Israel were soon divided), and record the destruction of them both.

The books that follow are no longer historical books in the strict sense except for the complex unity *1–2 Paralipomenon-Esdras-Nehemias,* discussed above (§ 110). *Esdras-Nehemias* resumes the narration at the chronological point where the books of *Kings* left off, i.e., at the Babylonian exile; it recounts the return from the exile and the work of restoration in the homeland up to about the middle of the fifth century B.C.

113. Were the books composed in a chronological order corresponding to the matter they treat? To phrase it differently, are the books of the Hebrew Canon arranged according to the dates which should be assigned to them?

However many and important the questions which are raised about the different books of the Old Testament, none can compare in seriousness with this one. Here is the core of biblical criticism, and these questions lurk, more or less, behind all the others.

To limit the inquiry to the first section of the Hebrew Canon taken as a block — "the Torah," "Early Prophets," and "Late Prophets" — ancient Hebrew tradition has constantly replied in the affirmative. The Torah is older than "Early Prophets" and these in turn are older than "Later Prophets." Modern criticism in the main has given a negative answer; briefly, a good part of "Later Prophets," which are prophetic writings, is older than "Early Prophets," which are historical; the Torah, in its present form, is not as old as the "Prophets" in general. While therefore the Hebrew tradition maintains generally the chronological order: Law-Historiography-Prophetism, modern criticism has inverted this order, replacing it by Prophecy-Historiography-Law.

It is not the task of this work to relate the steps by which criticism has arrived at this conclusion, nor the battle fought between it and the upholders of the traditional opinion. The battle, now about a hundred years old, gives no indication of abating, for while the traditionalists cling to more or less the same defensive positions, the critics direct their offensive from new sectors under the form of successively renovated hypotheses and theories. Only the last sector from which the attack was launched and the most recent maneuvers which seem to point to its abandonment will be indicated.

114. The theory commonly attributed to Wellhausen[1] can be briefly summed up as follows.

"In ancient Israel there was no written law"; there were only some traditional norms, some of them very ancient, which, circulated orally, controlled by their indisputable authority both civil and, especially, religious life; in doubtful cases the living oracle, the priest, decided and applied this fluid Torah. *Deuteronomy* (conventionally signified by *D*) "discovered" and published under Josias (621 B.C.; cf. § 510 ff.) was for that period the book of the Torah: "it was also the first and only one of its time." This first text may have included certain decisions then put into writing by the priests, but the innovation lay in the fact that the book "was edited with evident purpose of not remaining a private piece of writing, but of attaining public value *as a book*."[2] With the appearance of the new codex "the ancient liberty" which up to then had been dominant in the religious spirit and cult "ended"; the new "supreme objective authority . . . was the death of prophecy." — But "Deuteronomy was also the program for a reform, not for a restoration," that is, it was an introduction of something new, not a return to the old. On the strength of this program progress was made toward further codification, especially in matters of cult and genealogy, but on the other hand this led to a revision of the historico-religious writings already existing in Israel. The driving force behind this activity originated in the sacerdotal circles which, during the Babylonian exile, recognized Ezechiel as their leader. The work of codification produced the Sacerdotal Code (or Priesterkodex, signified by the initial *P*); the work of revision went as

---

[1] Cf. J. Wellhausen, *Die Komposition des Hexateuchs und der historischen Bücher des Alten Testament,* 3 ed., Berlin, 1899; *id., Prolegomena zur Geschichte Israels,* 6 ed., Appendix, Berlin, 1919; *id., Israelitische und jüdische Geschichte,* 8 ed., Berlin, 1921. The quotations are taken from the *Prolegomena,* pp. viii, x, 401, 408. Cf. also J. Coppens, *The Old Testament and the Critics,* Paterson, N. J., 1942.

[2] The italics are in the German text (*Prolegomena,* p. 402). Cf. Coppens, *The Old Testament and The Critics,* Paterson, N. J., 1942, p. 30 ff.

far as a double modification of documents, the first according to the spirit of *Deuteronomy*, the second according to the spirit of the Sacerdotal Code. Later on, by a process of editing and fusion, the fixation of the Canon began, in that "in time 'the Books' were added to 'the Book.'"

115. The *Book* could not be anything else but *Deuteronomy*, which continued to grow and increase until it evolved into our present-day Torah. The first edition was an historical part. A codex of such character which was destined to become the *magna charta* of the theocratic nation, could not remain a simple formulary of laws, but had as it were to justify itself in the events which happened to the nation itself, and by which those laws were, it was claimed, occasioned. This historical part was made up of two documents long in circulation in Israel: the Yahwistic document (J)* and the Elohistic (E), so called because the words "Yahweh" and "Elohim" were used to name the God of Israel. The Yahwistic document arose in the kingdom of Juda about the middle of the ninth century B.C.; the Elohistic in the northern kingdom, about a century after the Yahwistic. Both documents are popular narratives: they relate the origins of the people of Israel (of the human race even: J) in a simple and naïve way, fixing in writing what was certainly on the lips of all. They have been called the "two twin brothers," so great is their generic affinity, a statement that does not, however, preclude certain subtle details which often enough distinguish them. Often, but not always, for in some undetermined era — probably after 720 B.C. — the similarity of the two documents inspired their fusion, and there resulted only one account. This came to be called the "prophetic account," because it arose in times when prophecy flourished, and before any written Torah existed; it is signified by the initials R^{JE}, to signify that an R (redactor) in explaining the documents had fused them together. The initials are necessary in practice because in many cases, for the reasons just indicated, the two documents fused into one work are no longer distinguishable today. This "prophetic account," after it had received the modifications just mentioned, was united with *Deuteronomy* during the exile, with the result that the Torah was then constituted thus: $D + R^{JE}$.

116. The Sacerdotal Code was a still later addition. "The Sacerdotal Code must have been composed in Jerusalem and in Juda," if not by Esdras himself, certainly in his time. During the same era or shortly thereafter it was fused with the existing Torah; the formula, then, was: $D + R^{JE} + P$; quantitatively P played a predominant part. "Perhaps also Esdras ought to be regarded as the editor of the Pentateuch," as the one who completed the ultimate fusion which is, substantially, our

---

* The Hebrew letter "Yod" is transliterated by "Y" rather than "J."

present Torah. This does not rule out the fact that "later on, additions and changes of every kind have been made," to the redaction of Esdras also.

The Canon therefore begins with the Torah. After it the other parts of the Canon follow in order. The book of *Josue*, first of the "Early Prophets," is not part of these, but has undergone the same process as the Pentateuch, forming with it a so-called Hexateuch. The other books, historical and prophetical, were incorporated into the Canon later, when the historical books were editorially revised according to the spirit of the last stage of the Torah, especially that of *P*.

Comparing, therefore, the Law on the one hand and the historical and prophetic books on the other, we reach the following conclusion: "Since the historical and prophetic books existed in part long before they became canonical, something similar must have been the case with the Law. It is, however, essentially different in regard to the Law. The Law *demands* a legal value, it *demands* recognition as a community book;[3] between Law and Canon there is no distinction. Hence, although the Torah as a literary work is more recent than the historical and prophetical books, it is older, as Law, than those writings which originally and by themselves have no legal character but have acquired it in an accessory manner, being joined to a true and existing Law."

117. Up to this point we have presented the thought and words of Wellhausen, and more or less those of his followers. The arguments adduced from philology or literary criticism or from history to support his theory can be examined in his writings or in the writings of those who have accurately expounded them in order to refute them. No matter whence they are derived, his arguments are weak because of their underlying philosophic presuppositions. This is a point which will always make agreement impossible between scholars who, even though they apply the same methods of analysis and arguments, are nevertheless separated by opposite philosophical principles employed in tracing the broad outlines of Israel's history, which is essentially a religious history.

There is no point in self-deception or dissimulation here. Two scholars, equally masters of the scientific apparatus, will reconstruct the history of Israel in two fundamentally different ways, depending upon their different philosophical principles. The Hegelian who is an accomplished Orientalist will contemplate such a history under an entirely different light than a Thomist who is likewise an accomplished Orientalist. They might agree on many details of the superstructure, but on the founda-

---

[3] "Das Gesetz *will* gesetzliche Geltung haben, *will* Gemeinbuch sein," *Prolegomena*, p. 408 (italics in the German text).

tions, never. The reason is evident. For one the first and most fundamental facts of that history are "possible," for the other they are "impossible," and must therefore be rejected and some kind of explanation for their genesis given. The crucial point which always divides scholars is the antecedent philosophical "possibility" of a history of Israel as it is presented in its general lines by the Bible itself.

In this connection a sentence of Wellhausen's may be quoted although it does not refer to the whole history of Israel but to a particular question: "The Israelite tradition on this point is of greater value than any objection. If it is even *possible*, it would be folly to prefer any other possibility." If this particular "possibility" is extended so as to include the general development of the history of Israel, we enter into the depths of philosophy. It is clear that if one has philosophical principles which differ from those of Wellhausen, he can rightfully admit the very "possibility" which Wellhausen would deny.[4]

118. The theory of Wellhausen however, which has so triumphantly dominated the field for over thirty years, is today undergoing a grave crisis; and the point at which it is falling apart is precisely that presupposition which is its foundation stone, namely, the "impossibility" of the Israelite tradition. The pivotal point of the question is not whether in the redaction of the Hexateuch, or, better, the Pentateuch, previous sources were utilized, for there is a general consensus today on this point and even the most traditional scholars admit that ancient sources were incorporated or utilized in such a work. The pivotal point is the period or time which is assigned to these sources, and what historical value can be attributed to them. It is very significant that those who are responsible for the crisis in Wellhausen's theory are principally those scholars who do not profess any dogma or systems, but are simply men dedicated to archaeological research. To these, the theory of Wellhausen, especially in its chronological assertions, appears to be pretty much a matter of armchair thinking. To his subtle, learned, but aprioristic skill, they have opposed factual data, especially that which has come to light during or after Wellhausen's reconstruction: as for example, the codex of Hammurabi (§§ 4, 246), and the Hittite codex (§§ 46, 248), the Amarna letters (§ 43 ff.), the recent discoveries in Palestine (§ 74 ff.), and, in a word, with all the documents which lay underground when Wellhausen fashioned his theory. The spade of the archaeologist has been digging away at the fundamental stone of the pretended "impossibility." If the stone has not yet been broken into pieces, it has at least been greatly weakened and its foundations shaken. The basic issue raised above concerning the date

---

[4] *Komposition des Hexateuchs*, 347.

of the sources of the Pentateuch and their historical value, may now be given this answer: In proportion as one recedes from Wellhausen's position, he approaches closer to tradition.[5]

119. To verify this one has only to juxtapose, even superficially, the two "histories of the people of Israel" written by Stade and Sellin. Stade, a dyed-in-the-wool Wellhausenian, wrote in 1887; Sellin, many times a director of excavations in Palestine (§§ 78, 80, 88), wrote in 1924. For Stade, solid ground in the history of Israel begins somewhere around the time of the monarchy; another safe point is the time of the Israelite invasion and conquest of Canaan, bearing always in mind that "the Ephraimite legend of the conquest of the country to the west of the Jordan on the part of all the people of Israel under the leadership of Josue, is not founded on any historical tradition." Moreover, "one cannot talk seriously of an era of Judges as preceding that of the kings." The preceding era then fades into full legend, so much so that Stade does not even consider it worth while to put the Wellhausenian "impossibility" of the Israelite tradition to the test. "Joseph, Jacob, Isaac, Abraham, are tribal heroes"; "both the dwelling of the patriarchs in the country to the west of the Jordan and that of the people in Egypt are historically suspect"; if then there was a dwelling in Egypt, it must have happened in a manner entirely different from that narrated in the legend; "from this it can be concluded that the researches regarding the pharaohs under whom Israel emigrated from Egypt, are nothing but useless calculations and names," just as "historical tradition is lacking concerning the route the Israelites took in their flight from Egypt. In a word, what we read in *Exodus* is a mythical legend, a travesty of history camouflaged by historical and geographical details."

The blustering dogmatism of a Wellhausen is not evident in the archaeologist. Sellin admits the historical reality of the patriarchs, their sojourn in Canaan, and the dwelling of a part of the people in Egypt; he determines approximately the time of their stay there, of the exodus, and their subsequent itinerary; he treats at length of the events in the wilderness and of Sinai, of Moses and his death, dwelling at length, with understandable archaeological complacency, on the conquest of Canaan. If even he often speaks of "sagas" (in the sense which the word has in the German language), he does attribute to these sagas, generally speaking, an historical credibility such as would have scandalized Wellhausen.[6]

120. It would be naïve to claim that all this has definitely scuttled the Wellhausen theory, and that his followers are returning *en masse*

---

[5] Cf. the letter to Cardinal Suhard from the Secretary of the Biblical Commission, P. Vosté, in *Homiletic and Pastoral Review*, 1948, 567–574.

[6] Cited by Stade, *Geschichte des Volkes Israels*, Berlin, 1887; Sellin, *Geschichte . . .*, Leipzig, 1924, 4 f.; Kittel, *Geschichte*, 6 ed., 1923, 6 ff.

to traditional positions. As Sellin justly observes, criticism is passing through a period of transition and uncertainty; the approach to tradition is manifested above all in raising the date of the sources utilized by the Pentateuch, and in conceding to them an ever increasing historical value. Both are, anyhow, quite far removed from those assigned to them by tradition. Thus for Sellin the Pentateuch contains some very ancient parts, some which are also Mosaic: *J* is of the times of David and Solomon, *E* of the time of Solomon, *D* of about 700 B.C., *P* contains elements of various epochs, some of them ancient; the ultimate compilation, after preceding liturgical redactions, was effected under Esdras.

U. Cassuto in his "Studi sulla Genesi," upholds, at least for *Genesis*, the unity of origin; he dates it from Davidic times.[7]

121. W. Roberton Smith, in his preface to the English translation of Wellhausen's *Prolegomena*, declared: "The Old Testament does not offer us a history of Israel, but it does furnish the materials from which that history can be constructed."

This is, in substance, the criterion which, when applied to documents, guides modern historiography in regard to the Greeks, Romans, and other peoples of antiquity. Its second and positive part can be subscribed to by students of any opinion. The first and the negative part is typically Wellhausenian, if applied to the fundamental outlines of the history of Israel. The practical consequence is that one who accepts the theory of Wellhausen will throw these outlines overboard at his pleasure, and will discard most of that matter in his construction of the history of Israel. On the contrary, anyone who does not accept the theory in question will retain the outlines, and will dispose the critically appraised matter according to them.

Critically appraised, to be sure; this does not mean, however, that the one possible critique is that based on the philosophical principles presupposed by the theory of Wellhausen. A real critique might even reject the negative part of the above-mentioned criterion, that is, by accepting as historical the fundamental outlines of the history of Israel as proffered by the Bible. The non-Wellhausenian scholar could dispose the matter offered by the Bible along lines critically appraised but not discarded *en bloc* as by Wellhausen. For the rest, however imprudent from a critical viewpoint these discards *en bloc* may be, it is clear that yesterday's fable may today turn out to be history, and that up-to-date archaeologists carefully handle biblical material which was disdainfully discarded by the Wellhausens of yesterday.

It would be hazardous to an extreme to attempt to predict the direction future criticism will take, but it is perfectly safe to assert that any

---

[7] E. Sellin, *Einleitung in das A.T.*, 4 ed., Leipzig, 1925, 19 ff.; U. Cassuto, "Studi sulla Genesi," in *Giornale della Soc. Asiat. Ital.*, I, 1925–1926, 193 ff.

future critical history of Israel, if it is to enjoy more than a passing existence, must take into account the basic outlines of that history as they are sketched in the Bible. Not that all will then be easy and clear; on the contrary, questions will arise concerning many passages in the narrative. But a question mark has never, in any science, justified the amputation of limbs.

This is, therefore, the scientific reason which obliges us to follow, step by step, the unfolding of the biblical narrative; future knowledge will bring the awaited light to illumine the obscurities of that story.

THE HISTORY OF ISRAEL

THE PATRIARCHS

122. The history of Israel is based upon an essentially mystical fact: the call of Abraham.

Abraham was of the family of Terah (see the following table), which is described in the Bible as idolatrous (Josue 24:2; Judith 5:6 ff.; cf. Josephus, *Antiquities*, 1, 7, 1). Terah lived in Ur of the Chaldees (§ 2); after his son Haran died there he, together with his other son Abraham, Sara, the wife of Abraham, and his nephew Lot, moved to Harran (§ 2), where he died.[1]

123. The emigration of the Terahites from Ur to Harran was surely not an unusual event, but rather a mere illustration of the close ties existing between the two cities. The Chaldean tribes concentrated around Ur of the Chaldees were ethnologically related to the Aramean tribes near Harran: besides this, both cities were special centers of the cult of the moon-god, Sin (§§ 2, 16). The cult had doubtless spread from Ur to Harran, since this latter city was on the road (*harranu*, "road") leading from Mesopotamia toward the Syro-Palestinian region. It was consequently controlled by Ur until the end of the third millennium (§ 3). The names of the Terahites show clear traces of the predominance of the cult of the moon-god. One example among others is the name of Laban, which brings to mind the Hebrew *lebhanah*, an epithet for the moon (cf. also § 132). At any rate the direct occasion of the emigration of the family of Terah may perhaps have been the wars which upset Chaldea in the last decades before Hammurabi (§ 4), and from which the city of Ur especially suffered.[2]

124. It was against this background that Abraham's call took place. Although not subject to archaeological control, the call must be judged in the light of its historical consequences. In effect, God commanded Abraham to go out from his country and his relatives

---

[1] Cf. R. de Vaux, "Les patriarches hébreux et les découvertes modernes," *Revue biblique*, 1946, pp. 321–348.

[2] Concerning the times of Abraham, cf. E. Dhorme, "Abraham dans le cadre de l'histoire" in *RB*, 1928, 386 ff.; 1931, 346 ff.; R. de Vaux, *art. cit., loc. cit.*, 321–348; 1948, 321–347. For interesting and enlightening parallels, cf. C. H. Gordon, "Biblical Customs and the Nuzu Tablets," *BA*, 1940, 1–12.

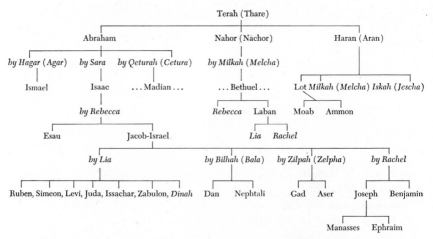

NOTE: The names in parenthesis are the reading of the Vulgate; those in italics are
the names of women. Some ancient writers (Josephus, *Antiquities*, I, 6, 5;
Targ. Jon.; St. Jerome, etc.), followed by some modern authors, identify
Iskah (Jescha) with Sara; cf., however, Gen. 20:12.

to a place to be indicated to him. It was God's will to make him the
head of a great nation, the object of divine benedictions, and the
person through whom all the nations of the earth would be blessed. The
call took place in Ur (cf. Acts 7:2–3; the *wayommer* of Gen. 12:1 can
be translated as usual, according to Hebrew grammar, as the plu-
perfect "had said"). The circumstances mentioned above were favorable
to this emigration but it was actually decided by this mystical fact. It
was a decision of momentous consequences, but understandable in view
of the great importance attached to religion by the ancient, and especially
the Semitic, peoples. Babylonian documents record the waging of wars
over the possession of a sacred image. The details of the manner in
which Abraham was called are lacking, but the fact was accepted
reverently and without question by his idolatrous parents when they
decided to leave Ur with him. Other examples of men profoundly
convinced of a special mission frequently occurred in Israel in the era
of Prophetism (§ 418 ff.). Outside of Israel the success of Mahomet
shows what influence a man could exercise among Semites if he stepped
before them as one invested with a divine mission.

125. The Terahites intended to emigrate to Canaan (Gen. 11:31),
the stop at Harran being an intermediate resting place. After the
death of his father, Abraham resumed his westward journey with
Sara, Lot, and their servants. Leaving Harran when he was already
seventy-five years old (cf. § 127), he entered the land of Canaan
from the northeast.

Here the conditions of the el-Amarna period were not yet realized (§ 43 ff.). Some rather contemporary information can be gathered from the Egyptian *Tale of Sinuhe*[3] (c. Twelfth Dynasty; § 30) where mention is made of southern Palestine (§§ 205, 359). The population must have been very* sparse; the Canaanites lived in cities and fortified places, allowing nomadic tribes to pasture their flocks in the neighboring countryside. Abraham's group must have appeared to be one of these tribes, and he himself to be one of many sheikhs driven by political fortune or nomadic instincts into the open country. He was not, however, an insignificant sheikh, for, counting relatives, household, and other servants, his group numbered more than a hundred (Gen. 14:14), by no means a puny force, considering the population of the land.

126. These two factors made it possible for Abraham to move about quite freely in that region. He traveled Canaan from north to south, stopping at Sichem (§ 88) — where he received the promise from God that the land of Canaan would be given to his descendants — then at Beth-el, and afterward advancing toward the Negeb (§ 65). A widespread famine forced Abraham's group to go down into Egypt.[4] The Egyptians, noticing the beauty of Sara, reported it to an unnamed Pharoah. Sara was seized and taken to the court of the Pharaoh, who showered Abraham with munificent gifts of slaves and animals because of her. But Pharaoh, punished by God in a manner not described, sent Sara back to Abraham, complaining because he had not declared Sara to be his wife but had pretended that she was his sister.

127. The descent of Abraham into Egypt because of the famine rings true. In ancient times the desert nomads always looked upon Egypt as the land of abundance, since the regular flooding of the Nile (§ 23) saved it (except in rare instances [§ 16]) from the danger of famine — brought on elsewhere by drought. The monuments of Egypt portray Asiatic Bedouin marching toward Egypt, and hieroglyphic texts verify these traditional immigrations. The immigrants became so demanding,

---

[3] *ANET*, 18–22.

[4] Egyptian testimony concerning Israelite immigration into Egypt, in *ANET*, 229.

Caravan of Semites (men, women, and children) migrating to Egypt (Dynasty XII).

Semitic immigrants present themselves to an Egyptian official. The men prostrate themselves, the women remain standing behind them. (Thebes.)

however, that the Pharaohs were obliged to put a halt to their inroads and to defend their homeland by force. Abraham's attempt to pass Sara off as his sister (Gen. 20:2), rather than acknowledge her as his wife is understandable. She was actually his half-sister, as he explains (Gen. 20:12). His silence concerning her marital relationship to himself was inspired by a rather well grounded fear. More difficult to explain is Sara's comeliness at the age of sixty-five (cf. 17:17 with 12:4), when, it seems, she would hardly be likely to awaken the ardor of an Egyptian Pharaoh. A similar incident will take place when Abraham dwelt in the territory of Abimelech (Gen. 20); and yet again in the lifetime of Isaac (26:7–11). The whole matter is closely bound up not only with the extraordinary longevity of the patriarchs (cf. §§ 183, 222 ff.), but also with the maternity of Sara at the age of ninety, and more generally with the fecundity of the more than one hundred-year-old patriarchs. It is clear that the Bible intends explicitly to present these particular phenomena as the result of a privilege reserved to the progenitors of the people of God.

When Abraham went up to Canaan from Egypt he returned to Beth-el. In the meantime his group had notably increased; his flocks and those of Lot could only with difficulty find the necessary pastures; inevitable arguments flared up between the respective herdsmen. The group therefore divided; Abraham allowed Lot his choice, and he chose the region of the Jordan from north to south of the Dead Sea (§ 62 ff.), finally establishing himself at Sodom (§ 94). Abraham, however, journeyed to the terebinths of Mambre near Hebron (§ 91).

128. At this point the Bible narrates a very special event typically Babylonian in character and probably also in origin (Gen. 14). It

came about that 'Amraphel king of Shin'ar, 'Aryokh king of 'Ellasar, Kedhor-la'omer king of 'Elam, and Tidh'al king of Goim, made war on the five kings of the Palestinian Pentapolis — Sodom, Gomorrha, Admah, Seboim, and Bela-So'ar (§§ 94, 136) — who had remained tributaries of Kedhor-la'omer for twelve years and in the thirteenth rebelled. The battle was joined in the valley of Siddim, which is probably covered today by the Dead Sea; the kings of Pentapolis were routed, those of Sodom and Gomorrha took to flight and their cities were sacked; among those taken prisoners were Lot and his family. When Abraham learned of the affair, he selected and armed three hundred and eighteen of his servants and set out to rescue his nephew. He was joined by other forces of undetermined number from around Hebron (cf. Gen. 14:13, with 14:24). According to approved Bedouin tactics, he patiently followed the victorious troops northward to Dan on the border of Palestine (§ 60), and one night attacked them, striking probably at the rearguard which was slowed down and encumbered with booty and prisoners. Pursuing the army northward he succeeded in rescuing Lot and his possessions.

Half a millennium later Thutmose III conducted his great Asiatic campaigns (§ 34) with an average of less than twenty thousand men. The raid of the four victorious kings must then have been conducted with a much smaller force, so that Abraham's handful could in the circumstances and with the above-mentioned tactics accomplish what has been reported.[5]

129. The incursion of the four kings was hardly anything new, for from the middle of the third millennium monarchs of Mesopotamia, kings like Sargon and Gudea (§ 3) had exercised acts of *quasi* dominion on the shores of the Mediterranean. Innumerable attempts have been made to identify these kings. At present many hold that 'Amraphel, king of Shin'ar, is Hammurabi (§ 4) of Babylonia (Shin'ar = Shumer; according to others = Shanhar).[6] Other identifications more or less founded are: 'Aryokh, king of 'Ellasar, corresponds to Rim-Sin (read also Rim[or Riw]-Aku) of Larsa (§ 4); Tidh'al, king of Goim ("of the peoples"), is Tudhalijash I, king of the Hittites, a contemporary of Hammurabi; as for Kedhor-la'omer, as yet unidentified, the name is Elamite (*Kutir* ["servant" ?] of *Lagamar*, Elamite divinity): he is presented as king of Elam. The fact that Kedhor-la'omer is the only one named in Gen. 14:4, 5, 17, and the first named in 14:9, gives rise to

---

[5] Cf. *Cambridge Ancient History*, II, Cambridge, 1926, 67, for a description of an Egyptian army.
[6] For the identification of Shin'ar with Shumer, cf. A. Deimel in *Biblica*, 1921, 71 ff.; with Shanhar, cf. Dhorme, in *RB*, 1931, 507 ff. For the identification of the various persons named, cf. Deimel in *Biblica*, 1927, 350–357; Dhorme in *RB*, *loc. cit.*; P. de Vaux, *art. cit.*, 1948, 326 ff.

a suggestion that the expedition took place before Hammurabi had defeated the king of Elam in battle (§ 4) and was therefore still his vassal; nevertheless, at the very beginning of the narrative (Gen. 14:1) the first named is Hammurabi.

In conclusion, the identification of Hammurabi and 'Amraphel is not immune to grave doubts.

130. Melchisedech, who was king of Salem and also a priest of 'El-'elyon, "the most high God" (§ 178), came out to meet and congratulate Abraham and his warriors on their return from the victorious razzia. He offered bread and wine and finally blessed Abraham, who recognized his sacerdotal authority and gave him the tenth part of the salvaged booty. Salem is in all probability the Urusalim (uru = "foundation"?) of the documents of el-Amarna, i.e., Jerusalem (§ 57); some however think that there was a Salim on the bank of the Jordan (cf. Jn. 3:23). The name of its king Malkisedheq, "[my] king is justice," finds its parallel in that of Adhoni-sedheq, "[my] lord is justice," likewise king of Jerusalem in the times of Josue (Josue 10:1 ff.), and both names, together with other facts, lend a plausibility to the hypotheses that Canaanite Jerusalem was the center of the cult of a god Sedeq, "justice" (§ 97; cf. Isa. 1:26; Jer. 31:23).

Melchisedech himself is historically an indeterminate and isolated figure, but later Jewish tradition preserved a vivid recollection of him, perceiving in him an image of the future Messias. His indeterminate and isolated character is brought out in bold relief by the epistle to the Hebrews (7:2 ff.): "First, as his name shows, he is king of justice: and also he is king of Salem, that is, king of peace. Without father, without mother, without genealogy, having neither beginning of days nor end of life . . ." It is interesting on that account to note that similar phrases are employed by a successor of Melchisedech, Abdi-Hipa (§ 57). In one of his letters to the Pharaoh he says: "What have I done to the king, my Lord? They calumniate me before the king, my Lord, saying: Abdi-Hipa has betrayed the king, his Lord! Behold, as for me, neither my father nor my mother set me in this place; the arm of the mighty king has caused me to enter into the house of my father. Why should I commit rebellion against the king, my Lord? . . ." Some suppose that the "king" who had introduced Abdi-Hipa into the house of his father might have been a divinity ("king" = Melekh; § 107), and therefore he was at one time king and priest, like his predecessor, Melchisedech; but the rest of the letter does not support such a hypothesis. At any rate, elsewhere too he returns to the same idea: ". . . Behold, neither my father nor my mother has given me this land of Urusalim; the powerful hand of the king has given it to me. . . ."[7]

---

[7] Cf. the two letters of Abdi-Hipa ('Abdu-Heba), in *ANET*, 487 ff.

131. Meanwhile, the divine promises gave no indication of fulfillment. Abraham was still without the children who would be the beginning of that great nation of which he was to be the head (§ 124). He expressed his anxiety to God during a theophany, but God merely reaffirmed his promises. Abraham believed them, and his faith was reputed to him unto justice. God therefore made a regular pact or "alliance" or "testament" with Abraham, according to the usual Babylonian formalities (Gen. 15:9 ff.; cf. 34:18 ff.), by which the former promises of descendants and the possession of Canaan were officially confirmed.

Abraham's faith, however, was not shared by Sara, and with subtle design the Bible interweaves the story of Sara's incredulity with the faith of Abraham and her privileged fecundity (§ 127). Sterile herself, Sara gave Abraham her own personal servant, Hagar, to use as a concubine. The ensuing children would by law be considered as belonging to the mistress. Hagar was Egyptian (perhaps given by the Pharaoh: § 126), but being in the service of the Terahites she was subject to the law in force among them. This law must trace back to their native country, i.e., Babylonia. Articles 144–147 of the contemporary Code of Hammurabi (§§ 4, 246) consider the sterility of a wife as a reason for her offering one of her own servants to her husband. If the servant was also sterile, the code (art. 147) permitted that she be sold. If she bore children and boasted of them so as to become a rival of her mistress, the code (art. 146) did not permit her to be sold, because of the children, but only that she be reduced to her position as simple slave. This last applies in Abraham's case. By reason of a special privilege (§ 127) he was fertile at the age of eighty-six (Gen. 16:16), and Hagar conceived; she became puffed up with pride and scorned her barren mistress, who complained to Abraham. He simply reminded Sara that the servant was in her power and that she could do what she liked with her. Thereupon Sara, applying the Babylonian Law, "humiliated" (*watte 'aneha*, Gen. 16:16) the proud one, returning her to the condition of bondage. Humiliated thus, Hagar fled into the desert in rebellion; but warned by an angel (or by God himself; cp. Gen. 16:7 ff. with 16:13), she returned to her master and gave birth to Ismael (§ 137).

132. When Abraham reached his ninety-ninth year, another theophany occurred. The preceding promises were again confirmed with the added precision that the heir of the promises was not to be Ismael, already born, but another who would be born of Sara. As a confirmatory sign God imposed a new name upon him and his wife, and commanded him to practice the rite of circumcision.

His name up to that time had been 'Abhram, which is a contraction of the Babylonian form (Assyrian) *Abi-ramu* (cf. Num. 16:1; § 260): its meaning would seem to be "Father-is-exalted," in which "Father" is perhaps the name of a divinity (the moon-god, Sin?; § 123). This

Present-day Hebron.

name was changed to 'Abraham and was connected with the meaning "Father-of-numbers-of-people," a signification which does not seem to be based on any etymology of the Hebrew or related languages, but only on the assonance of the final syllable of the name with hamon, "quantity." It is therefore an etymological approximation of a popular type of which the Bible records several cases (§§ 203, 239, 283). The corresponding Babylonian form A-ba-ra-ma means "Has-a-Beloved-Father."

The name of Abraham's wife, Sarai, was perhaps an antiquated form (in Babylonian, Sa-ra-a-a); it was now changed into the newer form, Sarah, that is, "princess." The corresponding Babylonian word, Sharratu, was the title of the goddess Nin-gal, spouse of the moon-god, Sin (§ 123).

133. Circumcision, well defined in meaning among some peoples, is in itself and its origins a typical ritual of which the complete explanation has yet to be given. Far from being a rite peculiar to the Israelites or even to the ancient Semites, modern ethnological researches have disclosed its almost universal practice in our times. For antiquity it can be shown that it was practiced from the time of the Old Kingdom in Egypt (§ 29); today it is practiced by at least one seventh of the human race. This estimate includes many African tribes, especially of western and eastern Africa, among whom some are Christians, besides many peoples of Australia, Polynesia, and South America. It is also attested in pre-Columbian North, Central, and South America. In ancient Egypt it was perhaps universally practiced;

at any rate it was certainly widespread, especially in priestly classes and court circles. Herodotus tells us (II, 104) that the Phoenicians and the "Syrians who are in Palestine" (i.e., the Israelites, Edomites, Ammonites, Moabites; cf. Jer. 9:26) adopted it from the Egyptians, and wonders if the Egyptians in their turn had not copied it from the Ethiopians. The Arabs practiced it even before Mahomet and may have adopted it from the Ethiopians, and after the rise of Islam may have brought it as far as central Asia, although the Koran does not prescribe it or even mention it. However, though it was practiced all over the world, certain groups have always remained uncircumcised, as for example the Indo-European, the Mongolian, and Ugro-Finnish races. Not only this, but even among neighboring tribes, or even within one branch of a tribe such nonconformity is encountered. The Zulus, who live in the midst of the Kaffir tribes which circumcise, do not practice it. In ancient times it was the Philistines who ignored it in Palestine. Although most Semites have always circumcised, there is no documentary proof that the Assyro-Babylonians, who were also of Semitic origin, did likewise. According to *Gen.* 34:14 ff. the Canaanites there mentioned did not circumcise.

134. The rite of circumcision is not uniform among various peoples. Most common is circumcision of the male, which was either complete circumcision (*ablatio praeputii*) or a simple incision; circumcision of the female (*ablatio clitoridis,* etc.) is rather widespread also. Among the majority of peoples, especially the primitives, it is performed around the age of puberty; among many it is performed sooner, even at birth.

The enormous diffusion of this practice leads to the thought that in many cases the origin of the rite is not the same, hence the difficulty in trying to explain it in all cases by one common reason. Circumcision might later assume, among various peoples, a well-defined religious or civil meaning which would cause them to forget the older signification. Herodotus gave cleanliness as the reason for circumcision among the Egyptians (II, 37), but few modern ethnologists accept this hygienic reason, nor do they accept the explanation that circumcision was thought to favor fecundity and the sexual act. Hence they look for the explanation in some primitive or successively attenuated sacrificial motive or some symbolical reincarnation; or it may have had a social significance as a prematrimonial rite (§§ 148, 211), whereby the male becoming capable of generation is accepted into the community of warriors, and takes his leave from that of the women, the custodians of infancy. Other motives, all of them more or less probable, have been proposed also.

135. Whatever its primitive significance, circumcision among the Israelites assumed a fundamental importance as a nationalistic and religious rite. Modern Abyssinian Christians who still practice it

attribute to it only a social and nationalistic, not a religious, significance. Abraham, because he was a Babylonian, was not circumcised. He may have become acquainted with the rite during his stay in Egypt, but he later accepted it as a sign of the pact with Yahweh, through which he was destined to become the head of Yahweh's nation. "The uncircumcised male . . . that soul shall be destroyed out of his people; he has violated my covenant." Thus spoke God to Abraham (Gen. 17:14), and this has been the constant Hebrew tradition (especially during the struggles for Yahwistic nationalism in the period of Hellenism).

Among the Israelites circumcision was performed only on the males, including those who were adopted into their national-religious society; no equivalent ceremony was provided for the females. Circumcision usually took place, in ancient times at least, on the eighth day after the birth of the child. This solicitude is not found in the majority of other peoples, who perform the rite after some years have passed (thus, usually, the present-day Arabs), and it highlights the symbolism of the rite through which the Israelite was born to Yahweh.

The formalism through which it came to be considered as a *quasi-magical* act, endowed in its materiality with infallible power, was decidedly repudiated both by the Torah (Lev. 26:41–42; Deut. 10:16; 30:6) and by the prophets, who insisted on the circumcision "of the ears" and "of the heart," that is, on the spiritual dispositions which should accompany and vivify the material rite (cf. Rom. 2:29; Phil. 3:3; etc.).

136. The rite was performed on Abraham and all the males with him when he was ninety-nine years old.

Not long after this he was favored with another theophany. Three men (which the consequent biblical account explains as an apparition of God in human form with two angels) presented themselves at his tent, near the terebinths of Mambre (§127), where they accepted his hospitality — something sacred for every oriental. While they conversed, they announced to Abraham that Sara would have a son within a year. Sara, listening, laughed (in Hebrew, *yishaq*, masculine form) at the announcement because of her advanced age; the Bible records, with pointed comment (§ 127), that she was in her menopause. To Abraham as to a confidential friend (§ 91) God revealed the destruction he was about to wreak on Sodom and Gomorrha, in punishment for the vices against nature which flourished there (cf. § 338). Because of Abraham's intercession, God promised to be lenient with that city for the sake of even a very small number of virtuous people — if any such could be found. Two of the men, the two angels, then proceeded from Mambre to Sodom, where they were given hospitality by Lot (§ 127), and when the wicked citizens tried to abuse

The "Terebinth of Abraham" near Hebron.

them, they immediately made Lot and his family depart, and a catastrophic ruin was visited upon the entire region. Lot's wife[8] dallied along the way and was suffocated and covered over by the saline fumes of the cataclysm (§ 62). The Bible indeed presumes that a large portion of the ruined region is now covered by the Dead Sea (Gen. 14:3; § 94).

137. After this, the Terahites increased in numbers. It is through Lot's branch, now separated from that of Abraham, that the Bible traces the incestuous origin of the progenitors of the Moabites and of the Ammonites.

Abraham then moved from Hebron, perhaps because of a drought, and proceeded southwards to Gerar (§ 92), where Abimelech was king. Here too Sara was involved in an incident as she had been in Egypt. Presented by Abraham as his sister, Sara was seized and brought to court, but the king, warned by God as to her real char-

---

[8] Cf. *BA*, V, 1942, p. 23 ff.

acter, restored her intact. The author of *Genesis* wished to show clearly how unlikely it was, humanly speaking, that Abraham should ever see the posterity so many times promised to him; at every step it was imperilled, but this only brings out into bolder relief how unfailingly God came to his aid (cf. § 141).

It was the final test. Sara brought forth her son, and he was named Isaac, "He-laughs" (*yishaq;* § 136), not so much in memory of the incredulous mirth of the mother, however, as in testimony of the joy his birth brought to the household. On the eighth day the boy was circumcised. The Bible does not forget to record (§ 127) that Abraham was exactly one hundred years old at that time.

The jealousy which arose between Sara and Hagar on account of their sons drove Sara to demand of Abraham that he send away the slave and her son, Ismael. The proposal "very much displeased Abraham for the sake of his son" (Gen. 21:11), all the more so since his paternal affection found a full guaranty in the ancient law (Code of Hammurabi, art. 146; § 131). Nevertheless, at God's behest he expelled the mother and son, leaving them in the desert. Ismael is portrayed by the Bible (Gen. 25:12–16) as the progenitor of twelve Arab tribes. Abraham then made an alliance of friendship with Abimelech and made him accept seven lambs in testimony of his (Abraham's right of proprietorship over the well of Beersheba ("Well of the Seven," or "of the oath" of alliance; § 60).

138. Although the divine promise in regard to posterity had been fulfilled, Abraham's faith was put to the test once more; the biblical

Ancient well of Beersheba.

narrative immediately following records the divine request for the sacrifice of the heir. God unexpectedly commands Abraham to take his son Isaac and to offer him as a human sacrifice on a mountain in the "land of Moriah."

The name is a controversial one. In 2 *Paralipomenon*, 3:1, the hill where the temple of Solomon (§ 96) was built is called "Mount" Moriah; but a "country" of such a name is not recorded elsewhere. The Syriac Peshitta, instead of Moriah, has "Ammorites," a reading preferred by many moderns; others correct it to "Madian," referring to Sinai (§ 234 ff.).

The sacrifice of his first-born was certain to remind Abraham of the sacrifice of the first-born as practiced by the Canaanites (§ 103) in the midst of whom he lived. The fact that such a sacrifice was requested of him by God justified its fulfillment in his own conscience. To obey meant the destruction of his only son, and would again return Abraham to a state wherein humanly speaking there was little hope for future sons. It was indeed a new and more difficult test of his faith. In fact the biblical author says that God "put Abraham to the test" (Gen. 22:1), and this expression is the key to the incident. The test was passed, the sacrifice was not carried out. At the very moment he was to slay his son, Abraham was stopped by God, and a ram substituted for the human victim. Thus, while Abraham had demonstrated the firmness of his faith and the heroic quality of his obedience, God manifested his rejection of the widespread practice of human sacrifices which was based on a perversion of these two virtues. After a long sojourn at Beersheba, Abraham returned to Hebron, where Sara died at the age of one hundred and twenty-seven. In order to bury her, Abraham bought from the Hittites who lived there (§ 45) the grotto of Makhpelah and the terrain around it facing Mambre (§ 91).

139. Isaac was thirty-seven years old when his mother died, and Abraham thought to provide him a wife. She must not be a daughter of the surrounding Canaanites, from whom Abraham considered himself quite different for ethnological or religious reasons; she had to be of his

Present-day mosque on the grotto of Makhpelah. (Vester, Amer. Colony.)

country and his lineage. He then thought of the descendants of his brother Nahor, of whom he had recently received news (Gen. 22:20 ff.) and who was established at Harran. He dispatched the superintendent of his house in haste to Aram Naharayim (§ 51) and he returned with Rebecca, daughter of Bethuel son of Nahor, who became the wife of Isaac.

Abraham later took unto himself another wife named Qeturah. As descendants of this union the Bible indicates the ancestors of various tribes living in the wilderness to the south and southeast of Palestine. The best known of these was Madian (§ 206).

Abraham finally died at the age of one hundred and seventy-five and was buried in the grotto of Makhpelah (§ 138) near Sara by his sons Isaac and Ismael. Before he died, however, he made Isaac his full heir; to his other sons he made bequests and commanded them to settle far from the heir: even here the atavistic law (§ 131) had already contemplated similar cases (Code of Hammurabi, art. 165; Sumerian law, 14: § 247).

140. The figure of Isaac is faintly sketched by the biblical narrator. In some respects, however, Isaac strongly resembled his father.

Like Sara, Rebecca was sterile, and remained so until Isaac's sixtieth year (cf. Gen. 25:20 with 25:26). Then, through his prayers, God removed her sterility and she conceived. During her pregnancy she remarked that "the sons within her were struggling" (Gen. 25:22); and when she consulted God she was told that she carried within her two nations struggling against each other, and that the older of these would serve the younger. The two nations, i.e., the twin progenitors, were then born. The first was reddish and hairy, because of which he was called Esau, "hairy"?, and later on also Edom, "red." The second appeared with a hand clasping the heel of the first, and because of this was called Jacob, *Ya'aqobh,* "he-holds-the-heel"; but since "catching the heel" meant also morally to "supplant" someone, the name of the second-born signified "he-supplants," and later on he supplanted his brother in the birthright (cf. Gen. 27:36). When they were grown, "Esau became expert in the hunt and a man of the fields, while Jacob was a quiet man, living in tents" (Gen. 25:27).

As a matter of fact, of the two peoples — the Edomites (Idumaeans) from Esau, and the Israelites from Jacob — the first had a politico-monarchial organization before that of the Israelites (Gen. 36:31); nevertheless their precedence yielded to that of the nation of "him-who-supplants," which then assumed in the history of Palestine the importance of a first-born. The region of the Edomites was the wilderness which extended south of the Dead Sea and east of the Wadi el-'Araba (§ 61); there a man "lived by his own sword" (Gen. 27:40), hunting animals or men in traditional raider fashion. The Israelites, on the contrary, lived in a region suited to a "quiet people living in tents."

141. Economic and especially religious privileges (§ 139) were intimately linked with the primogeniture among the Terahites. Isaac's first-born son, Esau, returning one day from the hunt sick and "near to death" (Gen. 25:32), asked Jacob for a dish of lentils which he had prepared. Jacob agreed to do this on condition that Esau cede his birthright to him. The condition was accepted, the bargain fulfilled, and "he-supplants" was from that day onward legally the first-born in place of his now supplanted brother.

An incident similar to that of Abraham's in Gerar (§ 137) occurred in the life of Isaac. Like his father, Isaac too was driven by famine to the city of Gerar, and he too circulated the information that Rebecca was his "sister" (she was in fact his cousin). But King Abimelech surprised the two of them displaying affection toward one another, and realizing the true state of affairs publicly guaranteed the status of Rebecca, and still later entered into a friendly alliance with Isaac near the well of Beersheba, as he had also done with Abraham. Clearly the parallel of the two traditions extends not only to the events, but also to the name of the place and the person. The mutual influence exercised by the traditions, and the precise, original data presented by each cannot now be determined by even the best-intentioned research (cf. § 149).

142. An important fact is that, in the meantime, the Terahites began to introduce agricultural practices into their nomadic life. Isaac sowed seed in the fields and reaped an abundant harvest (Gen. 26:12). The fact is also noteworthy and is purposely emphasized by the biblical writer, that the supplanted first-born, Esau, began the movement away from the ethnologico-religious integrity of the Terahites by marrying Hittite wives (§ 44 ff.) "who were bitterness to the soul of Isaac and Rebecca" (Gen. 26:35).

Having supplanted his brother in the birthright, Jacob could supplant him in the rights which went with it, chief of which was the paternal benediction. With his mother's help he disguised himself and presented himself as Esau to his blind father (Gen. 27). Thus the paternal benediction, fount of every kind of prosperity, was his. The tension between the two brothers was naturally heightened. Esau's explicit intentions of mortal vengeance were reported to Rebecca. To prevent any such tragedy she sent Jacob to Laban, her brother, in her native Harran, where, moreover, he would have a chance to find a wife from the same stock, instead of taking a Hittite, as his brother had done (Gen. 27:46 ff.).

143. During his journey toward Harran, Jacob stopped one night at Luz. In a dream he saw a ladder which united earth to heaven, from the top of which God spoke to him, confirming for him the promises already made to Abraham and Isaac. "And Jacob, arising in the morning, took the stone which he had put under his head as a pillow and set it up as *massebah*, pouring oil on the top of it; and he called the name of that place *Beth-el*" ("house of God"; Gen. 28:18–19); he had in fact exclaimed when he awakened from sleep: "Indeed, Yahweh is in this place, and I knew it not!" (Gen. 28:16.) "He made a vow, saying: If God shall be with me, and shall keep me in the way by which I walk . . . and I shall return safe to my father's house, Yahweh shall be my God, and this stone, which I have set up as *massebah* shall be *beth-elohim*" ("house of God") (Gen. 28:20 ff.). The terminology is well known in Canaanite usage (§ 104), but here *massebah* was a memorial of an extraordinary event, almost like the menhir (§ 72); it was also a testimonial (§ 145) of the vow which was made, by reason of which the *massebah* had to be replaced later by *beth-elohim*, a true "sanctuary" to Yahweh (for the use of this name cf. § 210).

144. Jacob remained twenty years with his uncle Laban in Harran (Gen. 31:38). Lia and Rachel, daughters of Laban, became wives of Jacob, while Zilpah, Lia's handmaid, and Bilhah, handmaid of Rachel, became his legal concubines according to the Babylonian-Terahite law (§ 131). The twelve male children born of the four women (Benjamin was born later: § 150) are the eponyms of the Israelite tribes (for the list see the Table: § 122). It should be noted that among the Terahites there are likewise only twelve sons of Ismael (§ 137), and also of Nabor (Gen. 22:20 ff.); the number seems to be computed in some conventional manner (§§ 169, 291) which naturally cannot be checked today. During this time Jacob, wisely industrious, acquired great numbers of cattle, a fact which aroused the jealousy of his miserly uncle. The jealousy increased and finally led to an open break between the two families. Jacob and his two wives secretly set out to return to his father in Canaan. Laban heard of the unexpected departure too late to prevent it so he followed him, overtaking him in Galaad (§ 66). His intention was twofold: to settle personal and economic questions, and get back the teraphim (§ 106) which were missing from his house after the sudden departure.

These teraphim, called also "gods" (Gen. 31:30, 32) were smuggled off by Rachel without her husband's knowledge. Even a search through the baggage of the caravan did not discover where a clever woman, who wanted to carry these good-luck charms with her to the new country she was about to enter, had hidden them.

145. Various personal questions were settled satisfactorily, and the meeting terminated in an alliance of friendship. The ceremonial is very

interesting. After an exchange of explanations "Jacob[9] took a stone and set it up as a *massebah*. Jacob then said to his brethren: Gather some stones. And they gathered some stones and made a heap, and then ate there upon the heap. And Laban called it *Yeghar-Sahadutha*, while Jacob called it *Gal-'edh*. And Laban said: This heap is a witness between me and thee today! — therefore the name of Gal-'edh was given to it and also Mispah, since he added: Yahweh judge between me and thee when we shall be gone out one from the other" (Gen. 31:45–49). Jacob then offered a sacrifice, followed by a sacrificial banquet in which the relatives took part. It is clear that here the *massebah* has the value of a testimonial memorial (§ 143); steles of this kind, with the above signification, were most frequently used in Assyria under the name of *kudurru*. Heaping up stones was an ancient custom, and is related to the use of the cairns (§ 72). Laban, an Aramean (§ 49), called this monument by its Arabic name: *Yeghar-Sahadutha*, "pile of the testimonial." Jacob naturally gave it a Hebrew name, "heap of the witness." Argument rages over both names, which mean the same thing, just as it does about the Hebrew *Mispah*, "place of watching."

146. Noteworthy, too, are the names given to the divinity. Laban, confronting Jacob's group, had spoken of the "God of your father" (Gen. 31:29); Jacob in reply spoke of the "God of my father, the God of Abraham, the Terror of Isaac" (Gen. 31:42; cf. § 178). On the point of ratifying the alliance, Laban invoked the divinities of both families, "the God of Abraham and the God of Nahor,"[10] but Jacob swore by "the Terror of his father Isaac" (Gen. 31:53). The divergence of religious beliefs between the two Terahites is unmistakable. Jacob invoked and recognized only the God of Abraham and Isaac; Laban, with polytheistic syncretism, makes room at His side also for the God of Nahor (cf. Josue 24:2, 14, 15). This explains the theft of the teraphim by his daughter Rachel, and her motive in stealing them (§ 144). Rachel must have shared the religious beliefs of her father, and for that reason had stolen the teraphim, carefully concealing the fact from Jacob, who was so far from suspecting the truth that he declared himself ready to put the culprit to death (Gen. 31:32). The teraphim will reappear many other times in the history of Israel, even in much later times (2 Kings 23:24; Zach. 12:2).

147. The rite completed, Laban and Jacob separated, the latter resuming his journey southward toward his father and also toward a threatening unknown. When twenty years before "He-supplants" had

---

[9] Some critics correct the text to read *Laban* instead of *Jacob*.

[10] The phrase which follows the *God of their father* is lacking in the Greek of the Septuagint, and is thought to be a later addition by most modern critics; it is omitted from the Italian translation (Vaccari) of the Pontifical Biblical Institute, in which a note states: "Nachor was also infected by idolatry."

The Jabbok. (Vester, Amer. Colony.)

departed from that region to escape the vengeful brother he had supplanted, the only things he could then depend on were the staff which helped him ford rivers (Gen. 32:11) and the mighty arm which wielded it. Now he was returning rich with wives, children, servants, cattle, and possessions, intending to display all his blessings to his old father so as to make him proud of his son, and then to enjoy a patriarchal life at his side. But at the side of the old father there stood Esau, whose old rancors would undoubtedly blaze anew and fiercely at the sight of this prosperity of "He-supplants" — stolen prosperity, because it was the fruit of the birthright and the blessing stolen from the first-born. The supplanted one was reduced to the desolate wilderness of Edom, and there like an outcast "he lived by his sword" (§ 140), but that very sword, which labored because of the supplanting, could be the instrument of vengeance on the supplanter. For an oriental, vengeance is justice. The messengers Jacob had sent to his brother out of courtesy announced on their return that Esau was coming out to meet him with four hundred men.

"Jacob was much terrified and distressed" (Gen. 32:8). He decided to face it out and divided his people and possessions in many groups with instructions to meet his brother at intervals and placate him with gifts. Coming down from the north, he found himself on the right bank of the Jabbok (§ 66), and that night had his company cross the torrent so as not to be surprised in passage by his brother. The crossing certainly was not brief and at the end of the night Jacob, who had to direct the crossing, remained alone, the last to leave the old encampment.

That moment of solitude, an interlude in a period of intense activity, was God's moment. Jacob was disturbed in mind both by the fear of his brother and by other more important and profound anxieties. He had recently been comforted by a vision of angels (Gen. 32:2–3), and in the fear of his approaching brother had prayed to the God of Abraham and Isaac, reminding Him of the ancient promises.

These promises, however, were the crux of his torment. If he were the legitimate heir, why had he been separated from the land of the divine promises for these twenty years? Why had he been obliged to go to an idolatrous country and family (§§ 144 ff., 149)? Was the somber menace which attended his return prepared by the justice of God? Did it indicate perhaps that God had rejected him, and had reestablished the supplanted one in his natural rights? It was therefore not so much a question of one brother advancing to meet his brother, as it was of a man who was

Sichem — site of the Well of Jacob.
(Vester, Amer. Colony.)

meeting his God. In that nocturnal solitude the man was burdened by such thoughts and he was in agony. Agony or "struggle": not death. In fact, armed by his faith "he contended with God . . . and conquered" (Osee 12:4–5).

This struggle is described by the Bible in a literary style which has in it much of the Dantesque. "And Jacob remained alone. And a man struggled with him until the break of day. And [this man] seeing that he could not overcome him he struck him on the socket of his thigh, and the socket of his thigh was dislocated while he struggled with him. [That man] then said: Let me go, for it is break of day. But [Jacob] said: I will not let thee go except thou bless me. — And he said: What is thy name? — And he replied: Jacob. And he said: Thy name shall not be Jacob anymore, but Israel ['Fights-God'] because thou hast contended with God and with men and hast prevailed. — And Jacob asked him, saying: Tell me, I pray thee, thy name? — And he replied: Why dost thou ask my name? And he blessed him. Jacob then called the name of that place Peniel (Penuel) ['Face of God'] since [he exclaimed] I have seen God face to face and my life has been spared" (Gen. 32:25–31).

Who was the victor in that struggle, the Unknown Man or the known? The Bible accords the victory to them both. The Unknown is vanquished by the known because he is held captive by him and is not allowed to go free except he first bless him. But the known is in turn vanquished because the Unknown has changed his name, which in the Old Testament is synonymous with personality (for men, Gen. 17:5 ff.; Isa. 62:2; Num. 16:2; Job 30:8; etc.; for God, Isa. 18:7; 30:27; 48:9; Ezech. 20:44; Ps. 74:7; etc.; § 207 ff.). From that night, one might say, "He-supplants" disappears, to give place to "Fights-God." The strokes by which the Bible portrays the man who is known before and after his struggle with God reveal the great change which took place in him: once a shrewd, energetic activist, he emerges from the encounter tranquil and serene.

148. Contrary to all expectation, the meeting with Esau was a friendly one, and the supplanted brother afterward returned peaceably to the steppe. Jacob, stopping first at Sukkoth, crossed the Jordan and repaired to Sichem (§ 88), where he pitched his tents in front of the city and purchased some ground, "and erected there an altar, calling it 'El-'Elohe-Israel (*God-the-God-of-Israel*)" (Gen. 33:20).

It happened one day that Dinah, daughter of Jacob, wandering out of curiosity through the district, was violated by Sichem, the son of Hamor ("ass": totem name, §§ 167, 316), ruler of the land. Loving her

Greek crypt enclosing the Well of Jacob. (*Dictionn. de la Bible.*)

even after the deed, he sought her hand from her father and her
brothers, offering them a kind of citizenship (Gen. 34:10, 21). The
brothers deceitfully imposed circumcision upon him as a condition of
acceptance (§ 133 ff.), explaining it to be a national, not a religious
custom (Gen. 34:14); their real motive was hidden. The condition was
accepted and the rite performed on the men of that place. The third
day after the circumcision, when the wound was most sensitive, Simeon
and Levi, fully armed and followed later by the other brothers,
burst into the city and slew the violator of their sister and the other
men. The entire city was looted. Some centuries later, the Habiri
(§ 54 ff.) did almost the same thing. Jacob nevertheless rebuked the
group which had undertaken this reprisal. The slaughter must have
included a large number of families (cf. Gen. 34:24), which, if they
could not react immediately, had other ethnic groups related to or allied
with them. Hamor was a Hevite, but Jacob feared also the Canaanites
and the Perezites in the territory (§ 258).

149. For this reason the group moved on to Beth-el, or Luz (§ 143),
the sacred place of the prosperous years of Jacob. The memory of the
vow there made to the God of Abraham and Isaac added to the succeeding prosperity led Jacob to take religious inventory within his
family. The teraphim stolen by Rachel (§ 144) were not the only
products of the idolatry of the Terahites of Harran; there were besides
the statuettes of "strange gods," also "earrings," that is, magical amulets,
possibly with some figures on them. They were all given to Jacob, and
he buried them at the foot of the oaks of Sichem.

When he arrived at Beth-el, he "built an altar, and called the place
'El-Beth-'el (God of Beth-el)" (Gen. 35:7). Here another theophany
occurred, similar in part to that of the nocturnal struggle: God changed
his name for him from Jacob to Israel; but the account this time does
not give the historical or etymological reason for the change. Another
parallel, relative to the preceding visit of Jacob (§ 143), can be seen
in the fact that this time he also erects a *massebah*, pouring upon it a
libation and oil and calling the place Beth-el (Gen. 35:14-15). The
similarity of this group of traditions with those preceding is clear; but
even here the possibility that they refer to identical facts, rather than
similar ones (cf. § 141) escapes verification.

150. Leaving Beth-el and moving southward, Jacob became a father
for the last time, but Rachel died in childbirth near Ephrata
(Beth-lehem?). As she was dying she gave the newborn child the
name Ben'oni, "Son of my pain," but the father, wishing to erase the
sad memory, changed the name to that of Ben-yamin, "Son of the
right," the arm of good fortune. Soon after this a scandal occurred
when Ruben, the first-born, violated his father's bed by lying with

Bilhah (Bala), handmaid of the deceased Rachel and concubine of Jacob (§ 144). Jacob, naturally, learned of the incident.

Finally the group arrived at Mambre, where Isaac still lived. When he died at one hundred and eighty years of age (§ 127), he was buried at Makhpelah by his sons Esau and Jacob (§ 138; cf. Gen. 49:31).

151. While Esau on the steppe allowed his descendants to mix with the Horites (§ 58) drawing farther and farther away (§ 142) from the Terahite clannishness, Jacob remained at Hebron, the site cherished by his forebears. There for many years this tranquil conqueror of God could now lead that patriarchal life which he had earned in the travail of his youth; and perhaps in his eyes every passing year appeared to be a new bond linking his lineage to the lands promised to him by God. Instead "He-supplants" had in turn a supplanter; not that he was supplanted in his character as heir of the divine promises and eponym of the people of god, but insofar as this character of his had to be actualized through the work of another, of an "addition" to his mission. This other was his son Joseph, *Yoseph* "[God] adds [issue]" (Gen. 30:24): he was in fact the great multiplier of the progeny of Israel.

152. The story of Joseph is one of the most beautiful in all literature; its splendor and power have long been recognized by *literati* of all kinds. One should, of course, read the story in the Bible and according to the Bible, for it inevitably suffers from the retelling. A résumé of the facts is as follows.

Joseph, first-born of Jacob's favorite wife, Rachel, and the blood brother of Benjamin, was his father's favorite. This favoritism aroused a jealousy on the part of his brothers which afterward was to turn into hatred, either because he reported their evil conduct to their father or because at a certain period he began to relate to them certain dreams of his which were, to say the least, irritating. Once he dreamed that while he was binding sheaves in the field, his sheaf had remained upright, but those of the brothers bowed down to do him reverence; another time, that the sun and moon and eleven stars — that is, father, mother, and brothers — bowed down before him. His father rebuked him for these tales, but did not understand the matter clearly. The brothers who had slain Sichem (§ 148), and the adulterous firstborn, Ruben (§ 150), began to consider ways of ridding themselves of their presumptuous brother, who was then seventeen years old. One day his father sent him to inquire after the brothers who were a long way from the pasture. He departed from Hebron and sought them toward Sichem and finally found them at Dothan. Seeing him afar off, the brothers decided to act. Some wanted to kill him, and then simulate an accident, but the judgment of the first-born, sustained by Juda, prevailed. After defiling his father's bed Ruben did not want to stain his hands with his brother's blood. The boy was thrown into a dry cistern,

Nile Delta from Gizeh.

and when some Arab merchants (Ismaelites or Madianites, the tradition is not certain) bearing aromatics and spices to Egypt passed by, he was sold to them. Joseph's coat, presented to him as a sign of particular affection by his father, was dipped in the blood of a kid, thus giving some plausibility to the story that a wild beast had torn the missing boy to pieces. While the father wept inconsolably, Joseph was resold by the merchants in "Egypt to Potiphar, a eunuch of Pharaoh, and head of the butchers" (Gen. 37:36).

153. In his new surroundings Joseph did not change; he was painstaking and prudent in the humble services at first confided to him, and when later on his master made him manager over the whole house, he kept his head, and was kind to the many slaves under him. He did not change. The tales which he had carried to his father about his brothers may have concerned certain wicked practices of theirs which they were not disposed to give up. It is recorded, for example, that while Joseph was in Egypt his brother Juda, whose Canaanite wife had died, went in to a sacred prostitute (§ 108), or to what he thought was one (Gen. 38:21 f.).

Joseph was also a handsome youth, and his physical comeliness was a suitable setting for his high moral character. His master's wife allowed her imagination loose rein where he was concerned. She desired the youth and made definite advances to him, but her invitation was rejected in justice to his master and because he did not want to "sin against God" (Gen. 39:9). The refusal served only to whet her desire and her invitations were repeated "day after day," and daily rejected. Finally the woman became exasperated, and naturally sought revenge; showing the cloak left in her hand by the youth when he fled from her, she offered it as proof that he had attempted to violate her. Joseph was cast into prison.

154. In his new surroundings the prisoner endeared himself to the inspector by the way he performed his various duties. When the chief cupbearer and chief baker of the Pharaoh were cast into prison (probably because of some plot to assassinate that monarch), Joseph was assigned to them. After some little time had passed, each of them had a dream which he could not interpret. Joseph interpreted the two dreams, foretelling that within three days the cupbearer would be restored to his rank and the baker would be handed over to justice. Thus it occurred, but although Joseph had commended himself to the cupbearer, the man forgot him.

Two more years passed, and the Pharaoh dreamed that he saw seven fat cows and seven lean ones come up out of the Nile; the lean ones devoured the fat ones. He also saw seven full ears on one stalk and seven withered, and the latter swallowed up the former. When the wise men of the country were consulted they were quite unable to satisfy the agitated Pharaoh. It was then that the cupbearer remembered his own dream and the one who had interpreted it, and so Joseph was called into court. "He shaved himself, changed his clothes, and came to the Pharaoh" (Gen. 41:14). Then speaking in the name of God, Joseph explained the two dreams: both had reference to one imminent event, seven years of abundant harvests, followed by seven of want. The explanation ended with the counsel that the Pharaoh should prepare himself against the seven years of want by filling storage places with provisions during the seven years of abundance and should depute a commissioner to oversee the provisioning of the whole of Egypt.

155. The Pharaoh with all his court considered this explanation of the dreams satisfactory and the advice excellent. The choice of the commissioner was therefore spontaneous — Joseph himself. The prisoner of yesterday became through the will of the Pharaoh the viceroy of Egypt: he was invested with the insignia of his office; he received the seal of the Pharaoh; he ascended to the second chariot of the realm and at his passage *abhrekh!* was shouted. The Pharaoh renamed him *Saphenath-pa'neah*, and gave him 'Asenath, daughter of Poti-phera', priest of 'On, as a wife.

All this happened thirteen years after Joseph had been sold by his brothers; he was now thirty years old (Gen. 41:46), and entering upon his new and exalted office he acted with vigor and dispatch. His intelligent eyes fixed on the predicted famine, he traveled through the whole of Egypt during the period of abundance, setting up strategic centers with reserve granaries. The chaste man was also fecund; his wife bore him two sons, to whom he gave names which to himself, as a son and father, meant many things: the first-born he called Manasses, *Menashsheh*, "Make-forget," since he reasoned: "God has made me forget

all my travail and all my paternal household"; the second he called
Ephraim, "Double-fecundity"? since he reasoned "God renders me
fecund in the land of my affliction" (Gen. 41:51–52).

Then came the scarcity. The Pharaoh sent the hungry to Joseph and
Joseph put his reserve provisions on the market. It was thus that Egypt
met the crisis, and other countries nearby, unable to cope with it, came
to seek food in Egypt. The stage was now set for the doing of justice.
And so, in fact, it was done.

156. Joseph's brothers were among the hungry who went down to
Egypt. Jacob, however, had kept his favorite Benjamin with him, for
safety's sake. When the brothers presented themselves before Joseph he
recognized them, but they had no inkling that the magnificent viceroy
was their brother. Joseph now had them in his power, but before using
that power to bring home to them the enormity of their crime, he first
wished to play with them, thus insuring the success of his plan. Feigning
complete ignorance of Hebrew, he spoke to them through an interpreter,
but he understood the comments they made in their own tongue. He
accused them of having come into the land in order to spy upon it. With
the veracity born of fear they related the state of their family, referring
even to Benjamin who had remained with his father, and to the other
brother "who is not living." Joseph pretended not to believe them, and
demanded that they return home and fetch Benjamin back to him.
Simeon was imprisoned until their return, but the money they had paid
for the grain was secretly placed in their sacks, by Joseph's orders.

When they told Jacob what had happened, his sorrow knew no bounds:
Simeon had been left in Egypt, and to obtain more grain he would have
to allow Benjamin to go down to Egypt. The matter of the purses made
the whole thing very mysterious also. But the famine continued, and they
were forced to decide that Benjamin would have to go. Ruben the first-
born and Juda promised their old father that they would bring his son
back to him. They took the mysterious purses with them.

157. This time they were received affably. The viceroy invited them
to banquet with him, although he observed the Egyptian custom which
forbade that he eat at their table. Benjamin was singled out for
attention. The next day the guests were given leave to depart; the
purses of the first trip had been refused under some pretext when they
were returned, and this time also the money was placed in the sacks;
lastly, the silver cup from which Joseph drank and with which he performed divination with water (Gen. 44:5, 15) was placed in Benjamin's
sack. Soon after they had left the city the brothers were stopped by
the King's steward, who rebuked them for the theft of the cup. This was
energetically denied by the brothers, but when the sacks were opened
the cup was found in Benjamin's sack. Shaken by this discovery they

returned to implore mercy from Joseph and to declare themselves his slaves. Joseph, who now had their hearts as well as their persons in his grip, struck the final blow: he did not wish them to be his slaves, but would be content with only the guilty one — Benjamin; the others were free to carry the news back to their aged father.

Juda, who had guaranteed Jacob of Benjamin's return, arose to protest against this judgment. The thought of the father awaiting at home inspired him to make a speech of impassioned grief which is a miracle of literary power. Joseph then put an end to the game, having sufficiently explored the feelings of his brothers, and, weeping, made himself known to them. They were dazed by the turn of events, and only after successive demonstrations of his affection were they assured that it was Joseph, and that he pardoned them.

He then sent wagons and robes to help his father make the journey to Egypt. The father decided to comply when God appeared to him in a dream. "He-supplants" was in his turn supplanted as an instrument in the plans of the God of Abraham. Jacob, then one hundred and thirty years old (Gen. 47:9), went down into Egypt with all his descendants. The Pharaoh assigned the fertile land of Gessen to the immigrants (§ 193 ff.) and there, with the passage of centuries, the small group of the Terahites of Jacob became, thanks to Joseph, the people of Israel.

158. The story of Joseph has many counterparts in Egyptian literature and it has none; none entirely like it, and many which resemble it in some details. Ever since Egyptology has added a new light to what had already been learned from Herodotus about ancient Egypt, scholars have recognized the fact that the biblical account of Joseph breathes a genuine Egyptian atmosphere and that in its details it agrees exactly with the customs of the country. No Egyptian account of Joseph, however, has ever come down to us, nor do Egyptian sources ever mention his person or his deeds.

Attention is usually drawn to the *Story of Two Brothers*,[11] a piece of imaginative writing made up of tales loosely joined together, and probably compiled by court personages as entertaining literature. The papyrus which records it (Papyrus of Orbiney) dates from the end of the Nineteenth Dynasty (§ 33). The first tale tells of two blood brothers. The older, Anubi, was married; the younger, Bata, was not. The brothers lived together, and the older of the two was as a father to his brother, and made use of his services in the fields. One day as they were working he sent Bata back to the house for some seed grain. Off he went, and being strong, soon had a heavy load of grain on his shoulders. Anubi's wife was in the house, admired his strength, and made indecent proposals

---

[11] Cf. *ANET*, 23–25, for the "Story of Two Brothers."

to him. The youth then "became angry as a leopard" because of the evil
she had spoken, and she feared greatly. And he said to her: Thou art as
a mother to me and thy husband as a father, since he is older than I am
and has reared me. What a grave crime thou hast spoken to me! Do not
speak of it any more! I shall tell no one about it nor shall I allow it to
escape my lips to anyone!" The woman, however, did not put much stock
in his promise, and feared lest he accuse her before her husband. When
he returned, therefore, she poured out the whole story, depicting Bata,
naturally, as the tempter, and herself as the victim. She also exhibited
the bruises caused by Bata's striking her when she resisted him, and
besought her husband to save her from her brother-in-law by killing
him. Anubi became as "angry as a leopard," sharpened his dagger, and
hid behind the door, ready to dispatch his brother upon his arrival. But
one of the cows led by Bata spoke to him, warning him of his peril.
Other portents are then mentioned which provide matter for other tales,
but they need not be recounted here.

It is clear that the similarity of this account and that of Joseph is reduced to the theme of adultery proposed by the woman and refused by
the man, certainly not the most frequent, yet not an entirely unknown
theme in antiquity. The Lycian-Grecian world knew the story of Bel-
lerophon, which used the same theme (*Iliad*, VI, 152 ff.). From such a
vague resemblance it would hardly be legitimate to conclude to a literary
dependence, even abstracting from the chronological question involved,
for it would first be necessary to establish that the wives of the Egyptians
were all as noble as Lucretia.

159. On the other hand, many details are illustrated by Egyptology.
A few points will suffice. The aromatics and spices carried to Egypt by
the merchants to whom Joseph was sold were most commonly used in
Egyptian liturgy, medicine, and especially embalming (§ 164). The
name of Joseph's master, Potiphar, is typically Egyptian, *Pa-di-pa-Ra*,
"The gift from [the god] Ra"; the form *Pa-di-Ra* (meaning the same
thing, without the article *pa* in front of the name of the god) was
discovered in an inscription of the Eighteenth Dynasty: many other
forms were discovered which contained the names of other gods,
Pa-di-Amon, Pa-di-Bastit, etc. That he is called a "eunuch" does
not militate against his marriage: in biblical terminology that term is
often only a synonym for "employee of the court" without regard for
physical integrity, and this is most likely the case here. Even interpreting
the term strictly, other explanations are still possible, for not all such
mutilations were total, and there are examples in the Orient of eunuchs
with their own harems. The rank of "captain of the butchers" was
a court office known among the Babylonians (2 Kings 25:8, etc.);
perhaps at that time it was a simple title (cf. Keeper of the Seal, Chan-

cellor of the Exchequer, etc.) which originated in more ancient duties, probably the killing of animals wounded in the hunt by the king, or providing of meats for the royal kitchen (in favor of this last a similar official could be cited in the present-day court of Abyssinia). The offices of chief cupbearer and chief baker fit well the Egyptian picture; other documents speak of royal offices of "Accountant of the Serving Room" and "Pastry Cook."[12]

160. It was only natural that Joseph, the dreamer of dreams in his own country, should be regarded in Egypt as an interpreter of dreams. Dreams commanded great respect among the Egyptians, as one can gather from Herodotus (II, 141) or from documents of various epochs (Thutmose IV, Merneptah, "Stele of the dream" of Napata of the seventh century, etc.). For that matter respect for dreams was rather common among all oriental peoples, beginning with the Chaldeans. One notes that in the Bible "Chaldean" is synonymous with astrologer and diviner, and the oriental slaves, for the most part Egyptians, who practiced such crafts were called Chaldeans by the Romans (*Chaldeos ne consulito*). The ceremonial observed by Joseph in order to present himself before the Pharaoh, notably his shaving himself (head and beard), was court protocol, probably being required by the divine authority attributed to the Pharaoh. The same can be said of the ceremonial in which Joseph was adorned with his new dignity. The use of the coach and chariot of war was introduced into Egypt by the Hyksos (§ 31), to which nationality the contemporary Pharaoh also belonged (§ 162 ff.). The cry *abhrekh!* is a problem word for which a dozen explanations are given: one, for example, is that it is an adaptation of the Egyptian *ab(u)-rek*, "thy command is our desire!" It is well nevertheless to keep in mind that in the Semitic language the root B R K means "to kneel down." The name *Saphenath-paʿneah* is strictly Egyptian. The most probable explanation (Steindorff) is that in it is hidden the name *de(d)pnet(er) efʿonh*, "God spoke, and [he who bears the name] lived"; similar examples are formed by the names of gods: *de Amon efʿonh*, "Amon spoke and lived," and others. To speak of *God* without any name proper to him was more frequent from the Twenty-Second Dynasty on, but there are even earlier examples. That the Pharaoh should choose a name for Joseph without the proper name of some idolatrous divinity can be explained as a mark of the king's consideration for the monotheism of his favorite. The name of Joseph's wife, ʾAsenath, is certainly the Egyptian *as-Net*, "pertaining to Neith," the goddess of Sais; names of this type are encountered during the Eighteenth Dynasty. The name of her father, Poti-pheraʿ, is the

---

[12] Cf. Mallon, "Les Hébreux en Egypte" in *Orientalia*, 3, Rome, 1921, 75 ff., for Egyptian proper names in the story of Joseph.

Dam on the Nile at Assuan.

more complete transcription of the name of Potiphar discussed above (§ 159). That he was a priest of 'On (Heliopolis; § 24) was a great honor for his son-in-law, when one considers the exceptional political (Fifth Dynasty; § 29; cf. § 34) and cultural (cf. Herodotus, II; § 3) influence wielded by the priests of that city.

161. The two periods of abundance and scarcity have also been clarified by Egyptian documents. It is true that the fertility of Egypt is assured by the Nile (§ 23) and that this privilege of hers made Egypt the granary of the ancient world (§ 127), but the rich floods of the river were not always regular. If the floodwaters were regularly high they led to abundant harvests; if not, they were followed by want and hunger. So absolutely does this hold that modern ingenuity has cast about for some method of controlling the waters. At the close of the past century huge reservoirs were constructed at various points along the course of the river, for the purpose of balancing the irregularities of the floods. Similar attempts had been made in ancient times but naturally with little success; sometimes, then, even Egypt experienced hunger. Knowledge of more than one such period of want has come down to us: during the Twelfth Dynasty, through the inscriptions of Amenemhet I and the governor Ameni; during the Seventeenth Dynasty, through the inscription of the government employee Baba; the periods of scarcity of the Christian era described by Arabian historians, one in A.D. 1190 (Abdallatif) and one lasting seven years from 1064–1071 (Maqrizi), might also be mentioned. Of seven

years' duration also, as the one in Joseph's time, was a period of want which took place much earlier under Zoser of the Third Dynasty, but this is known only through a relatively recent inscription (third century B.C.), which some look upon as a deliberate invention of the priests of the time interested in demonstrating their historical rights to certain revenues. The Pharaoh speaks in it in this manner:[13]

Winnowing and storing grain in Egypt.

"I am very much grieved at those who are in the Palace. My heart is sorely distressed at the misfortune, since in my time the Nile has not reached [flood stage] for seven years. Products are scarce, greens are not bountiful, foodstuffs are lacking. Everyone robs his neighbor. . . . The reservoirs(?) were opened, but . . . and all that was there has been consumed." Whatever may be the value of this text, it is certain that there were reservoirs of grain ever since the Ancient Empire; not only their ruins, but also small reproductions of them, deposited as symbols in the tombs, have come to light. Hence when Joseph multiplied his granaries in view of the coming scarcity he only intensified a measure long in use.

162. The most important question in the story of Joseph regards the Pharaoh. To what dynasty did he belong?

If one chooses to follow the chronology offered by the Bible, he may take as his point of departure the fact that Abraham and Hammurabi were contemporaries (§ 129), and in a wholly hypothetical manner establish that the call of Abraham (§ 122) occurred in the first year of Hammurabi's reign, i.e., in 1955.[14] One would then get the following dates: for the birth of Isaac, 1930 (§ 137); for the birth of Jacob, 1870 (§ 140); for the descent of Jacob and his family into Egypt, 1740 (§ 157); summing up the years, which, according to the Bible, elapsed from the call of Abraham to Jacob's descent into Egypt, one obtains 215 years (1955 − 215 = 1740). The Pharaoh, therefore, who

---

[13] *ANET*, 31.

[14] According to Albright, *op. cit.*, Hammurabi governed from 1728–1686 B.C., cf. § 4.

welcomed Jacob, and who had made Joseph viceroy some years before, must have reigned around the middle of the eighteenth century, and this would be the period of the Hyksos (§ 31).

163. A very late tradition (in George Sincella's *Chronographia,* ed. Dindorf, I, pp. 115, 129, 201 in *Corpus Scriptorum Historiae Byz.,* Bonn, 1829) puts the elevation of Joseph in the seventeenth year of the Pharaoh Aphophis — one of the three Apopi (perhaps Apopi II) of the Hyksos. Whatever the value of this tradition, it is certain that the various elements of the story of Joseph converge to indicate that his Pharaoh was one of the Hyksos. These, in fact, were foreigners in Egypt who, when they began to assimilate the civilization of the country, preferred to surround themselves with high officials who were not Egyptian, and upon whose fidelity they could count with greater assurance. This is the basis for Joseph's success at court. He was the Asiatic favorite of an Asiatic sovereign; just as Nehemen, whose sarcophagus was found at Saqqara,[15] was an Asiatic in the service of a Hyksos Pharaoh — another Apopi. The powers conceded to the favorite were not exaggerated; in the Egyptian court at other epochs were very influential ministers created by the benevolence of the Pharaohs, the most significant example being the Vizier Janhamu (§ 57) from the period of el-Amarna. Although of Semitic ancestry, as his name testifies, and living in times in which hatred for Asiatics in general ran high in Egypt (§§ 31, 198 ff.), he succeeded nevertheless in becoming all powerful at court. So striking is the analogy that some scholars with vivid imaginations have considered identifying Janhamu with the biblical Joseph.

164. Jacob lived seventeen years in the new land governed by his son, and died at the age of one hundred and forty-seven (Gen. 47:28). Before he died he adopted as his own the two sons of Joseph (§ 155), giving preference to Ephraim, who was the second; he then blessed all his own sons one by one (Gen. 49:2–27) with invocations which are a synthesis of their past and future deeds and of their respective descendants (cf. § 275). He also made Joseph swear that he would bury him, not in Egypt, but at Makhpelah with his fathers (§§ 138, 150). When he died he was embalmed in the Egyptian manner, the process requiring forty days (cf. Herodotus, II, 86; Diodorus Siculus, I, 91; § 159). The corpse was then brought to Makhpelah with great pomp, and was buried there (§ 197).

Joseph died at the age of one hundred and ten and was also embalmed and laid in the coffin (Gen. 50:26), doubtless the usual Egyptian coffin of an anthropomorphic type which is found in all museums of Egyptian

---

[15] Cf. Mallon, *op. cit.,* 37 f., 58.

Tomb of the Patriarch Joseph near Nablus.

antiquities. His mummy remained in Egypt for many centuries (Exod. 13:19; Josue 24:32), and afterward was buried at Sichem (§ 88).[16]

*   *   *

165. The history of the Terahites up to this point has been presented in the Bible as a true history of persons and facts. Modern criticism has interpreted it in various ways, all of which prescind more or less from the idea that it is a true history. Thus, the names of the persons and events described are thought to have a value more symbolic than real, since they portray in a concrete way some ethnological or religious idea or historical fact. The process of symbolic representation was probably more subconscious than deliberate, in accordance with historical laws more or less common to all ancient peoples, for whom the concrete replaces the abstract, leading to the creation of fictitious images of persons and events complete with details. In the creation of these pictures other rather common ethnological factors, such as totemism, mythology, etc., would naturally be added, complicating more and more the value of the end product and deforming in varying degree its symbolic signification.

166. A system much in vogue up to a few years ago, and today generally abandoned, was the mythologico-astral interpretation. It was

---

[16] Cf. *ibid.*, 87 ff., for particulars on Egyptian methods of embalming.

based on the idea that in both Egypt and Babylonia astral cults had a fundamental importance in the creation of mythical persons and cycles. That principle was then applied to the Bible. Astral motives, mythical themes and others were seen everywhere in the story of the patriarchs. Thus Abraham is the moon-god; his passage from the Orient (Babylonia) to the Occident (Canaan) is a lunar passage; the various halts, as at Harran, are lunar stations; the incursion of 'Amraphel and his colleagues against the five kings of Pentapolis symbolizes the victory of spring over winter, which concludes with the five days added to the lunisolar calendar; Jacob, who flees to Laban and then returns to Canaan, is the moon which disappears and then reappears; the twelve sons of Jacob are the twelve signs of the Zodiac, and so on.

On the other hand some scholars do not hesitate to liken the patriarchs to the Moslem *wely*, or the guardian genii of a given locality. The various places connected with the history of the patriarchs in the Bible account would be in reality the places in which these demigods were venerated, and sometimes their presumed tombs were preserved. Small clans devoted to them would then assume the name, and would weave around them a legend of human deeds.

167. Another system sees in the patriarchs eponymous heroes who represent the people of Israel in its formation and increase; hence its history is not one of individuals but of ethnic groups designated by collective names. Just as it is still said today "the Turk was defeated," or "Israel was led into exile," to indicate the peoples, so the apparently personal biblical designations indicated special clans or tribes; often indeed such designations would be those of the *totem* animal of the clan, as Lia, *le'ah*, "wild cow"?; Rachel, *rahel*, "sheep," etc. (§§ 148, 316). Thus would this system translate the various eponymous accounts into modern language, sifting as much as possible the real facts from their symbolical explanation. Marriages between eponyms would be fusions of ethnic groups; and their personal dislikes were wars or rivalries among the tribes.

168. A third system, today winning an increasing number of adherents, admits that the patriarchs were historical persons, but considers this historicity as a tiny nucleus around which is woven much legend under the influence of diverse ethnological and above all religious factors.

Several maintain that the Jacob-Israel figure is the result of a legendary fusion of two elements: the eponymous Israel represents a warlike and absorbing tribe; the other is the real person of Jacob, sheikh of a peaceful tribe of shepherds. Some of the wives and descendants of this two-faced Janus would be real, others eponymous, insofar as they represented the fusions or divisions of the ethnic group of Jacob-Israel.

Other interpretations multiply as the principles of the system are applied to Abraham and Isaac, or to Jacob and his brothers. Thus for some the figure of Jacob belonged to the sagas of the northern and Transjordanian (kingdom of Israel) territory, which was familiar only with his descent into Canaan from the northeast (Harran); in southern territory this was later joined to the legend of the rivalry between Jacob and Esau which justified Jacob's coming from the northeast, and to the tradition of his stay in Hebron. For others, however, Isaac belongs to the southern sagas (kingdom of Juda), which center about Beersheba and Gerar.

The figure of ·Abraham is more complex, and is usually interpreted as originating in the regions to the south. It is said to have been altered and contaminated at a later date by other sagas: by that of Isaac (the stay in Gerar and the episode of Abimelech [§§ 137, 141]), and of Jacob-Israel (the stops in Sichem, Beth-el, etc.).

169. The sons of Jacob are interpreted as eponymous personifications of the twelve tribes of Israel. The number is schematic and conventional, being found in other biblical genealogies of related peoples (§§ 144, 291). Certain discrepancies, moreover, have been discovered in the various lists of the Israelite tribes, explicable only by a long period of annexation and progressive organization. The most ancient document in this connection would be the canticle of Debora (Judg. 5), then the blessing of Jacob (Gen. 49), then that of Moses (Deut. 33), etc. These various eponymous clans could have been in great part divisions of some one of the patriarchal tribes which wandered into Canaan and out of it, preserving in their sagas certain faint recollections of the regions they inhabited, and these crop up here and there in the biblical account. One of these clans, that of Joseph, could have even pushed on into the borders of Egypt (but perhaps only into its adjacent territory, the Negeb: § 65) to return later on, re-enforced in numbers, into Canaan and to draw other less important clans in its wake.

These various interpretations were more directly based upon the above-mentioned historical and ethnological laws which were derived from other ancient peoples and then applied in exactly the same way to the Israelites. To a lesser degree other conclusions have come to be adopted. Among these one that derives from literary criticism (§ 115) is well thought of; the various documents which are woven together in the biblical account reflect the various legends in diverse stages of formation, sometimes agreeing sometimes conflicting with one another.

The advances of archaeology are continually clarifying the historical background of the age of the patriarchs, and are beginning little by little to confirm occasionally the biblical dates relative to them (§ 118 ff.). The vague uncertainty which has always seemed to favor the formation of such theories is being progressively dissipated.

170. Even for this period modern discoveries have supplied some factual material.

In the first place, extra-biblical documents have preserved names which are typically Israelite, though previously known only from the Bible. Abstracting from the mention of "Israel" made by the stele of Merneptah (§ 35) which appears there as a name of a nation and not of a country (§ 231), geographical names have also been discovered. The mention of a *h q r i - ' i b r m*, "Field of Abraham," made by the Pharaoh Sesac in his inscription on the temple of Karnak, is not of exceptional importance, since it certainly refers to a locality conquered by him during his foray into Palestine (§§ 36, 416) in the tenth century, but at least it shows that at the period when the traditions were supposedly unformed and only beginning, the name of the head of Israel was so widely diffused as to be part of geographical designations.

171. Other examples go back to more remote periods. The inscriptions of Seti I and Rameses II (§ 33) name *'A-sa-ru*, a region of the hinterland of central Phoenicia which corresponds to the zone later assigned by the Bible to the Israelite tribe of *Aser*. In the first half of the fifteenth century, Thutmose III, enumerating in the inscription of the temple of Amon at Karnak the localities conquered by him in Palestine after the battle of Megiddo (§ 34), mentions as number 78 a *Y s p - e r(l)*, which certainly corresponds to a *Y o s e p h - ' e l* (§ 151),[17] and as number 102 a *Y q b - e r(l)* corresponding to a *Y a ' q o b h - ' e l* (§140). Inscriptions on scarabs dating from the period of the Hyksos have preserved theophoric names formed by this *Ya'qobh*, "Jacob," in composition with other elements; for example *Ya'qobh-'ar*, *Ya'qobh-ba'al* (for *ba'al*, cf. § 107), and similar forms. The interpretation of this material in regard to the people of Israel is difficult and much discussed. It is sufficient to remember that in the times of Seti I and Rameses II the biblical Israelites, according to the more common opinion today, had not yet settled in Palestine (§ 228 ff.); furthermore, that in the time of Thutmose III they were certainly still in Egypt. The most reasonable explanation is perhaps to perceive in these names which up to the present seemed to be typically Israelite, not indeed onomastic derivations from the Terahite group, but ordinary products of the wider Semitic onomastic process. Indeed, the Semitic element predominated among the Hyksos (§ 31), and on the other hand names were discovered in Babylonia corresponding not only to Abraham (§ 132) but also to Jacob (*Yakub-ilu, Yakubum*). These names must have been common and widely used and so could easily enter into geographical designations without any dependence on the Terahites (with the probable exception of the "Field of Abraham" in the inscrip-

---

[17] *Ibid.*, 41 ff., 188 f., on Semitic names in Egyptian documents.

tion of Sesac, whose later date rather suggests an Israelite background). That such names afterward assumed in the history of the patriarchs a special symbolic significance does not raise any greater difficulty than that of the symbolism of circumcision, which was more ancient than Abraham (§ 135).

172. Other questions have arisen with regard to the name of the nation itself. The most common designation in the Bible is simply "Israel" (§ 147), or, according to the Semitic manner *Bene-Israel*, the "Sons of Israel." Much rarer is the designation "Hebrews," which is usually but not always preferred in the biblical narrative when a foreigner speaks of the Israelites (cf. *Hebreasque terras* of Tacitus, *Hist.*, V, 2), when an Israelite speaks to foreigners, or when the Israelites are compared to foreigners by the narrator.

The etymology of this word *'Ibhrim*, "Hebrews," is disputed. Some think that it belongs to an ancestor *'Ebher*, descendant of Sem and remote progenitor of the Terahites (Gen. 10:24 ff.; 11:14 ff.); grammatically such an etymology is possible, and ethnologically has support in the mention of the *Bene-'Ebher*, "Sons of Eber" (Gen. 10:21; cf. Num. 24:24?). Others, however, hold that it is a geographic appellation and is derived from the word *'ebher, beyond, across*, the country "on the other side" of some barrier (sea, river, etc.); the designation is indeed frequent even among other peoples ("*ultra*montane," "*trans*teverino," etc.), and the word is understood in this way by the Septuagint which translates *Abraham the Hebrew* of Gen. 14:13 by Abraham ὁ περάτης, "the one going over." Some believe that the barrier to which this *trans* refers is the Jordan, in which case the word would be of Canaanite origin, but most hold that it refers to the Euphrates, in which case it would be of Babylonian origin.

The Bible itself, however, presents Eber as the father of many other races besides the Terahites; hence, according to the first opinion, the Israelites would not be the only descendants of Eber, that is, the only Hebrews, nor would the term "Hebrews" be synonymous with "Israelites," but would be to this as genus is to species. Later on, it is true, the two terms were usually employed by the people as synonyms, but the Bible itself has preserved traces of the ancient distinction. In speaking of the wars between the Israelites and the Philistines in the time of Saul, it says: "The Hebrews [who] had been on the side of the Philistines as in the past, [and] who had gone out together with them to war, also revolted[18] to be with Israel which was with Saul" (1 Sam. 14:21; cf. 4:9–10; 13:3–4, 19; § 350).

173. Two names furnished by contemporary extra-biblical documents have been thought to approximate the word "Hebrew."

---

[18] This is the reading of the word as rendered by the Septuagint and the Syriac.

Egyptian documents from the time of Thutmose III (Eighteenth Dynasty) to the time of Rameses IV (Twentieth Dynasty; § 33), that is, for more than three centuries, frequently mention a foreign people dependent upon Egypt and called 'P R W, 'P W R Y W, 'Aperu, 'Apuriu. Under Thutmose III they were present at the capture of Joppe in Canaan. They are again mentioned as being in Canaan, probably as allies, in a stele of Seti I found at Beisan (§ 86). Under Rameses II they were obliged to transport stones for a temple south of Memphis; during the reign of Rameses III they formed a strong group at Heliopolis, and Rameses IV, when visiting the caves of Hammamat, was accompanied by several hundred of them. For more than fifty years it was believed that they might have been the Hebrews. Actually the approximation of 'P R W with the Hebrew 'B R Y, "Hebrew," presents serious philological difficulties. The identification was welcomed at first with great enthusiasm, but upon reflection it was seen that chronological factors plus the wide dissemination of this unknown people over all Egypt and Canaan, rendered it hardly probable that they were the same as the Hebrews; it became even less likely when, in accordance with the principles of philology, the word was explained as the name of the Aphri (the Phoenicians of the Carthaginian coasts), · or as a common name (approximately, "miners," "diggers"). In any case, even if the equivalence were demonstrated it would designate the Hebrews, not the Israelites.

174. An even more fervent welcome was extended to the identification of "Hebrews" with "Habiri" (§ 54). The Habiri of the letters of el-Amarna were either the Israelites themselves coming up from Egypt and conquering Canaan, or, at least, certain tribes related to the group of the "Sons of Israel," which preceded them as first waves of the numerous nation of the "Hebrews" in the migration from the desert toward Canaan. This time also the primitive fervor quickly chilled. The purely philological question, whether in the abstract the Hebrew form 'Ibhrim, "Hebrews," can be considered the same as that designating the Habiri in the documents of el-Amarna, matters little; it is certain that the interpretation of this name as "allies," from the root Ḥ B R (§ 54), is philologically more normal than the other from 'B R (from which "Hebrews" is derived). It seems to be also more in accord with history, since the Habiri are spoken of in an age and region quite distant from that of el-Amarna and of Canaan, for example in the period of Rim-Sin of Larsa (§ 4) and in documents of Hittite origin (§ 44 ff.). The evidence seems to indicate that the word is an adjective used in different places and times as an appellative, applicable to diverse peoples, somewhat as the term "revolutionary" is in modern history. The identification of the "Hebrews" with "Habiri" rests therefore on a shaky philological foundation.[19]

❉   ❉   ❉

175. The Bible portrays the religion of the patriarchs as essentially dependent on the call of Abraham (§ 122). As Abraham was a chosen person, so his religion and that of his descendants was a religion of the elect. It is not described as a family heirloom as was, for example, the religion of Hammurabi, nor yet as the product of theological speculation, as that of Amenophis IV (§ 34) but as an immediate consequence of the mystical act through which Abraham was selected by God, and of the pact (§ 131) drawn up by God with him.

The biblical narrator brings out clearly God's faithfulness to the promises made to Abraham and sealed by the covenant, a fidelity which is prodigious, in view of the grave and unexpected difficulties which threatened the fulfillment of those promises (§§ 131, 137 ff.). On the other hand, the patriarchs, bearers of those promises, are represented as sincere men, co-operative and entirely dedicated to their fulfillment. In this sense their whole life is religious. When they emigrate, trade, beget children, bless, these actions all take place under the increasingly luminous plan of God. Without the pact of God with Abraham, the biblical history of the patriarchs does not make sense; once presupposed, their history becomes an historical demonstration of a religious thesis.

176. The religion of the patriarchs was a new religion but the cult which was proper to it was not entirely new. Naturally the simple elementary forms of worship — prayer, oblation, sacrifice, already in use more or less by all men and corresponding in every age to the most intimate needs of the human soul, did not change. Less general usages were modified and adapted as in the case of circumcision (§ 133 ff.) and the use of the *massebah* as a religious memorial (§ 143). Naturally accepted also was the current religious terminology which formed a part of the everyday language and preserved the ethnico-religious traditions; both terms and tradition, however, were carefully sifted from anything openly opposed to its new character.

Thus the history of the patriarchs showed them praying to the divinity, offering him ritual libations and animal sacrifices upon the altars they built. As in more ancient and simpler forms of worship, the offerer was also the sacrificer who completed the ritual act without the help of a priesthood. The prayers of the patriarchs were true dialogues with the divinity, a privilege in which the narrator sees another consequence (§ 127) and proof of their election. The divinity furthermore also spoke to the patriarchs and manifested his wishes to them by means of dreams.

---

[19] *ANET*, 22, n. 4; P. de Vaux, *RB*, 1948, 337 ff.; Dhorme, *ib.*, 1930, 171, n. 1.

177. The divinity is called *'El,* a term pertaining to the most ancient forms of the Semitic languages. Some modern scholars link this term with the idea of "being the first" (root, 'Y L through V'L?), but most connect it with the idea of "being strong, powerful" (root, 'V L); even recently Sellin was able to write: "That the fundamental meaning of EL is 'the strong, powerful Being,' cannot be denied; it is a common name which became a proper name certainly in the last millennium B.C." The other two terms, *'Eloah* and *'Elohim,* are generally admitted to be secondary forms of 'El: it should be noted that 'Elohim is grammatically a true plural, but is used in the Bible either to express the plural notion of many "gods," or to indicate the singular idea of one true "God."

In the history of the patriarchs "the Powerful One" is often given a second name which associates him with a certain event, place, or quality. Thus the designations, *'El-ro'i,* "God of the vision" (Gen. 16:13), on the occasion of the theophany accorded to Hagar (§ 131); *'El-olam,* "Eternal God" (Gen. 21:33; cf. Isa. 40:28) on the occasion of the alliance of Abraham and Abimelech at Beersheba (§ 137); *'El-beth'el,* "God of Beth-el" (Gen. 31:13) in connection with the divine dream which Jacob had at Beth-el (§ 143); *'El-'Elohe-Israel,* "God-the-God-of-Israel" (§ 148). The most frequent designation, however, and the one which appears also elsewhere in the Bible (in the book of *Job* alone, which makes use of archaic language, it appears some thirty times) is *'El-S D Y* vocalized by the Massora into *'El-shaddai.* The word has not only created difficulty for the ancient versions which translated it differently even within the limits of the same version (the Septuagint alone has five or six ways), but the Massora itself gives a vocalization based on a false analysis (S-D Y; cf. Aquila, Symmachus, etc., ἱκανός); the Vulgate, in conformity with the most frequent translation of the Septuagint almost always renders it as "Omnipotent-[God]." Some modern scholars derive it from the Hebrew root S D D, "to act violently," "to destroy," supposing the word derived from it to have almost acquired the meaning of "formidable"; others however approximate it to the Babylonian *shadu,* "mountain," the Mountain of the North, which among various peoples was held to be the seat of the divinity, and this can be verified in regard to the Babylonians from Isa. 14:13.[20]

178. At any rate these designations do not represent a use common only to the Terahites. The Bible records this use among the Canaanites also in the expression *'El-'elyon,* "most high God," whose priest was Melchisedech (§ 130; Gen. 14:18 ff.); this usage is also confirmed by Philo of Byblos, who, in regard to the Phoenician theogony, speaks of an

---

[20] Sellin, *Geschichte,* 47. For the name El-Shaddai, cf. Zorell, "Der Gottesname 'Saddai' in den alten Uebersetzungen" in *Biblica,* 1927, 215 ff.

Ἐλιοῦν χαλούμενος "Ὕψιστος (in Eusebius, *Praepar. evang.*, I, 10; in Migne, *P.G.*, 21, 80 [82]; cf. Epiphanius, *Adv. haer.*, I, 3, 40 [20] in Migne, *P.G.*, 41, 685). Later on, however, the Canaanites generally substituted Ba'al for 'El (§ 107), so that Ba'al is coupled with other divine designations.

In the history of the patriarchs the divinity is also designated by means of expressions which do not include 'El, such as the "Terror of Isaac" (Gen. 31:42, 53; § 146), clearly expressing the awfulness involved in the idea of divinity; "the Mighty One of Jacob" and "Rock of Israel" (Gen. 49:24), the metaphorical acceptation of which seems to be certain among the Terahites (cf. § 104 for the Canaanites), especially when "rock" is interpreted as a place of escape or refuge, i.e., "cliff" (Hebrew *ṣur*, applied frequently to God, refuge of the people).

179. It is almost superfluous to observe that the various designations of the divinity which occur in the history of the patriarchs do not imply other divinities but only the memorial of an event, a place or a quality in relation to 'El. The fact that the Canaanites multiplied the 'El[im] as so many local deities does not prove that the same thing happened in the case of the patriarchs; this is expressly ruled out by the fact that these various designations refer more or less directly to a single and unique fact, namely, the call of Abraham, and to the promises made to him, and therefore always refer to the same God who was their author. This position is essential for the correct interpretation of these titles, just as (to cite the trite but modern example given by Renan) the Christian position is essential if one is not to consider the Madonna of Loreto, of Lourdes, etc., as different Madonnas. Thus even if it were to be proven, and it has not been, that the form "'Elohim" (grammatically a plural, § 177) was traceable to the ancient 'El [im] which implies a plurality, it does not then follow that the plurality implied by the concept was intended by the patriarchs. They made use of the term, now crystallized in its plural form, to express a singular concept. The plurality of the concept would, if proven, apply to the Canaanites; the patriarchs consistently used the invariable plural form which may have derived from the Canaanites, but gave it a singular meaning. In view of the position taken above, this point is indisputable; the patriarchs corrected the terminology — or better, its use — in the light of their religious principles (§ 185). Nor is this the only example. The term "Ba'al" had once been used in Israel, but was later repudiated and its place taken by other terms, for it had come to have an idolatrous signification (§ 107).

*   *   *

180. Corrections too of the traditions preserved by the Terahites were made in the light of religious principles. When they emigrated

from Ur (§ 122) they brought with them the two inevitable patrimonies of dwellers of the desert, whether ancient or modern: the material heritage of servants, cattle, and utensils and the moral heritage of traditions. The juridical traditions already mentioned depended on the traditions of Babylonia, cradle of the Terahites (§§ 131 ff., 139); besides these there must have been others of various kinds, above all those which concerned primitive history and which by analogy may be presumed to be related to those of Babylonia. These traditions can be perceived in various passages of the Bible and especially in the first chapters (Gen. 1–11), which link the origins of the world and of the human race with those of the Terahites. It is not within the present plan to treat of these traditions, which are so often discussed in an extremely *a priori* manner. Only some of the conclusions which flow from comparisons with Babylonia will be pointed out.

An over-all comparison of the two groups of traditions confirms the presumed existence of juridical traditions; between the two groups there is clearly a generic similarity. In dealing with particular traditions, however, the comparison should be accurate and precise. In some cases the affinity is so close that the correspondence is almost

Accadian seal. (British Museum.)

verbal; in others it is recognizable in certain general concepts only; in still others it can only be detected in secondary or extremely vague tendencies; in others, finally, there is no correspondence whatsoever.

181. One of these last-mentioned cases is the tradition of the sin of Adam and Eve (Gen. 3). Nothing like it has yet been discovered in Babylonia despite the earnest efforts of scholars. On an Accadian seal of the third millennium, two personages, one with horns, the other possibly a woman, both dressed, are seated on benches on either side of a tree. Behind the woman (?) and at some distance from the tree there is a serpent, stretching from the top of the seal to the bottom. Some look upon this as a portrayal of the sin of Adam and Eve, but a more extensive study of Babylonian documents and a closer examination have much discredited such an interpretation. Today a "learned ignorance" is professed regarding the true meaning of the scene.

More recently a brief text from Nippur, called the little poem *En-e-ba-am*, has been published by Langdon,[21] under the title "Sumerian

---

[21] S. Langdon, *Sumerian Epic of Paradise, the Flood, and the Fall of Man*, (University of Pennsylvania Museum), Philadelphia, 1915; opposed are J. D. Prince, in *JAOS*, 1916, 90 ff.; M. Jastrow, *ibid.*, 122 ff.; Dhorme in *RB*, 1921, 309. Text in *ANET*, 38 ff.

Epic of Paradise, the Flood and the Fall of Man," but the text is quite other than the title. Actually, Assyriologists (Witzel, Dhorme, etc.) have concluded that in the text "there is not the least trace of paradise, flood or fall of man." It is, as a matter of fact, a mythical poem dealing with the god of waters, Enki, and his spouse, Ninella; it may perhaps refer to a drought that desolated the region inhabited by the divine couple. It seems to speak of abundant and beneficial waters, not of a flood. The fall of man is not so much as mentioned.

182. At other times the similarity exists in matters of secondary importance or is very vague. Such is the case of the Babylonian poem of creation, so named from its opening words, *Enuma elish,* "Time was when above," compared with the cosmogony of the Bible (Gen. 1–2:3). The identity of theme, the origin of heaven and earth, naturally leads to the treatment of some parallel points (formation of the firmament, the stars, moon, creation of man, etc.), but the material of the two accounts, the facts narrated, the manner of explanation, and especially the basic religious ideas, entirely differentiate the two traditions. There must have been several traditions concerning the Babylonian cosmogony. Indeed, leaving aside other works which are rich in cosmogonic information, it may be noted that the cosmogonies of Berossus and Damascius do not fully harmonize with the redaction of the *Enuma elish* which has come down to us. Our version of it dates from the Neo-Assyrian period (§ 17); the poem itself was composed probably in the First Dynasty of Babel (§ 4); and possibly depends on a shorter and more ancient Sumerian work.[22]

183. More noteworthy is the schematic correspondence between the primitive genealogies which the two traditions contain. The traditional genealogy given in the Bible (Gen. 5) links Adam with Noah, i.e., from the beginning of the human race to the Flood. These persons had a life span of about eight hundred years. To this genealogy is added the account of the deluge (Gen. 6 ff.), after which the narrator, restricting himself to that part of the human race which will be the object of his account (§ 111), furnishes another genealogy, that of the Semites (Gen. 11:10 ff.) which however assigns to the persons mentioned a much shorter life span which gradually decreases from Sem (six hundred years) to Terah, the father of Abraham (two hundred and five years according to the Hebrew text, but one hundred and forty-five according to the Samaritan: cf. Gen. 11:26, 32; 12:4; Acts 7:4; §§ 122, 125). Reducing the biblical tradition to an outline, there is first the antediluvian genealogy recording a life span of centuries; a *hiatus,* represented by the Flood; postdiluvian genealogy, with a shorter and constantly diminishing life span.

---

[22] Text of *Enuma elish,* in *ANET,* 60 ff.

The same schema with its three parts appears also in the Babylonian tradition. The first part is composed of the series of antediluvian dynasties, in which each monarch reigns many thousands of years (for example, Enmeduranna, king of Sippar, seventy-two thousand years, or according to another recension, twenty-one thousand); then comes the *hiatus* of the Deluge, which completely separates the preceding story from the following; at the end, the third part of the schema, composed of the postdiluvian dynasties of the various cities (Kish, Erech, etc.; § 3); to these personages there is assigned a shorter and diminishing life span (from an average of ten centuries for those of the first dynasty of Kish, to an average of much less than a century for those immediately following).[23]

184. It is, however, in the story of the flood that the correspondence between the two groups of traditions is greatest, and in some points, identical.

The biblical tradition is contained in Gen. 6–9:17: modern critics commonly consider it among the Jahwistic (J) and Sacerdotal (P) documents with some editorial additions (R; cf. § 115 ff.).

Over and above the account of Berossus, there are a number of Babylonian texts which mention the Deluge; they are, of course, of different periods and vary in length. The classical text is the eleventh of the twelve tablets which comprise the *Epic of Gilgamesh*, a masterpiece of Babylonian literature widely known in ancient times throughout anterior Asia. There were not only various local versions of this but also foreign translations (in the Hittite dialects since the middle of the second millennium B.C.). The most famous copy, which alone will be considered, comes from the library of Ashurbanipal (§ 484), but the epic itself dates back at least to the period of Hammurabi (§ 4). In Tablet XI, the deluge is an episode quite incidental to

Tablet containing the Babylonian account of the Flood. (British Museum.)

---

[23] The threefold scheme of old Babylonian chronology is treated by Dhorme, "L'aurore de l'histoire babylonienne" in *RB*, 1924, 534 ff.; 1926, 66.

the plot of the poem, which is a speech directed to the hero of the epic, Gilgamesh. Because of this many have considered the episode to be a later insertion influenced by one of the various versions of the flood story then in circulation. In the prologue Gilgamesh, wishing to assure himself of immortality, sets out upon a long and adventurous journey to obtain the secret from his ancestor Utnapishtim, who was favored with immortality by the gods after the deluge. When he arrives at the island on which his ancestor lives, Gilgamesh asks him concerning the "secret of life" and receives in reply the account of the deluge.

Utnapishtim, a devotee of the god Ea, lives at Shuruppak (§ 2). The gods decide to destroy humanity by means of a flood, but Ea warns his devotee by giving him this command:

Epic of Gilgamesh	Genesis
Tablet XI[24]	
23. Man of Shuruppak, son of Ubara-Tutu,	And God said to Noe . . .
24. demolish [thy] house and build [from it] a ship.	Make an ark of resin-wood (6:13-14).
25. Leave thy riches, take thought for thy life!	
26. Reject thy possessions, save thy life!	
27. Bring seed of life of all kinds aboard the ship.	And of every sort of living creature of all flesh you shall bring two into the ark (6:19).
28. The ship that thou must build,	
29. Let its measurements be [well] measured:	And this is [the measurement] how you will make it:
30. Let the length and breadth correspond;	
31. Upon the Apsu[25] must thou launch it.	

Utnapishtim sets about building the ship. A brief lacuna occurs at this point, and then the hero relates the following of himself:

57. On the fifth day I raised its frame.	
58. Its surface (?) was 1 *iku*,[26] its walls were 10 *gar*[27] high.	The length of the ark [shall be] 300 cubits: its width 50 cubits: and its height 30 cubits. You shall make an
59. The extent of its roof corresponded (?) to 10 *gar*.	opening (?) for the ark, and finish it a cubit from the top, and set a door in the side of the ark
60. I laid down its hull; I designed it.	
61. I covered it with six stories;	[with three floors], lower, middle and
62. I divided [its length?] seven times;	third (6:15-16).

---

[24] Cp. the complete text of Tablet XI, in *ANET*, 93-97.

[25] The name of the primordial ocean; here however it signifies the Persian Gulf.

[26] About 4000 square yards. (The German translation in *Altorientalische Texte*[2], p. 176, has 12 *iku*, but this must be a typographical error; the cuneiform text has 1 *iku*.)

[27] About 65 yards high because 1 *gar* was about 6 yards; since a *gar* corresponds to 12 cubits, the total height was 120 cubits (cf. the respective measurements of the biblical account).

63. Its [interior?] I divided nine times;   Make little rooms in the ark.
64. I set water-plugs in its middle
    against the waters;
65. I chose a rudder and procured what   Take with you every kind of food (6:21).
    was necessary.
66. Six *sar*[28] of bitumen I put into the   Cover it with pitch inside and out
    furnace;   (6:14).
67. Three *sar* of asphalt . . . within.

Utnapishtim, when the ship is finished, celebrates with a festive banquet. Then he continues:

81. [All that I had] I stowed [aboard].
82. All that I had I stowed [aboard] —   Noe and his sons, and his wife, and
    silver.   his sons' wives went together into the
83. All that I had I stowed [aboard] —   ark, to escape the waters of the flood.
    gold.   Of clean animals and unclean, and of
84. All that I had I stowed [aboard] —   birds, and of every creature crawling
    seed of life.   on the ground, pairs, male and female,
85. I brought into the ship all my fam-   entered the ark with Noe (7:7–9; cf.
    ily and kindred;   13–15).
86. beasts of the field, the wild crea-
    tures of the field, craftsmen, I
    brought all in.

94. I entered into the ship and closed   And the LORD shut him in (7:16).
    my door.
95. To the master of the ship, to the
    pilot Puzur-Amurru,
96. I entrusted the palace [of the ship]
    with all its possessions.
97. When a glimmer of the morning
    shone forth,
98. There arose from the horizon a   All the fountains of the Great Tehom[29]
    black cloud: burst forth,
99. Adad[30] roared in its midst,
100. Shullat and Hamish strode before,
101. went on as heralds over mountain
     and country.
102. Nergal uproots the [dam] posts,   and the floodgates of the heavens were
                                         opened (7:11).
103. Ninurta strides forth, makes the
     dike to flow,
104. The Anunnaki lift up the torches.
105. With their flame they ignite the
     country.
106. The fury of Adad reaches even to
     the heavens,
107. Turning every light into darkness.

---

[28] As there was no measure of volume, *sar* is only a numerical figure with a value of 3600.

[29] The Great Tehom (cf. the Assyrian *Tiamat*) was the impassable lower ocean which surrounded the earth; above the firmament there was another gathering of waters, contained by the dikes or cataracts of the heavens (cf. the next part of the verse).

[30] This and the following are Babylonian divinities; for Adad cf. § 107.

The polytheistic description is continued. The gods, presented in Homeric style, are terrified by the deluge and take refuge in the higher heaven of the god Anu. There, outside the flood, "they pack together like dogs," afflicted by the extermination and protesting against it. Meanwhile the deluge continues.

128. Six days and nights

And the flood continued 40 days upon the earth (7:17).

129. The wind blows, the deluge rages: the storm ravages the country.

130. When the seventh day arrived, the storm, the flood, was defeated in the battle

131. Which it, like an army, had fought.

132. The sea grew quiet, the tempest abated, the deluge ceased.

133. I watched the weather, there was silence.

The waters rose higher and higher on the earth, so that the highest mountains everywhere under the heavens were covered; the waters rose 15 cubits above the mountains so that they were covered (7:19-20).

The waters rose on the earth a hundred and fifty days (7:24).

134. The whole human race had become clay.

135. The countryside had become as level as a roof.

Every living thing on the earth was wiped out, from man to beast, from reptile to bird of the air: they were wiped from the earth (7:23).

136. I opened the window, and the light fell upon my cheek;

137. I fell upon my knees, I sat down, weeping;

138. Down my cheeks coursed my tears.

139. I looked about for coast lines, in the expanse of the sea.

140. At 12 [distance?] farther on, an island emerged.

Noe opened the window [of] the ark (8:6).

141. The ship came to a halt on Mount Nisir:

142. Mount Nisir held the ship fast, allowing no motion.

The ark rested, on the seventeenth day of the seventh month, upon the mountains of 'Ararat (8:4).

Mount Nisir, according to later documents, was situated between the Tigris and the lower Zab (§ 1); there the ship rests six days.

146. When the seventh day arrived

147. I made a dove go out. I released it.

148. The dove went out but came back,

149. There being no place to rest it came back.

150. I made a swallow go out, I released it:

151. The swallow went out and came back.

152. There being no place to rest, it came back.

153. I made a raven go out, I released it;

154. the raven went out, he sees the drying-up of the waters:

155. he eats, shakes himself, caws and does not return.

At the end of forty days, Noe opened the window he had made in the ark, and released a raven. It flew to and fro until the waters had dried off the earth. Then he sent forth a dove to see if the waters had abated from the surface of the ground. But the dove found no place to alight, so she returned to him in the ark; for the water covered the whole earth. He put forth his hand and caught her, and drew her to him into the ark. He waited another seven days, and again sent forth the dove from the ark. The dove came back to him in the evening, and there in her mouth

was a green olive leaf; so Noe knew
that the waters had abated from the
earth. Then he waited another seven
days, and sent forth the dove: but
she did not return to him any more
(8:6–12).

156. I made [all] go out to the four winds, I offered a sacrifice,

Noe went forth with his sons and his wife and his sons' wives. All wild animals, all cattle, all birds, and all creatures crawling on the earth, according to their kinds they went out of the ark. Then Noe built an altar to the LORD; he took of every clean animal and of every clean bird, and offered holocausts on the altar,

157. I poured out an oblation on the top of the mountain;
158. Seven and seven cult-vessels I arranged.
159. Into their cups I scattered cane, cedar wood and myrtle;
160. The gods smelled the savor,
161. The gods smelled the sweet savor
162. The gods crowded like flies above the sacrifice.

And the LORD smelled the sweet odor (8:18–21).

185. Comparison of the closest points of the two accounts yields much valuable information. It shows that the biblical account, which in its present state is several centuries posterior to the Babylonian, depends upon that patrimony of ethnic traditions (§ 180) which the Terahites had brought with them from Babylonia. Thus the link with Babylonian civilization, already seen in the matter of laws (§§ 131 ff., 139; cf. § 246) and other ethnological elements (§§ 123, 131 ff., 145 ff.), is once more confirmed. Yet the divergences of the two accounts also show that the Babylonian tradition has been passed through a spiritual filter, by which the dregs of polytheistic thought and the excessive anthropomorphisms were strained out. That polytheistic ideas would multiply in number in the Babylonian transmission of the Flood story is only what we might expect, but we lack sufficient evidence on this for us to form a judgment; such ideas, however, must have been widespread at the time in which the patriarchs lived. It is not difficult to discover the idea behind this religious filter: Jacob's selective inventory of the sacred objects in his own household (§ 149), and the choice and correction of religious terminology accomplished by the patriarchs (§ 179), were also motivated by the same idea. It is the idea of the vocation of Abraham and of his pact with God, which alone give meaning to the biblical story of the patriarchs (§ 175).

186. It has long been known that various traditions concerning some kind of a flood are discernible among many other peoples: the deluge of Deucalion among the Greeks; the many stories of pre-Columbian America; the traditions still preserved today in Australia, Polynesia, India, Kashmir, Tibet, Lithuania, etc. Faced with these facts, many accept the attractive theory that the fact which lies at the bottom of both the Babylonian and Terahite traditions lies behind these traditions also. A more judicious view, however, associates the various deluges with geological *diluvia* which, frequently following glacial phenomena, have during the quaternary geological era profoundly modified the surface of the globe and divested it of living beings.

On this point some very recent[31] discoveries have been made and once more the question of the deluge is the order of the day. During excavations conducted at Ur and Kish (§ 2) from 1928 onward, there came to light material evidence of the cause of the hiatus in the ancient Babylonian or biblical (§ 183) genealogies. In both localities the excavations reached the lowest stratum known up to that time, and the ceramic finds led the excavators to date this level at the very dawn of Babylonian history, i.e., the era of the first local dynasties (§ 3). Continued excavations led to a stratum which at Ur was of virgin clay deposited by water; at Kish it was of fine sand interspersed with evidence of fresh-water shellfish and fish. Going below these strata, there unexpectedly came to light the remains of a civilization which, although evidently more ancient than the earliest Babylonian, nevertheless contained colored ceramics of a more perfect type. The Anglo-American excavators immediately informed the English newspapers and magazines, which at once confidently blazoned forth with "The biblical deluge a proven fact" and other headlines in similar vein. They decided that the stratum which constitutes the *hiatus* was the "level of the deluge." Indeed the simultaneous proof from both places seemed as indubitable as it was clear, although later on its importance was more accurately determined.[32]

187. The explanation of the fact is open to the discussion of specialists and in the meantime we can only wait for more precise information.

Dhorme meanwhile speaks of the "river *par excellence*, the Euphrates, which with an immense flood . . . has covered over, silted up, and invaded those cities which once flourished on its banks. It is not at all surprising if the record of a similar flood has been preserved by the people and the wise men of Chaldea." In a conference at the Pontifical Biblical Institute of Rome, Deimel attempted to fit the data of these excavations into documented history and Babylonian chronology. The conference was not published, but the following is an authorized

---

[31] Cf. Burrows, *What Mean These Stones?* (New Haven, 1941), pp. 26, 70; also C. L. Woolley, *Ur of the Chaldees*, London, 1929; S. Langdon, *Excavations at Kish*, 1929; J. Finegan, *Light from the Ancient Past*, Princeton, 1947, pp. 23–27.

[32] Dhorme, in *RB*, 1930, 481–502; Woolley, *op. cit.*, 22–29.

résumé. "Penetrating into the twilight of Babylonian prehistory, we encounter the great and ancient Babylonian king list [§ 183], which enumerates the kings of Babylonia from the creation of the world up to the deluge, and from the deluge up to the time of Hammurabi, that is, toward the latter part of the third millennium B.C. Other cuneiform texts and the laws of sound paleography are of great help. These lead to the conclusion that the line of demarcation between history and prehistory is very near the period of the large collection of the texts of Fara [§ 2], the fatherland of the Babylonian Noah, that is, toward the close of the fourth millennium B.C. The most ancient list of the kings, above indicated, allows us to determine the approximate chronology of the great biblical deluge. In the hypothesis that the first half of the 139 kings, who, according to the list of rulers, lived from the time of the deluge up to the time of Hammurabi, governed as long as the second half[33] (which time interval can be approximately calculated by means of contemporary texts), the great deluge of the Bible would have occurred four thousand years B.C. This conclusion, drawn from the king list, may possibly be confirmed by the new excavations. In the excavations at Ur, the fatherland of Abraham, the excavators came upon a thick stratum of clayey deposit some seven to ten feet deep, apparently the result of an inundation. On digging through this, they discovered another cultural stratum, and then the bedrock upon which the earliest inhabitants had settled. These facts led Woolley to conclude that the Flood could have occurred 4000 years B.C. Deimel continued his lecture by asking whether the Babylonian deluge was to be identified with the one described in the Bible, and concluded that this cannot be reasonably denied. The two accounts agree [excluding, of course, the polytheistic nature of the Babylonian account, § 185], not only in the main points, but also in many particulars [§ 184]. A hundred years ago Christian exegetes would not have had any difficulty in admitting this data concerning the flood. In the meantime, however, so much certain information has been made available to us about man's prehistory, that today it is impossible to include all such data within so narrow an interval of time. Under the circumstances one should await from modern excavations, archaeologists, and students of cuneiform, a chronology which is solidly established. At present we are far from having any such chronology. If some day it materializes, Catholic exegetes will find an answer which will resolve the apparent discrepancy

---

[33] It has been noted (§ 183) that the first half of the Babylonian genealogical schema assigns to each ruler fantastic and untenable life-spans. Not so, however, the second half, which follows the *hiatus* of the deluge; taken in its entirety (not in the duration of each single reign), the life-spans are more likely. Cf. Burrows, *What Mean These Stones?* (New Haven, 1941), pp. 26 f., 70.

between the biblical and the Babylonian account of the deluge and will show clearly the historical exactness of Sacred Scripture in this particular also."[34]

188. Another question, not trivial from the historical point of view, comes to mind: how were the traditions of the patriarchs preserved and transmitted? Within very circumscribed limits a written transmission is certainly possible. There is no need to resort to a problematical alphabetic writing (§ 100), for today it is certain that cuneiform writing was internationally known and employed (§ 43); besides the documents of el-Amarna (§ 52 ff.), the cuneiform tablets discovered in Palestine itself, at Tell el-Hesy (§ 74), Ta'annak (§ 78), etc., are fresh proof of it in the territory of the patriarchs. It is perfectly legitimate to suppose that in the baggage of the nomadic patriarchs, in which the teraphim stolen by Rachel (§ 144) were hidden with such care, one might also have found a certain number of cuneiform tablets inscribed, perhaps, with authoritative juridical norms (§§ 131 ff., 139), or religious formulae (similar to those discovered by the thousands in Babylonia), or records and traditions gathered in Babylonia and which concerned only the Terahites. These tablets were a kind of strong-box which contained a part of their moral patrimony, something not less precious to these dwellers in the desert than was their material heritage (§ 180); and the patriarchs watched over it with a diligence inspired by their vocation (§ 185). Strictly speaking, one could even abandon the hypothesis of transmission by writing; if there was a written transmission, it was certainly very limited. Cuneiform writings on clay tablets were sufficiently cumbersome to discourage nomadic peoples from collecting them. The greater part of the traditions had to be preserved on a different kind of tablet, the "memory."

189. Only with extraordinary effort can we moderns realize the important part memory played among ancient peoples. The immeasurable output of both manual and mechanical writing today has almost atrophied this faculty in our social life, and the extensive and methodical use made of it by the ancients seems improbable to us. Yet the facts are incontrovertible. The point need not be labored by quoting numerous examples among other races (the Homeric poems are the classic example of this; they were entrusted only to the memory of the rhapsodists for centuries. A modern counterpart of this is had in the Finnish *Kálevala*, likewise entrusted only to the memory of the Finnish *laulaiát* for centuries). There are typical examples in Semitic circles also. The *Koran* was not "written" by Mahomet (and this was in the seventh century

---

[34] Cf. the *Osservatore Romano*, February 2–3, 1931. Woolley's interpretation is discounted by most scholars today; cf. *BA*, 1942, 55–62; Ceuppens, *Hist. Primaeva*, Rome, 1947, 336 f.; Burrows, *loc. cit.*; A. Parrot, *The Flood and Noah's Ark* (London: 1955).

A.D.!); its text was "recited" by the author to the first proselytes, and for some years was entrusted substantially to the memory of the so-called "bearers of the Koran," who could recite it in its entirety. Only when that first generation began to disappear was it decreed that the entire work be set down in writing. Yet up until that time the preservation of the text had been so literal that divergences encountered among the copies of the first writing (due more than anything else to the imperfection of the contemporary Arabian script), caused painful surprise. Even if the Israelites alone are considered, there are other striking proofs, to be taken in chronological order. It is well known that the enormous material which constitutes the Talmud and the various Targum[im] was transmitted for centuries by memory alone (noteworthy is the norm laid down by Rabbi Haggai, in Talmud Jer., *Megill.*, IV, 1, which expressly forbids "writing" the targum for the synagogal service). Even before that, the activity of the prophets was concerned principally with "reciting" publicly their songs. If in certain cases these were written down by the authors or dictated to a disciple (Jer. 36:2 ff., 32), this ordinarily took place later, for at first they were entrusted to "memory" (§ 527); in other cases they never passed from "memory" to "writing."

190. The ordinary storehouse for thought was, then, memory, not writing; living thought was preferred to a lifeless document. A writing would, of course, be in demand if one wanted an exact statement as in a contract, a law, a monument, and the like, but to preserve the ordinary individual and private records, memory was not only better adapted, but also more prized. Two modern examples of Semitic memory are very instructive, inasmuch as they reflect exactly the mentality of a profoundly conservative race.

Massaia tells of his visit in 1868 to a high school installed at Fekerié-gemb, in the domain and by the order of King Menelik, who had appointed a famous teacher, Tekla Tsion, to the office of Alaca (director); he was "reputed to be the most learned man in Abyssinia." A reception with a recitation of poetry was given in honor of Massaia, whose words tell their own story. "When that academic exercise was over, I manifested a desire to have those poems in writing but, strange as it seems, not one of the fifty youths who studied there knew how to write! I have already mentioned above that the Abyssinian schools do not use books and that the teachers themselves sometimes cannot read or write; furthermore in the high schools writing is not considered a very honorable occupation. The Alaca himself, the teacher of that large group of students, did not know how to write. There was a scribe present, but only to take care of correspondence; he had nothing to do with the school. This seems strange to us, but we have only to go back a few centuries to a time when the printing-press had not been invented to encounter learned men who did not know how to write. It was no more a disgrace for them than it is for us not to know how to print, or how to write with a fine hand. In those days the duty of communicating ideas by means of writing was entrusted to copyists, a salaried class, belonging more to the working classes than to that of the learned and the thinkers. The centuries roll on and customs change or are transformed, but Abyssinia has remained as it was, with its patriarchal traditions and its ancient customs." Massaia then calls attention to the prodigious memory of the students educated in that school. What he says concerning the similarity between the ancient and modern customs of these Semites is perfectly true. From many passages of the Amarna letters it can be argued that the "mummy" of thought was often distrusted; sometimes along with the letter there went a messenger who, for sake of greater security, would repeat the "writing" (§ 242) from "memory."[35]

191. The second example is of a somewhat different nature, but it likewise shows how important a use was made of memory for many centuries, and how marvelously accurate were the results. The following quotation needs no further comment. "While the avid interest of the world was attracted to the discoveries which brought to light the material wealth of ancient Egypt, Professor E. Newland Smith quietly went about his investigations into some of the spiritual riches of that ancient and great civilization. He turned to its music, for it is in music that the soul of any people finds expression. His researches soon revealed the inaccuracy of the theory that great music is a relatively modern art, for he found a musical treasure. In his researches, the *Times* reports, he worked back from the choral songs used today in the ceremonies of the Coptic Church. The choral music heard in Coptic services has never been written; for centuries it has been transmitted orally from singer to singer. There is a large college of music connected with the Coptic Church, where the singers spend some years learning the traditional music used in the cathedrals. The fact that almost all of these singers are blind helps to explain their extraordinary facility in memorizing music of such unusual complexity. Although entire days were required for the singing of certain hymns which are marvels of beauty, tiny faults of execution were rare. It was in 1927 that Professor Smith betook himself to Egypt for the first time. He spent one whole winter on a ship on the Nile, listening to the music which the director of music for all the Coptic churches, and other singers, sang for him. He returned to Egypt several times thereafter, and finally, in 1930, for the first time in history, succeeded in transcribing this music. The completed work filled seven large volumes."

---

[35] G. Massaia, *I miei 35 anni di missione nell Alta Etiopia*, Vol. IX, Rome, 1891, 78 ff. Concerning the usage whereby letter carriers were made to learn the contents of letter by heart, cf. *Cambridge Ancient History*, II, 334 ff.

EGYPT AND MOSES

192. The scanty information which the Bible provides concerning the sojourn of the Israelites in Egypt can be summarized as follows. The Terahites who entered Egypt with Jacob (Gen. 46:26 f.; Exod. 1:5; cf. the Septuagint and Acts 7:14) were about seventy in number, counting only the direct descendants. Settling in the land of Gessen, they led a life that was predominantly pastoral. When they had been there for many generations and their number had greatly increased, a new Pharaoh began to persecute them, setting them to work, among other things, on the construction of the cities of Pithom and Rameses. Finally, under the leadership of Moses, a numerous people went out from Egypt. In the light of archaeological discoveries, various questions can be raised concerning this meager information.

193. The first is a geographical question. Where is the land of Gessen? It is called in Hebrew *Goshen,* and in Gen. 47:11 is also called "land of Rameses." From what is known of the Hyksos who made fortifications in the Delta, making Avaris their stronghold (§ 31), it can be supposed that Goshen was in the Delta, and more precisely in its eastern part, about which the Hyksos were most concerned, because it was the road communicating with their native Asia.[1]

The designation "land of Rameses" involves a difficulty, for the Pharaohs who bore the name Rameses, from the second of whom the name is certainly derived (§ 33), commence only with the Nineteenth Dynasty, that is, almost three centuries after the Hyksos, yet it is stated that the designation is in use in the time of Joseph. The difficulty, however, is only apparent, and the anachronism can easily be explained as an anticipation, which means that the biblical narrator employs, in referring to the time of the Hyksos, a term which was current in his own day, much as we might now say that Julius Caesar waged war in France, instead of in Gaul.

The more exact location of Gessen, in this area suggested by history, has been attempted in view of later and rather vague indications. Many

---

[1] Mallon, *op. cit.,* p. 98 ff., studies the meaning of the Egyptian *gesem,*

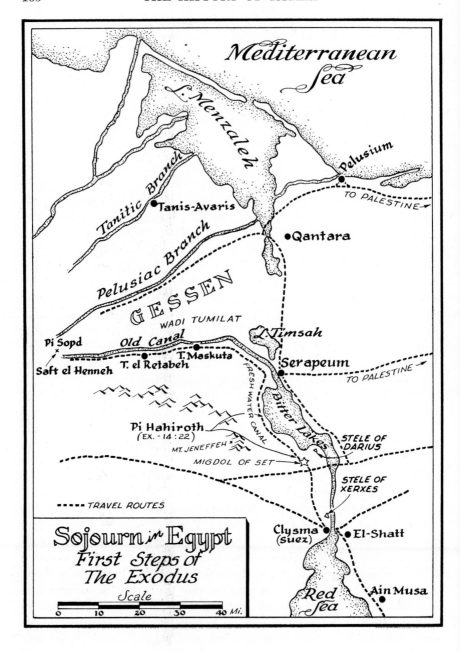

Sojourn in Egypt
First Steps of
The Exodus
Scale

0   10   20   30   40 Mi.

Egyptologists feel that the name of Gessen is recognizable in the word *g s m* (*gesem*) which documents of the Ptolemaic era would attribute to the twentieth nome of the East. Recent and more accurate studies, however, seem to have demonstrated that the hieroglyphic in question should be read *shesmet* (*shesem*) and refers to the region of Sinai.

A widely held opinion is that Gessen was situated at the western mouth of Wadi Tumilat, which traverses horizontally the eastern Delta about halfway up, and opens to the east into Lake Timsah at about the halfway point of the isthmus of Suez; in this case Gessen was included in the XX Egyptian nome, or province. Yet there are good reasons to suppose that it was situated somewhat more to the north, in the regions south of the city of Tanis (§ 24): in that case it was included in the XIX province, or better, in the XIV province. The question could be decided if scholars could identify with assurance the two cities of Pithom and Rameses, which were built by the Israelites and were the first stops in the itinerary of the exodus (§ 217 ff.), but they can only guess at the answers to these questions.

194. The key to the situation would be the location of the city of Rameses. That it was situated within the "land of Rameses" is to be taken for granted because of the identity of name, but precisely where? The question becomes complicated because it is connected with another no less problematical, the identification of Avaris. This "residence of the Hyksos has been located in every part of the eastern Delta from Heliopolis all the way to Pelusium" by the archaeologists. It is well known that the Pharaoh Rameses II had a passion for building, which led him shamelessly to inscribe his own name on many buildings put up long before his time, an evident plagiarism which has provoked the scorn of modern archaeologists. At any rate, which was the "city of Rameses" *par excellence,* the *Pi-Rameses* of the hieroglyphic documents? Until recently Pelusium seemed to have won a wide acceptance over Tanis, but new studies and documents (1930) have made a return to the older opinion advisable, since "we have most cogent reasons for locating at Tanis both the city of the Hyksos, Avaris, and the residence of the Rameses, Pi-Rameses." This would harmonize well with the expression used by the Bible when it describes precisely the territory occupied by the Israelites within Egypt as the "country of Tanis" (Ps. 78[77]:12, 43).[2]

195. The other city built by the Israelites, Pithom (*Pi-thum* in hieroglyphics, "dwelling of Tum," the god Atum) is located by many archaeologists at Tell el-Maskhuta, halfway along the Wadi Tumilat; by some however at Tell er-Retab (Tell Artabi), about ten miles to

---

[2] For the much-discussed identification of Avaris, cf. P. Montet, "Tanis, Avaris, et Pi-Ramses" in *RB*, 1930, 5–28; the two quotations given are from 6 and 28.

Semites and Asiatics brought to Egypt as prisoners. (Thebes.)

the west of Tell el-Maskhuta. The Bible calls the two cities built by the Israelites "supply cities" (Exod. 1:11); it is likely that since they were frontier cities, such stores were intended for the military; ruins of granaries have been found at Tell el-Maskhuta, and inscriptions which mention local warehouses either there or at Tell er-Retab, besides the many construction projects of Rameses II at Tanis (cf. also § 205). Tell el-Maskhuta was also called *Theku*, which is generally regarded as the biblical Sukkoth (Exod. 12:37; 13:20) and was the first stop of the exodus (§ 217).

196. In the land of Gessen the Israelites must have found things to their liking: in the first place the region was fertile and suitable for grazing (Gen. 45:18; 46:32 ff.; 47:3 ff.; etc.); moreover, especially in the beginning, they were more or less segregated from the Egyptian world. An interesting reason is assigned for this: "all the shepherds of flocks [of smaller animals] are an abomination to the Egyptians" (Gen. 46:34). This aversion of the Egyptians is also attested by Herodotus (II, 47) for the keepers of pigs, and by monuments, for the cowherds, and in both cases the aversion probably sprang from religious reasons. On the other hand, the aversion for shepherds of the Israelite type must have been based above all on nationalistic grounds; nomadic shepherds certainly had come down into Egypt in great numbers after the invasion of the Hyksos (§ 31), and in the eyes of the Egyptians these barbarian intruders would surely be looked upon as an abomination. Their condition of isolation must have helped the small group which was in the process of becoming a people; its national consciousness became more compact as a result, for its ethnic and religious traditions were preserved from infiltrations.

197. After many years the Israelites, by reason of their numbers, could no longer be contained within the land of Gessen (Exod. 1:7); it undoubtedly remained their principal center until much later times (Exod. 8:18[22]; 9:26), but groups of Israelites occasionally went forth to settle in the midst of the Egyptians, pasturing their cattle along with theirs (Exod. 9:4–7), and living openly with them (Exod. 12:13). This expansion of a prolific population makes it likely that groups of Israelites emigrated at intervals from a now overcrowded Gessen long before the general exodus, and rather than settle in the midst of the unfriendly Egyptians, preferred to return immediately to Canaan, the land to which they were bound by so many ancestral and religious traditions. At one time, in the early period, almost all of them had returned for a brief spell, when Joseph went up from Egypt into Canaan with a large following to bury Jacob (Gen. 50:7–14; § 164); certainly after that their ties with the promised land were not severed. This fact is not attested by the Bible, it is true, but is a possibility which must be remembered in view of future hypotheses (§ 231).

198. Much later, when the increase of the people was very great and their expansion in proportion, "a new king arose in Egypt, who knew nothing of Joseph" (Exod. 1:8). The expression is not difficult to understand: the new Pharaoh did not "remember" the services rendered to Egypt by Joseph, and accordingly changed the treatment until then given to his countrymen. This certainly does not mean that he was the first Pharaoh after the time of Joseph, nor that his predecessors had been as beneficent as Joseph's Pharaoh. The new Pharaoh initiated a different policy primarily out of national and political motives; he reasoned as follows: "Look how numerous and powerful the Israelite people are growing, more so than we ourselves! Come, let us deal shrewdly with them to stop their increase; otherwise, in time of war they too may join our enemies to fight against us, and so leave our country" (Exod. 1:9–10). He did not want to expel them from Egypt, since their herds and in general their manpower amounted to considerable wealth. At the same time, however, he feared their numbers in case of a war. He therefore adopted a policy of repression, hoping to reduce them to a condition of absolute inferiority in relation to the native population, and so keep them under control. Judging from this, it is not unreasonable to conclude that the new Pharaoh did not belong to the dynasties of the Hyksos, as that of Joseph, but to some other of the native dynasties which expelled the Hyksos and followed it up by making war upon them in Asia (§ 32 ff.). His measures against the Israelites were dictated by

Egyptian occupations; below, brickmaking. (Thebes, period of Thutmose III.)

his inveterate hatred of Asiatics as much as by political prudence (§ 31).

199. What role did the Israelites play in the Egyptian war of independence which terminated with the expulsion of the Hyksos? It might be expected that they would be on the side of their benefactors and neighbors, but it is probable that they took no part in it, maintaining a prudent neutrality which was fostered by their generally isolated condition. In Gessen life for them was very attractive and pleasant (Exod. 16:3; Num. 11:5), and they had no reason to take one side or another, since they were not called into the fray by either party: *quieta non movere.* Moreover, whoever the future Pharaoh might be, he would not expel them from their comfortable region; a Hyksos would certainly not do so, nor would a native Pharaoh, for the same reason that the "new" Pharaoh did not wish to expel them.

200. The first measure of persecution was to employ the Israelites in the making of bricks for the building of the cities of Pithom and Rameses (§ 194 ff.); next the persecution was stepped up, and they had to procure even the straw which was used in the interior of the brick to strengthen it. Their labors were supervised by inspectors armed with clubs, and their production was carefully checked.

Another measure of persecution aimed at drying up the very fountain of their increasing population: an order was given to the midwives to kill the males born of Israelite women but to allow the females to live. Since the midwives evaded the order, a more general command was given to throw the newborn male Israelites into the river.

The persecution must have lasted a long time, certainly for almost a century (cf. Exod. 2:2, 11, 23; 7:7): the respective intensification of both measures demonstrates that the persecution developed in two phases, the second more savage than the first. The second phase seems also to indicate a period in which it was possible to conduct a profound reorganization in the structure of the state whereby these foreigners, who reminded them so much of the abhorred Hyksos, had to be reduced to mere human machines for the good of the country.

201. Systematic oppression of a whole people succeeds only with great difficulty, as the history of mankind in general and that of the Israelites in particular teaches. The Israelites must have opposed the oppression in a passive manner, for the most part, but sometimes even actively as is clear from the incident of Moses, who killed an Egyptian oppressor (§ 204). The blows which the people received awakened a national consciousness which had been dulled by the easy life of Gessen, and their bitterness, rising to its climax, prepared them to detach themselves from the land of ease. Meanwhile "the Israelites groaned and cried out because of their slavery. As their cry for release went up to God, he heard their groaning and was mindful of his covenant with Abraham, Isaac and Jacob" (Exod. 2:23–24); in other words he sent a deliverer.

❃ ❃ ❃

202. Moses, the liberator of the Israelites, was, like his ancestor Abraham, a cultured wanderer. Educated in Babylonia, Abraham went out and took up a nomadic life because of a religious ideal; Moses, educated in the court of Egypt, abandoned it in protest against human injustice and found God in the desert. Both were driven to the wilderness as a result of their experiences with city life, but these experiences were invaluable to them when they came to put their social and religious plans into practice.

Moses was born of the house of Levi (§§ 210, 276) in the time of persecution. Instead of casting him into the river according to the edict, his mother hid him for three months. Then, unable to hide him any longer, she put him in a basket of papyrus smeared with asphalt, placed him in a bed of rushes alongside the river, and commanded his sister to guard him. When the daughter of the Pharaoh came down to bathe, things happened as the mother had perhaps planned, for she was probably acquainted with the habits of the princess. The basket was found, and the tenderness of the princess was aroused at the sight of the baby, evidently a Hebrew. She commanded the sister to find a nurse, and naturally the boy's mother stepped forward. Then when he had grown up she brought him to the princess, who "adopted him as her son, and called him *Mosheh;* for she said, I drew him out of the water" (Exod. 2:10).

203. This is a popular type of etymological explanation and is found elsewhere in the Bible (§§ 132, 239, 283); it derives the name Mosheh from the root of the verb *mashah*, "draw," "draw out," and the inter- pretation perhaps was also favored by the consideration that the personage was in reality "extracting" (active participle: *mosheh*) his own people from the land of servitude. Otherwise, since the name had been applied originally to the baby "drawn out" of the water, one would expect a passive form; and so Josephus favors an Egyptian etymology, affirming that "the Egyptians call water μῶ, and those saved from the water ὺσῆς" (*Antiquities,* II, 9, 6). Modern scholars generally do not accept this etymology, and prefer to trace the name to the Egyptian *m s(w)*, *mosu*, which means simply "boy," "son," and enters into the formation of proper names which are purely Egyptian (Ahmose, Thutmose, etc.).

Granted that this name demonstrates the Egyptian origin of the account, it is interesting to note that there is a somewhat similar Babylonian story concerning Sargon (Sharru-kin) of the third mil- lennium B.C. (§ 3).[3] He tells the story himself: "Sharru-kin, mighty king, king of Agade am I. My mother was a priestess;[4] I did not know my father; the brother of my father dwelt on the mountain. My city was Azupiranu, which lies on the bank of the Euphrates. My mother the priestess conceived me; she gave birth to me in secret; she placed me in a basket of reeds, and closed my door with asphalt. She abandoned me to the river which did not submerge me. The river carried me along, etc." Egyptian literature, however, has not yielded anything analogous to the story of Moses; the so-called *Tale of the Predestined Prince,* which has been considered in this connection, is not like it at all.

204. Moses remained at court for many years, perhaps forty in all (Exod. 2:23; 7:7; cf. Acts 7:23); the environment in which he lived certainly must have had a profound influence on his spiritual forma- tion, but did not make him indifferent to the lot of his fellow country- men. While he was enjoying a life of ease at court, he could not help coming into contact with Israelites in the vicinity who were being forced to make bricks and to labor at the building of Pi-Rameses (§ 200). His ears, which were habitually soothed by the skillful music of the court harpists and by the caressing voices of handmaids reading aloud their fantastic Egyptian stories, were suddenly assaulted by the cries of pain uttered by the builders, his brothers, as they were beaten by

---

[3] Cf. *ANET,* 119, for the account of the birth of Sargon of Agade.

[4] In Babylonian *enitu* (*entu*), "spouse of the god"; the Code of Hammurabi (art. 110; 127, 178 ff.; cf. also § 325), concerns itself often with this caste, which was greatly esteemed.

the Egyptian inspectors. The city that arose was indeed beautiful, but to the eyes of the reflective courtier its brick dripped blood. "On one occasion, after Moses had grown up, when he visited his kinsmen and witnessed their forced labor, he saw an Egyptian striking a Hebrew, one of his own kinsmen. Looking about and seeing no one, he slew the Egyptian and hid him in the sand" (Exod. 2, 11 f.). The deed did not pass unnoticed, and he was reproached for it by one of his fellow countrymen whom he had tried to recall to his duty. This man was probably one of those sympathetic to the Egyptian labor policy. At any rate the murder was being talked about and reached the ears of the Pharaoh. It was a serious crime to kill a public official in the discharge of his duties (he must have been an inspector of the work), and it was a greater crime in that it was perpetrated by a member of the court who had every reason to be grateful to the king. Evidently the call of blood had prevailed over his obligation of gratitude, and justice as well as prudence demanded a punishment which would be an example to others; hence the Pharaoh "sought to put him to death, but Moses fled from him and stayed in the land of Madian" (Exod. 2:15).

205. Neither this flight nor its terminus were in any way something new. The territory beyond the eastern confines of the Delta was a kind of Switzerland for the Egyptian empire, where compromised and threatened persons sought refuge. The *Tale of Sinuhe* (§§ 125, 359) states that its leading character took the same road and for the same reason; even the adventures which befell him offer some points of resemblance to those which overtook the fugitive Israelite courtier. Better documented still is the bloody magnificence of Pi-Rameses. This city is described during the Nineteenth Dynasty in a letter of the scribe Paibes as follows: ". . . I have arrived at Pi-Rameses-the-beloved-of-Amon,[5] and find that it is most excellent. A magnificent place, which has no equal; the same [god] Ra has founded it according to the plan of Thebes! To sojourn there is a benefit to life; its fields are full of every good thing; it has foodstuffs and provisions every day. Its pools are full of fish, its lagoons full of birds, its meadows green with grass . . . its fruits have the flavor of honey in the cultivated fields (?). Its granaries are full of barley and grain (§ 195); they rise up to the sky. Onions and leeks for foodstuffs (?; cf. Num. 11:5) . . . pomegranates, apples and olives and figs from the orchards. Sweet wine from Kenkeme, that is more excellent than honey. . . . the Shi-Hor[6] furnishes salt and nitrate: its boats depart and return. Foodstuffs and provisions are there every day. There one enjoys living, and no one

---

[5] The complete name of the city of Rameses.
[6] The Pelusiac branch of the Delta (§ 23).

Sinai.

exclaims there: Ah, yes![7] The lowly are treated there like the great. — Arise, let us celebrate its festivities of heaven[8] and its beginnings of summer!" The description goes on to dilate upon various pleasures of the city.

Another hieroglyphic document has an even greater topographical importance: "His Majesty has constructed a castle, 'Great-in-Victories'[9] is its name. It is situated between Palestine and Tameri[10] and is full of foodstuffs and provisions. It is like Hermonthis,[11] its duration like Hikuptah.[12] The sun[13] rises in its horizon, sets in its interior. All peoples abandon their cities and take up residence in its territory. Its west is the temple of Amon; its south a temple of Seth; Astarte is situated to its east; Uto to its north. The castle which is there is like the horizon of the sky: Rameses, the beloved of Amon, is in it as God, etc." The temple of Astarte, the Semitic divinity (§ 107), on the eastern side of the city is noteworthy; the cosmopolitan city, at the gates of Asia, had provided even worship for Asiatic visitors.[14]

206. Moses took refuge in Madian, a territory north of the Elanitic Gulf, and southeast of Palestine; it was occupied by tribes related to the Israelites by marriage (§ 139), and like true nomads they were scattered out in all directions. Moses seems to have spent much of his exile in the southeastern section of the Sinai peninsula and was received very favorably there by a chief who — like Melchisedech (§ 130) — is described as a priest. His name was Jethro (Exod. 3:1, etc.), although elsewhere he is also called Hobab (Judg. 4:11), and Raguel (Exod. 2:18: but the gloss depending on Num. 10:29 must be a mistake). Moses married Jethro's daughter, Sepphora, and she bore him a son, Gersom. Thus he spent some forty years (§§ 204, 212),

---

[7] A vague expression of some unfulfilled desire.
[8] Probably the time of the rising of Sirius (§ 27) etc.
[9] A customary epithet; *His Majesty* is Rameses II.
[10] Egypt (§ 35), here especially upper Egypt.
[11] Thebes.
[12] Memphis.
[13] Perhaps the Pharaoh who made it his residence.
[14] *ANET*, 471. Cf. Mallon, *op. cit.*, 112 ff.

during which time the Pharaoh who had sought to kill him died after a long reign (Exod. 2:23).

It was during this period that Moses one day brought Jethro's flock to pasture, leading them into the region of Mount Horeb (§ 236). There God appeared to him in a burning bush which was not consumed, and manifested His intention of sending him to liberate His people from Egypt. The apparition said to him: "I am the God of your fathers; the God of Abraham, the God of Isaac, and the God of Jacob" (Exod. 3:6).

207. As the name "God," *'Elohim,* was a generic name (§ 177), Moses, being fully aware of his own unfitness for such a great mission (Exod. 3:11) and in order to reply to the inevitable objections of his fellow countrymen (Exod. 3:13), asked the specific name of the God of the patriarchs. Among the Israelites a name was synonymous with personality (§ 147) and therefore a sort of seal or signature of authenticity. In Moses' case the name would be, as it were, proof of the genuineness of his mission. God replied, "I am who am." Then he added, "This is what you shall tell the Israelites: I am (*'Ehyeh*) sent me to you." God spoke further to Moses, "Thus shall you say to the Israelites: The LORD (*Yahweh*) the God of your fathers, the God of Abraham, the God of Isaac, the God of Jacob, has sent me to you. 'This is my name forever; this is my title for all generations'" (Exod. 3:14–15). This famous passage should be compared with another similar to it. A short time after this vision, God appeared anew to Moses and said to him: "I am the LORD. As God the Almighty I appeared to Abraham, Isaac and Jacob, but my name Lord I did not make known to them" (Exod. 6:2–3).

208. Out of reverence for the special name of their God, i.e., *Yahweh,* the Israelites did not pronounce it at all, in later times, interpreting the second commandment literally (cf. 20:7; and in the Septuagint, Lev. 24:16). When the word occurred in reading, they substituted for it the name of *'Adonai* (§ 107); as the ancient Hebrew script consisted of consonants only, the letters of the name Yahweh remained the same, forming the ineffable tetragram, *Y H W H.* When in Christian times the "points" (signs which served as vowels) were added to the consonantal text, it was not the original vowels of the tetragram which were added, but those of *'Adonai.* From this circumstance there came about, in the 15th century after (!) Christ, the custom of reading the tetragram as if it spelled *Jehovah.* That such a pronunciation is a hybrid and false and that the true one is "Yahweh," can be urged not only on grammatical grounds, but also because of the transcription 'Ιαβέ handed down to us from Theodoret (*Quaest. XV in Ex.,* in Migne, *P.G.,* 80, 244; cf. Epiphanius, *Adv. haer.,* I, 3,

40 [20], in Migne, *P.G.*, 41, 685; Clement of Alex., *Stromata*, V, 6, 34, in Migne, *P.G.*, 9, 60). The form Y H W, *Yahu*, Yaho, is encountered in the papyri of the fifth century B.C. which, beginning in 1906, have come to light in the Jewish colony of Elephantine (§ 505); it is explained as a morphological variant of the Y H W H, but it may be, as some think, even older than that.[15] It is finally interesting to note how this divine name, although enveloped in reverent ineffability, was known in the times of Augustus also by Diodorus Siculus, who speaks of it with indifference: ἱστοροῦσι . . . τοὺς νόμους . . . διδόναι . . . παρὰ δὲ τοῖς Ἰουδαίοις Μωυσῆν τον Ἰαὼ ἐπικαλούμενον θεόν (I, 94, 2).

209. The exact translation of the name is given in the first cited passage. God, speaking of himself, calls himself "I am"; men, speaking of him, call him, "He is." The two forms are respectively the first and third person of the present of the verb H W H, *hawah*, "to be," whose less ancient form is H Y H, *hayah*. Since *yahweh* could be the present not only of the simple form *qal*, "he-is," but also of the hiphil causative form "he makes to be," the name was interpreted by some as a causative form, something like "he that causes to be," "he calls into existence," and a reference to the formative or creative action of God is perceived in this signification. However, the causative form of the verb H Y H is found nowhere else in Hebrew, and the passage cited (Exod. 3:14–15) does not interpret the name as a causative form, but as a simple enunciation of a fact, "he-is"; the fact of "being" is declared proper to the God of the Israelites. Nevertheless from this idea of "being" there is not entirely excluded the other of "fulfilling," "making actual"; on the contrary it is brought out in bold relief by reason of the fact that the name to be spoken to the Israelites must be for them a proof that the God of the patriarchs will be one who fulfills his promises. In other words, just as "he-is," so indubitably "will be" his promises, because the fulfillment of these is a fact as certain as the fact that "he-is." In this way the reality of the God of the patriarchs and of his promises is quietly contrasted to the emptiness of the foreign gods and of their promises: an emptiness which the Bible hammers home in many passages.

210. The Bible's explanation of the name is not acceptable to some modern scholars for reasons which are other than philological, the objection being that it is too speculative and philosophically too elevated. They offer as a philological substitute for the verb "to be," the Arab verb *hawa*, which among other meanings has also that of "to fall (from a height)" (cf. *Koran*, 53, 1, and the Italian [*ac*]*cadere*, hence "to be"), or "to blow" (as the wind), from which is derived the substantive *hawa'*, "air," "atmosphere," "eternal space." On the

---

[15] *ANET*, 491 f., letters of the Jews in Elephantine.

slender basis of this analogy which is philologically debatable, they would conclude that Yahweh is the God who wanders about in the air, the "he-hovers" in the ethereal regions.

That God was manifested to the patriarchs only as *'El-Shaddai* (§ 177), and not as Yahweh as the other passage says, is interpreted in the light of other data offered by the Bible, such as the fact that even before the time of Moses there were among the Israelites those who bore theophoric names formed with "Yahweh." Abstracting from corrupt (*'Abhiyyah,* in 1 Para. 2:24) or doubtful texts (*'Ahiyyah,* in 1 Para. 2:25), it is certain that Moses' mother was called *Yokhebhedh,* "Yahweh is glory" (?) (Exod. 6:20; Num. 26:59); this shows that, at least in the tribe of Levi to which the woman belonged (Exod. 2:1) the name "Yahweh" was already previously known (cf. § 143).

It has been proposed by some modern scholars that "Yahweh" was the God of the Qenites, a branch of the Madianites to which the father-in-law of Moses, Jethro, belonged (Num. 10:29; Judg. 1:16; 4:11; § 276 ff.), but this has no biblical foundation. That even outside Israel theophoric names were formed with "Yahweh" has been often asserted but always later rejected; that question remains an open one still.

211. Moses was reluctant to accept the mission entrusted to him by God, either because he was conscious of his own inadequacy or because he was "slow of speech and tongue" (Exod. 4:10), but God gave him miraculous powers which were especially linked to his shepherd's staff, and designated his brother Aaron, a good speaker, to be his companion. Taking leave of Jethro, Moses then began the march toward Egypt with his wife Sepphora and his sons,[16] and with the staff of God in his hand (Exod. 4:20).

On the journey an important event took place. "On the journey, at a place where they spent the night, the Lord came upon Moses and would have killed him. But Sepphora took a piece of flint and cut off her son's foreskin and, touching his feet, she said: 'You are a spouse of blood to me.' Then God let Moses go. At that time she said: 'A spouse of blood,' in regard to the circumcision" (Exod. 4:24–26). The passage is a very difficult one. The idea that Yahweh comes to meet Moses in order to kill him is generally considered an anthropomorphism which indicated a fatal malady (§§ 256, 379, 497) for on leaving Moses, Yahweh seems to allude to his recovery. Sepphora thought that the illness was brought on by the lack of circumcision. In whom? She circumcises

---

[16] Thus the Hebrew text, using the plural; others maintain that we should read the singular, *his son,* cf. Exod. 2:22; 4:25, looking upon the plural as a later alteration due to Exod. 18:2–4 (cf. § 242).

the son, uncircumcised until then, but sees to it that the part cut off touches "his feet," surely of someone else than the son. Since the expression is a euphemism found in other passages of the Bible to indicate the genitals, there naturally comes to mind the idea that the ceremony of touching compensated in some manner for the lack of circumcision; hence "his feet" would refer to Moses, in which case even Moses would have been uncircumcised. In fact, when the ceremony was finished, he recovered. It has been supposed that the uncircumcision of Moses was due to the Egyptian persecution during which the rite would have been neglected or abandoned (§ 200); but this explanation does not seem to be well founded, since it is certain that the Israelites of the exodus were, at least in the vast majority, circumcised (Josue 5:5; § 283). The expression "bloody spouse," and the use of it made by Sepphora, seem to allude to an interpretation of circumcision as a premarital rite (§ 134). All in all the episode is far from clear.

212. Accompanied by Aaron, Moses presented himself to his fellow countrymen and was acknowledged as one sent by God especially because of his thaumaturgic power (Exod. 4:30–31). He then presented himself to the Pharaoh to ask permission in the name of Yahweh for a three-day journey into the desert to sacrifice to Yahweh. But the permission was refused and the oppression aggravated and because of this the spirit of the people began to be alienated from Moses. At this time he was eighty years old (Exod. 7:7).

After the Pharaoh's refusal Moses is presented by the Bible in the full light of his wonder-working power, which, although it was manifested throughout his whole life, reached its highest intensity in the period of the exodus. In the presence of the Pharaoh Moses cast his rod upon the ground, and it turned into a serpent; the same thing happened to the rods of the magicians of Egypt, but these serpents were swallowed up by Moses' serpent. Other punishments, the so-called Ten Plagues of Egypt, followed this remarkable demonstration (Exod. 7:14–12:36).

213. The water of the Nile was changed into blood — Egypt was invaded by frogs — by gnats — by horseflies — was laid waste by a cattle plague — by an epidemic of ulcers — by hail — by locusts — by darkness — by the death of all the first-born of men or beasts.

The first two plagues were duplicated by the magicians of Egypt, but after an unsuccessful attempt to bring about the third plague, the gnats, they exclaimed: "This is the finger of God!" (Exod. 8:15). The Bible mentions explicitly that the majority of the plagues spared the land of Gessen where the Israelites were, but it is certainly to be understood that they were spared the others also. It is not recorded, for example, that the Israelites were spared the plague of gnats, while it is foretold that they are to be spared that of the horseflies. Likewise for the majority of the plagues it is recorded that the Pharaoh promised to yield and allow the people to depart and that when the disaster ceased he hardened his heart: in other instances the promise of the Pharaoh is not mentioned, but only the hardening of his heart.

214. It has long since been emphasized that the ten plagues are similar in many respects to natural phenomena more or less frequent or typical of the Egyptian countryside. For example, the first plague is similar to the phenomenon of the "Red Nile," which is caused for the most part by the flooding of the river; because of this the waters assume a reddish-black color (§ 22), somewhat like diluted chocolate, and in a certain way can be said to resemble blood; this coloring is apparently caused by sediment from the Abyssinian lakes which is carried along by the flooding waters. However, the redness is intense only in the higher part of the river, and before it reaches the Delta the water has deposited most of its colored matter along its course; this water is not harmful to men or animals, as was that of the plague. The multiplication of frogs, gnats, and other insects is likewise usual during the floodstage; nor were contagious diseases in men or beasts unusual in a hot country, and grasshoppers are a serious disaster of all too frequent an occurrence in oriental countries (cf. Joel 1:4 ff.). Hail, on the other hand, is very rare, although not entirely unknown. The winds of the sirocco and of the "simun" (§ 67) can produce a kind of darkness, by reason of the enormous quantity of hot sand which raises to tremendous heights and which not infrequently falls on Sicily and southern Italy (according to Herodotus, III, 26, a part of the army of Cambyses was buried by this sand). The death of the first-born, however, is without a parallel in nature.

It is also certain that the Bible considers all ten plagues as miracles, for Moses controls both their beginning and their ending, and because their intensity and manner far surpass those of any similar natural phenomena.

215. The tenth plague, the most extraordinary and severe, overcame the Pharaoh. It was the month of Abib, later called Nisan, which corresponds to our March-April period. Moses, departing from the Pharaoh after he foretold the tenth plague, gave orders to his fellow countrymen that during the night between the fourteenth and fifteenth of that month every family must immolate a male lamb one year old, perfect in every respect. The victim's blood was to be sprinkled over the posts of the door of each house, and its roasted flesh eaten hastily with unleavened bread and bitter herbs. Those who ate of it were to dress and act as if they were on the point of flight. The victim and hence the rite concerned with it was called the *pesah*, "pasch," that is "pass over." That night indeed Yahweh passed through Egypt and entered into the houses of the Egyptians, killing the first-born; but the doors of the Israelites, sprinkled with the blood of the "pass over" he passed over, sparing them from the slaughter. Hence Moses gave instructions to the people with regard to future generations: "When your children ask you, 'What does this rite of yours mean,' you shall reply, 'This is the Passover sacrifice of the LORD, who passed over the houses of the Israelites in Egypt; when he struck down the Egyptians, he spared our houses'" (Exod. 12:26–27; cf. vv. 11, 12, 23).

216. There are other places in the Bible where the verb *pasah* is used in its primitive meaning of "limping," "leaping," "skipping" (§ 434), but it is easy for a secondary meaning of "pass over," "omit," to be derived from it; for example in English also the verb "to skip" [a number in a sum] is employed in that sense. This second meaning is not only clearly attested by the passages cited in *Exodus*, but is also probably found in the name of the city of *Tiphsah* (I Kings 5:4 [4:24]), the Thapsacus of the Greeks and Romans, which was the place where the armies ordinarily "passed over" the Euphrates, as did those of Cyrus the Younger (*Anabasis*, I, 4, 11), Darius and Alexander (Arrianus, II, 13; III, 7). Some philologists reject this etymology of *pesah* and others look for a different explanation of the origin of the Israelite "pasch," and they usually find it in the lunar cycle (the feast of the full moon). It is a matter of record that up to the present time nothing similar has been discovered among ancient peoples.

There is only one Babylonian text — unfortunately severely damaged and reduced to a few lines, so that the meaning and connection with the lost parts is absolutely problematical — in which a sacrificial lamb is mentioned as a substitute for a man and can be said to resemble vaguely the role of the paschal lamb which substituted among the Israelites for the first-born in the slaughter commanded by Yahweh. It must be remembered, however, that the essence of any sacrifice contains a similar idea. The text reads: "A lamb is (?) a substitute for a man. He gives [*or:* he gave?] the lamb for his life; he gives (?) the head of the lamb for the head of a man; the neck of the lamb for the neck of the man; he gives (?) the breast of the lamb for the breast of the man."[17]

217. After the slaughter of the tenth plague the Pharaoh not only permitted but ordered that the Israelites depart from Egypt that very night. This they did under the leadership of Moses and Aaron. They took with them unleavened dough because of the haste of their departure; they also took with them the mummy of Joseph (§ 164), their cattle, and many precious things which the Egyptians had given them.

---

[17] *ANET*, 331 (but not a clear reference).

The trip began from near Rameses, and the first halt was made at Sukkoth, the second at Etham "on the edge of the desert" (Exod. 13:20). Nothing is known of the location of Etham, but if Sukkoth is identified with Theku (Tell el-Maskhuta; § 195), it must be situated to the east of Sukkoth, toward the desert, and probably even farther south. The Bible records explicitly that the road taken by the Israelites was not that "of the country of the Philistines," which goes to the north and would lead directly to Canaan along the Mediterranean coast (§ 58), but was "by way of the desert road toward the Red Sea" (Exod. 13:17–18), that is, toward the south.

218. At Etham the direction of their march was changed when the Lord said to Moses: "Tell the Israelites to turn about and camp before Phi-hahiroth, between Migdol and the sea. You shall camp in front of Baal-Saphon" (Exod. 14:2). These three places were evidently close to one another, but they have not been identified. It is possible that *Migdol* ("tower") was a fort which is mentioned in Egyptian texts (*miktol*) and that it was a military post on the caravan road leading to Sinai (different from another Migdol farther to the north, below Pelusium and Lake Menzaleh, which guarded the caravan trail toward Canaan). The ruins of this southern Migdol would be found at Abu Hasan, fifteen miles north of Suez and to the south of the Bitter Lakes, that is, on the geological threshold of Shalluft which separates these lakes from the present-day tip of the Gulf of Suez.[18]

219. While the Israelites were still encamped in that locality, they were overtaken by the army of the Pharaoh, who had repented that he had allowed them to go and who had set out in pursuit with his war chariots. The sight of the Egyptian army terrified the emigrants, who began to wail and complain to Moses for having induced them to leave; Moses reassured them by reminding them of the miraculous intervention of Yahweh.

Until then, during the journey the LORD "preceded them in the daytime by means of a column of cloud to show them the way, and at night by means of a column of fire to give them light" (Exod. 13:21), but when the Egyptian army came upon the scene, the column of protection took up a position between the Israelites and the Egyptians, so that the latter could not come close to them all that night. "Then Moses stretched out his hand over the sea, and Yahweh swept the sea with a strong east wind throughout the night, and so turned it into dry land. When the water was thus divided, the Israelites marched into the midst of the sea on dry land, with the water like a wall to the right and to their left" (Exod. 14:20–22). When the night ended the

---

[18] For this southern Migdol, cf. Mallon, *op. cit.*, 169 f.

Egyptians bestirred themselves to pursue the Israelites and they also went in through the midst of the sea; but Yahweh first slowed up the pace of their chariots which moved more quickly than did men on foot, and then he ordered Moses to stretch out his hand over the sea. "So Moses stretched out his hand over the sea, and at dawn the sea flowed back to its normal depth. The Egyptians were fleeing head on toward the sea, when the Lord hurled them into its midst. As the water flowed back, it covered the chariots and the charioteers of Pharaoh's whole army which had followed the Israelites into the sea. Not a single one of them escaped . . . and Israel saw the Egyptians lying dead on the seashore" (Exod. 14:27–30).

220. Where does the Bible locate this extraordinary event? Indications of place are too scarce and uncertain (§ 193 ff.); if Migdol corresponds to Abu Hasan it is logical to hold that the crossing took place in the vicinity. It has been proved that during the Eighteenth and Nineteenth Dynasties the Red Sea extended much farther to the north than today, connecting by means of a long arm with the Bitter Lakes and, according to some, also with the Lake Timsah; this arm would have barred the way from the vicinity of Abu Hasan to the desert beyond the isthmus.

Yet that arm, generally not very deep, must have provided fords which made it possible to communicate by caravan with the region beyond the isthmus; some traces of these fords have been found. It is possible that the Israelites, bearing toward the south, had intended using one of these fords. M. Bourdon, a marine official connected for many years with the Suez Canal and an expert on places as well as documents, concluded his careful investigations of the terrain with the following words: "We are persuaded that in historical times, during the period of the Exodus to be precise, there existed between the actual basin of the [Bitter] Lakes and the tip of the Gulf of Suez a communication, precarious without a doubt, and perhaps intermittent according to the average depth of the sea — which leaves the passage of the Israelites its full miraculous character — but still sufficient to constitute an important obstacle between Egypt and the desert to the East. A crossing through this low area with its lakes, lagoons, canals, and swamps was possible only at the ford of Suez (*i.e., between Tell Qolzum and the actual Suez*) which is still used in our own day — and is the principal crossing — or across the fords of Little Bitter Lake in the vicinity of its present-day southern extremity."[19] One of the last-mentioned fords would have been at Migdol, eventually called Abu Hasan.

---

[19] The quotation is from the last page of Bourdon's article, "Note sur l'isthme de Suez" in *RB*, 1928, 232–256, with accompanying maps.

Some scholars, however, hold that the passage was across the geo-logical bridge of the Serapeum which divides the Bitter Lakes from Lake Timsah, supposing of course that the Red Sea reached up to this last lake; others, again, locate the place of passage at Suez itself. It is not necessary to dwell on the opinion of one scholar who located it to the north, toward the Mediterranean coast and south of Lake Menzaleh, claiming that the Israelites marched directly toward Canaan.

221. The miraculous character of the crossing is most clear in the Bible; a simple reading of the account dispenses from insistence on this point. However, the very nature of this ford explains the fatal mistake committed here by the Egyptians. No one would have known better than they, not only of the existence of the ford at this place, but also of the many delicate (and not always realizable) conditions of its use. It must have appeared perfectly obvious to the pursuers that favorable conditions for a crossing really existed that morning, once they saw the pursued actually advance into the ford; moreover, the east wind which had blown all during the night would have told them that the ford would be passable the next morning, for ordinarily the east wind pushes the lower waters toward the Bitter Lakes (or if one so prefers, toward Lake Timsah) and thus facilitates the passage. But what the Egyptians did not know was something they could not know, namely that this was Yahweh's wind. What happened to the Egyptian army was certainly a serious matter, but not an irreparable disaster for the armed forces of the Pharaoh. From Exod. 14:7 it is clear that the pursuing army was selected from other troops. There were "600 first-class chariots" and also *kol rekhebh Misrayim,* but this need not be taken to signify *every* chariot in Egypt; it may be correctly understood as signifying every *kind* of chariot in Egypt, of the ordinary kind, that is, as opposed to the 600 of a special type. The army engulfed by the waves must have been slightly over a thousand in all (cf. § 128). It is probable that the Pharaoh himself took part in the expedition (cf. Exod. 14:6, 8, 10), but that he also was drowned is not affirmed by the Bible, nor does it say that he entered the ford in person (Exod. 14:23, 26, 28; 15:4).

❊   ❊   ❊

222. How long did the children of Israel remain in Egypt? This question bristles with difficulties whether one follows the chronology of the Bible or tries to fit this chronology into what has been recently discovered of the history of Egypt.

First the data of the Bible. Exod. 12:40 states that "the dwelling of the Israelites during which they lived in Egypt, was 430 years." Thus the Hebrew text. Against it, however, are other weighty texts: the

Samaritan text, together with the Septuagint, followed in turn by the Itala, likewise give the identical figure of 430 years, but include in that figure the dwelling of the patriarchs in Canaan. St. Paul assigns 430 years to the period from the call of Abraham until Moses (Gal. 3:16–17). On the other hand the figure 400 appears in other places, which does not make for any discrepancy since the years are evidently expressed in round numbers (Gen. 15:13; cf. Acts 7:6; Josephus, *Antiquities*, 11, 9, 1, etc.; Philo, *Quis rerum div. haeres*, 54). However, if the data of the Samaritan text, the Septuagint, and the Itala are accepted, 215 years, representing the stay of the patriarchs in Canaan (§ 162), must be subtracted from the 430. Thus exactly half, or 215 years, remain to cover the sojourn in Egypt (cf. Josephus, *Antiquities*, II, 15, 5; Eusebius, *Chronicon, I, ad annum Abrahae*, 362, in Migne, *P.L.*, 369; see also 617). What seems to be an exact figure in reality is not so. Only the Masoretic tradition assigns all the years to the sojourn; the Alexandrian assigns only half that number. Applying this double interpretation to the conventional data of the Bible concerning the descent of Jacob into Egypt, i.e., in the year 1740 (§ 162), the following dates would result: according to the Masoretes, the exodus took place in $(1740 - 430 =)$ 1310, and according to the Alexandrians in $(1740 - 215 =)$ 1525 b.c.

223. 1 Kings 6:1 states that in the fourth year of the reign of Solomon, 480 years had elapsed since the Israelites left Egypt. Since the fourth year of Solomon is the year 970 (in round numbers, for strictly speaking it would be 969; cf. § 388), the exodus took place in $(970 + 480 =)$ 1450. But this date is not certain even if this information is followed. The better codices of the Septuagint (B and A) give the figure 440; hence the exodus occurred in $(970 + 440 =)$ 1410. The opinion of Josephus will not be discussed except to mention that perhaps from a calculation of the partial sums in the Bible for the period in question he gives the figure 592 (*Antiquities*, VII, 3, I, etc.), so that the exodus would have occurred in $(970 + 592 =)$ 1562.

Despite the conventional and elastic character of the date 1740 (§ 162), which is susceptible of modification by some decades, the dates of the exodus computed from it, 1310 and 1525, cannot be reconciled with those obtained by beginning with Solomon, that is, 1450 and 1410.

224. An even more hazardous, and less conclusive method, is to work back from 970, totaling up the partial figures which the Bible assigns to the happenings of the period between the fourth year of Solomon and the exodus. It was this method that Josephus probably used (§ 223); adding these figures gives the result he obtained, 554 years according to the Hebrew text and 588 according to the Septuagint. Even in regard to these figures difficulties arise. Either they are incomplete (the duration of certain events such as the regency of Josue and the elders, the

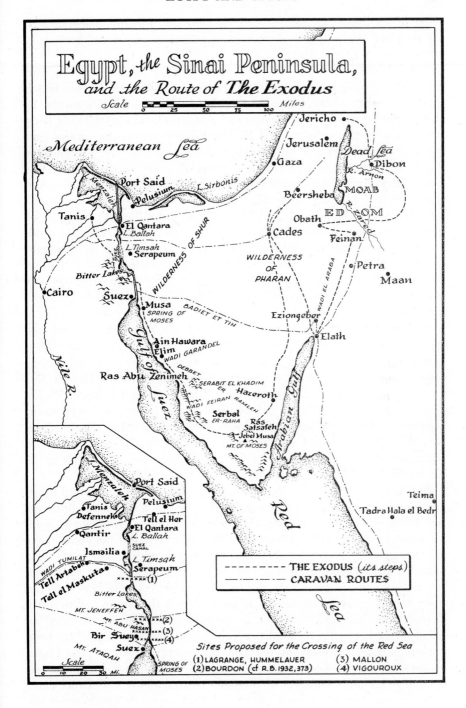

Egypt, the Sinai Peninsula, and the Route of The Exodus

Scale   Miles
0   25   50   75   100

THE EXODUS (its steps)
CARAVAN ROUTES

Sites Proposed for the Crossing of the Red Sea
(1) LAGRANGE, HUMMELAUER   (3) MALLON
(2) BOURDON (cf R.B. 1932, 373) (4) VIGOUROUX

188 THE HISTORY OF ISRAEL

reign of Saul, etc., are not given), or they are possibly too generous, for some of the judges and foreign oppressions may have been contemporaneous, at least in part.

225. Recently attention has been centered on another viewpoint. Did these figures have for ancient Israel the same mathematical value which they have for us today, or was their value only representative insofar as they might be multiples or fractions of a conventional cycle? It has been noted that in the events dated by the Bible between the exodus and Solomon, the figure 40 appears very frequently, or its multiples or fractions: Solomon and David each reign 40 years (according to Acts 13:21, Saul also), the judgeships of Eli (in the Septuagint, 20), Gedeon, Baraq-Debora, Othoniel, and the length of time spent in the desert, all lasted 40 years; the judgeship of Ehud (Aod) lasted for 80 years, that of Samson 20, the oppression of Jabin 20, and that of the Philistines 40. Hence it is thought that 40 might be a conventional term to designate the cycle of one "generation," and confirmation of this view is sought in the fact that the number 480, assigned by the Bible to the period from the exodus to Solomon (§ 223), corresponds exactly to 12 "generations" ($40 \times 12 = 480$).

Such an interpretation is questioned by others, for although the frequent use of the number 40 is a certain fact, it is also true that other numbers, in no way multiples or derivations of 40, are frequently used; for example, the 8 years of the oppression of Cushan-Rish'athayim, the 18 of Eglon, the 7 of Madian, the 18 of Ammon, the judgeship of Thola, 23 years, and of Jari, 22, etc. (§ 301 ff.). But it is not clear why these numbers should be given a plain numerical value, while the 40 alone should be a round and conventional number; on the other hand to consider them as fractions of 40 is as arbitrary an hypothesis as is the method by which such evolutions are excogitated.

226. It may therefore be rightly concluded in view of these and other considerations, that the data given by the present texts of the Bible do not provide a secure foundation for a systematic chronology, even allowing for a certain elasticity. For the most part the numbers given are of value as general and rather vague indications, and are to be taken as approximate determinations of a given period. This statement concerning chronological data in the Bible holds not only here, but for many other periods of the history of Israel. Nor is this broad and prudent distrust something modern; many centuries ago St. Jerome indicated as much when he wrote to Vitalis, a priest who had consulted him over a chronological difficulty of the Old Testament: "Read all the books of the Old or New Testament, and you will meet with a great discrepancy of years and confusion of numbers between Juda and Israel (i.e., between the two kingdoms); to spend time on such questions is an

occupation for those with leisure, but
not for scholars" (*Ad. Vit.*, ep. 71, 5;
in Migne, *P.L.*, 22, 676). The same
advice is applicable today to those
who would deal exclusively with
biblical chronology. — We now turn
to extra-biblical documents, to see if
they will help us determine this ever
fluctuating chronology with more
precision.

227. Who was the Pharaoh of the
exodus? Certainly he was not the
Pharaoh under whom Moses fled from
Egypt since this latter died after a
long reign during the time that Moses
stayed in Madian (§§ 204, 206). For
clarity's sake the preceding Pharaoh
of the long reign can be called

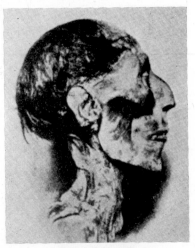

Head of the mummy of Rameses II.
(Cairo Museum.)

the "builder" Pharaoh, for the reasons already given; to call him the
"persecutor" Pharaoh would lead to confusion, since there was more
than one persecutor (§ 200), and there is no proof that the Pharaoh
under whom Moses was saved from the waters was the one under
whom he fled to Madian. Since Moses was born after the Hyksos were
expelled (§ 198) neither the builder Pharaoh nor the one of the
exodus was a Hyksos; passing over, therefore, the Seventeenth Dynasty
because it was restricted in dominion and time and entirely absorbed in
the fight for independence (§ 32), and the Twentieth Dynasty because
it was too late (§ 35), the choice lies between the Eighteenth and
Nineteenth (§ 33 ff.) dynasties.

228. Here again modern scholars are divided. Some see in Thutmose
III the builder and in Amenophis II or III the Pharaoh of the exodus;
others look upon Rameses II as the builder and on Merneptah as the
Pharaoh of the exodus. The question is highly debatable and is still open.
The choice of a solution will rest upon a mass of proof adjudged to
be strong, but not upon conclusive reasons. Today scholars incline rather
toward Rameses-Merneptah than toward Thutmose-Amenophis, for while
the chronology (§ 226) given in the text seems to favor the period of
Thutmose-Amenophis, the archaeological data seems rather to favor
the period of Rameses-Merneptah.[20]

229. Thutmose and Rameses both enjoyed long reigns. In favor of

---

[20] The latest information from Garstang's excavations at Jericho (see the note to
§ 82) would seem to favor instead, according to the opinion of the director, the
period of Thutmose-Amenophis. At the present time any judgment is premature.

Rameses is the certain fact that he was a great builder (§ 194), whereas Thutmose was continually engaged in military expeditions in Asia (§ 34), and was not much of a builder. During the reign of Thutmose (XVIII Dynasty), building activity was chiefly confined to Upper Egypt and Thebes, and the frontier-area was a military zone. Once the frontier was secure, Rameses (XIX Dynasty) saw to the building-up of the Delta. The name of the city of *Pi-Rameses*, on which the Israelites labored (§ 194), seems to point to its construction or at least its complete renovation under the Pharaoh whose name it bears.

Pharaoh Merneptah.   Pharaoh Rameses II.
      (Cairo.)   (Turin.)

It is true that even this name, strictly speaking, could be accounted for as a chronological anticipation, as in the case of the "land of Rameses" (§ 193); nevertheless, the abundance of hieroglyphic texts testifying to the name of the city (there were about forty of them until the recent discovery at Beisan of the stele of Rameses II, § 86, which likewise gives the name *Pi-Rameses*) seems to show that the "construction" typical of that locality was in the style affected by Rameses II, whose grandiose magnificence offers the better explanation for the oppressive slavery of the Israelites.

The latest archaeological researches undertaken to determine the chronology of the ruins of Jericho have as yet yielded nothing definitive (§§81, 82 note). If the famous inner wall was thrown down c. 1400 B.C., as Garstang would have it, the conquest of Josue could be assigned to that period, for it seems quite certain that the archaeological traces

of the destruction of the two parallel walls on the crest of the hill refer
to the Israelite conquest. If however this wall was destroyed shortly
before 1200 B.C. (Vincent), it would confirm the view that the Pharaoh
of the exodus was Merneptah. Between the conquest of Jericho and
the exodus there ensued, in fact, forty years in the desert. If then
Jericho fell in ± 1200, the exodus took place in 1240. As a certain
margin must be conceded these figures (cf. the remarks made about
Egyptian chronology in § 26), there would be a substantial agreement
between the date of the exodus (± 1240) and the reign of Merneptah
(± 1225–1215).

230. Prescinding from these dates and considering the general conditions of the two dynasties, it is clear that if the Eighteenth Dynasty
is favored, then the exodus occurred toward the beginning of the
el-Amarna period; but if the Nineteenth, then the exodus took place
right after Rameses II made peace with the Hittites. Now, during the
el-Amarna period the Egyptian rule was characterized by expediency,
half-hearted measures, and a temporizing attitude (§ 56 f.), and seems
to have lacked that inner firmness of administration which the policy
of persecution (of the Israelites) would demand (§ 200). Such strength
can more readily be imagined in the reign of Rameses II, who was free
from external worries about Asia by reason of his pact with the Hittites
(§ 35); he could afford to indulge his mania for building and at the
same time to aggravate the oppression of the Israelites for the political
reasons already given.

231. The famous stele of Merneptah, with its mention of "Israel"
(§ 35), calls for a very delicate interpretation, for it clearly shows
that before the last quarter of the thirteenth century B.C., there existed
an "Israel" outside of Egypt.

Where was it? That it was in Palestine is suggested by the fact that
it is mentioned immediately after places like *Canaan . . . Ascalon . . .
Gezer . . . Yanuʻam*, which are all in Palestine and well identified[21] (some
doubt existing only about the identification of Yanuʻam, which some
think is Jamnia, and others the present Tell en-Naʻameh situated in the
upper valley of the Jordan, and still others, the modern Tell en-Naʻam
more to the south), and then, as if to confirm this conclusion, a
sweeping mention of Palestine. On the other hand, in the hieroglyphic
writing of the document the names of the other Palestinian localities are
preceded by the sign which indicates "foreign nation" and likewise
by that of undulating mountains, which indicates a "foreign land"; *Israel*
is preceded only by the first sign and not by the second, which suggests
that for Merneptah it existed as a "foreign nation," but a nomadic and

---

[21] For the localization of Yanuʻam, cf. *Biblica*, 1926, 112, n. 2; *RB*, 1931, 477.

wandering one, i.e., lacking a "foreign land." From this it has been concluded that Israel, only recently gone out from Egypt, was still wandering about in the region of Sinai, before settling down in Palestine. The Pharaoh could boast of few real trophies of war, and may have added to the "foreign lands" of Palestine the "foreign nation" of Israel as well, thus making it appear that he himself had caused it to be nomadic and wandering. The phrase: *it is destroyed, it has no more seed* would be an allusion to this condition. The details served to enhance the prestige of Pharaoh himself.

Neither interpretation is certain. These last deductions would seem to demonstrate that the stele alludes to an Israel still nomadic and vagrant, and if this is true, the fact of a defeat inflicted by the Pharaoh on the greater part of the biblical Israel could be easily fitted into the biblical narrative (cf. § 263). If, however, the allusion is made to an Israel already settled in Palestine, this Israel would not necessarily be a people different from that of the descendants of Jacob, as the Bible itself allows for the possibility that even before the general exodus, some groups of the descendants of Jacob might have settled in Palestine (§ 197), where they could have multiplied as did their fellow countrymen who remained in Egypt. With the chronological uncertainty what it is, these various possibilities should not be forgotten when interpreting this famous inscription.

232. How many Israelites went out from Egypt with Moses? Our present text sets the number at (or slightly more than) 600 "thousand" men capable of bearing arms (Exod. 12:37; 38:26; Num. 1:46; 2:32; 11:21; 26:51); to these must be added not only the women, the old, and the children, expressly excluded from this counting, but also the many strangers who seized the opportunity to emigrate from Egypt (Exod. 12:38; cf. Num. 11:4; Josue 8:35). On the basis of these numbers a very modest estimate would be in the neighborhood of 2,500,000 persons, perhaps even higher.

Modern exegetes find this figure to be enormous, and it raises many difficulties of a practical order. How, for example, assemble such a multitude, and how get it across the sea in a single night? How provision the men and the cattle once they were on the other side? And Pharaoh's army (§ 221) was ridiculously tiny against such a host, etc. It is known that the Bible itself gives a much smaller figure for later times; at the taking of Jericho the number of armed men was "about forty thousand" (Josue 4:13; § 284). Forty thousand is also the total number of combatants given for the most populous tribes during the time of the Judges (Judg. 5:8). According to respectable calculations based on biblical and archaeological data, all Israel numbered less than half a million during the period of the Judges. Have we to deal here too with the phenomenon just seen in connection with the numbers of the chronology? The majority of scholars think so. As a result the number 600 "thousand" is judged to be exaggerated and is reduced in various ways. Von Hummelauer, for example, perceives in it an evident *error* and reduces it to 6 "thousands," which would yield a total of about 25,000 persons.

There are, of course, other solutions. Since the various texts are in substantial agreement as to the 600 "thousand," it has been claimed that the error is not one of transcription but rather one of interpretation. Thus the huge number would have been the result of a faulty mathematical resolution of a numerical sign which was based upon the Assyro-Babylonian sexagesimal system which proceeded as follows: 60×10; 600×6; $3,600 \times 10$; $36,000 \times 6$; etc. The number, then, would have been obtained by a triple progression along this sexagesimal scale, i.e., 36,000, which seems closer to reality (compare this with the 40,000 combatants of the time of the Judges).

Still others prefer to explain the difficulty by changing the meaning of the substantive "thousand." In the Bible the Hebrew word *'eleph* does indeed signify "thousand," but it also means a "grouping" of families or individuals in relation to a census of a people. Sometimes these groupings were described in relation to the "thousand," but often also as referring to a much smaller figure, as for example among the Romans the *centuries* contained 80, or 60, or even a lesser number of persons. If such is the case the 600 "thousand" of the exodus are really 600 "groupings," each one of a variable quantity, but altogether much less than 600,000. In consideration of another factor some scholars reduce the number of the emigrants still more; Sellin, for example, puts it around 2000.[22]

233. Modern scholars with good reason reject the account Josephus records out of Manetho (about 250 B.C.), concerning the Egyptian sojourn and the exodus of the Israelites. In an early section (*Contra Apionem*, 1, 73 ff.) the exodus is connected with the expulsion of the Hyksos; Avaris was not taken by storm by the Pharaohs of Thebes (§ 32), but ceded in treaties by the Hyksos, who retired in good order to Palestine where they founded Jerusalem. In another tract (*C. Apion.*, 1, 227 ff.), the preceding legend is intertwined with that of the "Lepers." When Amenophis was Pharaoh, Egypt was full of lepers and others with impure diseases. A priest, also named Amenophis, counseled the Pharaoh to cleanse the country. The Pharaoh then sent about 80,000 of them to work in the mines east of the Nile, but after a time he lightened their lot and permitted them to settle in Avaris, which had remained deserted after the departure of the Hyksos. There, under the

---

[22] Hummelauer, *Comm. in Numeros*, Paris, 1899, p. 225 f.; Sellin, *Geschichte*, 57.

leadership of a priest of Heliopolis named Osarsif the lepers were solidly organized and given religious laws of a monotheistic nature. The Hyksos, 200,000 strong, were invited to join them from Jerusalem, and war was begun against Amenophis, who, not being prepared for the attack, withdrew to Ethiopia. Thus the lepers and the Hyksos ruled Egypt for thirteen years, devastating the land. But then Amenophis came down from Ethiopia and drove them back into Palestine. The priest Osarsif then changed his name to Moses, by which name he was known from then onward. It is plain that such stories are but webs of fiction woven around some historical fact of Egyptian origin and others taken from the Bible. The late Alexandrian period, especially after the translation of the Septuagint had made the Bible available to Egyptian scholars, was a period favorable to the spawning of these and other legends of a more or less prejudiced nature.

* * *

234. Once the sea had been crossed, the Israelites pushed on in the direction of Sinai, beginning the wanderings in the steppe which were to last an entire generation.

The various geographical indications which the Bible gives for this period hinge on the principal question of the location of Sinai. Where was this mountain? Modern researches have done nothing about the age-old reply to this question except to place in clearer light the geographical foundations which are given either by the Bible or by ancient Jewish or Christian documents (Josephus, *Peregrinatio Silviae*, etc.).

Recently, however, the traditional answer has been supplanted by another, for reasons for the most part not geographical but suggested

Bedouin camp on the steppe. (Vester, Amer. Colony.)

by special principles which govern the different interpretations of the history of Israel. Hence it is that the locations of Sinai have multiplied to the point that there is hardly a place from southern Palestine downward where the famous mountain has not been located. One theory very much in vogue today places Sinai outside of the so-called Sinaitic peninsula and on the other side of the Elanitic Gulf, where a chain of mountains of volcanic nature is to be found. The basis for this location is, in substance, that one of the volcanoes,

Desert caravan.

then active, would have made a good background for the theophany of Sinai (§ 243) and only such a region could be the true location of Madian (§§ 206, 276).[23]

235. Tracing the itinerary of the Israelites according to the Bible and seeking as far as possible to ascertain the various stopping places, it is possible to discover the location of Sinai. Once they had crossed the sea, the Israelites pushed on into the steppe of Shur (Exod. 15:22)

---

[23] For the itinerary of the Israelites, cf. Lagrange, "L'itinéraire des Israelites du pays de Gessen aux bords du Jourdain" in *RB*, 1900, 63 ff.; *idem*, "Phounoun," *ibid.*, 1898, 112 ff. For the traditional Sinai and that territory, cf. *idem*, "Le Sinai biblique," *ibid.*, 1899, 369–392; R. Weill, *La presqu'ile du Sinai*, Paris, 1908; H. J. L. Beadnell, *The Wilderness of Sinai*, London, 1928.

Wadi Magharah. Dophqah. (Vester, Amer. Colony.)

which ran parallel to the isthmus. They descended therefore to the south, going between the Gulf of Suez and the chain of hills which flank it to the east. In this region they halted at Marah, where they found brackish water (Exod. 15:23), and then at Elim where there were 12 springs and 70 palms (Exod. 15:27; Num. 33:9). In this coastal zone even today there are more or less brackish springs, especially from 'Aiun Musa ("Springs of Moses") on down. Marah was probably farther south than 'Aiun Musa, and Elim a bit lower between 'Ain Hawarah and Wadi Gharandel. This was not a new road opened up by the Israelites on this journey, but was the route usually taken by the Egyptians to get to their important mines at Serabit el-Khadim (§§ 100, 277). Farther south of Elim, one branch of a fork in the road leads from the coast in the direction of Serabit, the other borders the Red Sea. The Israelites went along this second branch, and here must have occurred the halt beside the Red Sea (Num. 33:10). Then turning inland, they entered the desert of Sin (Exod. 16:1; Num. 33:11), and camped at Dophqah (Num. 33:12), a name in which some have thought to discern a derivation from the Egyptian *mafkat*, the name of the turquoise

'Aiun Musa ("Springs of Moses").
(Vester, Amer. Colony.)

Wadi Gharandel (Palms of Elim?).
(Vester, Amer. Colony.)

Steppe of Shur. (Vester, Amer. Colony.)

extracted by the Egyptians in these regions (Wadi Magharah, Wadi Baba, etc.), and designating at times the whole territory. Another halt was made at Alush (Num. 33:13), which is not known at all, then at Raphidim (Exod. 17:1; Num. 33:14), usually thought to be located near the present-day Feiran, whence they came out into the plains of Sinai. This is the traditional Sinai (§ 234), and it lies at the southern end of the peninsula of that name.

236. Sinai is part of the mountainous system Tur Sina. It is volcanic in nature, with its western spur culminating in Jebel Serbal (6730 feet), others to the east along the Elanitic Gulf, and a south-central group of red granite. In this latter group the following are noteworthy: Jebel Musa ("Mountain of Moses"), with a northern peak, Ras es-Safsaf (6934 feet), a southern peak (7360 feet) with the famous monastery of St. Catherine at its base, and Jebel Katerin (8548 feet) slightly more to the southwest. Jebel Serbal is joined to Jebel Musa by a plateau, er-Raha, above which Jebel Musa rises 2112 feet; this mountain is circled on the southeast by the plateau of es-Seba'iye.

In the Bible Mount Sinai is also called Horeb (§ 206). In most passages the two names are used interchangeably (except perhaps in Exod. 17:6, which may be an anticipation of the following episode of verse 8 ff.). A tradition preserved in both places, but especially in the monastery of St. Catherine, points to Horeb as the peak of Safsaf, and Sinai as the southern and higher peak. Such exactness may be suspect. Probably Horeb was the true name of the mountain, with Sinai referring either to the Steppe of Sin or even to the moon-god Sin (§§ 2,

Jebel Musa seen from Ras es-Safsaf. (Vester, Amer. Colony.)

123), who was possibly revered in the adjacent territory.

237. The region into which the Israelites entered when they departed from Egypt was a steppe, but not strictly a desert. It was not a vast expanse of sand with shifting dunes which would prevent the growth of any kind of vegetation; it was, rather, a hilly, uncultivated and uninhabited country, arid but yet not sterile, so that wherever water sprang from the earth an oasis was created, and the thirsty vegetation (grass and bushes are to be found almost everywhere in the steppe, and provide food for the flocks) was transformed into a luxuriant garden around the oasis. The oasis, or water, has always been for the nomads of the steppe the

Sinai and the Monastery of St. Catherine. (Beadnell, *Wilderness of Sinai.*)

meeting- or resting-place par excellence; the name for well (Hebrew: *be'er;* Arabic: *bi'r*) occurs most frequently in their place names.

238. At Marah the bitter water was made drinkable when Moses cast into it the stick which God pointed out to him (Exod. 15:25; see the

Jebel Serbal from the oasis of Feiran. (Beadnell, *Wilderness of Sinai.*)

Er-Raha plateau. (Vester, Amer. Colony.)

Ras es-Safsaf. (Vester, Amer. Colony.)

Sahara desert. (Wide World Photo.)

interpretation which Ecclus. 34:4–6, makes of it). After Elim, a month after the exodus from Egypt (Exod. 16:1), provisions grew short and the penury of the steppe caused the travelers to mourn the abundance of the Delta. When the grumblers among them demanded meat and bread, Moses promised them on the part of God that they should have them. "In the evening quail came up and covered the camp. In the morning a dew lay all about the camp, and when the dew evaporated, there on the surface of the desert were fine flakes like hoarfrost on the ground. On seeing it, the Israelites asked one another, "What is this?" (*man hu*) for they did not know what it was (*mah hu*). But Moses told them, "This is the bread which the Lord has given to you to eat. . . . The Israelites called this food manna (*man*)" (Exod. 16:13–15, 31).

239. This etymology of the name "manna" is probably of the customary popular type (§§ 132, 203, 283). If one were to translate it strictly, according to Hebrew grammar, the exclamation *man hu* would not make any sense. The context seems to require the question, "What is it?" but in such case the expression *mah hu* should have been used, and in fact was used farther on. It could be an Aramaic form, but this would be *măn* not *mān*, and would signify "Who [is it]?", and not "What [is it]?" Others have sought the etymology of "manna," with greater or lesser plausibility, in other than Semitic languages. The exclamation is not necessarily a strict question, but may also be merely an expression of surprise, "This thing, is it *man*?", in which case it might be pre-supposed that the Israelites already knew about *man* and its name be-

A watering-place. Palestine. (Vester, Amer. Colony.)

cause they heard it spoken of in Egypt (§ 240), and were now for the first time seeing it in reality; the uncertainty of the recognition was cause for wonder.

240. "Manna was like coriander seed and had the appearance of bdellium. When they had gone about and gathered it up, the people would grind it between millstones or pound it in a mortar, then cook it in a pot and make it into loaves which tasted like cakes made with oil. At night, when the dew fell upon the camp, the manna also fell" (Num. 11:7–9). Such was the manna according to the Bible, which reports that it was gathered during the entire wandering of the Israelites on the steppe (Exod. 16:35), and that it ceased as soon as they had eaten the produce of the Canaanite soil near Jericho (§ 283). Furthermore, what was gathered in the morning melted once the sun had arisen and the heat began. If it were kept more than a day it spoiled, so a *gomor* (about four quarts) was gathered for each one; in order to observe the following Sabbath, two *gomor* were gathered on Friday. Num. 21:5 states that in time the people became weary of the manna and despised it. Along with the manna they certainly consumed other foods furnished by the flocks or procured from the steppe (vegetables, fruits, game, etc.).

There is a tree among oriental flora which regularly produces a substance called by the Arabs *man es-sama'*, "manna of heaven"; the tree, called *tarfa*, is the *Tamarix mannifera Ehr.*, and is scattered about several regions of anterior Asia. It is particularly common along the western coast of the Sinai peninsula, where it sometimes forms forests of varying size. There are, seemingly, none of these trees on the eastern coast. Other species of trees also bear manna, but they are less widely diffused and less productive. The *Tamarix* grows up to about twenty feet in height. From its more tender branches, swollen with sap from May to August, there exudes during the night, through a puncture made in the bark by an insect, the *Gossyparia mannipara,* a few drops of a substance which, upon exposure to the air, condenses and falls to the ground. These grains are as large as a coriander seed, opalescent in color, of the consistency of virgin wax, and have a flavor reminiscent of honey. They melt on the ground under the heat of the sun and are absorbed.

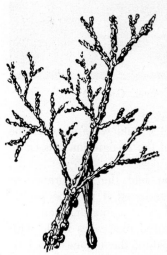

Sprig of manna.

The Arabs gather up these grains at dawn, and, after perfunctorily dusting them to free them from the twigs and dust, eat them. Manna is also sometimes harvested for export. The entire Sinai peninsula produces a very small amount of manna, however, and the yearly produce runs to about six hundred pounds. It cannot, obviously, be cooked, and its nutritional value is very low because of the lack of nitrogenous substances, but it can be preserved indefinitely.

The similarity of this botanical manna to the phenomenon described by the Bible was brought out even in ancient times (Josephus, *Antiquities,* III, 1, 6; S. Ambrose, *Epistles,* 64, 1, in Migne, *P.L.,* 16, 1271). The Bible, however, does not describe this event as something ordinary and natural; it is comparable in this regard to the ten plagues of Egypt (§ 214). The same may be said of the quail, which traverse the peninsula of Sinai in large flocks during their spring migration (it was then summer). They fly very low and alight tired out from crossing the sea (Josephus, *Antiquities,* III, 1, 5; Herodotus, II, 77).

241. Near Raphidim the water ran low and the people grumbled against Moses. At the divine command he struck the rock at Horeb (Exod. 17:6; § 236) with his rod and water gushed forth. Moses then called the name of that place *Massah,* "test," and *Meribah,* "quarrel," alluding to the behavior of the Israelites (cf. § 261).

At Raphidim also occurred the first clash of arms. The Amalecites, an Arabian tribe of the peninsula, attacked the travelers. Moses with the rod in his hand raised on high assisted in the fray from a nearby hill.

As long as he maintained this posture the battle went well for the Israelites, but when through weariness he lowered his hand the Amalecites would prevail. Moses was then made to sit down while others held up his arms, and the victory was won by Israel under the leadership of Josue.

242. There is given here an item of great importance. The Lord commanded Moses: "Write this down in a book as something to be remembered, and recite it in the ears of Josue" (Exod. 17:14). In this typically Semitic phraseology, "book" generally means any kind of "writing" to be preserved as a memorial. It could be merely a clay tablet, a strip of leather, a piece of palm bark, or something similar. It is worthy of note, however, that oral transmission of the event, as well as a written account, was prescribed; it was to be "put into the ears of Josue," so that it could be made known to others. This prescription, while it confirms the importance always attached by Semites to memory (§ 189 ff.), makes it clear that in the nomadic group of Israel there was being formed a small nucleus of documents which had a kind of official character (§ 190) and was a support to the numerous oral traditions (§ 180).

At this time Moses received a visit from his father-in-law, Jethro, who brought to him his wife Sepphora and his sons Gersom and Eliezer; of this latter son and of Moses' separation from Sepphora we have no other information. Jethro came to congratulate his son-in-law on all that Yahweh had accomplished for Israel; as a priest (§ 206), he offered a holocaust and sacrifices, sharing the sacrificial banquet with Aaron and the ancients of Israel. As one experienced in ruling he counseled Moses to appoint ancients in his stead to render judgment for the people, and then returned to Madian.

* * *

243. The third month after their departure from Egypt the Israelites arrived at Sinai and camped in front of it.

Moses commanded a preparation of three days and forbade anyone to go up the slope of the mountain under penalty of death. "On the morning of the third day there were peals of thunder and lightning, and a heavy cloud over the mountain, and a very loud trumpet blast, so that all the people in the camp trembled. But Moses led the people out of the camp to meet God, and they stationed themselves at the foot of the mountain. Mount Sinai was all wrapped in smoke, for the Lord came down upon it in fire. The smoke rose from it as though from a furnace, and the whole mountain trembled violently. The trumpet blast grew louder and louder, while Moses was speaking and God answering him with thunder. When the Lord came down to the top of Mount Sinai, he summoned Moses to the top of the mountain, and Moses went up to him" (Exod. 19:16–20). In this first theophany he received from God the Ten Commandments and a number of other prescriptions, some of them quite minute, which were augmented later on by other divine communications.

Later on the pact by which the people bound themselves to observe the law given by Yahweh was officially concluded. Moses raised up an altar at the base of the mount, and twelve *masseboth* (§§ 104, 143, 145) for the twelve tribes, and when the sacrificial victims were offered, he sprinkled part of the blood on the altar, then read the pact before the people, received their consent, and sprinkled the rest of the blood on them. He then ascended the mount with Aaron and the seventy ancients (§ 242) so that they could contemplate Yahweh.

When they returned to the camp, Moses enjoined the administration of justice upon the ancients and Aaron and Hur. Accompanied by Josue, he went back up the mountain, which was again covered by a divine cloud; into this cloud Moses entered alone. He remained on the mountain for forty days and forty nights, and during this time received from the Lord a number of prescriptions concerning worship, and also two tablets of stone on which the Decalogue was written.

244. The first nucleus of the Israelite legislation had now been formed. It was increased as time went on by the addition of other laws demanded by various circumstances and by the ever increasing organization of the nation. The fact that the legislation was drawn up on various occasions to meet different circumstances led to its lack of a comprehensive, methodical plan. As it stands now it contains many small codices and scattered laws. Additions, modernizations, adaptations, interpretations, oral and written transmissions (§ 242) are other factors which gave to the ancient Israelite legislation its present extension and disposition in the Bible. Its history is intertwined, on the one hand, with that of the nation which lived by this legislation; on the other, it overflows into the history of the writings from which the Bible was formed (§§ 109 ff., 510 ff.). It is enough for us to note that since other peoples had their own codes of law which were older than that of the Israelites, the Israelitic legislation was not, either in its material or in the disposition of that material, everywhere and in every respect original.

At this stage the new nation was indebted to Babylonia for some elements of the civilization it had received through the Terahites (§ 180). For still others it was indebted to Egypt, where the little group had remained for centuries while becoming a people. Moreover, in Egypt the descendants of the Terahites could easily have learned of the laws and customs of other peoples who had dealings with the Pharaohs; a case in point would be the Hittites, who as early as the first half of the thirteenth century had concluded an alliance with Egypt which was

The most ancient copy of the Decalogue. Nash papyrus. (First century B.C.)

reinforced by court marriages (§ 46). This dependence is confirmed by documentary evidence.

245. The Decalogue, which is presented by the Bible itself as its most ancient piece of legislation, has come down to us in two somewhat divergent forms (Exod. 20:2–17; Deut. 5:6–21; cf. Exod. 34:14–26); its briefer commands probably reflect the more ancient form, which had to be in the form of incisive precepts so as to be easily carved on two tables of stone (§ 243); the other more wordy precepts preserved the ancient substance under a form which is perhaps less ancient.

Whether the substance or the more ancient form of the Decalogue is considered, some extra-biblical documents are similar to it. Chapter 125 of the Egyptian *Book of the Dead* treats of the presentation of a dead man before the tribunal where Osiris, surrounded by forty-two gods, sits in judgment; before entering their presence the dead man makes a lengthy examination of conscience, contemplating among other things the following:

"I did not commit injustice;
I did not prey upon others;
I was not avaricious;
I did not steal;
I did not kill anyone;
I did not make the bushel smaller;
I did not commit any injustice;
I did not rob from the possessions of the temple;
I did not speak a lie. . . .
I did not dishonor [the] God. . . ."

and in another place:

"I did not kill;
I did not make anyone kill;
I did not act evilly against anyone;
I did not cut down on the oblation in the temple;
I did not damage the sacred cakes of the gods;

> I did not carry away the cakes of the dead;
> I did not commit fornication (?)
> I did not commit immodest acts [in the sanctuary of
>   the God of the city]. . . ."

Another document, this one from Babylonia, contains a ritual from Shirpu which prescribes that the following questions (among many others) be asked of the person who is to be exorcised:

> "Have you outraged a God?
>   have you despised a Goddess?
> Is your sin against your God?
>   is your misdeed against your Goddess?
> Do you have disgust for your ancestors?
>   rancor against your elder brother?
> Have you despised father or mother?
>   have you contemned your elder sister? . . .
> Have you said 'it is' instead of 'it is not'?
>   have you said 'it is not' instead of 'it is'?
> Have you spoken any impure things?
>   have you committed any inconsiderate action? . . .
> Have you penetrated into the house of your neighbor?
>   have you gone too close to your neighbor's wife?
> Have you shed the blood of your neighbor?
>   have you carried away the vesture of your neighbor? . . .
> Has your mouth been upright?
>   your heart disloyal?
> Has your mouth affirmed
>   and your heart denied? . . ."

Now the terse and incisive statements of these lists may very well have been replies to statements, equally terse and incisive, of some very famous code of laws, according to which such lists had been drawn up. In this case we would have, aside from the number of laws, a number of "decalogues" which in Egypt read:

> "Thou shalt not commit injustice;
> Thou shalt not prey upon others;
> Thou shalt not be avaricious;
> Thou shalt not steal;
> Thou shalt not kill; etc."

and in Babylonia:[24]

> "Thou shalt not outrage a God;
> Thou shalt not disdain a Goddess. . . .
> Thou shalt not disdain thy father and mother. . . .

---

[24] Text of the Egyptian document in *ANET*, 34 f.; of the Babylonian document, H. Gressmann, in *AO*, 324 f.

Thou shalt not say 'it is' instead of 'it is not.' . . .
Thou shalt not shed the blood of thy neighbor, etc."

246. A much greater number of similarities results from a comparison of the remainder of the Israelite legislation with that of the various peoples of anterior Asia. Some instances have already been pointed out in the history of the Terahites (§§ 131, 137, 139) with reference only to the Code of Hammurabi,[25] but besides this classic code, there have come down to us in various states of preservation other collections of Sumerian, Hittite, Assyrian, Neo-Babylonian laws. The abundance of material permits only a few of the more representative instances. The reference to the corresponding biblical law is given in parentheses.

Code of Hammurabi:[26] 3. "If a man in a trial has rendered false testimony, and has not proven his affirmation, if that trial is a trial involving a life, that man shall be killed." (Cf. Deut. 19:16–21.)

4. "If he has rendered testimony in a case of grain or money, he shall bear the penalty of that case." (Cf. Exod. 23:8; Deut. 16:19.)

9. "If a man, a piece of whose property has gone astray, finds the lost article in the hand of another, and the man in whose hand the lost article has been found says: A vendor sold it to me; I have bought it in the presence of witnesses! — and the owner of the lost article says: I will produce witnesses who recognize my lost article! — the buyer will produce the vendor who has sold it to him and the witnesses in whose presence he made the purchase, and the owner of the lost article (will produce) the witnesses who recognize the lost article. The judges shall examine their case; the witnesses before whom the purchase has been made and the witnesses who recognize the lost article, shall tell what they know *in the presence of God:* the vendor is a thief, he shall be killed. The owner of the lost article shall take the lost article, and the buyer shall take from the estate of the vendor the money which he has paid out." (Cf. Exod. 22:7–8, where the phrase "present oneself to

The Stele of Hammurabi (7.4 feet high). The bas-relief shows Hammurabi standing before the god Shamash. The code is inscribed on the lower section of the stele. (Louvre Museum.)

---

[25] Cf. R. de Vaux, *RB*, 1946, 328 ff.; *ANET*, 163 ff.
[26] *ANET*, 166–176; *RB*, 1901, 615; *ibid.*, 1903, 27–51.

God," *'el-ha 'elohim,* parallels the Babylonian "in the presence of God," *ina mahar ilim,* of the code.)

14. "If a man steals the young son of another, he shall be put to death." (Cf. Exod. 21:16.)

17. "If a man seizes a fugitive male or female slave in the field and brings him to his master, the owner of the slave shall pay him two sicles of silver." (Cf. Deut. 23:16 [15].)

21. "If a man breaks into a house, before the same breach he shall be put to death and buried." (Cf. Exod. 22:1–2 [2–3].)

57. "If a shepherd does not make an agreement with the owner of a field about pasturing his animals and without permission of the owner makes them feed in the field; when the owner of the field shall mow his field, the shepherd who without permission of the owner had made his animals feed upon the field, shall give over and above to the owner of the field for every *iku* (of ground; cf. note for § 184) twenty *kur* of grain." (Cf. Exod. 22:[4] 5.)

117. "If a debt has involved a man and he has sold his wife, his son and daughter for money, or has given them over to service for the debts, they shall work for three years in the house of their purchaser or temporary master, (but) in the fourth year they shall be set free." (Cf. Exod. 21:2–11; Lev. 25:39 ff.)

132. "If the finger of accusation is pointed against the wife of a man with regard to another man, and she has not been caught while lying with another man: for her husband's sake she shall be plunged into the river." (As can be gathered from other documents, especially from article 2 of this code, "plunging into the river" was the water ordeal [the medieval *ordalium,* from the Teutonic *Urteil*], a sacred ceremony by means of which a judgment of a god is provoked to decide on some particular accusations not convincingly proved. For the wife accused of adultery, cf. Num. 5:12 ff.: the law of "jealousy.")

138. "If a man wishes to divorce his wife who did not bear him children, he shall give her money to the amount of her *tirḥatum* (gift of the husband to the father-in-law) and he shall restore to her the dowry which she had brought from the house of her father and then he may divorce her." (Cf. Deut. 24:1.)

195. "If a son strikes his father, they shall cut off his hand." (Cf. Exod. 21:15, 17.)

196. "If a man ruins the eye of a free man, they shall destroy his eye." — 197. "If he breaks the bone of another, his own bone shall be broken." — 200. "If a man knocks out a tooth of another man of his own rank, they shall knock one of his teeth out." (Cf. Exod. 21:24–25; Lev. 24:20; Deut. 19:21: the "*lex talionis.*")

250. "If an ox, walking through the street, gores and kills a man, no penalty shall be incurred."

251. "If the ox of a man was a gorer and had shown that he has this vicious habit, and he has not docked its horns, or has not tethered the ox, and that ox gored and killed a free man: (the owner) shall give one-half mina of silver." (Cf. Exod. 21:28–32.)

247. Sumerian Laws:[27] D. 13. "If a second wife whom a man has married has borne him children, the dowry which she has brought from the house of her father shall be her children's. The children of the first wife and the children of the second wife shall divide the possessions of the father in equal parts." — 14. "If a man has married a wife and she has borne him children and these remain alive: and a slave also has borne children (to that man) her owner, and the father has declared the slave and her children free: the children of the slave shall not divide the house together with the children of her owner." (Note how Abraham acted in disposing of his heritage, § 139.)

248. Hittite Code:[28] 3. "If anyone strikes a free man or woman, and this person dies, (only) *his hand* doing wrong, he must take away this (cadaver), and besides must give two persons (in exchange). Thus his debt (?) will be resolved." (Cf. Exod. 21:13, where the expression *his hand* also appears as if the hand were a lethal instrument contrary to the intention of the agent; Deut. 19:4 ff.)

8. "If anyone wounds a male or female slave, or knocks out his/her teeth, he must give 10 sicles of silver. Thus will be resolved his debt (?)." (Cf. Exod. 21:27.)

10. "If anyone bewitches a man, so that he be confined to his bed and cannot work (?), he must give a man in his place, and (this latter) will work in the house of the sick man until he is well. When he recovers, he must give him 6 sicles of silver, and besides must himself pay the physician's fee." (Cf. Exod. 21:18–19.)

17. "If anyone causes a free woman to miscarry, if (it is) the tenth month, he must pay 10 sicles of silver; if it is the sixth month, he must pay 5 sicles of silver. Thus will be resolved his debt (?)."(Cf. Exod. 21:22.)

57. "If anyone steals a bull — if it is half a year old it is not a bull, if it is a yearling it is not a bull; if it is two years old, then it is a bull — formerly 30 oxen had to be given, now he must give only 15 oxen: that is, 5 two-year-olds, 5 yearlings, and 5 oxen of a half year. Thus shall be resolved his debt (?)." (The articles following consider the case of horses, rams, cows, etc.; cf. Exod. 21:37; 22:2–3.)

---

[27] *ANET*, 160, § 24 f.
[28] *Ibid.*, 189–196.

106. "If anyone makes a fire in his field and spreads it to (another) which has fruit, and burns (this) field, he who has burned it must take the burnt field for himself and give a good field to the owner of the field; he must furthermore irrigate it." (Cf. Exod. 22:5 [6].)

187. "If anyone does evil with a cow, (for) punishment, he must die. Let him be brought before the Gate (?) of the king: the king can kill him and the king can also let him live; but he must not [appeal to] come before [the person of the] king." (Cf. Exod. 22:18 [19].)

193. "If a man takes a wife and then the man dies, his brother shall take his wife, (then) his father shall take her. If in turn his father also dies, one of his brothers shall take her, whatever woman he has taken. There shall be no punishment." (Cf. Deut. 25:5–10; law of the "levirate marriage.")

194. "If a free man cohabits with a slavewoman, (whether) it be this one or that one, (there is for this) no punishment. . . ." (Cf. Exod. 21:7 ff.; Deut. 21:10 ff.; Lev. 19:20.)

195. a. "If a man has intercourse with his brother's wife while his brother is alive, (there is for this) punishment." (Cf. Lev. 18:16; 20:21.)

195. b. "If a man takes a free woman, then lies also with her daughter, (there is for this) punishment." (Cf. Lev. 18:17; 20:14.)

197. "If a man seizes a woman in the mountains, it is the man's crime and he must die; but if he seizes her in (her) house, the woman (also) has sinned, the woman must die; if the man (husband of the woman) surprises them and kills them, there is no punishment for him." — 198. "If he leads them to the Gate of the Palace and says: Let not my wife die! and spares his wife's life, he must let also the adulterer live, and shall mark his head. If he says: Let both die! then they must be punished. The king may order them killed, the king may spare their lives." (Cf. Lev. 21:10; Deut. 22:22–27.)

249. Assyrian Laws:[29] (VAT 10000). 8. "If a woman injures the testicle of a man in an argument, one of her fingers shall be cut off. If the doctor applies a binding and notwithstanding the other testicle becomes infected from her and begins to suppurate, or if she injures also the other testicle in an argument, both [her eyes?] shall be dug out." (Cf. Deut. 25:11–12.)

54. "[If a daughter of a man], a virgin, [who] dwells [in the house] of her father, is not asked (in marriage) from her (father), and is not deflowered [with vio]lence, nor betrothed, there is no legal cause against her father. (If) a man in the midst of the city or in the fields, or at night in a market-place, or in a hayloft, or during a festival of the city, has seized the virgin with violence and has lain with her, the father of the virgin shall take the wife of the man who lay with

---

[29] *Ibid.*, 181–185.

the virgin, and shall give her to be ravished. He shall not restore her to her husband; he shall take her. The father shall give his daughter to him who lay with her as in matrimony. If this man does not have a wife, he shall give triple the money of the price of the virgin to her father. He who lay with her shall espouse her, he shall not reject her. If the father is not willing, he shall receive triple the money for the virgin: he shall give his daughter to whom he pleases." (Cf. Exod. 22:15–16; Deut. 22:28–29.)

(VAT 10001). 8. "If a man changes the boundary of his field, let it be measured off, let it be certain; for all that by which he has diminished the field (of another) he shall give triple; let a finger of his be cut off, he shall be beaten with a hundred (blows of a) rod, and he shall put in a full month in the king's service." (Cf. Deut. 19:14; 27:17.)

250. Neo-Babylonian Laws.[30] 3. "[The man who has opened] his well for irrigation, (but) has not strengthened its cover (?) and has caused an overflow (?), and has put [under water] the field of his [neigh]bors, he shall give grain [to his neighbors] (according to the ordinary yield of the) neighbors." (Cf. Exod. 21:33–34.)

251. Intertwined with its social prescriptions, the Israelite legislation contains many others of a religious and liturgical nature. The collection contained in Exod. 25–31 illustrates this, as it gives instructions for the construction of the entire portable sanctuary, that is, the Ark, the table, the lampstand, the Tabernacle or sacred tent, the altar, the vestments, and also with regard to the person of the priests, and the like.

Even with regard to the liturgy of ancient Israel modern discoveries have brought new light, and — abstracting from the religious idea underlying the various rites — have revealed in the ritual of other more ancient peoples a large number of similarities, now described in the various manuals of archaeology. The internal divisions of the Tabernacle and of the surrounding area, and also the disposition of the liturgical furnishings, is substantially that of the Temple of Solomon (§ 391 ff.). A brief pause here to consider the most sacred and ancient object of the religion of Israel: the Ark.

252. The essentially amorphous character of Yahwistic cult did not allow it to revolve around any "sacred" object as was customary in other religions, that is, any sculptured or symbolic representation of the Divinity, such as an idol. Instead, it centered about a sacred location; in lieu of a divine object, it had a divine place, namely, the Ark of the Covenant or of the pact.

The Ark was the "footstool" of the invisible Yahweh (1 Para. 28:2; Ps. 99:5; 132:7); upon it and exactly between the two cherubim of

---

[30] *Ibid.,* 197.

the propitiatory, he was "seated" (1 Sam. 4:4; 2 Sam. 6:2); there he appeared (Lev. 16:2) and spoke to Moses (Exod. 25:22; Num. 7:89) and to other chosen ones.

The Hebrew *'aron* means "ark" or "chest," even in a profane sense. The sacred Ark was really a little chest, 2½ cubits long and 1½ cubits high; if, as is more probable, the lesser cubit was used (18 inches),

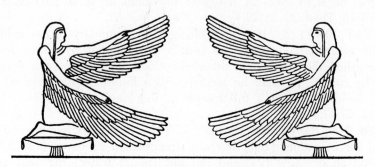

Cherubim of the Zodiac of Dendera. (Didelius, *Die Lade Jahves.*)

it was about 45 inches long and 27 inches wide. Inside and out it was overlaid with pure gold. All around the top was a border of gold in the form of a garland, and at the four feet were four rings through which two poles passed for carrying. On the top, probably imbedded in the garland, rested the "propitiatory," which seems to have been simply a plate of pure gold. It was the *kapporeth,* usually translated by the Septuagint as ἱλαστήριον (Vulgate, *propitiatorium*), although Philo, Josephus, and sometimes the Septuagint also use it in conjunction with ἐπίθεμα, "covering."

To the two sides of the propitiatory and joined to it were two figures of cherubim, likewise of gold; they were turned one toward the other, their wings fully extended and shading the propitiatory, their faces bent toward it. Whether these cherubim were of human, animal, or mixed form is not stated; some modern scholars claim they were of animal form, because of analogous figures of Babylonian cherubim (bull, lion, etc.; cf. Ezech. 1:5 ff.; 10:15, 20; etc.). Others, on the contrary, recalling similar Egyptian figures, suppose them to have been of human form. At any rate, these two were the only sculptured images lawfully admitted in the cult of Israel.

The interior of the Ark was hollow, but not entirely empty. "There was nothing else in the Ark but the two tables of stone which Moses put there at Horeb, the tables of the pact[31] which Yahweh made

---

[31] The words: *the tables of the pact* are lacking in the Hebrew but should be inserted according to the Septuagint.

Egyptian priests carrying the sacred barque.

with the Israelites, when they went out from the land of Egypt"
(1 Kings 8:9).

253. This reference to an historical fact provides us with the key
to the symbolism of the Ark. In fact, at the time of the exodus there
was a custom of placing in the temples under the feet of the statue
of the divinity, the texts of the pacts of alliance made between kings
or nations, as if thereby the god was made the guarantor or witness
of the bilateral contract; a treaty of Rameses II (§ 35) with the
Hittites has an express codicil to this effect. The custom, therefore,
is reflected in the symbolism of the Ark: Yahweh was "seated" on
the cherubim of the propitiatory; under his feet, within the Ark,
had been placed the text of that pact by which he made an alliance
with the nation of Israel. Hence the name, Ark of the pact or of the
alliance (§§ 243, 274) was entirely fitting.

Objects of cult similar to the Ark are known to have been used by the
Babylonians and the Egyptians. The Babylonian ark does not resemble
it much, since its form was rather a kind of seat or throne.
The Egyptian ark had a much greater resemblance: it consisted of a
coffer or small temple (ναός), of about the same dimensions as the
Israelite ark, containing inside some statue or sacred object, and with
figures on the outside of genii with spread wings; it too was carried
by means of poles in procession by the priests, as the Israelite ark
was borne by the Levites (Deut. 31:9, 25). It was not, however,

ordinarily placed directly on the poles, but on the sacred barque or *bari* which served as a sort of sedan.

254. During the long stay of Moses on the mountain (§ 243) the first defection of the people took place. Aaron was persuaded to fashion, out of feminine ornaments offered for that purpose, a calf of gold which was to be "their God" who brought them out of Egypt (Exod. 32:4). The invisible and immaterial "He-is" (§ 207) was too transcendent for people who in Egypt had witnessed the pompous ceremonial which surrounded the sacred bull Apis, and who also must have known of the Canaanite statues representing the divinity under the form of a bull (§ 106). The people did not understand why they could not represent "He-is" under the form of a bull, a form striking in its power. The bull, or calf, was fashioned, and Aaron constructed an altar before it; sacrifices were offered, and the people danced in its presence.

Moses, descending with Josue from the mountain, heard the noise and took in the scene. Filled with anger, he broke the two tablets of the law and destroyed the calf, and having the Levites on his side he effected a slaughter through them among the people; about three thousand people were slain. Moses then interceded for the people before God, went back up Sinai and was given new tablets of the Law.

255. The Israelites remained at the foot of Sinai for almost a year (cf. Exod. 19:1, with Num. 10:11). When the portable sanctuary and its fittings were ready, it was set up on the first day of the first month of the second year after the exodus from Egypt (Exod. 40:17); the pasch was celebrated in the same month (Num. 9:4 ff.), and after another month had passed, the people again set forth on their journey (Num. 10:11 ff.), this time leaving Sinai behind them.

❊ ❊ ❊

256. On leaving Sinai the Israelites headed for Canaan (Num. 10:29), intending to pass through Cades, which is about fifty miles south of Beersheba (§ 59); from Sinai to Cades it was an eleven day trip (Deut. 1:2). They therefore moved northward in the direction of the desert of Pharan, now called *Badiet et-Tih,* the "desert of solitude," whose northern part was also called, it seems, the desert of Zin (Vulgate, *Sin*). They skirted the eastern edge of this desert region, bearing toward the Elanitic Gulf.

A halt was made at Taberah, "burning" (Vulgate, *Incensio*), so called because the wrath of the Lord blazed up there against the people who were grumbling about the inconveniences of the journey; part of their camp was destroyed. Another halt was made at Qibhroth-hatta'awah, "graves of greed," and this name too evokes the memory of a particular event. Tired of the manna, the people petulantly cried out for meat, and there occurred another extraordinary flight of quail (§ 240), the time being once more the spring of the year. Greedily they gathered up large numbers of them, putting the meat out to dry. And then "the LORD's wrath flared up against the people, and he struck them with a very great plague" (Num. 11:33). This is another way of saying (§§ 211, 379, 497) that their gluttony led to a fatal epidemic which gave this place its name. The incident may have occurred at what is now Erweis el-Ebeirig. In that place also Moses chose seventy ancients to share with him the government of the people and as the spirit came to rest on them, they prophesied (§ 420). Another halt was made at Haseroth, perhaps modern 'Ain Huderah, somewhat toward the Elanitic Gulf. Here the jealousy felt toward Moses by Aaron and Miriam, Moses' sister, because of Moses' wife, occasioned the striking punishment of the sister and a confirmation of Moses' leadership. After Haseroth, Cades.[32]

257. The halts we have mentioned were in all probability only the more noteworthy ones; the list given in Num. 33 contains about the same number. The list is probably mnemonic, for between the point of departure, Rameses, and the last mentioned, that of the Steppe of Moab, exactly forty stops are enumerated, corresponding to forty years in the entire journey. The figure in both cases could be merely a conventional one (§ 225) and hence only an approximation. The connection between this list and other data in the Bible is very difficult to establish.

Cades, or Cades Barne (Qadesh Barne'a), is most likely the present-day 'Ain Qedeis, where, as the name indicates, water is to be found. It seems that in ancient times there were three springs there, although at some distance apart. Its proximity to Beersheba (§ 256) made Cades an opportune place to prepare for the invasion of Canaan; hence the Israelites stopped there for the first time as they came from Sinai (Deut. 1:19; Num. 32:8). Other biblical data create difficulties, e.g., designating the stay of the Israelites in Cades as having occurred in the desert of Pharan (Num. 13:1.4) or in the desert of Zin (33:36). It may be that a generic designation was employed, insofar as Cades was more or less between Pharan and Zin (Num. 13:27; 21:1; 27:14; Deut. 32:51; 33:2). In treating of desert regions and nearby places (§ 256) it is not surprising to find that place names vary; nor was the generic designation unfounded. At any rate, the different terminology is a proof of the variety of documents used in the biblical narrative.[33]

258. From Cades Moses sent out spies to reconnoiter the land of

---

[32] For a description of this area, cf. C. L. Woolley and T. L. Lawrence, *Wilderness of Zin* (Palestine Explor. Fund, Annual), London, 1914.
[33] On Cades, cf. *RB*, 1922, 55–81.

Canaan, and this shows his intention of beginning the campaign of conquest not far from there (Num. 13:2 ff.). The spies went up the desert of Zin and then the Negeb (Num. 13:21–22; § 65), then went through Palestine up to the "entrance of Emath" (§ 60), and returned after forty days with a glowing report of its fertility, and bearing with them as proof some of its unusual fruits. But what they said of the strength of the inhabitants and the fortified condition of their cities (§ 101) was conducive of fear.

When it treats of the inhabitants of Canaan, the Bible here and there employs various names: Canaanites (§ 52), Amorrites (§ 47), Jebusites (§ 96), Amalecites (§ 241), Hevites, Perezites (§ 148), Gergasites, Qenites (§ 210), and Qenizites (§ 291). Besides races of "Giants," the *Nephilim*, it mentions other strange names such as the 'Anaqim ("those of the [extended]? neck"), the (Zuzim) Zamzummin (the "Mumblers"?), the Emim (the "Terrible"?), the Rephaim (the "Specters"?). Of the peoples designated by these names practically none are known except the first. Some must have lived in the adjacent regions rather than in Canaan itself. In the races of "Giants" can be seen perhaps traces of ancient pre-Semitic ethnic elements, now disappearing, a people of a larger stature than was then usual. It is certain that in this regard fantastic exaggerations were bound to circulate, just as the description which the returning scouts from Canaan gave were bound to be colored by their motives: "All the people we saw there are huge men, veritable giants (the 'Anaqim [Enacim] were a race of giants [Nephilim]); we felt like mere grasshoppers, and so we must have seemed to them" (Num. 13:32–33). This description is in the same category as the other given by these same scouts, according to whom the walls of the Canaanite cities reached "to the sky" (Deut. 1:28).

259. The effect of such talk was immediate. Appalled by the difficulty of conquering the promised land, the people rose up against Moses, the deceiver who had misled them. In vain did Josue and Caleb, themselves members of the patrol, protest against the exaggerations of their companions; the people threatened to stone Moses and wanted to return under another leader to Egypt. At this the Lord, angry, threatened to destroy the people, but he was placated by Moses. As a punishment, however, all the spies with the exception of Josue and Caleb were to die, and all the people over twenty years of age, Josue and Caleb again excepted, were to be excluded from entering into the promised land, and were condemned to wander for forty years in the desert until the last of this insolent generation had died (§ 271). Slightly more than a year had passed since their exodus, and entry into Canaan was set back for more than thirty-eight years. By this peremptory divine com-

Tip of the Elanitic Gulf. (Hyamson, *Palestine old and new.*)

mand the direction of march was reversed, and they were obliged to head back toward the sea.

Presumption, however, was to teach them a lesson. The very next morning many of them (if not all) set out with warlike intent to take Canaan. But the Amalecites and Canaanites met and defeated them, driving them back as far as Sephath (later called Horma), which is perhaps the present town of Sebaita, about twenty-five miles north of Cades. From here they returned to Cades, from which neither Moses nor the Ark had moved.

260. Now the wandering began, and this time it was a kind of punishment. Moving to the south, the Israelites made a number of stops which are listed in Num. 33:19–35, going from near Cades to Ezion-geber on the tip of the Elanitic Gulf. Num. 33:36 mentions a stay at Cades after Ezion-geber, but the order is inverted in Deut. 1:46, 2:8. There were probably two stops at Cades, one of several months' duration at the end of the Sinai-Cades trip (Num. 13:27); the other occurring after the trip to Ezion-geber and before they succeeded in penetrating into Canaan (Num. 20:14, 22); this latter stay would be the one which lasted for many years (Deut. 1:46) until the condemned generation disappeared. Probably during this second stop Cades became something of a center, from which the nomadic Israelites would periodically sally forth in search of pasturage and other necessities.

The "Cades period" however seems jealously to guard a secret. The connection of the sources which allude to it is perplexing, and, as a whole, they suggest an intentional incompleteness which invites a closer scrutiny.

Although it is not known where it took place, the rebellion of Core certainly occurred during this period, but it was rather an isolated incident. Core, a Levite, rebelled with Dathan, Abiram (= Abraham; § 132), and other followers, against the monarchical rule of Moses and the sacerdotal prerogatives of Aaron; but Yahweh miraculously confirmed these two in their supremacy, and destroyed the revolters. As an affirmation of principle, the rebellion did not then have any aftermath, except that the next day the people manifested its disapproval of the divine punishment meted out on the rebels, and was punished by a plague. This scourge was checked thanks to the intercession of Moses and Aaron. At Cades, however, something happened which had more profound and lasting results than the rebellion of Core.

261. "The whole Israelite community arrived in the desert of Zin in the first month, and the people settled at Cades. It was here that Mariam died and here that she was buried" (Num. 20:1). In this account mention is made of the "first month" but not of the year, and it is very difficult to see how this could have been the fortieth year, for the remainder of the account presupposes events for which time could not then be found before the definitive advance toward Canaan. It may perhaps have been the third year after the exodus, antecedently named the second at the foot of Sinai (Num. 10:11). If, however, the present text be taken as an isolated one, there is no need for continuity in the events related, and the text could take for granted other happenings such as the move upon Ezion-geber and also the rebellion of Core. It is then possible and perhaps more probable also that the reference is to the first month of a year, following at no great interval the third year after the exodus.

It was in this undetermined year that the people complained against Moses and Aaron because of the lack of water, and voiced the usual regrets for the comforts of Egypt. Moses and Aaron turned to the Lord, who commanded Moses to take up his wonderworking rod, assemble the people, and speak before them in front of the rock which would gush forth water. When the multitude was assembled Moses spoke: "Listen to me, you rebels! Are we to bring water for you out of this rock? Then raising his hand, Moses struck the rock twice with his staff, and water gushed out in abundance for the community and their livestock to drink" (Num. 20:10–11). Up to this point there is nothing strange on the part of Moses the wonderworker, who in his brief address evidently wishes to prepare the rebellious multitude properly to appreciate the miracle he is about to work. The strange part follows at once: the Lord reproved the brothers because they "were not faithful" to him in showing forth his sanctity before the Israelites (Num. 20:12), and because of this they were denied the honor of leading Israel into the promised land. The text ends by saying that the place was "the waters of *Meribah*" ("*contest*," cf. § 241), for the Israelites contended with the Lord where he "revealed his sanctity among them" (Num. 20:13). The gravity of the punishment inflicted on the two presupposes a proportionate fault. Wherein lay the fault of Moses and Aaron? Is it to be sought in this miracle, because Moses struck the rock twice instead of only once, or did he in his brief address manifest some skepticism, etc.? The accusation "of not having had faith" in Yahweh is reasserted and emphasized later by Yahweh himself, when he reproves Moses and Aaron for "having been rebellious" to his orders at *Meribah* (Num. 20:24; cf. 27:14; Deut. 32:51). Such grave accusations are certainly not justified by two blows on the rock nor by Moses' words. There must rather have been some scandalous incident known to all which involved the great law-giver of Israel; later, out of reverence for Moses, a veil of silence began to be drawn over it (cf. Ps. 106[105]:32–33). The same idea may lie behind the omission of that painful passage in later redactions of the documents, which thus acquired their present edifying tone (§ 260).

262. How were the forty years in the desert spent? For a little more than a year — until the first stop at Cades — many details are given. From Cades on, more than thirty-eight years passed concerning which, except for the episodes of Core and Meribah, there are no details at all. A veil covers the period of Cades. Nevertheless, a glance through this veil is possible, thanks to Amos (Amos 5:25–26; repeated in Acts 7:42–43), who reproves the Israelites for not having offered sacrifices and oblations to Yahweh for forty years in the desert and for having served idols. Perhaps some apostasy from Yahweh and from Moses took place then? The precise and unequivocal words of Amos would be a surprising removal of the pious veil cast over this period, the purpose of which was to hide the opprobrium of the nation of Yahweh. The fact that for forty years circumcision, the fundamental rite of Yahwism, practiced by the old generation in Egypt (Josue 5:4–7; §§ 211, 283), was not practiced on the new generation suggests a serious apostasy. An echo of this apostasy can perhaps also be discerned in a remark in the Jerus. Talmud, *Taanith*, III, 4 (ed. Schwab, Paris, 1883, t. vi, p. 168; cf. *Baba Bathra*, 121 b) according to which the people of Israel, excommunicated as it were, did not speak to Moses during those thirty-eight years.

263. At any rate, is there not perhaps some connection between the "fault" of Moses veiled through reverence, and the apostasy of Israel veiled out of piety? Nothing certain can be said about what constituted that "fault"; but the pious reserve which covers both it and the apostasy of Israel give rise to a legitimate suspicion that the first was — not the direct cause exactly — but an occasion or the provocation of the second. Meribah indeed is the place of the "fault" not only of Moses (Num. 20:24; Ps. 106:33) but also of the people (Ps. 106:32; 81[80]:8). From the praises which are accorded the descendants of Levi in Deut. 33:8–10, Hummelauer argues that the Levites were the only ones faithful to Moses during the general apostasy.[34]

Meribah is to be located with certainty in the region of Cades (Num. 27:14; Deut. 32:51); it was probably one of the three springs there (§ 257). It was here, then, that there began the split-up of the people which would last for thirty or thirty-five years. When and why the "apostates" rejoined the tiny group which had remained faithful to Moses, cannot be even vaguely determined, but it may have taken place some years before the definitive march on Canaan. It is perfectly possible that, following on bitter disillusionment, the reconciliation was also due to a crippling defeat inflicted upon the wanderers toward the west by Merneptah, which might fit in with one of the interpretations already given to the stele of that Pharaoh (§ 231).

The reorganization of the group on the basis of Yahwistic legislation must have been begun at Cades after the reunion. This may have required several years, and during this time the old and obstinate generation continued to die off. Toward the fortieth year from the exodus the advance from Cades on Canaan was begun, and this time it was definitive.

Mount Hor. (Vester, Amer. Colony.)

*   *   *

264. From Cades, Moses sent ambassadors to the king of Edom, asking free passage through his territory. This being refused, and not wishing to come to grips with the descendants of Esau (§§ 140, 151), he decided to go southward again toward the

---

[34] Cf. Hummelauer, *op. cit.*, 168 ff.

Steppe of Moab.

Elanitic Gulf and then to ascend farther eastward, giving Edom a wide berth. However, either because the people were so sure of obtaining passage that they had already proceeded northward, or because they were attacked as invaders, they were obliged to fight in the Negeb with the Canaanite king of Arad, and the Israelites were victorious.

Not far from Cades they reached Mount Hor (probably Jebel Madurah), where Aaron died at the age of one hundred and twenty-three. It was the first day of the fifth month of the fortieth year after the exodus (Num. 33:38 f.). Going down then along the mountains of Seir along the Araba (§ 61), they went up it more to the east, stopping

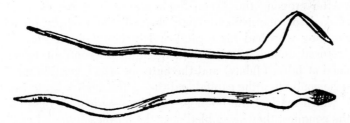

Bronze serpent found at Gezer. (Macalister, *Excavation of Gezer.*)

at Salmona, Phunon (Khirbet-Feinan), Oboth, Iyye-Abarim, all in eastern Edom. Then, skirting the southeastern extremity of the Dead Sea, they crossed a wadi north of Wadi el-Hesa called Zared, and reached the Arnon (§ 66), the torrent dividing the land of Moab from the region to the north, which was occupied by the Amorrites (§ 47 ff.) but still retained its ancient name of the "steppe of Moab."

265. This march must have lasted a few months, and yet the only event reported in the Bible is that of the "fiery serpents." When the Israelites had departed from Mount Hor, they again began to complain about traveling in the desert and the wretched food, and the Lord sent among the people fiery serpents which by their bite, probably, produced a high fever and often death. At Moses' intercession Yahweh provided the remedy: "Moses made a bronze serpent and mounted it on a pole, and

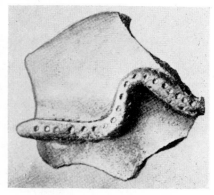

Figure of a serpent on a ceramic fragment of Teleilat Ghassul. (*Biblica*, 1930.)

whenever anyone who had been bitten by a serpent looked at the bronze serpent, he recovered" (Num. 21:9). The context does not mention the symbolism of this serpent, but in this connection there come spontaneously to mind various Palestinian artifacts, especially the many ex-voto objects adorned with the figure of a symbolical serpent found in the excavations of Beisan, and the important bronze serpent found at Gezer (§ 106): this amulet or ex-voto pertaining to the Israelite epoch (about 1000 B.C.) is six and three quarters inches long and very similar to another, nine and three quarters inches long, found at Susa. In Ezechias' lifetime (§ 481), the Israelites (§ 48) were reported to have worshiped the serpent made by Moses.

266. After crossing the Arnon the conquest by force of arms began. Moses asked for permission to pass through the territory of Sehon, an Amorrite king who had his capital at Hesebon (present-day Hesban). Sehon refused and descended with his army to confront Israel. Battle was joined at Jahsa (Jahas) and the outcome was favorable for the Israelites, who conquered the capital and the entire country up to the Jabbok (§ 66), which marked the boundary of the kingdom of Basan above it. After the conquest they assembled near the northeastern end of the Dead Sea, on the plains of Phasga between the Abarim mountains and in front of Nebo (Jebel Neba). From here they went out against Og, king of Basan; they defeated him at Edrei and conquered the country. In this manner the Israelites became masters of Transjordan from the Arnon to Hermon (§ 59). Then, awaiting a propitious moment for penetrating into Canaan itself, "they encamped in the plains of Moab on the other side of the Jericho stretch of the Jordan" (Num. 22:1).[35]

---

[35] For a description of the region north and east of the Dead Sea, cf. *RB*, 1931, 214 ff.; cf. N. Glueck, *The Other Side of the Jordan.*

267. The victory gave the Israelites the ancient territories of Moab, which had been previously conquered from the Amorrites (Num. 21:26), and made them neighbors to the tribes of Madianites who had pushed toward the north from their southern center (§ 206). The successes of the newcomers alarmed Balac king of Moab. With the approval of the "elders of Madian" (Num. 22:4), that is, the heads of the allied tribes, he decided to resort to magic to avert the danger against which his arms gave him little encouragement. The means chosen were not considered inadequate in those times, when the occult arts were very often closely connected with religion, and magic, whether in Egypt or Babylonia or in the intermediate provinces, occupied a prominent place in social life. Balac called upon a soothsayer named Balaam.

268. The story of Balaam is typical of the actual ethnic background of Israel. The poems preserved in it are also literary documents of the first order and had a long life on the lips of the people, who, when they recited or sang them, intended to exalt the deeds of Yahweh, God of Israel, whose great power was recognized even by foreign nations.

According to Josue 13:22, Balaam was a *qosem*, a word which always has an evil connotation in the Bible, meaning a "dealer in spells," "magician," or "soothsayer," almost invariably a foreigner. Balac sent messengers to "Balaam, son of Beor, at Pethor on the Euphrates, in the land of the nation of his people, summoning him with these words: 'A people has come here from Egypt who now cover the face of the earth and are

The site of ancient Hesebon. (Vester, Amer. Colony.)

settling down opposite us! Please come and curse this people for us; they are stronger than we are. We may then be able to defeat them and drive them out of the country. For I know that whoever you bless is blessed, and whoever you curse is cursed'" (Num. 22:5–6).

Pethor, the city of Balaam, seems to correspond to the *Pitru* of the Assyrian documents (Salmanassar II) and to the *Pedru* of the Egyptian documents (Thutmose III). It stood on the right bank of the "River," that is, the

Euphrates; in fact Deut. 23:5 (Hebrew) specifies that Pethor was in "Aram of the Two Rivers" (§ 51). That would make Balaam an Aramean, and Balac sends to call him from such a distance because he is in the land "of the nation of his people," that is, of his fellow countrymen, and thus he is also an Aramean. Some Hebrew manuscripts and ancient versions, among which is the Vulgate, instead of "his people" ('ammo), read ('ammon) the people of the Ammonites bordering on the kingdom of Balac, in which case Balaam would be an Ammonite.[36]

269. The first attempt to procure him was not successful, for Balaam consulted Yahweh at nighttime (it is remarkable that this foreigner is acquainted with the God of Israel) and was forbidden to depart. Another delegation was sent and this time Yahweh permitted the soothsayer to go, provided that he will do what he is commanded. Balaam saddled his ass, a noble mount in the east, and set off. However, along the road, "the anger of God flared up at him for going, and the angel of the LORD stationed himself on the road to hinder him" (Num. 22:22). The reason for this anger, after the granting of permission, is not explained by the text; the narration perhaps utilizes two documents from one of which the verses giving the reason have dropped out. When the ass saw the angel it became frightened and turned off through the fields. Balaam had not yet noticed the angel, and so struck his steed with a will, but in vain, because the angel stood always in front of it. Then "Yahweh opened the mouth of the ass," which began to speak, and bewail such treatment. Balaam, not at all surprised at the beast's speaking, gave answer to him. Only after some time did Yahweh open the eyes of Balaam so that he could see the angel. The discussion with the angel ended with permission to continue the journey.

When Balaam reached the end of his journey, he was made to ascend successively three heights from which could be perceived in the distance the camp of the Israelites: Bamoth-Baal, the field of Sophim, and Mount Phegor, all three in the environs of Phasga (§ 266). In each place he commanded that seven altars for the immolation of victims be built, and in his mantic state, he each time pronounced not a curse but a blessing on Israel. To the remonstrances of the king he replied that Yahweh had put in his mouth the prophecy of benediction. After the third prophecy, the king requested Balaam to leave. Before doing so he spontaneously pronounced a fourth prophecy, foretelling the humiliation which, at a future time, the peoples of Moab, Edom, Amalec, and the Qenites, and finally even Assyria and the peoples beyond the Euphrates, would undergo because of Israel. After this Balaam departed and returned to his own region (Num. 24:25).

---

[36] E. F. Sutcliff, "De unitate litteraria Num. XXII" in *Biblica*, 1926, 3–39.

270. We have, however, a better picture of Balaam from documents which concern the later history of Israel. At Shittim, in the environs of the camp of the nation of Yahweh, perfumes of the incense of Canaanite cults scented the air. Not only incense, but women skilled in seduction were also there (§ 108). The name of one of the heights of Balaam, Bamoth-Baal, is eloquent in itself (Bamoth, § 104; Baal, § 107); near another of those heights, Phegor, there must have been a sanctuary especially dedicated to the Ba'al of the place, the Baal-Phegor, represented no doubt in phallic form (§ 104). Thus it came about that "the people degraded themselves by having illicit relations with the Moabite women. These then invited the people to the sacrifices of their god, and the people ate of the sacrifices and worshiped their God" (Num. 25:1). With the Moabites were also the Madianites, the two races being allied (§ 267). Once a sacred Madianite prostitute of noble family (as they often were in Babylonia) was brought by an Israelite, Zamri, into the camp itself, under the very eyes of Moses, but a zealous Yahwist, Pinehas (Phinees; § 293; cf. § 340), transfixed them both *in flagranti delicto* with a thrust of his lance, thus executing the order of Yahweh who, after the first disorders, had decreed death for scandalous conduct and had sent a plague among the people. The scourge ceased after the action of Pinehas, but Moses proclaimed war also against the Madianites.

The report of this war (Num. 31) states that it was Balaam who had counseled the Madianites to seduce the Israelites to licentious worship (31:16) and that the soothsayer himself was killed in that war (31:8). The presence of Balaam among the Madianites is not clear. It is pure conjecture to say that on his journey home he stopped with some of them who were his friends. Others think that here are two independent traditions whose harmonization is not clearly evident in the texts. His evil counsel is readily explained, for despite the prophecies of blessing which he was forced to give, this foreign soothsayer was always opposed to Israel.

271. The war against the Madianites was a holy war, conducted according to the principles of a war of extermination. It yielded much booty; among the prisoners only the children and virgins were spared. In a word, it was the classical *herem*,[37] codified in Deut. 7:2; 20:14.

Shortly before this war a new census of the people had been made: the members of the old generation were all dead except Josue and Caleb (§ 259; Num. 26:65). The total number 601,730 was slightly lower than at the time of the exodus (Num. 1:46; for the value of these figures, cf. § 232).

---

[37] For a discussion of the *herem,* cf. A. Fernandez, "El herem biblico" in *Biblica,* 1924, 3–25.

272. The conquest was of considerable extent and provided the basis for a stable organization of at least a part of the people. Middle and lower Transjordan, rich in pastures (§ 66), were well suited to tribes with many cattle, such as the tribes of Ruben and Gad (Num. 32:1); on the other hand, if a certain number of the people were to settle permanently in Transjordan, this would mean that a notable force for the proximate conquest of Canaan proper would be missing (Num. 32:6). This serious difficulty was obviated by a formal pledge on the part of the tribes under discussion to participate with an undiminished number of troops in the future conquest, and with this the partition was made. Lower Transjordan from the Arnon on the south, up to about Wadi Hesban to the north was assigned to Ruben. To Gad was assigned a part of middle Transjordan, from about Wadi Hesban to the south, up to the Jabbok to the north. The upper and remaining part of Middle Transjordan, from the Jabbok to the Yarmuk, that is, a good part of Galaad (§ 66) was given to half the tribe of Manasses.

Thus the Israelites had arrived on the soil of that promised land, entry into which had been denied Moses as a penalty for his mysterious fault (§ 261 ff.). His task being finished, he could now bow out.

273. His last acts were still those of a legislator. If he could not in person enter into the land of his ancient ancestors and of his future nephews, he could at least do so in spirit. He gave rules to guide them in the division of the territory shortly to be conquered (Num. 34), providing cities for the Levites also (§ 291), and cities of refuge for unintentional murderers (Num. 35). He then summarized, modified, and brought up to date the various laws which had arisen on different occasions during the forty years of wandering in the desert. His experience had taught him that a young theocratic nation needed civil and religious norms for its spiritual consolidation as much as it needed territorial expansion; part of this juridical material of the legislator was that which became, in an oratorical form, the codex of *Deuteronomy* (§§ 114, 510 ff.). The legislation, based on the ancient Yahwistic foundations, called for an official renewal of the alliance or pact which bound the nation to Yahweh, so much the more so now that the old generation which had witnessed the solemn pact at the foot of Sinai (§ 243) had disappeared (§ 271). Moses renewed the pact of Horeb in the land of Moab (Deut. 28:69; cf. 1:5). He also decreed that a solemn manifestation of this renewal should be celebrated with special ceremonial in Canaan itself on the mountains Gerizim and Ebal, which flank Sichem (§§ 88, 285; Deut. 11:28–29; 27:2 ff.; cf. Josue 8:30–35).

274. The juridical collection was put into writing (Deut. 17:18; 28:58 ff.; 29:19 ff.; 30:10; 31:9, 24) and deposited near the Ark (31:26).

Mount Nebo. (Vester, Amer. Colony.)

This writing down of the law was called for by its character as a public document (§ 190); its deposition near the Ark was due to the religious character of the alliance attested by the Ark. Hence the "Ark of the alliance" (§ 253) was called also "Ark of the witness" (Exod. 25:22 ff.; 30:6; Num. 4:5; etc.), because it "bore witness" (Deut. 31:26) against Israel for every violation of the pact. Within the Ark were the tablets of the Law (§ 252); outside of it were the juridical norms which interpreted and applied those tablets. Such an arrangement was not new; the stele of the classical Code of Hammurabi (§§ 4, 246) was from the very beginning set up, by way of promulgation, in the temple of the Sun at Sippar (and copies of it in the temples of other cities), whence it was borne away as a trophy of war by the Elamites, to be placed by them in the temple of Shushinak at Susa (cf. also § 511 ff.).

Likewise as a testimony, that is, to check on the observance of Israel, Moses arranged for a future and periodical reading of the collection of laws in the presence of all the people, and specifically in the seventh or sabbatical year, on the occasion of the feast of the Tabernacles, or Booths (Deut. 31:10 ff.). To celebrate the Pasch, Pentecost, and Tabernacles, every male of legal age was required to make a pilgrimage, to stand "before Yahweh" with the rest of the people (Exod. 23:14–17; Deut. 16:16). Finally, as his successor in the office of supreme ruler of the nation, Moses designated Josue, the Ephraimite, son of Nun, one of the old generation who was to be permitted to enter into the promised land (§ 259), and who had already often served on several important missions.

275. The biblical narrative then portrays Moses reciting a canticle which sums up the history of Israel. In it the magnanimous fidelity of Yahweh and the stubbornness of Israel are emphasized. Moses then pronounced a series of benedictions for each tribe, similar to those uttered by the dying Jacob on his sons, the progenitors of the same tribes (§ 164). After this Moses ascended Mount Nebo (§ 266) near Phasga of the Abarim mountains, from which he could distinguish

Canaan proper from nearby Jericho and beyond (Deut. 32:49; 34:1 ff.). This distant view substituted for the entrance into that land, forbidden him because of his fault. On that height, his eyes on that vista, he died. He was one hundred and twenty years old, but "his eyes were undimmed, and his vigor unabated. . . . Since then no prophet has arisen in Israel like Moses, whom the LORD knew face to face"(Deut. 34:7, 10).

❅   ❅   ❅

276. Recent criticism finds much more historical data in the biblical narrative concerning Sinai and Moses than did the criticism of half a century ago (§ 118 ff.).

According to one rather widespread opinion, the account of the wandering in the desert had its origin in the joining of two cycles of traditions. The more ancient cycle recorded events which occurred near Cades, the more modern, those around Sinai. If the Israelites had headed directly for Canaan on leaving Egypt, they would have gone straight to Cades, for from it there issued one of the principal roads of communication with Canaan. It is supposed that at Cades (Qadesh, "holy") there was a famous sanctuary served as to cult by a special caste. This caste is said to have been the "levites," since the name is held to be originally not the name of a tribe — much less of an Israelite tribe — but of the sacerdotal office. In proof of this it has been alleged that in Minean inscriptions found at el-ʿOla, southeast of Madian (on the road to Mecca), the priest and priestess of the god Wadd are designated respectively by the title *L wʾ* and its feminine form *l wʾt*, from which the Hebrew *Lewi*, "Levi," "Levite," would be derived. When then the Bible designates Moses as a "levite" (§ 202), and as dwelling in Madian, and finally as the son-in-law of Jethro, priest of Madian, a key is provided to his historical reality. He was a priest, perhaps the principal one, of the caste dedicated to the Madianite sanctuary of Cades. When the Israelites who had just fled from Egypt invaded the oasis, he, with his fellow levites, organized them and became their head.[38]

277. How the cycle of stories which revolved about Sinai arose is explained in a still more doubtful manner. Generally speaking, it is thought that this location, so unusual geographically, came into use because of the sanctuary venerated at Serabit el-Khadim (§§ 100, 235) as far back as the first Egyptian dynasties, and which was later continually renewed and enlarged by the Egyptians who came there to exploit the mines. Others link up the two sets of traditions by supposing that

---

[38] Gressmann, *Mose und seine Zeit*, Göttingen, 1913; M. Vernes, *Sinaï contre Kadès*, Paris, 1915; E. Sellin, *Mose und seine Bedeutung für die israelitische-jüdische Religionsgeschichte*, Leipzig, 1922. Note Sellin's hypothesis concerning the death of Moses in his *Geschichte*, 77 ff.

Moses really went from Cades to Sinai after first attempting to organize
the fugitives at Cades, being thwarted however by their obstinacy.
At Sinai he succeeded in his purpose with a small group of faithful
followers. In these hypotheses, therefore, the religion of Yahweh would
be substantially of Qenite, that is Madianite origin (§ 210), more or
less modified by Moses and adopted by the Israelites at his command.
It must be noted, however, that the above interpretation of the solitary
Minean inscription, *l w'*, *l w't*, and much more its etymological relations
to the Hebrew "levite," are rejected by some scholars on purely
philological grounds; the dating of these Minean inscriptions is most
uncertain, and today a much lower date is assigned to them than in the
past, so low in fact that one scholar has even proposed that the Hebrew
terminology is reflected in the Minean.

278. Moses is considered almost unanimously by modern criticism to
have been an historical person, although numerous reservations are
made on particular points; his death especially is said to have been
dramatized in the usual manner. On this point Sellin (§ 119) has recently
proposed a hypothesis which he considers proved by such passages as
Osee 9:7-13; 12:14 ff.; 5:2; Amos 5:13; and others. According to him,
Moses opposed the participation of the people in the obscene cult of
Baal-Phegor and was killed with his family at Shittim (§ 270). His
martyrdom was the great fault of Israel to which veiled allusions were
made in the above-mentioned passages of the prophets. To escape divine
punishment a small number of his faithful disciples departed from that
infamous place and crossed the Jordan.

Some of the passages mentioned can be interpreted in a manner
entirely different from Sellin's; others — which are supposed to have
greater proving force — have been touched up by him for presumably
critical reasons, so that they say what he wants; the unvarnished text
tells an entirely different story. This is the method of textual criticism by
which Cheyne succeeded in demonstrating that the religion and civilization of ancient Israel are derived from the tribe of Yerahme'el, which
settled to the south of Canaan. Of course, his demonstration convinced
no one, for while he found the name Yerahme'el an infinite number of
times by tampering with the biblical texts, the Bible really mentions that
name a scant ten times and that in a quite incidental way.

JOSUE AND THE JUDGES

279. The period which extends from the death of Moses to the rise of the monarchy in Israel includes both the penetration into Canaan, and its conquest. The pace of the conquest was slow and insistent, like the beating of waves, but it had to reckon with the material and moral reaction of the conquered populations. The penetration under Josue began the conquest; it was continued under the Judges. The latter period was still one of conquest and consolidation, but likewise one of adjustment and compromise.

The history of this period is sketchily traced in the Bible. Facts are sometimes thrown together, superimposed one upon the other, or at other times are synthetically presented. The chronology is a problem, and it seems the author has frequently omitted some of the intervening facts. This period is like a mountain range seen upon a distant horizon: the peaks glow in the sun, but darkness fills the valleys and the perspective is extremely obscure.

280. At the time of Moses' death, the political situation was favorable for a break-through into Canaan. If the exodus occurred under Merneptah (§ 227 ff.), the settling of Israel in Transjordan about forty years later approaches the time of Rameses III (1198–1167). It is the time in which the sovereignty of Egypt, at grips with the "Peoples of the Sea" (§ 35), was felt slightly or not at all in Canaan. To the north the Hittites were on the decline; the same waves of peoples which had pushed the Peoples of the Sea back to the eastern Mediterranean were now battering a breach in the Hittite Empire, which was destined to fall at the end of that century.

From these circumstances it appears that Canaan underwent a period similar to that of el-Amarna (§ 52 ff.). Unchecked by a strong overlord, the little kings and local princes must have torn each other to pieces in their rivalries. The thicker the web of little states, city states, lands, etc., each with its own head, the more numerous their struggles must have been. In Josue 12 alone there are enumerated thirty-one kings who were overthrown by the victory of Israel (half of

The Jordan near Jericho.

these are not named in the detailed account). It is easy to see that the territories of several of these "kings" were limited to a few square miles.

281. It was in this region of turmoil that Israel, a young people now sufficiently numerous to face the coalitions of several Canaanite states, longed to settle. Unpracticed in the art of laying siege to the strongly fortified Canaanite cities (§ 101), it was nevertheless inured to the hardships and privations of the desert. The task therefore, although not easy, was yet not too difficult.

News of their arrival in Transjordan (§ 266 ff.) soon made its way across the Jordan, and certainly did not inspire any confidence in the little states most exposed to the invasion. The main force of the Israelites was still concentrated at Shittim, opposite Jericho (§ 270), and there was every reason to suppose that an attempt would be made to break through across the river there. The king of Jericho watched uneasily.

282. He had reason to be vigilant. He knew that, one day, two men from the threatening people encamped across the Jordan had penetrated during the night into the city and had found asylum in the house of Rahab, a prostitute and probably also an innkeeper (the two occupations often went together), whose house adjoined the walls of the city. These are the walls which, according to the latest word of archaeology, constituted the inner enclosure (§ 82). The fact of espionage was obvious, and he ordered the arrest of the two spies. The innkeeper saved them by saying that the two had gone out that evening but that they could certainly be caught if pursued. The king's agents hastened toward the fords of the Jordan, where they reasoned the spies should have fled. Meanwhile the spies who had been hidden on the woman's roof were let down by a rope outside the walls of the city. They fled to the mountains, recrossed the Jordan, and returned to Shittim. Josue had indeed sent them, and the information they brought him determined him to act.

283. First he arranged for the moving of the people from Shittim to the banks of the Jordan. The crossing of the river is the exact parallel to the miraculous crossing of the Red Sea, since it demonstrated to the people that Yahweh was with Josue as He had been with Moses (Josue 3:7; 4:14, 23). The column of people was preceded by

The site of Gilgal. (Vester, Amer. Colony.)

priests carrying the Ark; as soon as these touched the river, which was swollen by the usual melting of the snows of Hermon (§ 61), the water from above stopped, up to Adam (Vulgate, *Adom*) — probably the present-day ford of el-Damiyeh — while the water below continued to flow toward the Dead Sea. Thus the river bed became dry, and the Ark remained there until the people had completed the crossing. Once this was finished the water resumed its ordinary course. From the miraculously dried river bed Josue commanded twelve stones (the number of the tribes) to be taken and erected as a memorial of the event at Gilgal (Vulgate, *Galgal*), the first camping place of the Israelites in the promised land.

The name is probably still preserved in the present-day *Tell Gilgiul*, situated about halfway between the Jordan and Jericho, and seems to refer to the circle (root, *G L L*) of stones which formed the cromlech (§ 72). Another interpretation was given to the name according to one of the usual popular etymologies (§§ 132, 203, 239). At Gilgal the rite of circumcision was performed with stone knives on the new generation, which being born in the desert was as yet uncircumcised (§§ 211, 262): on that occasion "Yahweh said to Josue: Today I have rolled away (Hebrew — *gallothi*) the reproach of Egypt from you. And the name of this place was called Gilgal even to the present day" (Josue 5:9).

There also on the night of the fourteenth of Nisan the Pasch was celebrated. On the following day, when they tasted the products of the Palestinian soil, the manna ceased (§ 240). The armed force, held in readiness there, numbered about 40,000 men (Josue 4:13).[1]

---

[1] Sellin, *Gilgal, ein Beitrag zur Geschichte der Einwanderung Israels in Palästina,* Leipzig, 1917.

284. The strategic point for the conquest of Canaan from the east was Jericho, but the city had barred its doors "before the Israelites: no one went out and no one entered" (Josue 6:1); the massiveness of its walls (§ 80 ff.) allowed them to meet any attack with a peaceful mind, even from besiegers much more expert than the Israelites. Despite this the city was captured, but thanks to a miraculous power. Obeying a command of Yahweh, Josue for six consecutive days made his armed forces circle around the city, preceded by the priests who carried the Ark and sounded the trumpets. To circle the city did not take very long, as the city was not very large (§ 101); hence it was possible on the seventh day to march around it seven times. At the seventh time on that day, when the priests sounded the trumpets, the people, spread out in procession around the walls, shouted a great cry at a sign from Josue, and the walls crumbled. The earthquake of Yahweh is here parallel to the wind of Yahweh in the crossing of the Red Sea (§ 221). The processional circle then drew in upon the now defenseless city, and destroyed it. All the inhabitants there were killed according to the *herem* (§ 271), but the life and possessions of Rahab the prostitute were spared and she was associated with the people of Yahweh. The city afterward remained ruined and deserted for centuries because of the anathema which Josue pronounced on it. It was rebuilt by Hiel (§ 80).

285. A certain Achan failed to observe the total *herem* of Jericho by taking some things for himself. When soon afterward an assault was made on Hai, situated near Bethel, northwest of Jericho, the Israelites were repulsed with losses, although the undertaking should have been easy. When Yahweh was consulted, the sacred lots indicated Achan to be the guilty one, and both he and his whole family were stoned. Then Hai was taken. The account of the clever ambuscade by which the city fell (Josue 8:1–29) offers grave difficulties both on account of the divergences between the Hebrew text and the Septuagint, and the usual confusion of numbers (§§ 222 ff., 232 ff.) in the Hebrew text. At any rate, the result of the campaign is clear enough: the city was burned and all the in-

Ruins of ancient temple on Mount Gerizim.

habitants killed; the king was captured and this time the booty was distributed to the combatants.

Josue next provided for the solemnities attendant upon the renewal of the pact, as Moses had prescribed (§ 273). He erected an altar on Mount Ebal upon which sacrifices were offered. "And there he wrote on stones a copy of the Torah of Moses" (Josue 8:32; § 273 ff.), and read it in its entirety before the people, part of whom were on Ebal, and part on Gerizim opposite it. To the solemn proclamation of each commandment the people replied and assented.[2]

286. Meanwhile the victories of Israel had aroused serious apprehension among the chiefs of the little states of Canaan, several of whom joined in an offensive and defensive league against Israel. The inhabitants of Gabaon, the present-day *El-Jib* slightly north of Tell el-Ful (§ 85), did not fall in with this and had recourse instead to a stratagem in order to save their lives. Disguising themselves as travelers from far-off lands, they presented themselves at Josue's camp, saying that they had come to make an alliance with Israel, being attracted thereto by the fame of Yahweh. Josue and the leaders believed them and swore not to do them any violence. A few days later it was discovered that the self-styled wanderers were in reality Canaanites who lived a short distance from the camp; their villages were recognized and visited but because of their oath the Israelites did not harm the inhabitants. Instead, they made them their servants, detailing them to perform the menial work in the camp. It was the first case of official toleration of and cohabitation with Canaanites.

The defection of the Gabaonites from the Canaanite fold was learned with sadness by the other cities. A punitive league was formed with Adhoni-sedheq, king of Jerusalem (§ 130), at its head; he was joined by the kings of Hebron (§ 691), Jarmuth, Lachish, and Eglon (§ 74). The Gabaonites turned for help to Josue, and he promptly came to their aid and overthrew the five kings, whose rout was aggravated by a terrible hail storm which fell on the fugitives and killed them.

287. On the occasion of this victory, so rapid and extensive that there hardly seemed time to profit by it, the biblical account reports a passage from an ancient triumphal song which comes from the "book of the *Yashar*" (Just?; Valiant?), also mentioned elsewhere in the Bible and surely part of an old collection of nationalistico-Yahwistic songs (for which reason some scholars following the reading of the Septuagint in 1 Kings 8:53 *bis,* want to correct it to "Book of the

---

[2] Cf. A. Tricot, "La prise d'Ai" in *Biblica*, 1922, 273–300; R. Tonneau, "Le sacrifice de Josué sur le mont Ebal" in *RB*, 1926, 98–109; Vincent, "Les fouilles d'et Tell = 'Ai" in *RB*, 1937, 231–266.

Shir," of the *Song*). In this passage Josue exclaims in the fervor of the victory:

> "O sun, move not over Gabaon!
> and [thou], moon, over the valley of 'Ayyalon!
> And the sun stopped, and the moon stood still,
> until the people revenged themselves upon their enemies!"

The narrator then adds, by way of comment: "And the sun stood still in the center of the sky, nor did it hasten to set for almost an entire day; and there was not a day like that one,[3] neither before nor afterwards" (Josue 10:12–14).

288. Scholars of various camps, including Catholics, have attempted to tone down the meaning of this passage — or at least of the song — by supposing that in it was expressed only the desire that the triumphal day would be prolonged, or that it affirmed metaphorically that the sun and moon seemed to be held back by some miracle. Hebrew cosmology, however, with its quite definite ideas and precise terminology, would seem to attribute an absolutely literal sense to the song and much more to the commentary (cf. Ecclus. 46:5; Josephus, *Antiquities*, V, 1, 17). To suppose that the author speaks in the style of Horace when he says: *Alme sol . . . possis nihil urbe Roma — visere maius* (*Carmen saecul.*, 9–12), seems to imply a stylistic anachronism, aggravated by a psychological confusion which equates Semitic realism with Greco-Roman abstraction. This question is purely an exegetical one and from this point of view the opponents of Galileo were more justified in their course of action than is commonly thought today.

The scientific question is quite different. From this viewpoint there comes a rather widely held theory based on meteorological phenomena, namely, that the phenomenon had some connection with a hailstorm. Some say a cloud hid the sun as at sunset, and that after a hailstorm the sun reappeared; or its rays were refracted by a cloud. Other hypotheses of this kind are also offered. The point on which all agree is that there was no real astronomical disturbance, a fact which must be remembered when appraising the results of the exegetical question.

289. The five kings, who in defeat had sought refuge in the cave of Maqqedah (Maceda), were then dragged forth and killed.

Josue enlarged his conquest by becoming master of Libna, Lachish, Eglon, Hebron, and Debir, and slew the king of Gezer (§ 74 ff.). Following this he completed two campaigns of vast proportions which are reported by the Bible only in a very condensed fashion. One was directed to the south, where Josue took possession of the territory "from

---

[3] The translation of the Vulgate, *tam longa dies*, is an interpretation.

Cades Barnea to Gaza" (Josue 10:41). The other was directed to the
north, where another league of small Canaanite states had been formed
with Jabin, king of Hasor, as head. Josue fell upon the armed forces
of the league in a surprise attack and struck them down to the "waters
of Merom" (in the neighborhood of the Lake el-Hule?; § 61). Hasor,
"which had been of old the capital of all these kingdoms" (Josue 11:10),
was captured; its king and all the inhabitants were killed and the city
burned. The rest of the region was also conquered "up to Baal-Gad in
the Lebanon valley at the foot of Mount Hermon" (Josue 11:17; cf.
§ 309).

290. The conquest was therefore accomplished, but circumstances
made it more an armed occupation than a conquest. In the first place
it was far from being complete. In many central points, especially the
more fortified ones, the Canaanites remained undisturbed. The situation
was worse at the periphery, where various peoples had not even come
into contact with the Israelites. Furthermore, the conquest had been a
violence visited upon the local population, rather than a stable domination imposed upon them. Under Israelite pressure these had been dis-
placed, or hemmed in, forced to yield space to the newcomers. No
attempt seems to have been made to establish a stable rule over them
(except over the Gabaonites; § 286). Up to this point Israelite arms
were superior but the tide might turn in favor of the Canaanites. And
as the Canaanite civilization was more developed and cultured, it was
always possible that it might win another kind of victory, a spiritual
enslavement of the newcomers.

At any rate what had been accomplished was enough for Josue to
proceed to the partition of the territory, which had been conquered by
the nation as a whole. After its division among the various tribes, each
would organize its own territory as best it could.

291. There were thirteen tribes, because the tribes of Ephraim and
Manasses were substituted for that of Joseph (§ 164), but, practically
speaking, there were only twelve (the typical number, § 144), as the
tribe of Levi remained without a special territory. The Levites were to
reside, however, in determined (Levitical) cities, located in the territories
of the various tribes; their maintenance was to be provided for by the
tenth part of the harvests. Some tribes had increased their numbers by
the absorption of heterogeneous ethnic elements. Aside from the case
of the Gabaonites who were slaves, groups of families are known to
have fused with Israel and enjoyed equal social rights with them. For
the most part these were of Edomite stock, like the Calebites, the
Qenizites (§§ 258, 306), the Yerahmeelites (§ 278), and especially the
Qenites to whom Moses was related by marriage (§ 276 ff.). Such
additions may have first occurred during the desert period, and may
occasionally have been repeated in Canaan in the case of wandering

clans well-disposed toward Israel. At times an amicable union was occasioned by a recognition of the ancient favors which Israel had received, as was the case of Rahab (§ 284) and the Qenites (1 Sam. 15:6).

292. Two and a half tribes were settled in Transjordan (§ 272), the remainder in Palestine. A first partition of what is now modern Palestine was made at Gilgal. The territory to the west of the Dead Sea, from the southern border of the Negeb to Jerusalem which lay to the north, was assigned to the tribe of Juda. Central Canaan, made up of the land from Gezer and a little above Beth-el to the south, northward to Sichem, was assigned to Ephraim. Half of the tribe of Manasses was placed farther north, extending from the northern border of Ephraim almost to the plain of Esdraelon.

Meanwhile the Tabernacle with the Ark was transported from Gilgal to Silo (§ 87), in the center of the territory allotted to Ephraim. Silo thereby became the politico-religious capital of Israel.

The narrow territory between Juda and Ephraim, from the Jordan to about midway to the Mediterranean was assigned to Benjamin. Besides Jericho and Gabaon it contained the as yet impregnable Jerusalem. To Simeon was assigned the Negeb, or extreme southern part of Juda, although a part stretched northward toward the Mediterranean. To Zabulon was given the region to the west of the Lake of Tiberias, from the heights north and south of the lake in the direction of the Mediterranean. Issachar was located between the half-tribe of Manasses to the south and Zabulon to the north. Aser had the coast of the Mediterranean from a little to the south of Carmel northward. Nephtali received the territory to the north of Zabulon between Aser on the west and the Jordan on the east. To Dan was assigned the narrow territory between Juda, Benjamin, Ephraim, and the Mediterranean. Later on, however, it emigrated and became the northernmost of all the tribes (§ 336). Finally, forty-eight Levitical cities were established (§ 291), plus six cities of refuge for unintentional murderers (§ 273), three on each side of the Jordan.

293. When the land was conquered and partitioned, the two and a half tribes of Transjordan were free to return to their settlements, and did so. First, however, they raised an altar in the vicinity of the Jordan. When the other tribes learned of this, they immediately interpreted the act as one of religious schism with political implications. The altar could be interpreted as a move to oppose the altar at Silo, with the design of driving a wedge into the nation's ethnico-Yahwistic unity. An assembly held in Silo considered the situation a *casus belli;* meanwhile, a delegation headed by Pinehas (§ 270), son of the high priest, Eleazar, was sent to demand an explanation. It was explained that they did not intend to raise this altar for the offering of sacrifices and oblations to

Yahweh, hence it was not intended to be a substitute for the national altar at Silo. It was merely a "testimonial" (Josue 22:27) whereby future generations would remember their obligations of loyalty to Yahweh. It was meant as a "memorial" like similar monuments (§§ 143, 145). Whether the explanation was sincere or not, it was accepted and the matter was dropped.

294. Toward the end of his life Josue convoked the representatives of the people, the first time at Silo, apparently, where he exhorted them to be loyal to Yahweh; and a second time at Sichem, locality of the patriarchs (§ 88), where he summarized the history of the nation from the patriarchs onward, and then made the people publicly renew their pact with Yahweh. After certain laws to suit different circumstances were promulgated at Sichem, Josue wrote these things "in the book of the law [§ 285] of God. Then he took a large stone and set it up there under the oak that was in the sanctuary of the Lord [§ 148]. And Josue said to all the people, 'This stone shall be our witness, for it has heard all the words which the Lord spoke to us. It shall be a witness against you, should you wish to deny your God'" (Josue 24:26–27).

A little while later Josue died, at the age of one hundred and ten. He was buried at Timnath-serah (Vulgate, *Thamnat-sare*) "in the mountainous region of Ephraim, to the north of the mountain of Gaash" (Josue 24:30) in the land assigned to him by the partition of the country (Josue 19:50).

295. With regard to the sepulcher of Josue the Greek text of the Septuagint (24:30 *bis*) has a special note lacking in the Hebrew text: "There were placed together with him in the tomb which was excavated there for him, the knives of stone with which he had circumcised the Israelites in Gilgal . . . and they have been there up to this day." Only the Septuagint (21:42 *d*) had previously mentioned that Josue, on receiving his property in Timnath-serah, gathered up the stone knives used for the circumcision (§ 283). The location of Timnath-serah is thought by some to be the present-day Haris, about ten miles southwest of Sichem, or Khirbet el-Fahahir, near Haris, but others hold it to be the present Tibneh, situated in the same direction (some ten miles northwest of Beth-el); near Tibneh, in fact, are *Kefr Ishu'a*, "village of Josue," and many tombs excavated in the rock. In one of these were unearthed in 1870 several stone knives which the discoverer, Richard, believed were the ones put in Josue's tomb.

*   *   *

296. Josue was at one and the same time the leader of the army and the ruler under whom the moral unity which Moses had given to Israel was still preserved, although not so compactly. In virtue of that unity the people had advanced from the foot of Mount Sinai to the interior of Canaan. Israel, however, was not one single force; it was a bundle of forces held together by the unity imparted to it by Moses and preserved by Josue. When the bundle came to rest in Canaan the bonds were, to a great extent, loosened.

Ethnical unity remained, despite numerically unimportant foreign additions (§ 291); there was legislative uniformity, despite customs peculiar to the different tribes; religious unity persisted, despite tendencies toward individualism more or less latent (§§ 315, 319, 334 ff.) and sometimes even open (§ 293); but after Josue, there was no unified government capable of organizing and co-ordinating the interests of the separate tribes. These interests often clashed, especially when they settled in Canaan, for then the traditional haughtiness of certain tribes, Ephraim for example, often made them forget that they were sons of Israel on a par with the other less fortunate and weaker tribes. The possession of a fertile valley or of an abundant spring oftener still led to forgetfulness of every trace of tribal and racial ancestry.

297. At any rate, the breakup of national unity was inevitable, and further conquest of Canaan could be continued only on that condition. Each tribe held its possessions for the most part in theory only. To complete that possession, dogged efforts were required over a period of many years, depending on the times and as opportunity offered. Obviously the entire nation could not so act; that was to be the task, and the reward, of each separate tribe.

Such was the social background of the period of the Judges which determined the political organization in accord with Semitic preferences. It was neither monarchy nor republic: there were no dynastic successions, no democratic elections. Its foundation was the patriarchal regime preferred by Bedouins — a primitive regime usually somewhat monarchical, but not rarely evolving into a democracy. In a wider social sphere dictatorship was also often encountered.

The father-of-the-family, often a sheikh and head of many families, was a genuine monarch, small but absolute. His commands were limited for the most part by traditions, or by existing formal laws, and resistance on the part of his subjects who could rebel or at least betake themselves out of his jurisdiction further limited his authority. The monarchical authority of the father-of-the-family was hereditary: it was transmitted to the first-born, or to one who had the right to it.

298. A group of families (Hebrew, *mishpahoth*) under the command of a sheikh was the cell of the tribe, as the tribe was a member of the nation. Clans and tribes had their flocks, and sometimes their farms, but they were rather shepherds than farmers and only rarely were they artisans or members of the professions. The tribes had their respective territories within which their families roamed. The spirit of unity which should have existed between clan and tribe was latent and implicit in normal times and was not the direct object of consciousness, but rather slumbered in the subconscious of the various groups, large or small. At certain moments, however, it flared up. When, for example, private interests within the nation clashed, appeal was made to the judgment of the ancients, the traditional representatives of the group authority. But let outsiders begin to oppress one of the tribes, and it showed its power and vigor afresh. In such a case, the nation of Yahweh, driven both by the instinct of preservation and nationalistic and Yahwistic courage, would react fiercely against the oppressor. Indifferent members eagerly rallied to the defense, even making serious sacrifices to do so, and renouncing their own autonomy. While the danger lasted they became one body again under one leader. These temporary heads of the whole nation or of the greater part were the dictators. The Israelites called them "Judges," *Shophetim*.

The name is not a new one. The Carthaginians, also Semites, likewise had *suf[f]etes*, as is mentioned by the Latin authors (Seneca, *De Tranquill.*, IV, V; Livy, XXVIII, 37, 2; XXX, 7, 5); they were the supreme magistrates of Carthage. The active participle of the verb *shaphat*, the word ordinarily signified "judging," but in the fuller Semitic sense, a judging by him who settles an argument according to justice, and hence also a judging by him who is the head of a people and saves it from danger according to justice. It is very doubtful if the term was commonly used as a title during the time of the Judges; the ancient texts designate them, more in conformity with their dictatorial character, with derivations of the idea of "saving."

299. The justice according to which these "judges" acted was the justice of Yahweh. The nation of Yahweh is trampled upon; it must therefore be raised up in virtue of Yahweh's justice. If the territory given by Him to His nation is invaded by foreigners, it is a religious theft for which compensation must be made by reason of the justice of Yahweh. Thus the Judges are the executors of the law of Yahwism; they translate into act — or they should — the spirit of that which Moses had put in writing.

The Yahwistic dictator was therefore the man of Yahweh. From this fact he derived his authority to recall the bickering members of Israel to unity. From the moment that the people, with a national and religious act of faith, recognized in him the messenger of Yahweh, he was a *quasi* monarch, with absolute powers; it was a theocratic choice on a democratic basis.

300. The period of the Judges began with the death of Josue, but this does not mean that the Judges arose at once. The Bible does not give an organic and connected history of this period, but an anthology of separate episodes. In fact the intention of the principal narrator of this period who used ancient sources in editing the Book of *Judges,* was not the exposition and analysis of the events which happened to Israel, but to drive home a powerful lesson from the facts which he used: namely, that every time the nation drew away from Yahweh, it fell into the power of enemy oppressors, and, on the contrary, every time it sought to return to him, He saved it by means of a Judge. This intention not only appears from the manner in which the separate episodes of the anthology are introduced and terminated, but is also clearly expressed in the brief general introduction with which the editor prefaces the whole history (Judg. 2:11 ff.).

Consequently, the anthology is schematic. The editor chooses from the various tribes six personages about whom he elaborates a history in some detail; these are the "major Judges," so-called because they are better known; together with these he names six others who are called "minor Judges" because substantially nothing about them is known except their names. There are then twelve judges, exactly the number of the tribes of Israel. (The usurpation of Abimelech is not a different judgeship from that of Gedeon, of which it is a consequence; he never was in reality nor was he ever considered to be a "Judge.")

301. The following schema presents the Judges according to the plan of the Book of *Judges:* those in parentheses are the minor Judges.

Oppressor of Israel	Liberating Judge
Cushan-Rish'athayim, king of Aram-Naharayim: 8 years	Othoniel, of Qenizite stock: 40 years
Eglon, king of Moab: 18 years	Ehud, of the tribe of Benjamin: 80 years
Philistines (?)	(Samgar)
Jabin, king of Hasor, with his general Sisara: 20 years	Baraq, of the tribe of Nephtali, together with the prophetess Debora: 40 years
Madian: 7 years	Gedeon, of the tribe of Manasses: 40 years. Usurpation of Abimelech: 3 years
?	(Thola, of the tribe of Issachar: 23 years)
?	(Jair, of Galaad: 22 years)
Ammon: 18 years	Jephte, of Galaad: 6 years
?	(Abesan: 7 years)
?	(Elon, of the tribe of Zabulon: 10 years)
?	(Abdon: 8 years)
Philistines: 40 years	Samson, of the tribe of Dan: 20 years

Eli and Samuel, the "Judges" who usher in the era of the monarchy, lie outside the schema of the Book of *Judges*, but the judgeship of Eli at least may have been contemporaneous with the others.

302. About this schema two things should be remarked. In the first place, the authority of the Judges extended almost always to one or a few tribes; none of them, probably (except, it seems, Samuel), was recognized by the entire nation. In the second place and as a consequence of the first, a goodly number could have been at least partially contemporaneous. Attempts have been made to find proof of this in the text of the narrative itself. For example, Judg. 10:7, states that because Israel sinned Yahweh delivered them "into the hand of the Philistines and the hand of the sons of Ammon." There immediately follows the story of Jephte, who fought only against Ammon, and not against the Philistines; against these it was Samson who fought. It is therefore concluded that the judgeships of Jephte and Samson were contemporaneous.

Whatever may be the value of the figures dealing with the oppressions and respective judgeships (§ 222 ff.), they cannot be considered as numbers which have only to be added in order to yield the duration of this period, since what has been left out is not known. It is sufficient for us to presume that, as the exodus is preferably supposed to have taken place under Merneptah, the whole period (including the judgeship of Eli and part of that of Samuel) runs from Rameses III (§ 280) up to about the middle of the eleventh century B.C., when the monarchy of Israel was established in the person of Saul (§ 349), which would mean a century and a half, more or less.

303. Prefacing the general introduction to the anthology is a narrative introduction (Judg. 1–2:5) which in its present form begins with the death of Josue. From this it would seem that the book was to record events occurring after the death of Josue. However, immediately after this prologue comes the anthology, which begins anew with a résumé of the last days of Josue and of his death (2:6–10). Judging from this, then, the preface records things that happened before his death. Nor is this all. The events when analyzed seem to fit into the conquest of Canaan under Josue as more detailed reports within the larger and more general summary; in that case Judg. 1:3–20 would describe how, after the conquest of Jericho by the whole nation, the tribes of Juda and Simeon detached themselves from the others and turned to the south to conquer their territory, and Judg. 1:22 ff. would record the conquests made in the north by the descendants of Joseph (with Josue personally at the head), and elsewhere by the other tribes. On the other hand, the two and one half tribes of Transjordan are missing from this detailed list, and yet they had surely taken part in the conquest under

Josue. Such an omission would prove that they had already returned to their territory (§ 293) and that therefore the events in question took place later. It also can be seen that they occurred after the partition of the territories among the different tribes (Judg. 1:3) and therefore soon after the conquest under Josue (§ 292), for it seems unlikely that a country would be divided up before its conquest had started.

304. The question cannot be settled definitely. It is probable that the introduction tells of events which occurred for the most part before and to some small extent, after the death of Josue. Its internal structure and also its position after the Book of *Josue* and before the anthology of *Judges* rather suggest a random collection of scattered, fragmentary documents, referring to the various tribes. Hence it is so much more difficult to figure out their chronology and the correct relationship with other documents. Two examples will illustrate.

In Judg. 1:4 ff. it is stated that the tribe of Juda, advancing toward the south, put to rout at Bezeq the Canaanite king, Adhoni-bezeq, who, after being mutilated by the Israelites, was taken (the text does not say whether by the Israelites or by his servants) to Jerusalem, where he died. "Bezeq," as the name of the king indicates, could be a Canaanite divinity not known elsewhere; it was also the name of a place; it is difficult to see how it could be the present-day Ibziq, situated to the northeast of Sichem and hence too far north; although it might be Bezqah to the west of Jerusalem. Where was Adhoni-bezeq king? His death at Jerusalem suggests that this was his capital, in which case one is tempted to identify him with that Adhoni-sedheq, king of Jerusalem, who was killed in Josue's conquest (§ 286 ff.); especially as the Septuagint (Josue 10:1 ff.) reads for the name of that king, Adhoni-bezeq, exactly as does the Hebrew. Is this the same person, whose name has undergone alterations traceable to the usual copyists' errors? Are they two different personages, one of whom is Bezeq, or does one succeed the other in the kingdom of Jerusalem?

305. The other example is even more obscure. Immediately after the mention of Adhoni-bezeq's death, it is related that the tribe of Juda "attacked Jerusalem and took it, and put it to the edge of the sword and set the city on fire" (Judg. 1:8). Shortly after (1:21) it is stated that the tribe of Benjamin was unsuccessful in driving the Jebusites from Jerusalem and that, therefore, the Jebusites and Benjamites dwelt together in Jerusalem "until this day." While the fact that Jerusalem was not then stormed and taken is confirmed by many contemporary passages such as Josue 15:63, Judg. 19:11–12, and in other later ones, the other report that it was taken by storm contradicts what the Bible and archaeology affirm concerning the extraordinary difficulty in subduing Canaanite Jerusalem (§§ 96, 98). The passage, therefore, which

cannot refer to the capturing of the city in the time of the Judges, is probably an anticipation of the seizure of the city by David (§ 358). Anticipatory accounts of this kind (in the form of parenthetical remarks) are not unknown in biblical writing and the present example was perhaps called to mind by the previous mention of Jerusalem.

306. The plan of *Judges* is concerned almost always with the tribes of the north. Yet, the first of the greater Judges, Othoniel, is a southerner, belonging to the Edomite clan of the Qenites (§ 291), who from the earliest times were united with the tribe of Juda and later on definitely incorporated with it. It is known of him only that he liberated his people from the oppression of Cushan-rish'athayim, king of Aram-Naharayim. Both names have been called into question. The name of the king signifies "Cushan-of-the-double-wickedness" and seems to be a popular derogatory epithet, similar to a Babylonian designation found in Jer. 50:21 ("twofold rebellion"). The name of the kingdom designates the Syria of the Two Rivers (§ 51); by some, however, it has been considered unlikely that a king of those regions would penetrate into southern Palestine at that period. Hence it is supposed that, instead of 'R M (Aram), the true reading should be 'D M (Edom) the country bordering the south of Palestine. The two words are frequently interchanged in the Bible (§§ 440 note, 451 note).

307. More details are supplied about the second major Judge. Eglon, king of Moab, aided by the Ammonites and the Amalecites, had occupied the territory of Benjamin to the west of the Jordan and subjected the inhabitants to tribute. One year a courageous Benjamite named Ehud (Aod) was included among the bearers of the tribute. He had prepared his plan; since he was left-handed (Hebrew — '*itter*, better translated perhaps as "ambidextrous") he had hidden a long double-edged dagger under his garments on the right side in order the better to conceal the weapon. After the ceremony of presentation, he departed with the others, but after a few paces he returned, on the pretext of telling an important secret to the king. Received in a separate room, he killed the king with a single thrust, closed the door, and went away undisturbed. After he arrived unharmed in his own country he incited the people to revolt and controlled the fords of the Jordan, where he killed the Moabite oppressors trying to escape to their own country.

308. The third episode of the anthology takes place farther to the north, in the valley of Esdraelon (§ 64), and the principal tribes involved are those settled from that valley on up: the half-tribe of Manasses, Issachar, Zabulon, Nephtali. Cades, a village of the territory of Nephtali (lying to the west of Lake el-Hule; § 61), was the place of origin of Baraq ("thunder"), the Judge of this episode, but the part he plays is a secondary one. The real protagonist is a woman, Debora ("bee").

Air view of the Valley of Esdraelon seen from the west.

She was the wife of a man named Lappidhoth, and enjoyed extraordinary authority over her fellow countrymen. A "prophetess," and universally recognized as such in Israel, she was sought out by people from the various tribes in the hope of receiving inspired replies to their queries. She had located her tribunal under the "palm of Debora," midway between Beth-el and Rama to the north of Jerusalem. Here she exercised her theomantic magistracy, giving decisions concerning religious and political, public and private affairs (§ 420).

Meanwhile, the Israelites who had located in and north of Esdraelon were oppressed by the Canaanites, who had remained masters of important centers and above all of the strong places commanding the key roads crossing the valley (§ 64), even after the Israelite conquest. Expanding little by little from these fortresses, they succeeded first in stifling the activity of the Israelites and finally in enslaving them.

309. Who was this oppressor? There are two sources of information concerning the judgeship of Debora: one in prose (Judg. 4), and the ancient poem known as the "Canticle of Debora," one of the most precious monuments of ancient Israel (Judg. 5). According to the prose account the oppressor was "Jabin king of Canaan who reigned in Hasor, and the leader of his army was Sisara, who resided at Harosheth-haggoim" (Judg. 4:2); this is confirmed a bit later (verse 17) where Jabin is called "king of Hasor." Yet only a moment before (verses 23–24) he was called only "king of Canaan" (cf. Ps. 83[82]:10). The poem however makes no mention of Jabin at all, and speaks only of Sisara.

The Israelites, however, had under Josue already killed a Jabin, king of Hasor, and burned his northerly city (§ 289), which seems to have been a capital of some importance. Who, then, is the present Jabin, king of Hasor? It would be easy to make of him a descendant of the

Mount Tabor.

ancient victim of Israel whose city had been rebuilt, but several considerations, and especially the chronological uncertainty, render this explanation most doubtful. Rather, it could be that two different cities are involved notwithstanding the same name; the Bible knows for certain of five different cities of the name of Hasor and there could be even more, since originally it was a common name, "[fortified] enclosure," "a place closed in [by a wall]," which came to be applied to various localities (like the Italian *castle*, the German *Berg*, and similar names). It seems more likely that the statement, "Jabin was king of Hasor," is a gloss, added by someone who was surprised to see that the prose account calls Jabin "king of Canaan" only, and who therefore added the other title, supposing Jabin to be the same king as in the time of Josue, although he was actually a later king bearing the same name. At any rate, this Jabin, whoever he may be, does not appear in the development of events.

310. From her tribunal under the "palm" Debora followed affairs closely and the cry of pain from the oppressed northern tribes aroused a lively response in her Yahwistic spirit. She decided to act. Summoning Baraq, she commanded him to gather the armies of the tribes of Nephtali and Zabulon on Tabor. It was not possible to ignore the command of the "prophetess," so Baraq agreed, but desired that the prophetess go with him, which she did.

Baraq had cleverly relied on the effect which the presence of such a woman would have upon his armies. Among the Semites, women ordinarily occupied a very secondary place in public life, but sometimes they came to the fore, and then their efficacy was so much the greater as their pre-eminence was so unusual. Abstracting from the Semitic Dido of Carthage and Zenobia of Palmyra, as well as from women leaders

Torrent of Qishon (Cison); above, the slopes of Mount Carmel. (Vester, Amer. Colony.)

of the desert tribes whom some Assyrian kings boast, in their inscriptions, of having subdued, there are many classic examples among the Arabs. Even before Mohammed the Christian Mawiyah (fourth century A.D.), queen of the dynasty of the Ghassanides, seriously annoyed the Byzantine Empire with raids conducted under her personal leadership; under Islam, there was the valiant Umm Ziml, killed in combat; and the self-styled prophetess, Sagah, revolted vigorously against the Caliph Abu Bakr. More resolute still was the widow of Mohammed, 'A'ishah, who, after siding against 'Ali, harangued the crowds at Mecca, joined with the combatants, and in the "battle of the camel" rode her camel to the fray. Nor did she desist until the enemy succeeded in hamstringing her mount, so that she fell to the ground. Even then she inveighed vehemently against the conquerors who ran to assist her. This 'A'ishah was the "mother of the believers."

311. In the ancient poem, Debora also is called "Mother in Israel" (Judg. 5:7). As mother of the nation she went to the north among the tribes of Nephtali and Zabulon which were rising in revolt; other nearer or more co-operative tribes like Issachar, Ephraim, Benjamin, and the important clan of Makir pertaining to the tribe of Manasses in Canaan, responded to the call. It was recorded with regret that Ruben, Gad, Transjordanic Manasses, Dan, and Aser did not answer the appeal; no information is given concerning Juda, Simeon, and Levi. In all, some forty thousand men gathered together, but they were not well-armed, for their oppressors had cautiously deprived them of arms, as the Philistines were to do so also, later on (§ 350). What they lacked in weapons, however, they made up in enthusiasm, being aroused by the presence of the "mother in Israel." Sisara descended to the field with his soldiers and nine hundred Canaanite war chariots. The battle took place in the center of the valley of Esdraelon, a little above the line between Ta'annak (§ 78) and Megiddo (§ 79), along the Torrent Qishon (Cison) which

runs through the valley. The armed Canaanite forces were thrown into confusion because of the spirit of the Israelite fighters, and Sisara himself escaped the rout only by taking to his heels.

312. In fleeing, Sisara no doubt intended to take refuge in his city, Harosheth-haggoim (probably the present-day el-Haritiye on the southeastern slopes of Carmel), and so, to avoid the battlefield, he set out southwards. When he arrived at Cades (modern Tell Abu Qudeis) exhausted by his labors and consumed with thirst, he sought water and a chance to rest in a clan which had been hospitably received by the Canaanites of that area. Heber, the head of the clan, was a descendant of the Qenites, among whom was the father-in-law of Moses (§§ 210, 276 ff., 291), and hence was a friend of the victorious Israelites. The fugitive king, received with the appearances of kindness by Jahal, wife of Heber, quenched his thirst, and was allowed to rest in the tent. When he was fast asleep on the ground, Jahal came softly to him, and with one blow of a hammer drove a tent peg through his temples so that his head was nailed fast to the ground. Death at the hands of a woman was the most ignominious death a Semite could suffer (§ 320).

313. Once the valley of Esdraelon and the adjacent regions were definitely liberated, the fertility of that section, again exploited by the Israelites, brought about good results. There ensued a period of comfort and material well-being which made the nation appreciate ever more and more the stability of an agricultural life. Ease and comfort, however, brought with them the usual consequences, fostered also by contact with the agricultural and now peaceful Canaanites. There did not seem to be any need, as there had been in the past, of the wonder-working intervention of Yahweh; things were now going along well. It was sufficient for them that they be able to complete their agricultural labors, that rain come at the right time, that the fertility of the soil continue as usual, that there be no plague of insects, and so on. If only these things were assured, the Israelite would see his dream fulfilled. But who was it who sends all these benefits? Was it really Yahweh? Or was it not rather the group of local gods worshiped by the Canaanites? Surely these who had dwelt century after century in the region were more expert than the Israelites who had just arrived! If, therefore, *they* turned to the local Baal to obtain water for their fields, if they prayed to Astarte to make the soil fertile, if they made their respective Baal (§ 107) intervene to control invasions of harmful insects, their customs and rites must have some sound basis and it would be grave stupidity to neglect them. Yahweh was indeed the wonder-working God who intervened at solemn moments in the history of the nation such as at the Red Sea, Sinai, the Jordan, and he should certainly remain "the God" of Israel. In the

ordinary routine affairs of daily life, however, why should there not be
a place beside him or, if one so wished, a somewhat lower place, for
these other Canaanite divinities who performed such opportune services?
Then too, their rites (§ 108) were so attractive, they offered such complete satisfaction and an enjoyment so spontaneous that the whole man,
body and spirit, was enraptured. The cult of the invisible Yahweh had
too much mystery in it; there was nothing to be seen, nothing one could
touch. And so there came about in Israel a mixture of rites and beliefs,
a "syncretism." It was the moral victory of the Canaanites.

314. Yahweh, however, many times called the "jealous God," began
to remove the pastoral ease which was the occasion of this attitude
of his nation. The raids of the Bedouin were only a carrying-out
of his plans. The true Bedouin did not cultivate fields; the hoe and
the plow were as dishonorable to him as the lance and shield were
honorable; the more so since the lance and shield — if well used in a
well-planned raid — could produce as much grain and provisions as
the hoe and the plow. The agricultural wealth of the Israelites of the
valley of Esdraelon must have become proverbial; at the same time word
must have gone abroad that the life of the fields had somewhat dulled
their fighting spirit. It was a real opportunity: the prey was not defended,
and the human jackals came promptly in from the desert.

Madianites, Amalecites, and other nomads, generically called "sons
of the East," organized regular raids. They set out from their Transjordanic bases of operation with the mobility of nomad tribes. Crossing
the Jordan at the usual fords of Jericho, before every harvest they
poured into the Israelite territory "like locusts" (Judg. 6:5) carrying
away everything — produce of the field and cattle. The intensity and
violence of the raids drove the unwarlike victims to excavate caves in
the rocks where they could hide provisions and even their very persons.
This state of affairs endured some years until "Israel was reduced to
great misery by reason of Madian: then the Israelites raised a cry to
Yahweh" (Judg. 6:6).

315. At that time in the tribe of Manasses, a certain Joas, of the clan
of Abiezer, lived at Ophra (Ephra; perhaps the present-day Tell el
Far'ah, along Wadi Far'ah to the northeast of Sichem; but cf. § 84a), with
his son Gedeon. The father had an altar in honor of Baal (Judg. 6:25)
although he was not very enthusiastic about that cult (6:31–32); the
son, in turn, was so embittered over the misfortunes of Israel that
he began to lose faith in Yahweh (Judg. 6:13). Nevertheless he was
the chosen one of Yahweh, the new Judge who would liberate his
people. Assured of his mission by a vision (Judg. 6:14 ff.), he tore down
his father's altar to Baal — during the night, out of prudence — and
erected an altar to Yahweh, immolating upon it a holocaust with the

Mount Gelboe.

wood of the broken asherah (§ 105). When the deed became known the following morning, the indignant inhabitants wanted to put the perpetrator to death. Joas, however, owner of the destroyed altar, protected his son, remarking dryly that he expected Baal to safeguard his own interests. Hence, from that day on Gedeon was called *Yerrubbaʿal*, "let Baal protect himself."

316. The bold action of Gedeon, which went almost unchallenged, won him his authority and recalled to the oppressed Israelites the ancient wonders of Yahweh, whose new champion had arisen. As a result when the usual raiders again crossed the Jordan the clan of Abiezer was first to respond to Gedeon's appeal for support. Then successively Manasses, Aser, Zabulon, and Nephtali also joined him. The two forces joined at Harod ('Ain Jalud), in one of the eastern outlets of the valley of Esdraelon: the Israelites on the slopes of the mountains of Gelboe, the Madianites a little farther to the north and lower down. Gedeon preferred surprise and stratagem to a general attack. Choosing three hundred men, he drew near to the enemy's camp during the night at three points; as the signal was given, Gedeon's fighters uncovered the lamps which they had hidden under pitchers, waving them about and sounding their trumpets. The unexpected clamor and the surprising lights all around the camp made the enemy think that their encampment had been entered. This produced what is not infrequent among bands of loosely organized raiders — panic. In the darkness one could not distinguish friend from enemy, so they began to kill each other until those who were left scattered in flight toward the fords of the Jordan. Gedeon and the rest of Israel gave chase; two leaders of Madian bearing totemic names (§§ 148, 167), Oreb ("raven") and Zeb ("wolf"), were captured and put to death near the Jordan; two other kings, Zebah and Zalmunna were seized and killed in Transjordan, for Gedeon had pursued the fugitives. On his return he severely punished the Israelites of Sukkoth and Penuel in Transjordan because they had refused — probably out of fear of reprisal — to furnish supplies to his soldiers while pursuing the enemy.

317. Aside from the victory which made the property of the region safe, the spoils gathered from the fugitives were immense. To the author of such a signal success the dignity of kingship was offered for himself and for his children. But Gedeon replied: "I shall not rule over you, nor will my son rule over you; Yahweh will rule over you!" (Judg. 8:23.) The reply is not as clear as it sounds. Apparently it is negative but it could be a mere formality, for Gedeon actually accepted the power and promised to employ his new authority with the understanding that the true king of Israel was Yahweh, and he, Gedeon, was only his vicar. Probably the people were divided into two factions: one in favor of a monarchy, such as flourished among the surrounding peoples (§§ 140, 339) and which with its stable organization seemed able to offset such evils as the periodical raids of Madian (§ 314); the other against a monarchy, having traditional and Yahwistic ideals for its foundation. Gedeon and his family did in fact wield a monarchic power (cf. Judg. 9:2), even though they did not have the title. It was a compromise between the two factions, even as the reply of Gedeon had been.

318. Of the spoils collected from the enemy Gedeon asked only for the ringlets of gold which amounted to 1700 sicles (about 60 pounds), and with these "Gedeon made an *ephod* and put it in the city of Ophra; and all Israel fornicated with it so that it became a scandal for Gedeon and for his family" (Judg. 8:27). It is disputed exactly what the *ephod* was, even though it was also used in the legitimate worship of Yahweh. Certainly it was a liturgical object, by means of which the will of Yahweh was ascertained in special cases. By putting in his native city this instrument for divination Gedeon evidently wished to have at his disposal a religious sanction for his future decisions as governor; also with it there grew up a center of a special cult which gave meaning to the expression "fornicated" employed here by the sacred writer; elsewhere this expression refers to an idolatrous worship.

In keeping with Semitic regal splendor and over and above the capital and the place of worship, Gedeon also had a harem (§§ 372, 400) and seventy sons. He died at a ripe old age and was buried at Ophra.

319. The *quasi* monarchy of Gedeon could not continue unchanged in his family: it either had to burgeon into a real monarchy or disappear entirely, and that is why the episode of Abimelech is inserted in the "anthology" of the Judges; it is the natural conclusion of the judgeship of Gedeon.

Abimelech was the son of Gedeon from one of his wives of the second class who lived at Sichem. After the death of his father, Abimelech, who seems to have resided at Ophra, repaired to Sichem among the relatives of his mother in order to further his cause. The seventy sons of Gedeon had succeeded to their father's place as a corporation which held authority in common, but Abimelech was excluded from the corporation because he was born outside the paternal harem or because he was not content to share the authority with the others; at any rate he schemed at Sichem to be recognized as king alone. His proposals easily found followers, enthusiastic because of their own interests and because of their vehement loyalty to their clan. Action was not long in coming. To finance the pretender seventy sicles of silver were provided, drawn from the temple of Baalberith, or Baal "of the pact," in Sichem. The function of this temple is significant; its origin was certainly Canaanite (§§ 88, 107), yet the fact that money was drawn from it to help an Israelite suggests that the Israelites dwelling in Sichem were at least part owners. After the Israelite conquest it either belonged completely to Israel or served indifferently for the Israelites ("El-berith"; Judg. 9:26) and the Canaanites ("Baal-berith"; Judg. 8:33; 9:4) since it is very difficult to imagine that two different temples are involved here. The incidents in Ophra which involved Gedeon and his father (§ 315) were therefore not isolated; the temple of Baal-berith is a fresh proof of the widespread syncretism of those times (§ 313), which the Bible designates here also by the term *fornication* (Judg. 8:33; § 318).

Having won over the rabble, Abimelech marched on Ophra and destroyed the ruling corporation by killing all seventy of his brothers. Only the youngest one, Jotham, escaped. On his return to Sichem, therefore, Abimelech was proclaimed king.

320. The throne acquired by such means was not very stable. Immediately after the proclamation of Abimelech, Jotham circulated a fable (Judg. 9:8–15) in which the evil choice made by the Sichemites and their ingratitude toward the family of Gedeon was set forth. Furthermore the subjects were divided among themselves; the Canaanite element which was very influential soon began to look with a jaundiced eye on the regime of an Israelite. Abimelech knew the state of affairs and did not reside at Sichem, but left in his place a trusted lieutenant by the name of Zebul. After three years of rule the rebellion broke out openly. The Sichemites began to molest the caravans which traversed the country, on which the king demanded the right to levy a toll. There arose then a leader of the people, a certain Gaal who had many followers. He placed himself at the head of the movement, but Abimelech, who had moved promptly to Sichem, in one operation drove the rebels inside the walls; he captured and then destroyed the city and, proceed-

Grinding wheat as in ancient days.

ing as far as the "Tower of Sichem" (§ 88) where the people had sought refuge in the temple of El-berith, burned it.

The insurrection was not entirely suppressed; it was flourishing at other points. Abimelech had to rush to Thebes (now Tubas, to the northeast of Sichem in the direction of Beisan) which was also revolting. He seized the suburbs, but in the assault on the central tower of the city, he was struck on the head by a millstone thrown from above by a woman. On the point of expiring, he made his shield-bearer kill him, to avoid the disgrace of having died by a woman's hand (§ 312). His kingdom fell with him, and the Israelites who had followed him dispersed.

321. Notwithstanding these facts, religious syncretism continued to flourish among the Israelites. They served "Baal, and the Astartes and gods of Aram and the gods of Sidon and the gods of Moab and the gods of the Ammonites, and the gods of the Philistines"; in fact syncretism was so prevalent that they practically "abandoned Yahweh and did not serve him any longer" (Judg. 10:6). This last passage of editorial origin sums up the real state of affairs.

This time the punitive oppression occurred in Transjordan. The people of Ammon who pressed from the east on the territory of the Transjordanic tribes, recovered their ancient rights (§ 268) and occupied a good part of the region to the south of the Jabbok, up to Galaad (perhaps a city but not identified). The best part of the pasture-lands were being lost: repeated raids toward the west disturbed also the other Israelites, filling them with forebodings of future losses in territory. In time the Israelites began to react and gathered together at Mispah (Maspha), a locality not identified, to the north of the Jabbok. Fighting spirit rose high, especially at the memory of their past leaders, but a leader who could measure up to them was lacking.

322. As a matter of fact there was a bold and energetic leader, but he lived a long way from the regions which then needed him. He was Jephte (Yiphtah) originally from Galaad, but expelled out of hatred by

his own family. Being the son of a prostitute, the legitimate sons of the household had driven him away when he was grown; he had then taken refuge in the land of Tob to the north of Galaad, in the region of the sources of the Jordan (§ 61), and there he had captained a band which lived the classic life of the Bedouin: raids, prowess, adventure. The fine reputation of Jephte's raiders testified to the ability of their chief. Here, then, was the leader who was needed for the willing but disorganized Israelites gathered together near Mispah.

Some of the elders were sent to invite Jephte to come. At the formal proposal that he become head of Galaad and defeat Ammon, the ancient wrongs faded from his mind; he came to Mispah, the promises were renewed before Yahweh, and he assumed command of the army.

The experienced sheikh of the Bedouins did not attack at once, for he wanted to study the situation and to await possible re-enforcements from the rest of Israel. He therefore began discussions with the Ammonites. When these failed, he proceeded to action.

323. The course of action, however, did not seem easy to the meditative captain. The re-enforcements which he expected, especially those from Ephraim, did not come, and the forces at his disposal did not inspire too much confidence when compared with those of the enemy. But his cause was a kind of judgment of God: the victor would be one who fought for the right. The authority of the God of the nation was pledged and since Israel was in the right, Yahweh would be at his side. The primitive religious sentiment of the Bedouin then overflowed in all its strength "and Jephte made a vow to Yahweh saying: if thou givest the Ammonites into my hand, whoever shall first come out from the doors of my house when I return as victor over the Ammonites, shall be Yahweh's and I will offer him in a holocaust" (Judg. 11:30–31). The memory of human sacrifices which the sheikh had seen offered many times by the Canaanites (§ 103) did not seem strange to him in his exalted state of mind; he must have reasoned that the seriousness of the situation called for such an extraordinary vow.

The enterprise met with success. The victory was as swift, in accordance with Bedouin tactics, as it was extensive; probably they attacked the enemy on the flank instead of the front. Jephte crushed them from the east toward the Jordan in as many separate skirmishes as were necessary for victory. Transjordan from north to south was free again: twenty cities which had passed over to the Ammonites were reconquered.

324. When the victorious campaign was concluded Jephte returned to his house in Mispah. His vow had certainly been secret so that Yahweh himself should designate the victim by causing him to come out first from the house to meet the victor. And behold, among joyous virgins ready to perform the customary victory "fantasia," was his own daughter, his only child. A violent cry, the lament of a father, burst forth

from the victor when he perceived the victim of his vow, but his vow
was even stronger than his paternal affection. "And it happened that
when he saw her, he rent his garments and said: Alas! my daughter!
Thou hast indeed grieved me! Thou hast become my sorrow! for I
have opened my mouth to Yahweh and I can not retract!" (Judg. 11:35.)
When the girl learned of his vow she consented to its fulfillment
asking only two months' postponement and liberty to roam about the
mountains with her companions to mourn her virginity. Her request
was granted and "the two months having expired she returned to her
father, who fulfilled his vow upon her, as he had promised. And she
did not know man" (Judg. 11:39).

325. Even in ancient times some exegetes, misguided by a sentiment
that is anachronistic because it is entirely Christian, supposed that the
immolation of the daughter of Jephte was symbolic, that the child was
only forced to lead a life of virginity. This opinion has been revived by
some modern scholars but on a quite different basis. The immolation
would allude to the consecration of the virgin, not as a *qedheshah*
(§ 108), but as a vestal (similar to the *enitu* [*entu*] among the Babylonians, § 203, note), in some idolatrous sanctuary of Yahweh. Similar
traditions of non-Semitic peoples are well known: there is the story of
Idomeneus and his son, *Virg. Aen.*, III, 121; or that of Menander, in ps.
Plutarch, *De Fluviis*, IX; or that of Iphigenia, in Euripides, *Iphig. Taur.*,
17 ff. Yet aside from these, the example of the Moabite king, Mesha, who
immolated his son in circumstances exactly parallel to those of Jephte
(§ 440; cf. the probable case of Achaz, § 452), is too clear to allow
of any doubt, since Mesha fought at the border of Palestine and against
the Israelites about the middle of the ninth century B.C. Jewish tradition (Josephus, *Antiquities*, V, 7, 10; Talmud Babli, *Taanith*, 4 a) has
looked upon the incident as being a true sacrifice. The lamenting of
her virginity emphasized by the biblical account renders the symbolic
interpretation possible, but such a lament would be entirely spontaneous
for Israelites, who considered that a woman who died without issue
had lived in vain.

The event, moreover, made so great an impression in Israel (a fact
which brings out the extreme rarity of such a deed, in contrast to its
frequent occurrence among the Canaanites; § 103), that thereafter
Jewish maidens dedicated four days a year to the commemoration,
with mournful wailing, of the maiden who was sacrificed (some traces
of this custom were still in existence at the time of Epiphanius,
Adv. haer., XXXV [LV], 1, in Migne, *P.G.*, 41, 973; and LVIII
[LXXVIII], 24, in *P.G.*, 42, 736). This has prompted some recent scholars
to interpret the episode as an historical revamping of the Adonis-
Tammuz myth (cf. Ezech. 8:14).

326. The success of Jephte caused rejoicing throughout the nation, but it seemed to cast a reflection on the tribe of Ephraim which, through its own fault (§ 323) had taken no part in it. The Ephraimites, unwilling to admit their fault, crossed the Jordan without further ado to attack Jephte, to punish him for not having called them. But they were routed and pushed back toward the river. The fords were guarded by Jephte's soldiers, who cross-examined the fugitives as they arrived, all of them naturally disclaiming any connection with Ephraim. The various tribes had slight variations of language which differentiated them one from another (cf. Mt. 26:73): the Ephraimites, for example, pronounced the sibilant-palatal *sh* (as in the English word *shore*) as a sibilant-dental *s* (as in the word *sun*). This peculiarity became the test for the fugitives; when they approached the fords, they were craftily

Philistine types on Egyptian monuments. (Rameses III.)

engaged in conversation about the river so that their replies would employ the word *shibboleth,* "current of water" (elsewhere also "ear of corn"). The false pronunciation *sibboleth* betrayed the Ephraimites, and they were killed. In like manner the French were betrayed by their pronunciation of *ceci* at the Sicilian Vespers, March 31, 1282.

327. Samson, last of the major Judges, is the popular hero *par excellence;* his deeds must have been the preferred theme of the traditional stories of Israel, which were derived from different sources and varied in length. In him Yahwistic religious sentiment, fiery nationalism, and a fondness for heroic tales found full expression.

The target of Samson's undertakings was the Philistines. After the defeat inflicted on them by Rameses III when they attacked the Delta (§ 35), they settled on the seacoast of southern Canaan and for about a century were contained in their holdings on the seacoast. Shortly after 1100 B.C. they began to branch out into the northeastern hinterland, thus coming into contact with the Israelites who were there slowly consolidating their conquests, and who up to that time must not have had any hostile encounters.

328. Everything conspired from the start to make the Philistines the

Gaza, seen from the west. (Vester, Amer. Colony.)

typical enemies of Israel: diversity of racial stock, language, religion, and civilization. The Philistine was for Israel the "uncircumcised" *par excellence,* in other words, an inferior human being in every way. In matters of war and probably also in civil organization, however, the Philistines were from the beginning superior to the Israelites. Most expert in seafaring — in which the Israelites were completely inexperienced — noteworthy adventurers, they possessed an experience in the science of war inherited from the Aegean islands and Asia Minor whence they came (where in the meantime the period of the Trojan war was followed by the invasion of the Dorians). Of commanding stature, physiologically they were superior to the Israelites and suffered no serious inconvenience in adapting themselves to new surroundings. Their territory was made up of a pentarchy whose capitals were the five cities Ashdod (Azotus), Accaron (Eqron), Ascalon, Gaza, and Gath (Geth; § 75), all close to the Mediterranean. Their expansion into the hinterland, at the expense chiefly of the territories of Dan and Juda, was a slow and continuous movement which assumed in time the nature of an intolerable oppression. Then arose Samson, who, it must be noted, acted alone and for the most part on his own initiative.[4]

329. The biblical account describes the hero as being endowed with extraordinary strength; this is connected either with his birth which was foretold by Yahweh, or with his state as a religious "Nazarite" (Num. 6:1–21) to which his parents had consecrated him, and which obliged

---

[4] R. A. S. Macalister, *The Philistines* (Schweich Lectures, 1911), London, 1913.

him not to cut his hair (a quite common custom among ancient warriors) and to abstain from inebriating drink. As long as he remained
faithful to these conditions he would be granted extraordinary strength
but if he did not fulfill the obligations of his state or transgressed the
spirit of it, his strength would disappear.

In one account Samson loved a Philistine girl of the city of Timnah.
He wanted to marry her notwithstanding the reluctance of his parents,
scandalized that one chosen by Yahweh should be enamored of a
daughter of the uncircumcised; but "the affair [had been arranged] by
Yahweh, who sought an occasion [to attack] the Philistines" (Judg.
14:4). Once when going to visit his betrothed, Samson met a lion on
the road and tore it to pieces "as one would tear a kid to pieces." On
his return, he examined the carcass of the lion, and found that a swarm
of bees had gathered there and made honey. The incident later served
on the occasion of the marriage festivities as a riddle for his Philistine
guests, who agreed on the forfeit he suggested. Unable to solve the
riddle, they succeeded in learning the secret from Samson's wife and
so escaped paying the penalty. Samson paid the forfeit at the expense
of thirty Philistines of Ascalon, whom he killed and stripped for that
purpose. Sometime later Samson again visited his wife and finding
her given to another, vengefully burned the ripened crops of the
Philistines. He accomplished this by tying foxes together in pairs,
fastening torches to their tails and driving them through the fields
(similar means of vengeance were used elsewhere among the Semites;
according to Ovid [*Fasti*, IV, 679 ff.] the Romans had some such custom
as a circus game). In reprisal the Philistines burned Samson's wife and
her home, and he revenged her by slaughtering them.

330. These personal forays provoked a punitive expedition against
Samson. To avoid open war the Israelites persuaded the giant to deliver
himself to his enemies. He allowed himself to be bound with new ropes,
but as soon as he was in the power of the Philistines he broke the ropes
"like flax that has caught on fire," and seizing the jawbone of an ass,
killed a thousand Philistines with it. He threw down the jawbone, and
Yahweh caused a fountain to gush forth from it to slake the giant's
thirst. From that time on the name of the place was known as Ramath-
lehi, "height of the jawbone."

Later on Sampson visited a harlot in Philistine Gaza. The leaders
wished to avail themselves of this fine opportunity to do away with
their hated enemy, and closed the gates of the city at night, hoping to
kill him next morning. Awakening about midnight, Samson went to the
gate, lifted up the posts, crossbars and all, and carried them to the
top of a mountain.

331. His ruin was finally brought about by a woman named Delilah, of the valley of Soreq. She was in the employ of the Philistines to learn from Samson the secret of his strength. At first he gave her false leads, following which she first bound him with seven moist bow cords; then with new ropes; then while he slept she wove the seven locks of his hair in the warp of the loom which was firmly imbedded in the wall and ground, but each time she cried out that the Philistines were coming, Samson burst his bonds as if they were tow, and pulled up the loom as if it were a toy. The complaints of the disappointed woman became increasingly petulant and insistent, and Samson yielded, telling her that his strength lay in the fact that he was a Nazarite (§ 329); if his hair, as yet untouched by a razor, were cut, his strength would vanish. Delilah, while he slept, caused his hair to be cut; when the Philistines came this time, Samson was seized, blinded, led to Gaza, and put to turning the millstone, but safely bound in chains.

332. Time passed and the Philistines celebrated a great feast in honor of their god Dagon (according to some from *dagh,* "fish"; but more probably, according to Philo of Byblos [Fr. II, 16, in Müller, *Fragm.*], from *daghan,* "grain," hence an agricultural god). To make the ceremonies still merrier, their great enemy, delivered into their hands through the benignity of Dagon, was brought in. Along with the religious festivities there were dances and games in which athletic exhibitions imported by the Philistines from their Aegean contacts played an important part. It was a splendid occasion for an exhibition by Samson, blinded and conquered but still of gigantic frame. They had, however, forgotten one fact: his hair had grown back and he had regained externally his Nazarite state. Approaching Yahweh with a contrite spirit internally as well, he was again in full possession of all his extraordinary strength. He came to the feast. The sight of him was interesting and entertaining to the leaders and to the crowd gathered inside the temple of Dagon, on the roof, and all around. At a certain moment the blinded giant was led to the center of the temple, to the two pillars which were the key supports of the whole building. Arrived there he called upon Yahweh, felt the pillars, took hold of them, applied all his strength, shook them, and then pulled down the whole building with the pillars, burying himself and the spectators in the ruins.

333. From the heroic character of the deeds and from the name of the protagonist, Shimshon (from *shemesh,* "sun"; cf. the Babylonian Shamshanu), not a few modern scholars, followers of the astral myth theories (§ 166), are inclined to perceive in the figure of Samson a hero of a solar myth. On the other hand, the important part played by a foreign temptress in the history of Samson has not been sufficiently emphasized; under this aspect the activities of Samson illustrate the internal history of Israel in its private relations with the Canaanites and Philistines

rather than its international political history, as in the deeds of the other major Judges.[5]

* * *

334. The appendix which follows immediately after the schematic anthology (§ 300 ff.) of *Judges* also permits one to catch a glimpse of the internal history of Israel. This appendix relates two episodes which are not connected with the rest of the book nor related to each other. The first — concerning the Levite of Michas and the origin of the sanctuaries of Dan (Judg. 17–18) — provides instructive information about the ideas and religious customs in vogue among the people of that period; the second — concerning the crime and destruction of the tribe of Benjamin (Judg. 19–21) — gives an idea of the relations which prevailed among the various tribes, divided among themselves up to that point by their own particular interests. It also shows to what extent they all felt bound by the common bond of nationality.

335. Michas, an inhabitant of the mountainous region of Ephraim, secretly appropriated 1100 sicles of silver belonging to his mother. She, cursing the unknown thief, vowed to give to Yahweh whatever was recovered. The son then confessed, restored the money, and was blessed by his mother, who by reason of the vow, took 200 sicles and had them made into a statue of the divinity, one of those statues which the legitimate cult of Yahweh condemned on general principles (§ 252). Once the statue was made Michas had a "house of God," made an ephod (§ 318) and some teraphim (§ 144), and consecrated one of his sons a priest (Judg. 17:5). The "house of God," or sanctuary, was therefore set up with care and furnished with whatever was most likely to attract the people, and the enterprise proceeded satisfactorily but for one flaw: his son, the pseudo-priest, was not a man to command much authority, and he soon realized he would have to be replaced, as a genuine priest had to belong to the tribe of Levi (§ 276) whereas both he and his son belonged to that of Ephraim. A fortunate coincidence soon remedied that situation. A Levite of Bethlehem of Juda, a stranger (*ger*) in the tribe of Juda, left that region to look for better living conditions. Passing through the mountains of Ephraim, he came to the sanctuary of Michas, who received him with all the satisfaction of a businessman finding a long-awaited opportunity. A contract was quickly drawn up: Michas would give him ten sicles of silver a year, food, and clothing; the Levite was to give his services to the sanctuary. Everything now was or seemed to be in order, so that Michas could say: "Now I know that Yahweh will do well by me, since the Levite has become my priest" (Judg. 17:13).

---

[5] Smythe Palmer, *The Samson-Saga*, London, 1913.

336. Instead, another coincidence served to upset these plans, and the prosperous sanctuary of Michas disappeared.

It so happened that just at that time, five emissaries from the tribe of Dan passed by. The tribe had long wanted a different territory from that assigned to it, since the Danites were hemmed in between the Amorites and the Philistines; these five men were searching for such territory. When they arrived by chance at Michas' place, they recognized the wandering Levite and obtained from him a reply from Yahweh which promised success to their search. They pushed on up to the extreme north of Palestine, and there they saw that the region of Lais (§ 60) was most suitable for their needs. On returning to their tribe they related the results of their search, and six hundred armed soldiers with their families began the journey away from the old territory. Naturally they passed by Michas again, where they commandeered the ephod and teraphim from the sanctuary, and persuaded the Levite to follow them to their new settlement saying: "Which is better for thee, to be the priest of the house of one man alone, or to be the priest of a tribe and a clan in Israel?" (Judg. 18:19.) The protestations of the ruined Michas were silenced by the threats of the armed plunderers, and so in this way the priest and the sacred possessions moved on to the north. Lais was taken from the Canaanites and was called Dan; there the sanctuary of Dan (so called because its clients were chiefly Danites) was set up. In later times it was an object of censure because of its separatist and idolatrous character.

337. Such is the story as related in the appendix of *Judges*. Comparing it with that of the golden calf at the foot of Sinai (§ 254), one finds in both the same propensity of the people for a materialized cult of Yahweh but also a notable difference. At the foot of Mt. Sinai the reaction of authentic Yahwism was prompt and energetic; here, there was not the least reaction; instead the idolatrous sanctuary of Dan was accepted together with that of Silo, where the Ark itself, containing the text of the alliance between the nation and the immaterial Yahweh, rested (§ 253). Moreover, if even in the time of Gedeon national sanctuaries of this kind were erected by personages of note (§ 318), and if even in the altar erected by the tribes of Transjordan (§ 293) one can probably discover a similar attempt, it is permissible to conclude that at the time of this episode, particular sanctuaries, more or less important, must have been numerous, especially since, as Michas', they were probably intended for gain. A twofold circumstance had favored the rise of this state of affairs. There was, in the first place, the constant contact with Canaanite sanctuaries; even if this did not succeed in fomenting a formal apostasy from Yahweh, it readily induced the people to act toward Yahweh as they did toward Baal, Astarte, and other varieties of local gods. The altar erected to Baal by the father of Gedeon (§ 315) and the temple of Baal-berith at Sichem (§ 319) are typical examples differing in degree. In the second place, against this seductive and incessant danger the power of protective reaction had been diminished; the leader of Yahwism who had intervened so efficaciously at the foot of Sinai was now no longer present; the theocratic bonds which bound the tribes together existed still in theory, but practically they were much relaxed and national unity had suffered accordingly (§ 296). There was no strong leader to intervene and check the evil.

338. The second episode is more sinister. Another Levite, living to the north of the mountain of Ephraim, was returning home from Bethlehem, where he had been reconciled with a secondary wife who had been estranged from him. In order not to spend the night at Jerusalem, which was still in the hands of the Jebusites (§ 305), they continued on their way until they came as far as Gabaa (Gibe'a; § 85), where they were received hospitably not by the Benjamites of the place but by an Ephraimite stranger (*ger*) who had settled there. That night an event occurred which bears a strong resemblance to something that happened to Lot (§ 136). The Benjamites of the place went to the host and demanded that he hand the Levite over to them for their infamous purposes. The host refused, offering instead his own virgin daughter and the wife of the Levite, but they insisted. Then the Levite delivered to them his own wife, and she remained in their hands until morning, when she dragged herself to the door of the house, and there died with her hands outstretched toward the threshold. Her husband, getting ready to resume his journey, found her in the morning. He placed the corpse on his animal and took it to his house, and there cut it into twelve pieces. A piece was sent to each of the tribes of Israel to denounce and prove the crime.

All Israel was aroused "and gathered together as one man . . . before Yahweh" (Judg. 20:1) in the territory of the guilty tribe, i.e., at Mispah of Benjamin (Maspha; § 89). The punishment of Gabaa was decided upon, and also that of Benjamin which had taken the side of the inhabitants of Gabaa. The first attacks were repulsed by the valorous defense of the Benjamites, but Gabaa fell and was burned, and the whole tribe was killed except for six hundred who saved themselves by flight.

Later on, however, a certain sentiment of compassion was felt for the survivors. As they were now without wives, they were permitted to take four hundred virgins from Jabes in Galaad, a city which the Israelites had recently destroyed because it had not borne its share of the war against Benjamin; only these virgins had escaped the general slaughter. To fill up the number of wives, the Benjamites were also allowed to conduct a kind of Sabine rape at the expense of the inhabitants of Silo (§ 87).

SAMUEL, THE MONARCHY,
AND THE SCHISM

339. As the era of the Judges approached an end, the patriarchal and dictatorial regime was seen to be increasingly unable to cope with the changing conditions of the nation. The neighboring Edomites and Philistines could boast of political organizations which were both compact and centralized. Israel's inferiority in this respect must have been apparent to the people, for the proposal of a monarchical regime had found support as far back as the time of Gedeon and Abimelech (§ 317 ff.). But, side by side with the monarchical faction there was the very powerful and older conservative party (§ 346), to which the institution of a monarchy in Israel seemed an innovation, as dangerous in the political field as it was audacious in the religious. No one, however, could halt the march of events, and with the passage of the years and the succession of events the social constitution of the era of the Judges lost ground and the idea of a monarchy made ever more progress.

The menace of the Philistines became increasingly grave on the ill-defined frontiers. The exploits of Samson in his struggles with them had furnished good material for the traditional stories of the people, but had not scattered the ominous cloud forming in the southwest. That cloud in fact was getting blacker and would overshadow what remained of the period of the Judges and the first part of the monarchical era; in the shadow of that cloud and in great part provoked by it, arose the monarchical regime which finally dissipated it entirely.

340. Heli is presented by the Bible as the last Judge but one (1 Sam. 4:18 d: editorial note); but his judgeship is, from the little that is known of it, quite different from the typical ones of a Gedeon or a Debora. Neither a leader of soldiers, nor of the people, knowing how to instill enthusiasm in the masses, his pre-eminence in the nation was probably due solely to the fact of his dignity as high priest, through the line of Ithamar, in the national sanctuary of Silo (§ 292). In this dull period in which no one with leadership or spirit arose above the general plane of mediocrity, the eyes of the nation were turned toward the priest of Silo as if he, by his office, were something of a Gedeon or a Debora.

He was, instead, a weakling. A sincere Yahwist assiduous in office, he allowed himself to be controlled in his priestly functions by his two sons, Hophni and Pinehas (possibly Egyptian names, "tadpole" and "black"). Their cupidity led them to tamper with the offerings made by the people to the sanctuary, in clear violation of the laws of worship. According to one tradition (1 Sam. 2:22 b, missing in the Greek Vaticanus) they were also guilty of licentious acts on the grounds adjacent to the sanctuary. The complaints of scandalized pilgrims forced Heli to warn the two culprits, but his admonition was so weak that the scandal continued as before. The father, a feeble old man almost blind, and impotent in his sterile piety, continued as the head of the nation. Beside him stood the two active sons, "sons of *belial*" (2:12). Yet right under their noses, so to speak, Yahweh was preparing an unforeseen successor who would be ready to take over when Yahweh struck this sorry trio.

341. At the sanctuary of Silo a small child had been presented to Heli so that he might be reared in the service of Yahweh according to a vow made by his mother Anna. She was the wife of Elcana. Being sterile, she was taunted by Phenenna, another wife of Elcana, and she suffered bitterly. During one of the annual pilgrimages of the family to Silo, Anna prayed fervently in the sanctuary for a child, promising him to Yahweh. Her request was granted and she gave the child the name of Samuel (*Shemu'el*, probably "heard-by-God"); when he was grown up a bit she sent him as a Nazarite (§ 329) to Heli in Silo. There he was visited from time to time by his mother, all the while growing in stature and in goodness before Yahweh and before men (1 Sam. 2:26).

Although thrown into the company of Hophni and Pinehas at the sanctuary, the young Samuel did not yield to the suggestions which were made to him daily. The memory of his mother and her visits must have had a profound effect on his mind, but the personal example and the words of Heli certainly contributed to the spiritual formation of the young man, who was able to distinguish clearly between the father and his sons, and between Heli's irreproachable conduct and the weakness of his character. In such obvious contrast to his background, the figure of the young Samuel attracted more and more attention from those who frequented the sanctuary. They came from all sections and spoke well of him when they returned to their homes. It also was speedily broadcast that Yahweh had made the young priest the confidant of his revelations, although "the word of Yahweh was rare in those days, and there was no frequent vision" (1 Sam. 3:1). When he was still inexperienced in divine communications Yahweh confided to him one night the imminent punishment he was about to visit upon the scandalous sons of Heli and their weak father; Heli himself, obsequiously receiving the announcement, knew the divine communication to be genuine. With the passage of time, all Israel . . . recognized that Samuel was the established prophet of Yahweh; Yahweh continued to reveal himself in Silo, because Yahweh revealed himself to Samuel (1 Sam. 3:20–21). Heli's successor was ready.

342. Continuing their gradual occupation of Israelite territory, the Philistines provoked a reaction; Israel descended to the field of battle in goodly numbers and encountered the Philistines at Apheq but was put to flight leaving four thousand dead on the field. Although the defeat was not fatal it was serious; more serious, however, was the outlook for the future, of which this defeat seemed a portent. The defeated warriors then had recourse to a measure which seemed infallible to them: they sent to Silo for the Ark of Yahweh. The memories of ancient victories obtained by Moses and Josue, who kept the Ark close to the ranks of the combatants, were in keeping with this decision, but there also was a large measure of confidence in a supposed magical character of the sacred object. Centuries later that confidence would lead the inhabitants of Jerusalem to shout as a refrain "Temple of Yahweh" (Jer. 7:4), as if the Temple with the Ark within would magically suffice to stave off the destruction of the city by Nabuchodonosor (§ 523 ff.).

The Ark arrived at the encampment, carried by Hophni and Pinehas. Battle was joined. Not only was Israel routed and thirty thousand dead left on the field of battle, but the Ark itself was captured and the two sons of Heli killed.

That very same day a fugitive from the slaughter ran to Silo where Heli, now almost a centenarian and worried about the Ark of Yahweh, awaited word of the battle. When he heard the horrible news the old man fell backward from his chair, and died.

Never before had such a calamity befallen the nation of Yahweh: the enemy, strong and triumphant, the Ark in enemy hands, the national sanctuary of Silo bereft of its most sacred object and its high priest. As the new star of Yahwism arose it was confronted by this catastrophe, and Samuel, that star, was still too immature to be able to prescribe an efficacious remedy. Was this perhaps a general collapse, and the end of everything?

343. For many years no answer could be given to this question. A period of military disorganization followed the defeat as if in expectation of the end.

In the meantime the Ark, the greatest trophy of victory, was carried by the Philistines to Ashdod and placed in the temple of the god Dagon (§ 332) as if to testify to the inferiority of the defeated God. In the personal struggle between the two divinities, however, the roles were quickly reversed: the day after the Ark was placed in the temple it was found that the statue of Dagon had fallen to the ground in front of the Ark. It was put back in its place, but it was found the next day to have fallen again. Furthermore, its head and arms had been broken. But more than this, an unexpected invasion of mice damaged their crops and was followed by the usual bubonic plague, with loathsome swellings in the groin. This persuaded the people of Asdod better than any speculative theology to get rid of the Ark, the cause of all these evils. In order to keep the trophy in their country, it was sent to Gath (§ 328), but when this city was also struck by the plague the Ark went on to Accaron. Accaron was also afflicted, and on the advice of diviners, the trophy was put on a cart pulled by two cows without a driver, and on the cart were placed, as *ex-voto* offerings, five mice and five emerods of gold, according to the number of the Philistine cities (§ 328). When they were given free rein, the cows took the road toward the territory of the Israelites, and thus the Ark re-entered Israel, seven months after it had been captured (1 Sam. 6:1).

But the Ark did not return again to Silo, which had probably been destroyed meanwhile by the Philistines (Jer. 7:12–14). In any case it had lost its importance (§ 87). The Ark was first taken down from the cart at Beth-shemesh (§ 93) where the family of a certain Jechonias was severely punished by Yahweh (1 Sam. 6:19: Greek text) for failing to have respect for it. Next it was carried to Cariath-iarim, where it remained in the house of a certain Abinadab who deputed his son Eleazar to guard it, and there it remained until the time of David.

Twenty years passed (1 Sam. 7:2), a period of disorganization in which the Philistines enjoyed an absolute hegemony over the southern tribes of Israel, but the star of Samuel was continually rising.

344. In general the Philistine oppression served to recall Israel t, ancient Yahwism, especially through the intervention of Samuel, who led a campaign against the various syncretistic cults. The Philistines seized an occasion when the people were gathered at Mispah (§ 89) for a religious ceremony at Samuel's suggestion, to make the first hostile move. They attacked the assembled people, but, handicapped by a tempest, were repulsed and pursued by the Israelites. According to ancient custom (§ 145) Samuel erected a memorial stone on the spot to which the pursuit had driven, calling it the *'Ebhen ha-'ezer,* "stone of the [divine] help."

This clash of arms was more important as an indication than as a thing in itself; there seem to have been no others until the time of King Saul. Samuel had now become in fact the supreme authority in Israel, the Judge, who, if not a military leader like his predecessors compensated for this by being a legitimate priest. His actions in these two capacities developed into a consistent, methodical procedure; he "went about every year and made the circuit of Beth-el, Gilgal, and Mispah, and he judged Israel in all those places [*sanctuaries* in the Greek]; then he returned to Rama, for his house was there, and there he judged Israel and built an altar to Yahweh" (1 Sam. 7:16–17). As a matter of fact, Samuel's father Elcana was from Rama (§ 341), and according to 1 Para. 6:16 ff. seems to have been a Levite, a fact which made his priesthood legitimate. The activity, therefore, which Samuel engaged in was the profound work of a faithful reorganizer and, in part, innovator. While the other Judges had been principally political heads and secondarily religious leaders, he was above all a religious leader and only secondarily a political chief.

345. The above-mentioned inversion of the values of judgeship is especially noteworthy in Samuel, the last Judge. The Philistine domination must certainly have had its part in this, but the changed conditions had a greater. The regime of Judges who were at the same time military leaders no longer corresponded to the social life of the people now firmly established in Palestine; since, therefore, there were no military leaders, there remained only the person at the top of the religious hierarchy, i.e., in the case at hand, Samuel. It was vaguely felt, however, that something was missing in the supreme command. The religious regency was occupied but where was the political center, without a leader? Was not this vacancy perhaps a principal cause of the continuing humiliation of Israel before the Philistines? And if the ancient "Judge-General" did not arise, was it not time to think of a stable monarchy?

Samuel himself, understanding the new conditions, had made an attempt at a stable, organized regime: now that he had grown old he chose his own two sons to help him in his judgeship, setting them up as "Judges" at Beersheba, where they could attend to the needs of southern Israel (§ 60). What was before an extraordinary office dependent on the will of God, not subject to intrigue or transmissible, was by this transformed into something methodically bureaucratic. Yet the attempt at compromise, intended to accommodate the ancient regime to new circumstances, was a failure. Samuel's sons comported themselves differently from their father; they became corrupt in administering justice and ended by besmirching the good name which the judgeship still enjoyed because of the personal merits of Samuel. When the compromise failed, the majority of the people were convinced that there was no middle way: there would be either political anarchy or a stable monarchy. They turned, therefore, to the supreme religious authority, Samuel, and requested the official institution of a monarchy.

346. The example of the neighboring peoples who had monarchies (§§ 140, 339) was naturally one of the prime motives for the request (1 Sam. 8:5–20); nevertheless this and the other reasons mentioned did not win unanimous support, and side by side with the majority which was for the monarchy there was a powerful minority which did not approve.

Repercussions of this twofold partition are reflected in the double account which has come down to us about the institution of the monarchy (1 Sam. 8–11). In fact there is one account which can be called that of the majority (principally 9–10:16) all in favor of the monarchy: and another of the minority (principally 10:17 ff.; cf. 8:6 ff.) which, although it accepts the accomplished fact, carefully brings to light the shortcomings and inconveniences connected with it. These negotiations must have been long and difficult. It is certain, for example, that some episodes occurred at Mispah, others at Gilgal. It was natural, therefore, that there would be two accounts according to the political preferences: one which would emphasize the bright side of the events taking place; the other taking dour pleasure in showing the darker side, preferring to dwell on the episodes at Mispah. The two accounts in some respects may be complementary. Samuel personally was opposed to the monarchy from the beginning, according to the minority account (8:6 ff.; 10:19), but as the one who had charge of the situation, he submerged his personal opinion and yielded to the will of the majority. For this reason he appears in the majority account, if not as its spirited leader, certainly as a supporter of the new institution just sanctioned by him.

347. In Gabaa (§ 85), belonging to the tribe of Benjamin, was a family of a certain Cis, renowned for the sterling qualities and courage of its members. One son of Cis, Saul (*Sha'ul,* "asked [of God]"), stood out, a man of extraordinary stature, something which always made a deep impression on ancient peoples. It was the period of the great oppression by the Philistines who had a governor (*nesibh;* 1 Sam. 13:3 ff.) in Gabaa, surrounded no doubt by a small armed band; it is not unlikely that the renown achieved by the men of Cis was due to a number of small spirited skirmishes — similar to those of Samson — perpetrated here and there against isolated Philistine stations, and in which those courageous men must have found a willing help from the local populations. They were like sparks shooting up every now and then from beneath the ashes: unable as yet to start a fire, they neverthe-less attracted the admiring and encouraging glances of the oppressed.

They had attracted the attention also of Samuel, and his gaze rested especially on the gigantic figure of Saul. The physical pre-eminence of this man may have seemed to the Judge of Israel an indication of the designs of Yahweh, who had perhaps destined him to be the monarch requested by the people. Then one day Yahweh revealed to the "seer" (§ 419) in Rama (§ 344) that on the following day there would come to visit him the man whom he was to appoint as "ruler" in Israel (1 Sam. 9:16). The next day Saul, who was making a circuitous journey in search of his father's strayed asses, arrived at Rama. Samuel performed the Semitic elective ceremony on him in secret, pouring on his head the oil of anointing and constituting him "ruler" (10:1) in Israel. In Samuel's mind this election was not, apparently, definitive in character, nor did it confer the real dignity of "kingship." The secrecy with which it was performed and the title of "ruler" employed in the account gives it the appearance of a trial election. The task of the chosen one was principally that of being the leader in the struggle against the Philistines, i.e., he was to supply under the higher moral guidance of Samuel what was lacking in Samuel's judgeship. If he passed this test, and his valor gave every promise that he would, he would be publicly and definitively chosen as king.

348. Confirmation of this view may be seen in the exhortation which Samuel addressed to Saul immediately after the ceremony of election. Saul must act quickly and give a good account of himself. Yahweh is with him, as will be made evident in the encounters which await him as he leaves Samuel; when he arrives in Gabaa "where the governor[1] of the Philistines is" (1 Sam. 10:5) he will meet a band of prophets prophesying (§ 419) and the spirit of Yahweh will also envelop him (§ 361). When this happens, let him face any contingency with courage, because God is with him (10:7). This last exhortation, following upon the mention of Gabaa, must have seemed to Saul an invitation to begin his test at Gabaa.

In fact, some time after, "the governor of the Philistines who was at Gabaa" was killed by Jonathan, Saul's son (13:3). It was the signal for revolt, and Saul saw to it that the news was spread throughout Israelite territory. A gathering of the people at Gilgal was ordered. Taken by surprise the Philistines understood that the insurrection was serious. To cope with it effectively, they took time to recruit an adequate army. This pause was even more useful to Saul, since the Israelites were unprepared for a long war (§ 350).

349. The expedition against the Ammonites seems to have taken place during this time (it perhaps falls between verses 4 and 5 of 1 Sam. 13; at any rate its date is problematical). During this waiting period, probably seeking to profit by the threat which hung over Israel, the leader of the Ammonites, whose name was Nahas ("serpent": perhaps a totemic name, § 316, but cf. §§ 106, 265) attempted to reduce the Israelite city

---

[1] The ancient versions have the singular; the Hebrew has the plural.

of Jabes-Galaad in Transjordan. The inhabitants turned to Saul for help and, making a national issue of it, he laid the matter before the nation. Within a few days he hastened to Transjordan with the soldiers he was able to gather around him, and defeated the Ammonites.

This success raised the spirits of the nation and naturally furthered the candidacy of Saul for monarch. His public and definitive election to the kingship should probably be assigned to this period. Samuel must have felt that his period of probation (§ 347) had been passed success-fully and that the deeds already accomplished were a guarantee of future activities against the Philistines. When the people were gathered before Yahweh in Mispah, therefore, Samuel proceeded to the election of the king by means of the sacred lot; it fell to Saul. Samuel then laid down his official judgeship, receiving from the people ample recognition of the meritorious way in which he had discharged his office. He exhorted them to be faithful to Yahweh and obedient to the king. From that day on he restricted his activities to those of the religious leader of Israel, which implied sovereignty over and surveillance of even the new king. This decisive development in the history of Israel took place about the year 1040 (§ 302, cf. § 369).

350. The Philistines with a strong army had gathered in the meantime at Michmas, east of Beth-aven. But they were not the Ammonites, and it was only too clear that methodical war against them was much more difficult than the daring little forays which had succeeded so well at Gabaa (§ 348). Many Israelites, indeed, responded to the national appeal of Saul, but they were very poorly armed, having for weapons only hoes, spades, and other farming implements. The Philistines had allowed them to retain these, but had sequestered all arms (as in the time of Debora, § 311; a policy Porsenna followed against the Romans, Pliny, *Nat. Hist.*, XXXIV, 14). For a grand assault against the expert warriors of the Philistines they were hopelessly inadequate. Most of those who came to the gathering were bitterly disappointed and, as they were afraid, they disbanded, seeking refuge in desert strongholds or beyond the Jordan.

Nevertheless Saul wished to attack, but not before he offered sacrifice to Yahweh. When Samuel, who was to perform the ceremony, was late in coming, Saul, in order to prevent a further disbanding of his soldiers, himself offered the sacrifice. The rite was scarcely finished when Samuel arrived. He reproved Saul sharply as if for an act of usur-pation. Added to this Saul found that only six hundred men were left to him.

Under the circumstances, this was certainly not the moment to attempt a pitched battle with the enemy; guerrilla warfare and bold raids seemed indicated. A successful raid was accomplished at this time by Jonathan

(§ 348); the surprise produced in the enemy's camp by his unexpected appearance with his shield-bearer was followed by a certain confusion, and Saul seized that moment to attack. At the same time the Hebrews who were not Israelites (§ 172), imprudently engaged by the Philistines on this occasion, availed themselves of the opportunity to revolt. The defeat which followed, although not decisive, was a relatively grave one for the Philistines. It now seemed useless to them to keep a full army ready for battle when the enemy would not accept the challenge but would only conduct extensive guerrilla activities, so for the time being, the Philistines withdrew.

351. The suspension of hostilities was advantageous for Saul, because at that time it was most urgent that he have a military organization. This could be established with a permanent army as a nucleus. In fact "when Saul saw a courageous man or one fit for war, he took him to himself" (1 Sam. 14:52). His expeditions against Moab, Edom (or Aram?; § 306), and others (14:47) which were successful but of minor importance fit in here.

The progress of the military organization can be measured by the fact that later on Saul was in a position to carry the war into a rather distant region, and almost to encircle the Philistines. A campaign on a vast scale against the Amalecites had serious consequences for Saul. He had invited the Qenite inhabitants to withdraw from the Amalecites, the ancient enemies of Israel (§ 241), because Yahweh through Samuel had commanded him to carry out the *herem* (§ 271) in their regard, and he had no wish to involve the friendly Qenites (§ 291). The campaign was successful and the Amalecites were soundly defeated "from Hevila [or Telam?] up to Shur" (15:7), i.e., in the region south of the Negeb (§ 65), and their king, Agag, was taken prisoner. The booty was very rich but, either because the cupidity of the victors was aroused or because they saw an opportunity to recoup the losses suffered by the southern territory of Israel from the raids of the Amalecites (who had probably started the war), the fact remains that it was not totally destroyed as the *herem* demanded, but the more valuable items were spared and preserved.

The violation of the *herem* by the king himself was, Samuel thought, a grave crime, and when he met Saul at Gilgal he openly rebuked him. In the eyes of the religious head of Israel, the rebellion of Saul against the dictates of the *herem* imposed by Yahweh took on the malice of a "sin of [idolatrous] divination" and of a "crime of *teraphim*" (§ 146); Samuel concluded that as Saul had rejected the command of Yahweh so Yahweh had rejected Saul from his kingly dignity (15:23). The religious usurpation previously perpetrated by Saul (§ 350) was aggravated by the violation of the *herem*. However, at Saul's request

Samuel concealed the true state of affairs so as to save the kingly "face" before the people. After causing Agag to be killed in accordance with the *herem,* he departed and isolated himself at Rama (§ 344). He would not again see Saul during his lifetime (§ 364).

352. When Samuel and Saul had their falling out, the monarchy was quite solidly established in Israel and had begun to produce many benefits. One proof of this, among others, is that even the tragic end of Saul — which seemed to imply a catastrophe for the whole nation — did not cause them in any manner to reconsider a return to the regime of the Judges; the monarchy continued without upheavals and from the beginning the succession was hereditary (§ 367). The monarchy indeed had demonstrated that it was a decided advantage to the whole nation; the military organization, which had made possible the expedition against the Amalecites, was the child of the monarchy. The Philistines, always a threat because of their superiority in warfare, seem now to have been restrained from attacking the new regime because they perceived in it new possibilities of resistance and power.

The monarch personally had shown himself equal to his office. Apart from his religious arguments with Samuel, kept secret from the people (§ 351), he did not fail to live up to his previous fame as a; warrior. He was a wise leader in war, and in his private life had remained simple and humble. He continued to live on his lands at Gabaa, and they do not seem to have acquired any pre-eminence from the elevation of its citizen (§ 85). He had built neither palace nor court there, although an occasional banquet there (perhaps monthly on the occasion of the feast of the new moon; cf. 1 Sam. 20:5, but the Hebrew text is uncertain) also served for meeting his officials. Among these, the principal one and the head of the militia was Abner, the king's cousin and constant table companion. Saul usually distributed fields and vineyards taken from the enemy to the officials who had been outstanding in some feat of arms. Chiliarchs or centurions, they all formed a sort of military household of the king, a permanent nucleus which functioned, when need arose, as a framework for the quick mobilization of the people (1 Sam. 22:7). As for the family of the king, nothing but good could be said also (14:49–50); it seems that Saul had only one wife and therefore did not keep a harem (by which orientals judge the power of a king [§§ 318, 372, 400]; there is however a mention of one of his concubines in 2 Sam. 3:7; 21:8). Of his three sons (cf. however § 367) the eldest, Jonathan, had proved himself many a time worthy of the family traditions of valor (§§ 348, 350); of his two daughters, the younger was Michal (Michol).

353. The monarchy, however, encountered many difficulties, and some of them were serious. In the first place there was the permanent

threat of the Philistines who, if they chose to make a serious attack, might at any moment take over a good part of Israelite Canaan.

Then there were the Canaanites. Not that they were in any position to wage methodical, extensive warfare against Israel, but the disposition of their cities and lands, which had remained independent even during the time of the Judges, obstinately impeded the political cohesion of Israel which Saul so earnestly desired. More than one energetic effort was necessary to make these Canaanite islands disappear: there is a report of one assault against the Gabaonites, and even though the Israelites had a treaty oath with them (§ 286), Saul tried to exterminate them "in his zeal for the children of Israel and Juda" (2 Sam. 21:2). The results were not very satisfactory since the extirpated quickly sank new roots which contained a larger dose of poison for the exterminators (§ 364).

Again, the ancient rivalries among the tribes had not disappeared; even more than the tribal rivalries, the interests of this or that group were preferred to those of the general welfare, and as a result national unity suffered. Conflicts, indifference, and defections aggravated more and more the disunity of the kingdom.

354. Finally, Saul must have been very much affected by his break with Samuel and even more by the dark prediction Samuel made to him (§ 351). A sincere Yahwist like Saul, even if he was somewhat unrefined, would not take his relations with the religious head of the nation lightly, and would not consider this prediction as arbitrary or false, although it may have been conditional, and so could have been nullified by more zealous conduct toward Yahweh; it certainly was not ignored. The zeal with which Saul caused the disappearance of necromancers and diviners (1 Sam. 28:3, 9) supports this conclusion. The mental anguish which the rupture with Samuel and his prediction caused him must have been as a gnawing canker penetrating more and more into the heart of the monarch. There was, certainly, a psychopathic tendency in Saul's make-up. He was strong and rugged by nature, but in the recesses of his mind there were areas where he was fatally defenceless, and in these there grew a fixed idea, an obsession. The fixed idea around which his mind revolved found favorable ground in his religious spirit, agitated as it was by the vicissitudes of his realm and by the nerve-wracking cares of an office which he took very seriously. In the end he everywhere perceived, even among his most intimate friends, traitors who were attempting to usurp his regal prerogatives. As usual in cases of this kind, outbursts alternated with periods of extended depression, both caused by his morbid psychic condition. Hence there is mention of a "melancholy spirit" which Yahweh sent upon Saul. Attempts were made to lift up his spirits during these attacks with appropriate music (cf.

§ 423), but there is no mention whatever of any attempt to declare the unhappy monarch unfit to rule, or of any rebellion against him, so great was the affection by which he was surrounded and so many were the merits that all recognized in him. Then, on his tempestuous horizon, there arose a new star — David.

※　　　※　　　※

355. It is possible that his name, *Dawidh*, is a secondary form of *Dodhawahu*, "chosen one of Yahweh" (2 Para. 20:37), but it also has a counterpart in the Babylonian *Dawidanum;* at any rate the related term *dodh*, "beloved," "patron," is used as a name of the divinity in the Bible and in other Semitic documents (Isa. 5:1; Amos 8:14 [read D D K instead of D R K]; Cant. *passim* [?]; Stele of Mesha, line 12, § 439).

The principal sources for the history of David are to be found in the tract of 1 Sam. 16–1 Kings 2, to which can be added 1 Para. (2–3), 10–29, the titles of some Psalms and Ruth 4:17–22. The account of the Chronicler, however, is almost totally contained in the Books of *Samuel-Kings* and whatever details are added there concern statistical and liturgical data. The principal tract, in *Samuel-Kings,* contains the same phenomenon which was noted in treating of the institution of the monarchy (§ 346), namely, that even about a national hero like David there circulated in Israel traditions of different characteristics and provenience which were later incorporated into a single account. Thus either the same fact is recounted twice, or two are very similar (e.g., the slaying of the giant Goliath, in 1 Sam. 17 and 2 Sam. 21:19; origin of the proverb about Saul prophesying, in 1 Sam. 10:10–11 and 19:23–24; etc.); or an identical fact is reported with important divergences (David's entry to the court of Saul, in 1 Sam. 16:18–23 and 17:1 ff., especially verses 55–58; the death of Saul, in 1 Sam. 31:4–5 and 2 Sam. 1:9–10; etc.). It should be brought out also that the Greek version of the Septuagint, especially in a few important passages, presents a considerably different and generally briefer text than the Hebrew. The elimination of repetitions for the purpose of harmonization may be the explanation for this.

356. David was the son of Jesse (Isai), of one of the principal families in Bethlehem, of the tribe of Juda. He had seven brothers older than himself and perhaps two sisters. He was blond and of comely aspect, well knit, courageous, and also a skillful player of the harp; he had opportunities to develop these latter qualities as a shepherd tending his father's sheep.

Unknown to outsiders and treated with the usual benevolent indifference accorded young boys in their own home (1 Sam. 16:11), he

Present-day Bethlehem.

is portrayed in the Bible as the one chosen by Yahweh to succeed Saul. While Samuel was secretly mourning in Rama over Saul's rejection, he was told by Yahweh to go quietly to Bethlehem, and there choose the new king. When he arrived at the house of Jesse the older sons were first presented to him, but all were rejected. David was almost overlooked, and had to be summoned from his flocks to become the anointed king. This choice was not only private, but it seems not to have made a very serious impression on any of those present, including David himself (1 Sam. 17:28, 18:18, 24:6). Perhaps, marveling at the unusual rite performed by the venerable old prophet, the bystanders simply interpreted it as a strictly religious rite of hidden significance, and gave it no further thought.

357. The entrance of the newly-chosen king into the company of Saul is recounted according to two traditions. According to one, the courtiers counseled the agitated monarch to summon young David to court, where, being expert in playing the harp, he would be able to calm the violent attacks of the king with his music. Saul did summon David, who came and won the friendship of the king. Saul "loved him exceedingly and he became his armor bearer" (16:21).

The other tradition takes quite a different tack. When war broke out with the Philistines (the text does not give chronological references with regard to any preceding event), there was among the troops of the enemy a giant, Goliath of Gath, who continually defied the warriors of Saul to duel with him in order to decide the war. No one was willing to accept the challenge. The young shepherd David, who had been sent by his father to the camp to bring victuals to his three brothers enrolled in the army of Israel, heard the challenge and offered to fight the duel. Saul was skeptical at first, but changed his mind when he saw the self-confidence of the youngster. To prepare him for the fray, he clothed him in his own heavy armor, but the youth, hindered in his walking, cast it off and went out against the giant with only the equipment of a shepherd, a staff, a sling, and five smooth stones with sharp edges. The giant despised him and cursed him in the name of his gods; David attacked in the name of Yahweh. The first stone he flung struck and penetrated the forehead of the giant, who fell unconscious upon his face. David ran to him, unsheathed his sword, and cut off his head. After such a remarkable feat — according to this tradition — Saul asked about the person and family of David (17:55–58), as if until that day the youth had been a complete stranger to him. This shows that this second tradition is independent of the first, especially when it is recalled that according to this second tradition David joined the following of Saul precisely on this occasion; "and Saul took him to himself from that day and would not let him return to the house of his father" (18:2).

358. Some scholars have thought it possible to harmonize the second tradition with the first, by supposing that the residence of David at court as a harp-player (first tradition) was not continuous but broken by frequent absences (17:15; but cf. 16:21 with 17:55, 58). It is more reasonable, however, to suppose that the two traditions both supplied, along with the data preserved in the biblical account, other information — events or chronology — in virtue of which the two traditions were linked together and mutually integrated. The composer of the biblical narrative, presupposing the two traditions to be already known, selected only certain elements which today are no longer sufficient to give an exact picture of the relationship which existed between them. However, the discontinuity must have been noted long ago. The Septuagint (Codex Vaticanus), in fact, does not recognize any divergence between the two traditions, as it lacks the decisive passage of 1 Sam. 17:55–18:5, and does not give the text relative to the events preceding the duel (17:12–31). Such lacunae are revealing (§ 355), unless one could prove that the Seventy had hit upon a Hebrew text in a more ancient edition than the Masoretic.

In the text of the second tradition there is also the noteworthy remark that "David took the head of the Philistine and brought it to Jerusalem" (17:54), which city, however, was still in those times in the hands of the Jebusites. Here also there is a question of a chronological anticipation attributable to a later editor (§ 305); the skulls of slain enemies were preserved as trophies, as were their weapons.

There are differences of detail even about the killing of the giant

Goliath. According to 2 Sam. 21:19: "Elhanan son of Ja'ir [ ],[2] a Bethlehemite, killed Goliath of Gath," who had an unusually long lance. There is no reason to doubt that this Goliath of Gath is the same as the one in the story of David. To harmonize the two traditions it has been suggested that Elhanan was the original name of David. When then in 1 Para. 20:5, it is said that "Elhanan son of Ja'ir killed Lahmi the brother of Goliath of Gath," the victim of Elhanan would not, therefore, be Goliath, but a brother of his whose name was Lahmi. However, this description of the victory of Elhanan does not seem to constitute a different tradition from the preceding account. The text of *Paralipomenon* normally depends upon that of Samuel, and the reading of the

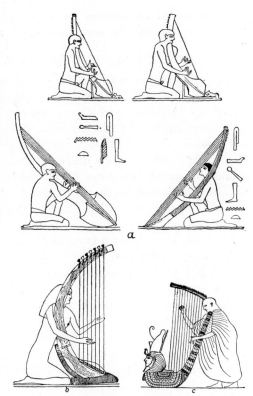

Egyptian musicians: a. Ancient Empire; b. Middle Empire; c. New Empire. (*Enciclopedia Italiana.*)

Chronicler (*'eth-lahmi 'ahi,* "Lahmi brother of") may well be a paleographic corruption of the reading of *Samuel* (*beth-hallahmi 'eth,* "Bethlehemite, the"). In this case the very existence of a brother of Goliath named Lahmi would be without foundation, while the tradition which makes Elhanan the conquerer of Goliath would be confirmed. Others however hold that the text of Samuel should be corrected according to that of *Paralipomenon* (but cf. 2 Sam. 23:24).

359. For the rest, combats between two warriors were frequent enough. Omitting the numerous examples of the Greco-Roman world, there is a highly instructive case in the Egyptian *Tale of Sinuhe* (§§ 125, 205),[3] in which the protagonist tells what happened to him in Palestine. "There came a strong warrior of Retenu (§ 58) to defy me in my tent. He was a valiant man who had no equal and

---

[2] 'Oreghim which comes after Ja'ar should be dropped, according to parallel passages in Para. (Greek); it comes from the end of the verse.

[3] The story of Sinuhe, in *ANET,* 18–22.

had vanquished all Retenu. He said that he wanted to fight me; he intended to rob me; he was thinking of appropriating for himself my flocks on the advice of his tribe." Sinuhe leaves the affair to the will of God and accepts the duel. "During the night, I stretched my bow and got my arrows ready, I sharpened my dagger and furbished my arms. When daylight came, the people of Retenu came up: he had stirred up his tribes and called together half of his countrymen; he made preparation for the combat. Every heart was with me; men and women shouted all together and everyone was anxious for me. They said: Is there really a brave man who can contend with him? Then he took his shield, battle-axe, his armful of lances. But after I had defied his arms, I allowed his lances to shoot by me without harm(?). When we were facing each other (?), he threw himself upon me. Then I let go with my bow against him, and my dart stuck fast in the nape of his neck. He uttered a cry and fell upon his nose: I dispatched him with his own battle-axe. I gave vent to my cry of victory upon his back and all the Asiatics clamored. I gave praise to the god Montu[4] but his people mourned for him."

360. The victory of David over the Philistine giant not only introduced him into the company of Saul and brought him high military rank, but also made him instantly popular in Israel. At court he was warmly welcomed; he became the close friend of Jonathan and also conquered the heart of Michal (§ 352). At the same time, however, difficulties arose which had their source in the brooding Saul. The refrain of the women who ran out to meet the conqueror and to perform the ceremonial *fantasia* (dance) was:

"Saul has slain his thousands;
but David his tens of thousands!"

To the disturbed brain of the king this had a derisive ring; it also clearly singled out his rival, whom up to that time he had only remotely feared. From that day Saul's violent fits became more frequent, focused now, however, on the popular hero. Once when David was playing the harp before him to soothe him, Saul attempted to pin him to the wall with the royal lance he held in his hand, but the attempt failed because of David's agility. Then the king, in order to remove him from the scene, promoted him to a higher military rank, assigning him at the same time to dangerous missions. But "David was successful in all his enterprises and Yahweh was with him . . . and Saul feared him" (1 Sam. 18:14–15). Later, when he learned that his daughter Michal was enamored of David, Saul promised her to him on con-

---

4 The Egyptian god of war.

dition that he should present as a dowry (among the Israelites it was paid by the groom to the father of the bride, cf. the Code of Hammurabi, art. 138: § 246) one hundred Philistine foreskins. The proposal was clever; on the surface it seemed to be a move to inflict a blow on the enemies of Israel; actually it exposed his future son-in-law to the dangers involved in killing a hundred mighty warriors. David sallied forth with his soldiers, however, slew two hundred Philistines, brought the desired parts to Saul, and so obtained Saul's daughter as his bride.

361. Despite this relationship, it was only natural that the king's jealousy should increase, and to such an extent that Saul "openly spoke to Jonathan his son and to all his ministers, to put David to death" (19:1). But Jonathan's friendship with David prompted him to remonstrate with his father. Saul relented. David soon reported another success against the Philistines, and Saul's fury again blazing up, he tried again to transfix David as he played. David dodged the throw and fled to his own house, but was obliged to run even from there, during the night, to escape the soldiers sent to capture him. His wife Michal let him down from a window and to gain time, put into his bed one of the teraphim (§ 144) camouflaging it as a human figure, then telling the soldiers who entered the house that David was ill in bed. Saul sent them back again with orders to arrest the sick man, bed and all, and the deception was discovered.

David sought refuge with Samuel at Rama, where there was a school of prophets (§ 422 ff.), but even here the messengers of the king and then the king himself overtook him, firmly bent on capturing him. But both the messengers and the king fell victims to prophetic contagion, and seized with a mantic exultation (§ 420), "they prophesied," giving David plenty of time to put distance between them and himself. At one time a somewhat ironical proverb was circulated in Israel: "What! Saul too among the prophets?" The proverb is linked, according to one tradition, to this incident; according to

Site of Adullam (?). (Vester, Amer. Colony.)

another, with a similar event which occurred to Saul at the time of his election (§ 348).

David finally was convinced, thanks to Jonathan, that it was impossible for him to remain longer at court without exposing his life to danger. From that day on, then, he began to lead a wandering life, as many in the Orient had to do once they had incurred the displeasure of the king. The Egyptian *Tale of Sinuhe* (§ 359) presupposes an identical motive for its hero's flight from Egypt and his adventurous life in Palestine.

362. A few of the more important episodes of the wandering life led by David were preserved in the popular traditions. He went first to the sanctuary of Nob, where the ministering priest Achimelech received him favorably, and gave him the loaves of proposition to eat. He also gave him the sword of Goliath which had been kept there. When Saul learned of this he took revenge by having Achimelech and his fellow priests put to death (only Abiathar escaped); nor were the people of the city spared. David fled from Nob and sought refuge with the Philistine Achis, king of Gath (§ 75), but in this city of the giant Goliath, he was quickly recognized. He therefore pretended to be mad, a condition which in the Orient apparently renders one's person inviolable, for it seems to make him a man possessed by a *djinn*. He next sought refuge in the cave of Adullam (probably the present-day 'Id el-miye, about fifteen miles southwest of Jerusalem); it must have been a locality suitable for a last-ditch defense. Besides members of his own family, many oppressed and adventurous men of the region gathered around him and made common cause with him.

Meanwhile Saul had been driven by his implacable jealousy to take up arms against his rival. When David, in a fortunate encounter, had repulsed a raid of the Philistines on Qeila, Saul moved against him, but David succeeded in fleeing in time with his men. From that time on he dwelt in the "desert of Juda" (§ 65) especially in the steppes of Ziph and Maon, and Saul continued to pursue him. Once David was betrayed by the inhabitants of Ziph, and had almost fallen into Saul's hands when a messenger brought Saul word of a sudden attack of the Philistines, which forced him to abandon the pursuit. Once the attack was under control, Saul resumed his hunt for David, who was still in the neighborhood of Engaddi; this time the king himself abandoned the pursuit, because David, finding him in a circumstance in which he could easily have killed him, refrained from doing so out of respect for the "Elect of Yahweh" (1 Sam. 24:7; § 366). Shortly thereafter David again showed his generosity in a similar manner, even though Saul had resumed the hunt (1 Sam. 26). During these troubled times, however, an idyllic romance blossomed for David. He espoused

Little Mount Hermon.

a new wife, the "beautiful and prudent" Abigail, recently become the widow of Nabal, a rich landowner who had treated David's men harshly, and had died soon afterward (1 Sam. 25).

363. To escape the unremitting persecution David again, and this time permanently, joined the Philistine, Achis of Gath who, knowing that he was a rival of Saul and the head of a band of six hundred valiant men, welcomed him, and assigned Siqelag near Gaza to him as his dwelling. Once David and his men were settled there, they began methodically to raid the southern peoples unfriendly to Israel, such as the Amalecites and other tribes of the desert. David was careful to leave no trace of these raids; no prisoners were taken, alive. Thus he could brashly tell King Achis that his incursions were directed against the Israelites and not against friendly tribes (1 Sam. 27). He was forced later on to join his company to a Philistine army which was on the point of engaging the Israelites in a pitched battle; but he was sent back because the other leaders did not trust him. On this occasion the Amalecites pillaged Siqelag, but David took out after them, defeated the raiders, and recovered the loot (1 Sam. 29–30).

Meanwhile "Samuel was dead; all Israel had mourned for him, and they had buried him in Rama, his city" (1 Sam. 28:3). Thus one cause of Saul's anger was removed, and the other, the rivalry of David, faded too as David went over to the Philistines. Yet his morbid fears did not cease on this account, for he had not forgotten the sinister prediction of Samuel (§ 351), nor David's popularity, nor the possibility of his return. Furthermore the Philistine storm, gathering more and more force, could not delay much longer in breaking over an Israel which was not yet able to meet it with a good chance of success.

364. The tempest broke forth with a roar. The Philistines, moving

Gelboe seen from the north. To the right of center, the village of Endor.

perhaps to help a Canaanite pocket which was then besieged by Saul (§ 353), went up with a strong force to encamp at Shunem in the valley of Esdraelon (§ 64). "Saul gathered together all Israel encamped at Gelboe" (28:4), that is, on the mountains which block off the valley to the southeast. From the heights Saul had time to contemplate and evaluate the enemy forces, and from what he saw "he was afraid and his heart trembled exceedingly" (38:5).

In the mental turmoil which enveloped him when his attempts to obtain a reply from Yahweh proved fruitless, Saul began to think anew of the dire prediction uttered by his great adversary who had recently died. Of a sudden he wanted to hear Samuel's prophecy again. Despite Saul's ban on necromancers and diviners (§ 354), one could still find hidden away in the country some practicers of this fascinating and (in ancient times) highly esteemed profession. Near Endor (modern *Endur* on the slope of Little Hermon), there was a genuine necromancer; Saul had himself taken there at night, incognito, and demanded that Samuel be evoked. The shade of the dead prophet actually appeared, spoke to Saul, confirmed the previous prediction, added another of the imminent catastrophe for Israel, and predicted that Saul and his sons would soon be where he was.

365. With his old valor now augmented by despair, Saul went forth to the catastrophe. He might perhaps have avoided it had he resorted to the old style of guerrilla warfare (§ 350) instead of a pitched battle, but guerrilla warfare demanded a strength of soul which the tragic monarch no longer possessed. Mentally exhausted, he wanted a showdown no matter what the outcome.

When the battle was joined "the men of Israel fled before the Philistines and fell down slain on the mountains of Gelboe. And the Philistines killed Jonathan, and Abinadad and Malchishua, the sons of Saul. And the whole weight of the battle was turned upon Saul; the archers overtook him [   ] with the bow, and he was wounded in the side.[5] Then Saul said to his armor-bearer: Draw my sword and run me through with it, so that these uncircumcised do not arrive [   ][6] and make sport of me! — But his armor-bearer was unwilling, because he was greatly afraid. Then Saul took his sword and threw himself upon it; his armor-bearer, seeing that Saul was dead, likewise threw himself on his sword and died together with him" (1 Sam. 31:1–5; cf. § 366). The following day the Philistines came to despoil the slain and found the body of Saul. They carried away his head and his armor, placing them as trophies in the double temple of Beisan (§ 86); the remainder of the corpse they affixed to the walls of the same city; it was taken down by the inhabitants of Jabes Galaad, who, in their piety, made a night raid to acquire possession of it. They buried the bones at Jabes.

Through the victory at Gelboe the Philistines became masters of the valley of Esdraelon. At the news of this defeat, the Israelite inhabitants fled from this place, abandoning their centers to the Philistines, who, established in that central valley, now exercised strategic control over Palestine.

The whole political edifice, which the tragic first king of Israel had begun to build and had so well advanced, collapsed with him. Compared to the beginning of his reign the situation had worsened, for at first there was only solitude — now there were ruins.

❋   ❋   ❋

366. One day, after the catastrophe at Gelboe, David returned to Siqelag from the pursuit of the Amalecites (§ 363), and learned of the turn of events from a fugitive from the camp of Saul. He was the son of an Amalecite and narrated how he happened to be on Gelboe at the moment of final defeat, when Saul, seeing that everything was lost, had ordered him to kill him. He obeyed the command and afterwards removed from the body the royal crown and bracelet, which he now brought to David. Whether the fugitive's story was true or false (§ 365), David commanded him to be struck down on the spot for having dared to lay hands on the "Elect of Yahweh" (§ 362). He and his followers sincerely lamented Saul's death, and David composed an elegy for Saul and Jonathan which is one of the most splendid examples of ancient Hebrew literature (2 Sam. 1:19–27).

Soon afterward, and no doubt with the consent of the Philistines,

---

[5] After *him* the word *men* should be deleted according to 1 Para. 10:3; the Hebrew text here is corrupt; the Septuagint reads: he *remained wounded in the side.*

[6] After *arrive* the words *and kill me* should be deleted according to the parallel passage in Para.

David went to Hebron, where he counted many partisans even among those who were heads of clans already associated with the tribe of Juda, and whose friendship he had been careful to maintain by his generous deeds (1 Sam. 30:26–31). Personal affection for him undoubtedly had its part in this adherence of the southern tribe of Juda to a fellow tribesman (§ 356), but another and perhaps not less important factor was the antagonism existing between that tribe and the others more to the north. Saul was a Benjamite (§ 347), only slightly to the north of Juda; but in the eyes of Juda he was a "northerner," and that was sufficient to prevent him from being the ideal king for the "southerners." The antagonism between south and north was of long standing, and although it receded into the background during the time of Saul, because of the perils of the moment and the benefits of the monarchical experiment, it was by no means dead. Now that Saul was no longer on the scene it again flared out in the preference shown toward a southern candidate. Even more grave consequences would follow from it, namely, a full break between north and south.

At Hebron, the place of many sacred memories for all Israel (§ 91), David was proclaimed king by his followers.

367. In the seven years or so that David reigned in Hebron, his jurisdiction was very limited, and did not extend beyond the tribe of Juda, which after the defeat of Gelboe was under the direct influence of the Philistines. These did not look with disfavor on the new king. Being already under their authority, and only a small vassal monarch of Philistia, David was not a serious threat to them, for the establishment of a new state in the very heart of Israel could only result in greater weakness for that nation. So they let him alone, following the ancient maxim: "Divide and rule."

The rest of Israel recognized as king Ishbaal (or Ishbosheth; § 107) the son of Saul (it is not clear whether he is a fourth son, according to 1 Para. 8:33; 9:39 or the second of the three sons mentioned in 1 Sam. 14:49, cf. 31:2; in this case he escaped and did not die in the slaughter at Gelboe, § 365). Abner (§ 352), having emerged unharmed from Gelboe, had Ishbaal elected king at Mahanaim in Transjordan, so as to be as far removed as possible from the Philistines. Ishbaal was king in name alone, and the reins of government were really in the hands of Abner.

368. Naturally there were rivalries between the two kingdoms, but no details of these remain except for a clash of arms which took place near Gabaon, at Helqah has-surim (Vulgate, *Ager robustorum;* 2 Sam. 2:16), in which Asael, brother of a general of David named Joab, was slain by Abner (Asael and Joab were sons of a sister of David). Internal conditions were quite different. In David's kingdom there

The site of Helqah has-surim (?). (Lemaire.)

was compactness and order, thanks to the external security which resulted from the friendship of the Philistines; in the kingdom of Ishbaal
there was disunity and dispersal of the tribes, uncertainty in the supreme
authority because of the false position of the king with respect to the
all-powerful Abner, internal repercussions of the Philistine peril. On
his part David tried to win the good will of the "northerners"; certainly
out of humanitarian zeal, but also with a political end in view, he sent
to thank the inhabitants of Jabes-Galaad for the piety they had
manifested toward Saul's dead body. David's fame as a valiant warrior and for generosity did the rest, diffusing itself among the disunited
northern tribes and, little by little, capturing their imagination.

Things went along thus until Abner, feeling that the foundation of
his power was becoming more and more shaky, seized the opportunity
of a private quarrel with Ishbaal to enter into negotiations with
David, with a view to extending David's authority over all Israel.
The "conversion" of the all-powerful minister seems to have been sincere, for he had already reached an agreement with the elders and had
persuaded them to pass over to David, but he was also looking out for
his own interests. A shrewd presentiment that the wind was about to
change prompted him to get on the right side. But he was not to enjoy
the fruits of his *volte-face*, for when he arrived at Hebron to work out
the details of the agreement he was treacherously slain by Joab, who
felt he owed it to his brother Asael to exact the blood vengeance
sacred to every Oriental. Not long afterwards Ishbaal also was killed by
two of his officials, who brought his head to David at Hebron, thinking
they were thus doing something pleasing to him. David, however, had
the two traitors put to death, as the fugitive from Gelboe had been, and
commanded that the head of his rival be decently buried. Previously he
had with sincere grief arranged for the funeral of Abner, and had him

buried at Hebron. This nobility of soul, and the lack of any leader in the dissident tribes, completed the task of winning over the rest of Israel. And so it came about that the ancients of the people convened in Hebron and elected David king over all Israel.

369. A little more than seven years had passed since the battle of Gelboe. Taking as the starting point the year 972 b.c., which is held with sufficient probability to mark the beginning of Solomon's reign, we get the following dates. According to 2 Sam. 5:4–5 (cf. 1 Kings 2:11) David reigned in all for forty years, the typical number (§ 225), of which about seven were over the tribe of Juda alone and the remaining thirty-three over all Israel. Therefore the year 1005 (972 + 33) would be the date of his proclamation as king over all Israel; the year 1012 (972 + 40) would be the date of his proclamation as king over the tribe of Juda alone and also the battle of Gelboe and the death of Saul. Saul had ruled (§ 349) some thirty years (later on it was computed as the typical forty; Acts 13:21). It need not be repeated that all these figures are subject to the limitations of prudent approximation (§ 226); from this period on, however, the ground becomes more solid.

The sudden enormous growth of the small vassal king annoyed the Philistines, the more so since the king was to show very shortly that as he had ceased to be small he no longer intended to remain a vassal. The sagacious adversary of Saul and the audacious ruler of Siqelag felt the urge to exercise his valor and to hold even the Philistines at bay. It may be that the Philistines attacked first, but the struggle was necessarily long and sporadic. David was careful not to repeat Saul's mistake of engaging in a pitched battle (§ 365). He imitated the Saul of early days, resorting to guerrilla warfare (§ 350). With this strategy he had everything to gain as time passed; with the Philistines it was quite the opposite, as they were probably then entering a period of internal decadence.

370. Only a few unconnected episodes of this long drawn-out contest have been recorded. In one, the Philistines, who had invaded the valley of the Rephaim to the south of Jerusalem, were beaten back by David in the place called Baal-perazim; in another, they were struck down from Gabaon (rather than Gabaa) to Gezer (2 Sam. 5:17–25). Other encounters are indicated elsewhere (2 Sam. 21:18–21), and show that battles were fought almost within the shadow of the Philistine capital of Gath (§ 343). At one point in the long struggle, then, the Philistines had retreated until they were defending their principal cities. In the time of Roboam, Gath had passed definitely into the power of Israel (2 Para. 11:8); there is some basis for the opinion of several modern scholars that it passed over to Israel during David's time. Whatever the fact, it is certain that the tactical and strategic procedure of David, plus the new spirit of his warriors and the internal crisis of the Philistines, reduced the enemy after a certain time to such a degree that they could no longer injure Israel; still later on they were to come under the hegemony of Israel.

371. As the external situation cleared little by little, David turned his attention to internal problems, the most imperative of which was the unification of the contending tribes. The new kingdom needed a capital, something to which Saul had never given a thought. Hebron was, of course, acceptable to the "southerners," but certainly not to the "northerners" (§ 366); moreover, it was not centrally located, and was so undefended that at the outbreak of hostilities against the Philistines David descended [from it] to the fortress, very probably Adullam (2 Sam. 5:17; cf. 23:13; § 362). It was therefore necessary that the capital be more to the north, that it be situated near the center of the entire territory of Israel, but most of all that it be strategically strong. The fortress of Sion-Jerusalem answered these qualifications excellently but it was considered quite impregnable, and the Jebusites who now occupied it (§ 358) boasted that the blind and lame sufficed to defend it (2 Sam. 5:6). Thanks perhaps to the daring of Joab (§ 98), David obtained control over the city. According to the present disposition of the documents incorporated into the biblical account, the conquest of Jerusalem (2 Sam. 5:6–16) seems to have been carried out before the war with the Philistines, but an examination of the contents of the documents and the very nature of the case suggest that it more probably came about during that long war, no doubt during a period of truce.

372. The new capital, Sion-Jerusalem, restricted as yet to the hillock of Ophel (§ 96), was called the "City of David." There was an element of theocracy in this personal appellation: the monarch made use of the prestige which his external victories and the rebirth, internally, of the nation of Yahweh, had built up in the eyes of the people; in fact "David recognized that Yahweh had established him as king over Israel and that He had exalted his reign for love of the people of Israel" (2 Sam. 5:12). As much could not be said of Saul.

In the construction of the new capital the Israelites, who were not very expert in matters of architecture, availed themselves largely of the services of Phoenician artisans and even of materials sent by Hiram, king of Tyre. The good relations between the two peoples seem to have been something recent and were perhaps strengthened by the common struggle against the Philistines.

The personal element which is reflected in the name of the new capital called for the further emphasis of a splendid court as conceived by an oriental mentality. In the Orient, a monarch's power was indicated by the number of wives in his harem (§§ 318, 400); David, then, as he had previously in Hebron taken new wives to himself (3:2–5), now also took more concubines and wives in Jerusalem . . . and sons and daughters were born to him (5:13). This practice also helped to establish family ties with neighboring peoples, which explains his taking of Maacha, daughter of Tholmai, king of Gessur, as a wife (3:3). The Hittite monarchs had acted in this way with the Pharaohs (§ 46), and the son of David, in his dealings with the Pharaohs, will imitate them in this (§ 383).

373. Another decisive undertaking of the clever new monarch was that of making the new capital also the religious center of Israel. The last center which had been relatively efficacious was Silo (§ 342); the Ark had been lost and recovered, and then had remained, unattended by any special distinction, at Cariath-iarim (§ 343). In this state of affairs the inclination to individualistic cults (§ 337) must naturally have flourished, and, for a theocratico-Yahwistic nation, this was a grave obstacle to spiritual unity. The centralization of the official cult depended upon the Ark, so David arranged for its removal from Cariath-iarim. After a three months' halt in the house of Obededom, he commanded that it be brought to Jerusalem. The king himself took part in the procession which accompanied the Ark. Girt in a linen ephod, David danced with all his might before Yahweh (?; § 318), and when the procession ended and the Ark was deposited on the pavilion pre-pared for it, he offered holocausts in the presence of Yahweh, and peace victims (2 Sam. 6:14, 17). In other words, this theocratic king also acted as a priest. When this is compared with the episode of Saul (§ 350), the different position of the two monarchs with respect to the sacerdotal class and its prerogatives (§ 388) becomes clear.

David also conceived the idea of building a permanent temple to Yahweh, but the Lord let him know through the prophet Nathan, that David was not to build a house for Yahweh — Yahweh would build one for him. "House" in Hebrew is also equivalent to "family." In other words, Yahweh communicated to David that he would solidly establish his dynasty over the nation of Israel, but that the time was not yet ripe for the construction of a house to Yahweh. The temple of the national God was also an indication of the power of an oriental monarch (§ 388), but David was only the artificer of that power, with his external wars and his internal reforms. Impressive exhibition of this power, however, was reserved to his son and successor, who would build the temple to Yahweh.

374. Later on David fought and conquered the Moabites, and still later the Ammonites. This second war, provoked by the insult which the Ammonite king, Hanon, had inflicted upon the ambassadors of David,

was long and difficult, as the Ammonites had for allies various small Aramaic kingdoms to the north of them such as Aram-Soba, Aram-Maacha, and also Aram of Damascus (§ 51). For all that, the war was ably conducted by Joab, who prepared the assault on the capital Rabbath-Ammon, and then yielded the honor of its capture to David. The city was then destroyed, enormous booty taken, and the inhabitants reduced to slavery and subjected to extremely heavy labors (such seems to be the meaning of 2 Sam. 12:31). Other successful campaigns were conducted to the south, against the Amalecites and especially against the Edomites, whose kingdom was destroyed and incorporated into David's, while their king, Hadad, fled and found sanctuary in hospitable Egypt (1 Kings 11:14 ff.; cf. § 383).

These wars, some of which were certainly carried on simultaneously (the exact chronological sequence eludes us) greatly increased the extension and power of David's kingdom. Along the Mediterranean, the Philistines no longer presented a serious threat, and farther to the north genuinely friendly relations with the Phoenicians (§ 372) prevailed. To the north, the various Aramaic states had become tributaries; to the east, Moab and Ammon were reduced to absolute vassalage; to the south, the Amalecites were dispersed and Edom was destroyed. David exercised direct power in Palestine from the Negeb to the Lebanon (§ 60), but the more or less powerful zone of his influence extended from the Red Sea to Damascus and beyond toward the Euphrates.

375. It would be an exaggeration to attempt a comparison between David's kingdom and the empires of Babylonia, Assyria, the Hittites, or Egypt; in comparison with these, his kingdom was only a respectable principality. Nevertheless, for one of the less numerous peoples it was certainly a grand kingdom, as it was undoubtedly the most extensive and the strongest which Israel was ever able to realize in all its history. It was certainly superior in its internal cohesion to the following reign of Solomon whose celebrated magnificence was only an external manifestation of the accomplishments of David.

The enterprising activity of the monarch gave rise to a military and civil organization. The rank and file of the army (sabha') was composed of valiant Israelites who were assembled on occasion by the sound of a trumpet or by proclamations of various kinds. These raw recruits were grafted into a permanent organization of soldiers, the principal cadre of which was a continuation of the six hundred warriors who were the companions of David during his stormier days (§ 363). There was also the royal bodyguard, composed of mercenaries of Philistine descent, the so-called Kereti ("Cretans," some of whom were Philistines: § 328) and Peleti ("Philistines" = "Palestinians"?; cf. § 58, and Beth-Pelet,

§ 92), the "Swiss" of their day, commanded by Banaias. Another permanent nucleus was that of the Gathites from Gath of Philistia (§ 343), headed by Ittai. Of all the warriors the group of the "Thirty" stand out most prominently (2 Sam. 23:13–39) and among the Thirty, the "Three" (23:8–12), of whom wonderful exploits are related. They were the so-called "valiant men (*ghibborim*) of David." The head of the whole army was Joab.

376. Of those who constituted the civil organization which was centered in the court we know something about the following: a *mazkir* ("one who reminds"), a kind of secretary-chancellor who probably had to "remind" the king of the affairs to be treated; a *sepher*, or "scribe," entrusted with the correspondence (cf. the duty of the writer in the service of Alaca the Abyssinian, in § 190) and perhaps also with the archives of the kingdom; an official assigned to the *mas* ("tribute labor"), or a kind of minister of public works (§ 405) to be built chiefly by slaves and subjugated peoples. There were also in court some "priests," among whom were the sons of David, whose duty it was to either administer justice or to assist the king with advice, consultation of Yahweh, and similar activities (2 Sam. 8:15–18; 20:23–26).

Mephibaal (Mephibosheth; § 107), the sole survivor of the family of Saul, and Jonathan's son, also lived at court. He was crippled from infancy, having fallen as his nurse fled in panic on hearing the news of the catastrophe at Gelboe. In memory of Saul and in loving memory of Jonathan, David had the royal survivor brought to his court and there treated him as his own son.

In his own family, scandalous and sorrowful events began to occur. Once his political power was well-consolidated and extended, family affairs became enmeshed in it and were to play an important part in the last years of his life.

377. During the war with the Ammonites, David had remained at Jerusalem, and there committed adultery with Bath-sheba, the wife of Urias the Hittite, who was then at the front. She became pregnant. To cover up what he had done, and pretending to seek information on the way the war was going, David had Urias return to Jerusalem. After some discussion, the king dismissed him so that he could go to his home and rest. But Urias must have suspected what had been going on in his absence; declaring that wartime was a time for austerity, he spent the night in a court of the royal palace. On the following day also, even though the king deliberately got him drunk, Urias stubbornly refused to visit his wife. After some thought, David then sent him back to Joab with sealed battle-orders. Joab was commanded that Urias be sent into the thickest part of the fray, there to be deserted and allowed to be killed. And so it was done. Urias was killed, and his wife became

a member of David's harem. The affair did not go unobserved in court circles; it caused something of a scandal which was timorously concealed. But the prophet Nathan (§ 425) courageously presented himself to the king, and with delicate prudence caused him to reflect on his crime by means of a striking parable. David acknowledged his fault before Yahweh and was pardoned, but he had to suffer as punishment the death of the son which Bath-sheba had in the meantime brought forth, and those distressing events which were to vex the royal family from then on.

378. Another scandal occurred in the royal household, of a kind not rare in oriental harems. Ammon, the first-born of David, had violated his sister, Thamar; Absalom, also the son of David and blood brother of Thamar, in order to revenge the outrage, trapped his wicked brother in a carefully worked-out snare and killed him, fleeing afterward to his royal relatives at Gessur (he was the son of Maacha, daughter of Tholmai, king of Gessur: § 372).

After three years he re-entered Jerusalem, where he remained two more years before being reconciled with his father. When the reconciliation took place, it was only pretense on the part of the son, for he intended to obtain possession of the throne for himself. He labored secretly and ably for a long time to obtain the support of a good part of the people, and when he judged that the opportune moment had arrived, he betook himself to Hebron and had himself proclaimed king. The first (and also the second) proclamation of David's kingship had occurred in the same locality. The separatist rivalry of the various tribes (§ 366), dormant during the renascence of David's power, revived at the first opportunity.

Caught napping by the insurrection, David fled hastily from Jerusalem to Transjordan, establishing at Mahanaim (2 Sam. 17:24: Hebrew text) the center of his resistance. Absalom occupied Jerusalem without a fight. To signify his capture of the throne in accordance with oriental custom (for the Persians cf. Herodotus, III, 68–69), he publicly violated the concubines whom he found in his father's harem. He did not, however, take the advice of his counselor Achitophel who urged him to pursue David immediately. David thereby gained both time and opportunity to obtain reinforcements. Thus when Absalom had crossed the Jordan and attacked David's army he was utterly defeated, and, even though his father had ordered the soldiers to spare the rebel's life, was killed. The insurrection under control, David returned to Jerusalem.

379. Once again the secessionist tendencies manifested themselves. Another insurrection was incited by the Benjamite Seba, who, to the chanting of a rebellious refrain (§ 411), tried to draw the tribes north of Juda away from the jurisdiction of David. It was easily quelled by Joab who also treacherously killed Amasa, to whom David had originally entrusted the task of subduing the revolt. The murder of Amasa reveals how jealous Joab was of his power; the murder of Abner (§ 368) had demonstrated his ruthless vindictiveness. So powerful in fact had the general become at court that he not infrequently imposed his will upon the king himself. Many times David disagreed with the overpowerful minister, but he could not depose him and was forced to tolerate him, for, besides being his own nephew (§ 368), he was a peerless head of the army and the real mastermind behind David's victories. Indeed for some time now the king had not gone out regularly to war.

The declining years of David's life were further saddened by two calamities. There came a famine which lasted for three years, and upon David's consulting Yahweh he learned that it was a punishment for Saul's massacre of the Gabaonites (§ 353). David then sent some descendants of Saul to the Gabaonites to suffer their vindictive justice, and these were hanged on the gallows. Another divine punishment was a pestilence which lasted for three days because David had dared to take a census in his kingdom; this, according to the oriental mind, signified that the nation belonged to the king, and not to the Lord. The cessation of the pestilence was announced by the same angel who had slaughtered the people (§§ 211, 497). The apparition occurred on the threshing-floor of Orna the Jebusite, which David therefore purchased and upon which he built an altar to Yahweh. Since this threshing-floor was located on top of the hill later selected by Solomon as the site of the Temple (§ 390), it is clear that this account is an attempt to explain that choice. As a matter of fact there were not lacking other places at Jerusalem where gatherings of a nationalistic and a liturgical nature were traditionally held (1 Kings 1:9 [19, 25], 33 [39, 45]). The altar erected by David added one more.

380. The last political act of David, now in full decline, was to decide the succession to the throne in favor of Solomon, begotten of the favorite Bath-sheba. Solomon had the support of his influential mother, of Nathan the prophet, of the high priest Sadoc, of Banaias and the *ghibborim* (§ 375). Adonias however was supported by the elder court ministers, men like Joab and that other high priest, Abiathar (§ 362); he was, moreover, the elder son. He then attempted to bring off a *coup de main* by allowing himself to be elected king by his followers. But while that election was going on, David at Bath-sheba's request had Solomon solemnly anointed king, and then led him to the throne. As soon as it was seen that law and power were on Solomon's side, Adonias' faction dispersed. And there it ended, for a time.

Before he died David recommended that Solomon be good to cer-

tain persons who had favored him, and also that he render justice
to certain others against whom for one reason or another he had been
unable to proceed, foremost among whom stood Joab, the murderer
of Abner and Amasa (§ 379).

381. Thus David died, after forty years as king (§ 369). He was
the real founder of the monarchy in Israel after the failure of Saul.
True, he did not succeed in unifying all the quarreling tribes, but his
courage, his initiative, and the political perspicacity with which he was
gifted allowed him to hold them together in a common framework
which resisted, during his reign and that of his successor, all attempts
at dissolution. Because of these gifts, David was far above the common
clay. Other fine qualities, such as his generosity of soul, chivalrous
temperament, poetic genius, and musical skill, must be added to these.
He towered above many others similarly endowed. His religious conviction was profound and vivid, and alone can explain many deeds of
his life. He also had many serious failings, among which were his
sensuality, cruelty, and an excessive indulgence toward the members
of his household; but in judging his character it must be remembered
that sensuality and cruelty were common in oriental monarchs, and it
is natural to suppose that the memory of his own experience and weakness caused in him that excessive leniency he displayed toward his own.

✻   ✻   ✻

382. David was above all a man of action, but his successor,
Solomon, was above all a king who enjoyed the fruits and exhibited
the splendor of this action (§ 375). The vital sap of the monarchical
trunk of David explains the efflorescence of Solomon, and later ages
have, as usual, admired with enthusiasm only the flower, giving but
a secondary thought to the strong stem from which it burgeoned.

As his first acts, Solomon followed out the recommendations of his
dying father, with eyes open wide for his own interest also. Adonias
had not entirely put aside his aspirations to the throne, and Solomon
kept close watch on him and his followers. When Adonias through
another requested of Solomon the hand of Abisag the Sunamite, the
companion of David's last years, Solomon saw in this an attempt
to assert his rights over the harem, and hence over the throne (§ 378) of
the dead king. He seized the opportunity to crush forever the faction
of his brother and rival. Adonias and Joab were executed and the high
priest Abiathar deposed from his office and confined at Anathoth, a
village about an hour and a half to the northeast of Jerusalem. Sadoc
alone remained as high priest (§ 380) and Joab's office went to
Banaias (§ 375), who had slain him in the Tabernacle of Yahweh, where
the old general had taken refuge.

383. In the matter of foreign relations, Solomon, quite unlike his warrior father, was a real diplomat. One indication that his diplomacy even in foreign affairs was able to extend the internal power created by David was his success in marrying a daughter of the Pharaoh, something which was not easy even for powerful princes. This Pharaoh seems to have been Siamon, the last but one of the Twenty-First Dynasty (§ 36); he gave his daughter the city of Gezer as a dowry (§ 76 ff.). Good relations with Hiram of Tyre (§ 372) were continued and further cemented.

Solomon solved the difficulties which arose in his foreign policy rather well. From the very beginning he had to face problems. Hadad, the king of Edom who had fled to Egypt (§ 374), had, on hearing of the deaths of David and of Joab, departed from Egypt, where he also was related by marriage to the Pharaoh, and had moved to reconquer his own country. His success in this enterprise was dubious. He may perhaps have been able to set up some kind of a domain, but it could not have been very extensive, as Solomon would traverse Edom without hindrance in the prosecution of his maritime enterprises in Ezion-geber (§ 385). It is probable that the good offices of a Pharaoh of the Twenty-First Dynasty who was related by marriage to both of them intervened to establish a *modus vivendi* between the two enemies.

Another difficulty faced him to the north where Rezon, once a captain of the king of Soba (§ 51), founded a new Aramean kingdom with Damascus as its center, using practically the same methods by which David had founded the kingdom of Israel. It is known of him only that he was the adversary of Israel during the whole time of Solomon (1 Kings 11:25). It was a case of jealous friction between two peoples, breaking out in border incidents and skirmishes, but never quite resulting in a complete war.

384. Characteristic of Solomon's policies was the development of commercial relations with other nations. This led him to build some forts for the protection of the international trade routes, and as a defense against the above-mentioned threats from the south and north. In the north, Hasor (§ 309) was fortified; lower down, the strategic caravan center, Megiddo; on a level with Jerusalem, Gezer, Beth-Horon, and Baalath; on the extreme southern border, Thamar (following the *ketib* of 1 Kings 9:18: cf. Ezech. 47:19; 48:28; the *qere* has "Tadmor," which would be Palmyra, in the middle of the desert between Damascus and the Euphrates) was fortified either against Edom or to protect the approach to Ezion-geber. Permanent garrisons of Israelites resided in these strongholds. Solomon also kept his war chariots and cavalry there, both innovations introduced by him into the Israelite army (1 Kings 10:26). It seems certain that the remains of Solomon's stables were discovered in the latest excavations of Megiddo (§ 79).

385. Solomon exported very few indigenous articles. The Palestine of that time was exclusively agricultural, and could produce few things of value in international trade. An enterprising king, he obtained articles for trade by importing, for example, horses from Qowe (Cilicia) and from Misrayim (Egypt, § 22; perhaps we should read Musri, a country near Cilicia: cf. Ezech. 27:14), and resold them to the Aramean and Hittite princes (1 Kings 10:28–29). His most profitable merchandise, however, came from those mysterious regions to the south and east of his realm which were the sources of precious articles in ancient times. Since these regions could be approached only by way of the sea, Solomon undertook the construction of a fleet of ships known technically as "Tarshish ships" (§ 462), at Ezion-geber on the tip of the Elanite Gulf of that time (about 18 miles farther north than it is today). Every three years these ships made the long voyage in order to obtain new supplies. Up to that time the Israelites had no familiarity with the sea at all (in later years they only once had a part in maritime history, and that a rather awkward one [§ 462]), but the industrious monarch solved this problem with the help of his friend Hiram, king of Tyre, who sent his sailors, men skilled in the ways of the sea, to help Solomon's men (1 Kings 9:27). No people of ancient times could compete with the Phoenicians in the art of navigation. The fleet reached Ophir, that enigmatic land located by scholars either in India, southern Arabia, or on the eastern coast of Africa (Madagascar); thence it returned laden with gold, silver, sandalwood(?), ivory, apes, and peacocks(?). Philologists suspect a Sanskrit origin for the Hebrew names of some of these articles (1 Kings 10:11, 12, 22).

386. The commercial relations of Solomon with the south occasioned a visit of the queen of the northern Arabian kingdom of Saba to Jerusalem. After business and political matters were taken care of, the queen followed an oriental custom by proposing various subtle and tricky questions to the monarch, for the fame of his wisdom had reached Saba along with his goods.

Sumptuous visits of monarchs were not rare: the one made by the Hittite king, Hattushil, to Rameses II, on the occasion of the marriage of the latter to the Hittite's daughter (§ 46), is a famous instance and is recorded on Egyptian monuments. Nor were the commercial enterprises of Solomon peculiar to him. The Amarna letters (§ 52 ff.) bring out the fact that among princes both great and small there was an extensive exchange of goods under the polite name of "offerings" which were in reality full commercial transactions. When the "offering" did not satisfy the recipient he would put an ordinary shopkeeper to shame with his loud complaints and protests.

387. Generally speaking Solomon's commerce must have been profitable, but with so much capital abroad and especially with so many costly building projects (§ 389 ff.), he was not spared the ordeal of meeting and recovering from economic crises with coffers that were half-empty. Not only did he pay the workers of Hiram with grain and oil (1 Kings 5:11) instead of gold, but to reimburse Hiram for loans amounting to 120 talents of gold (an astronomical sum), he was constrained to mutilate the territory of his realm by granting his creditors twenty cities of Galilee (9:10–14), a fact as grave as it is significant.

388. His commerce, in fact, was intended to provide part of the funds necessary for the costly construction projects which were demanded by his program. They were to be an exterior sign of the monarch's power inherited from his father, which up to that time had not the external magnificence so indispensable according to oriental standards. Who would have suitably appraised the power of the Egyptian dynasties without the sumptuous temples of their gods and the superb palaces of their Pharaohs? Who would have an adequate appreciation of the grandeur of Babylonia or Assyria were it not for their temples and palaces? The nation, in the Orient, was one unit with its national god, and the theocratic king was his national representative; hence the grandeur of the whole nation was measured by that of the temple and the royal palace together. In an oriental monarchy which had progressed beyond its beginnings and was well developed, a Cincinnatus dwelling in his little house and tilling his field was inconceivable, even as in the time of Solomon it was inconceivable in Israel that Saul remain in his modest Gabaa (§ 85) without a place of worship. No matter how powerful, such a monarchy would not engender belief in its strength at home and abroad when those things which passed for proofs of power were lacking. So Solomon began to build from the fourth year of his reign (1 Kings 6:1), i.e., in 970–969 B.C. (§§ 223, 369). Meanwhile, his royal dwelling place was the "City of David"; as for places of worship, the people sacrificed in the *bamoth* (§ 104). Solomon preferred the high place of Gabaon for his sacrifices, because it was the great[est] *bamah.* He offered a thousand holocausts upon that altar (1 Kings 3:2, 4; cf. § 373). But at Jerusalem, also, Solomon performed acts of worship before the Ark (3:15).

*   *   *

389. Solomon built the Temple and a royal palace, two distinct groups of buildings related to each other architecturally, and harmonized for practical reasons so as to form a single organic complex.

Imbued with his father's idea (§ 373), Solomon initiated the construction of the Temple and, like his father before him, turned to Hiram of Tyre for help, and for the same reason.

"Dome of the Rock" (Mosque of Omar) and the esplanade of the
Temple of Solomon.

The Phoenician king sent skilled workmen and the necessary materials. Cedars and cypresses from Lebanon were cut and floated as rafts as far as Jaffa (§ 63), whence Solomon's workmen carried them to Jerusalem. At the same time, many thousands of Israelite and Canaanite workmen labored at home to quarry, cut, and transport stones. Huram-'abhi (Hiram is not quite accurate), an artist of Tyre, was given charge of fashioning the objects of bronze; these he cast in a place where clay abounded, near Sukkoth in the valley of Jordan.

390. The location selected for the temple was the hill called Moriah, the northern continuation of Ophel (§ 96); the threshing floor of Orna the Jebusite was situated there and had been the scene of the theophany which the Bible indicates as the reason for Solomon's choice. There, too, David had erected an altar (§ 379).

This area is today occu-

The sacred rock in the "Dome of the Rock."
Top view. (Vester, Amer. Colony.)

pied by the Moslem holy-place, the Haram esh-Sherif, occupying an
area of circa 1053 x 1607 feet. The eastern (Cedron) and southwestern (Tyropoeon) sides were built up so as to form this area,
in the center of which there now rises the Qubbet es-sakhrah, the
"Dome of the Rock." This is commonly misnamed the "Mosque of
Omar" but the building is neither a mosque nor the work of Omar.
It covers a "rock," sacred to all Moslems, which measures about
45 by 60 feet, and rises 4 to 6 feet above the floor. It is quite possible
that the altar of holocausts set up by Solomon in his Temple (§ 393)
stood over this rock, and that an altar of David had stood there before
that. Nor is it unlikely that this same rock had once been a sanctuary
for the Jebusites of Sion.

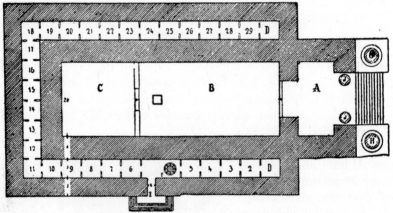

Plan of the Temple of Solomon. A, vestibule; B, hall; C, cell. The numbers
2, 3, 4, etc., indicate the small rooms. (Benzinger, *Hebr. Archäol.*)

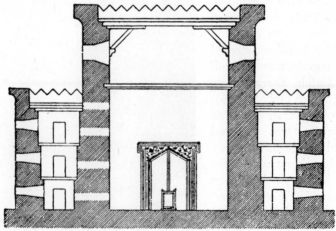

Cross section of the façade of the Temple of Solomon.
(Benzinger, *Hebr. Archäol.*)

391. The Temple proper, i.e., the "house [of Yahweh]," was a building consisting of three rooms. Entering the Temple from the front, which in conformity with the usual custom of the ancients was "orientated," i.e., facing east, one passed through the following rooms:

The *vestibule* (Hebrew, *'ulam*), c. 36 feet wide (20 cubits), 18 feet long (10 cubits); its height is not known exactly, but it must certainly have been more than 54 feet (30 cubits);

The *hall* (Hebrew, *hekhal:* from the Sumerian *e-gal*, "large house"); called also the "holy" (*qodhesh*), 36 feet wide, 72 feet (40 cubits) long, and 54 feet high.

The *cell* or *adytum* (Hebrew, *debhir*), called also the "most holy" (*qodhesh quodhashim*, "holy of holies," superlative), was a perfect cube measuring 36 feet in all three dimensions.

The total internal length of the building, from the façade of the *vestibule* to the rear of the *cell* was roughly 126 feet (70 cubits), with a uniform width of 36 feet.

392. On the outside the "house" was surrounded on three sides, north, west, south (the entrance was not), by a section which was joined to it. This consisted of three floors one on top of the other, each one about 9 feet (5 cubits) high, and each one subdivided into 30 small rooms. Since the wall of the "house" supporting the three floors was in the form of three large steps, the floors were wider as they were higher: the first floor was about 9 feet wide (5 cubits); the second 10½ feet (6 cubits); the third 12 feet (7 cubits) wide.

The house was illuminated by windows which were above the level of the third floor of the section annexed to it some 30 feet above the ground. These let light into the *hall*, but not into the *cell*, which was entirely dark and was separated from the *hall* only by a simple wall made of cedarwood, in which there was a pentagonal door; the

The massive columns at Thebes.

Lotus columns, temple at Luxor.

door which connected the *vestibule* and *hall*, however, was rectangular.

At the sides of the entrance to the vestibule were two pillars of cast bronze, each one about 32 feet (18 cubits) high and crowned by a round capital some 9 feet high (5 cubits), making 41 feet (23 cubits) in total height. The name of the pillar on the right was *Yakhin*, "will render stable," and on the left *Bo'az*, "in him is strength"(?). The signification of these two names should be referred to Yahweh in relation to the Temple, but according to indications of ancient variants it would seem that the original names were *Yakhun*, "it is stable," and *Be'oz*, "in power," both of which are to be referred to the Temple.

393. The entire edifice of the "house" was also surrounded at a certain distance, except on the west, by a wall; the open space between was the *atrium* (*haser*), called also "inner" or "upper" to distinguish it from the more ample lower one which surrounded the entire Temple-Palace group, and hence called "exterior" or "great" court. The wall of this "inner" atrium had three doors corresponding to the three cardinal points; in the midst of the open space, on the prolongation of the central apse of the "house," there arose from the sacred rock (§ 390) the altar of holocausts. The dimensions of the open atrium are not known; it is likely that they were at least double those of the "house."

Such are the basic features of the Temple of Solomon. It bears many similarities to the general plan of Egyptian and still more to Phoenician temples. As to its size, a brief comparison should prove interesting.

394. For Egypt, it will be enough to recall the huge exemplars to be found in the district of Thebes alone (§ 24); at Luxor the temple built by Amenophis III measured 180 by 623 feet, and was lengthened later to 853 feet by Rameses II. At Karnak, in the great temple of Amon built during the course of centuries, the Grand Hypostyle Hall alone (Seti

Colonnade of the Egyptian Temple of Edfu. (Vester, Amer. Colony.)

Central colonnade of the Grand Hypostyle Hall of the temple at Karnak.

I–Rameses II), which was only one fourth of the entire edifice, measured 337 by 170 feet. It had 134 pillars, the central twelve of which measured 11 feet 7 inches in diameter, 32 feet 9 inches in circumference, 69 feet in height with 11 foot capitals. The Column of Trajan at Rome has a diameter of 11 feet 5 inches and with pedestal and capital, is 96 feet high.

Recent excavations in Babylonia have made it possible to reduce legendary amplifications among other peoples to accurate measurements. At Ur, the Temple enclosure (§ 2) was a quadrilateral the sides of which measured 1246 × 813 × 1312 × 646 feet, and the tower annexed to it was a rectangle with a base of 213 by 141 feet. At Babel, the temple *Esagila* (§ 2; cf. Herodotus, I, 183) was a sort of square measuring 260 by 274 feet. *Etemenanki,* the tower of Babel, had the form of a square pyramid with seven receding terraces (cf. Herodotus, I, 181; Diodorus, II, 9; Strabo, XVI, 1, 5), and each side at the base measured 300 feet; it must have been at least that high.

From this it can be seen that Solomon's Temple was, in comparison to the great monuments of Egypt and Babylon, something like an ordinary parish church when compared to St. Peter's in Rome.

395. The inside of the Temple was very rich. The walls as well as the ceiling were covered with cedarwood and adorned with carvings of cherubim (§ 252), palms, and flowers; the floor was covered with cypress wood. The whole building was covered from top to bottom with gold.

Façade of the Temple of Rameses II at Abu Simbel.

In the dark and mysterious *cell* ("holy of holies") there was only the Ark. It was the dwelling place of Yahweh. The leaves of its pentagonal door (§ 392) were always open, but a veil hung on the door hiding the interior from the sight of mortals. On both sides of the Ark was a cherub 18 feet high, sculptured in wild olivewood and covered with gold. Their wings measured about 9 feet each, and were extended in such a manner that a wing of one cherub touched the corresponding wing of the cherub facing it and the others reached to the walls. Beneath the juncture of the wings of the cherubim was the Ark.

In the *hall* ("holy") were the gold altar of incense, the table of cedar covered with gold for the loaves of proposition, ten candelabra of pure gold, with accessories arranged on the two sides of the room.

In the *atrium* was the altar of holocausts (§ 393) made of bronze; there was also the so-called "sea," a large bronze water basin resting on 12 bronze oxen (the number of tribes), which faced the four cardinal points in groups of three; another ten vessels of bronze, which were made to fit little carts, were used to carry water from the reservoir to wherever it was needed for the flesh of the victims.

396. When the Temple buildings were completed, Solomon began on the Palace group. A very large atrium ("exterior" atrium; § 393), which contained them and the "inner" atrium of the Temple, cor-

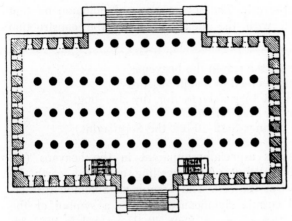

Plan of the House of the Forest of Libanus.
(Benzinger, *Hebr. Archäol.*)

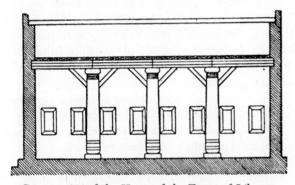

Cross section of the House of the Forest of Libanus.
(Benzinger, *Hebr. Archäol.*)

responded roughly to the area of the present Haram esh-Sherif (§ 390). The Palace group arose to the southeast of the Temple, connecting with its atrium and extending southward toward Ophel for an undetermined distance. The Palace group comprised:

The *House of the Forest of Libanus*, 180 feet long (100 cubits), 90 feet wide (50 cubits), 54 feet high (30 cubits), received its name from its 45 columns in three rows of 15 each, made of trunks of cedars of Libanus and adorned with larger and smaller shields of gold; it was probably used for solemn ceremonies.

The *vestibule of the columns*, about half as large as the preceding, seems to have been a kind of waiting room.

The *hall of justice* or *porch of the throne*, the name of which indicates its function; in it was the throne of ivory, with six steps on which stood twelve lions, six on each side, with a canopy above.

The *royal palace*, properly so called, situated between the atrium of the Temple to the northwest and the hall of justice to the southeast. It was divided into two parts, one of which was for Solomon and the royal harem, the other for the daughter of the Pharaoh, his wife.

397. It took twenty years to complete the whole project (1 Kings 9:10): seven years for the Temple group (6:38) and thirteen years for those of the Palace (7:1).

When the construction of the Temple was completed, Solomon celebrated its dedication with a solemn feast, transporting the Ark of

Sion to the interior of the *cell*. The solemn song of Solomon on that
occasion is impregnated with the idea underlying the construction
of the Temple:

> "Yahweh has set the sun in the heavens:
>   [but] he has decreed to live in obscurity!
> Yes, I have built thee a house for thy dwelling,
>   a place for thy stay forever!"
>   (1 Kings 8:12–13; cf. the Septuagint)

The glory of Yahweh is especially apparent in the heavens (cf.
Ps. 8:2–4; 19:2–7: Hebrew) but when dwelling upon the earth, he
dwells in the "obscurity" of the *cell*. The Temple of Solomon furthermore had a symbolical cosmic significance. It was a symbol of the
celestial Temple (Wisd. 9:8; cf. Exod. 25:9, 40; Hebr. 8:1–5; 9:23–24;
12:22); this celestial Temple was the prototype of the entire cosmos
which, according to Hebrew ideas, was conceived as being made up of
three parts — "heaven," "earth," and "sea" (cf. Apoc. 21:1–2). Hence in
the Temple of Solomon the *cell*, the habitation of Yahweh, corresponded
to "heaven"; the *hall*, with its enduring symbols of worship (altar of
incense, table of proposition, candelabra), corresponded to the "earth"
adoring Yahweh; the *atrium*, containing the "sea of bronze," corresponded to the "sea." This cosmic symbolism, which harmonizes with
many other details of the Temple of Solomon (and of the Tabernacle
of Moses: § 251), or of Egyptian and Babylonian temples, was never
lost sight of by Jewish tradition (Josephus, *Antiquities*, III, 6, 4; 7, 7;
Philo, *De Vita Mosis*, III, 4 ff. [ed. Cohn, IV, Berlin, 1902, II, 76 ff.])
and by Christian tradition (Jerome, *Epist.* 64, *ad Fabiolam*, 9 in Migne,
P.L., 22, 612–613; Origen, *Hom.* 9, *in Ex. n. 4*, in Migne, *P.G.*, 366;
Gregory Naz., *Orat.*, XXVIII, 31, in Migne, *P.G.*, 36, 69–72).

398. Another important construction project completed by Solomon
in Jerusalem, after he finished the palace (1 Kings 9:24), was that of
Mello. The term must have been originally a common name (cf. Sichem,
§ 88), signifying "filling," perhaps "terrace," "[earth] fill" (from *mala*,
"to fill"). An archaeological question arises concerning the location of
Mello. Recent discoveries have tended to confirm more and more
what had been supposed: namely, that it was a fortification to protect
the depression of the terrain which marked the attachment of Ophel
with the overhanging height of the Temple (§ 97), exactly where
the enclosure of the ancient City of David *was breached* (11:27)
in order to allow the expansion of the city to the north. Indeed it is
recorded at the same time that Solomon built "Mello and the walls
of Jerusalem" (9:15).

399. Herodotus (II, 124 ff.) while speaking of the pyramids of Gizeh

(§ 29) remarks that the labors connected with their construction were terribly severe, and stresses the enormous legacy of hate which the building Pharaohs left among the people. It gave rise to fabulous legends. The memory of the Pharaohs Cheops and Chefren was in truth held in hatred for centuries because of their tyrannical expenditure of men and material in the construction of these greatest monuments of all time.

The building projects of Solomon, similar to that of the pyramids of Gizeh although on a much smaller scale, entailed similar arrangements for labor, and had the same unhappy consequences. In fact, this is the real reason behind the events immediately preceding and succeeding his death, and explains the radical difference between the judgment rendered upon him by his contemporaries and by later generations.

A later Israel was more generous than the Egyptians, for, because of its nationalistic and Yahwistic ardor, it did not hold against Solomon the hatred which the Egyptians nursed against Cheops and Chefren. The nation of Yahweh was filled with admiration for the Temple and the Palace, and had only words of benediction for the hand which had constructed them. Their enthusiasm made them forget the sorrow that heavy hand had caused their ancestors and the lashes it could administer (1 Kings 12:11, 14; § 410). The gold glittering on the buildings of Solomon bathed his whole era in glory, but only because the bloody fiscal system which had produced that gold had been abolished for a long time. The builder of such great marvels, incomparable to Israelites who had never left Palestine, seemed to be the ideal king of Yahweh. He did not fare so well according to the clear testimony left us by his contemporaries, in whose eyes he appeared as neither an ideal king nor ideal Yahwist. Hence the difference in appraisal. The judgment of his contemporaries crystallized into rebellion and schism; that of posterity into admiration and idealization of his stature.

400. Solomon has gone down in history as the actualization of all that his name, *Shelomoh,* implies: he was the "perfect," "fortunate" king *par excellence* (for the feminine counterpart cf. *Canticle of Canticles,* 8, 10 d). Magnificence, opulence, and wisdom were his characteristics. Anything majestic or beautiful which made its appearance later on in Israel was in

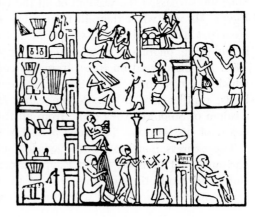

one way or other attributed to him, even though it were a book written in Greek shortly before the Christian era (e.g., the *Book of Wisdom*).

The harem was indicative of the power of an oriental monarch (§§ 318, 372). Tradition numbered 1000 women in the harem of Solomon, 700 of whom were wives of the first class, and 300 of the second (1 Kings 11:3). A different indication suggested by the context is that Solomon had only 60 wives of the first class and 80 of the second, and a third category consisting of "maidens without number" (Cant. 6:8), that is, of waiting aspirants (cf. Esth. 2:3–14).

A monarch's power was also measured by his opulence, and by the well-being of the people under his government. In the time of Solomon "silver was considered of no account" (1 Kings 10:21), for "he made silver as common in Jerusalem as stones, and cedar wood as abundant as the sycamores that grow in the Shephelah" (§ 63; 1 Kings 10:27). In fact, apart from many other occasional revenues, "the weight of the gold that came to Solomon in a single year, was 666 gold talents, besides [the revenues] from the merchants, the traffic of the traders and of all the kings of Arabia and the governors of the country" (10:14–15). The annual 666 talents are equal to several million dollars, and yet to pay Hiram one fifth of this sum, Solomon had to deed over to him 20 cities of his kingdom (§ 387). When later the nation divided into the two kingdoms of Juda and Israel, it is related that "Juda and Israel dwelt in tranquility, every man under his vine and under his fig tree, from Dan to Bersabee [§ 60], all the days of Solomon" (1 Kings 5:5 [Vulgate, 4:25]), and that "they were as the sand of the sea in number, eating and drinking and rejoicing" (4:20).

401. The head of such a happy state was not only an industrial expert, but also was most wise and learned, as well-versed in law and in literature so as to govern and to teach his people, as he was in the natural sciences in order to judge of merchandise. In fact, "the wisdom of Solomon surpassed the wisdom of all the Orientals and all the wisdom of Egypt. He was wiser than all men; wiser than Ethan the Ezrahite, and Heman, Chalcol and Darda, sons of Mahol, and his fame spread to all the neighboring peoples. He uttered 3000 proverbs; his poems numbered 1005. He discoursed on trees, from the cedar of Libanus to the hyssop which springs forth from the wall; he discoursed also on animals, birds, reptiles and fishes. People came from everywhere to hear the wisdom of Solomon; they came from all the kings of the earth, who had heard of his wisdom" (1 Kings 5:10–14: Hebrew [Vulgate, 4:30–34]).

The express mention of "the wisdom of Egypt" as a term of comparison is not unusual, for in Egypt sapiential literature was especially cultivated. Collections of proverbs (of the type of the Hebrew *Mashal*) are found there beginning with the Fifth Dynasty; an example of these is the *"Proverbs of Ptah-hope."* The most interesting is that of *Amen-em-ope,* going back perhaps to the Eighteenth Dynasty, and surely from before 1000 B.C. So similar both in conception and in method of expression is it to the biblical *Proverbs of Solomon ben David,* that many modern scholars believe that certain parts of this latter depend on the Egyptian collection.[7]

402. A typical example of Solomon's judicial acumen is afforded by the incident of the two harlots. These two lived together and became mothers at almost the same time. One of them while sleeping accidentally suffocated her infant; when she perceived the tragedy she took the other woman's baby, putting her dead child in the live one's place. When the other woman awoke the next morning and noticed the exchange she demanded her own child, but in vain. Both women then appealed to the king for judgment. When he had heard their pleas, he made as if to divide the live child in two with a sword, declaring that each woman should have half. The false mother agreed to this, but the true mother rejected the decision, preferring rather that the infant be given alive to her rival than that it should be killed. On the strength of this, Solomon judged her to be the child's real mother, and restored the infant to her. This psychological method which relied on maternal affection to discover the truth was considered to be typical and the fame of it spread abroad throughout Israel.

403. Yet there were personal failings which marred the record of the great monarch. Moabite, Ammonite, Idumean, Sidonean, and Hittite women entered his grandiose harem (§ 400), and, in the end, to please them Solomon neglected his Yahwism and adopted their idolatrous cults, taking part in them personally and building in the environs of Jerusalem sanctuaries to the Canaanite gods. The king of the nation of Yahweh, the tenacious builder of the Temple, the definitive conqueror of the Canaanites, could be seen prostrating himself before Astarte, Moloch (§ 107), Chamos, god of the Moabites (the god Kemosh of § 439), weakened and subdued by his women in his old age (1 Kings 11:1–8). Later tradition was as lenient as possible even with regard to this black stain; it was never entirely canceled or forgotten, not even in later times (Ecclus. 47:21–22: Vulgate). It was nevertheless concealed or not spoken of at all (by the Chronicler for instance), because this part of his life distorts the ideal figure of the "perfect" king of Yahweh (§ 400) painted by tradition.

404. What future generations were to forget in their generous nationalistic and Yahwistic sentiments was the real cause of the two judg-

---

[7] The Instruction of Amen-em-Opet, in *ANET,* 421 ff.; the Instruction of the Vizier Ptah-hotep, *ibid.,* 412 ff. Cf. Mallon, "La 'sagesse' de l'egyptien Amen-en-ope et les 'Proverbes' de Salomon" in *Biblica,* 1927, 3–30.

ments, namely, the heavy burdens necessitated by Solomon's building projects. These fell upon all his contemporaries. The expenses for the building projects, the army, and the court life could be met only in small part by the commercial revenues of the monarch; the greater part fell upon the people who, as in Egypt, had to furnish the basic materials and the manual labor. Hence a methodical system of taxes and requisitions was a necessity, and a suitable administration was created for the purpose. The country was divided into twelve new districts according to the number of the tribes, but the new districts coincided with the ancient territory of the tribes only in certain cases; in others he thought to increase them by the annexation of the Canaanite islands still independent in the time of Saul (§ 353). The Canaanites were now a very small and unimportant minority, and were incorporated into the political organism of the nation; naturally the burden of contributions pressed heavily also upon them. A prefect was at the head of each district, and each one had to provide maintenance for the court and for the King's horses for one month (1 Kings 4:7–28). It is noteworthy that the territory of Juda, the tribe of the monarch, does not appear in the list of the new districts; whether it was because Juda substituted some other contribution or enjoyed a special privilege, the fact was undoubtedly a source of bitterness and displeasure to the other tribes.

405. The furnishing of manual labor pressed heavily upon the Canaanites (9:20–21), as it had before upon the Gabaonites (§ 286), but it would be wrong to conclude (despite 9:22) that they alone had to help the skilled workmen of Hiram. From 5:27 ff. (Vulgate, 5:13 ff.) it seems that the contribution of manual labor was imposed on "all Israel." Three shifts of workers were set up under the command of Adoniram, of 10,000 men each. They took their turns cutting timber on Libanus for a month, one group laboring while the other two stayed at home. There were also thousands of other men set to cut and transport stones, the Canaanites being preferred for this task.

All this contribution of material and labor was a heavy burden both in itself and because of the time it lasted. It was particularly resented because up to that time the people were accustomed to giving a minimum, and that for the most part of their own free will. Nor did their enthusiasm cause them to forget these burdens, as posterity did. All things considered, so reasoned the northern tribes (§ 366), who benefits from all this pain and labor? The southerners alone, the royal tribe of Juda, which bleeds the other tribes, beautifies itself by their labors and has been unjustly exempted from the common burdens (§ 404). Such thoughts were as so much oil upon the fires of an ancient rivalry.

406. More disinterested and idealistic motives likewise fanned the flames. To certain circles which longed for an ideal of simple, austere Yahwism, as for example the dwellers of the steppe, the buildings of Solomon must have seemed something like a profanation, or compromise with the mentality of the great pagan nations. The scandalous idolatry of the head of the Yahwistic nation — a defection caused by the wiles of women — was, for all sincere Yahwists, utterly reprehensible and without excuse. These sincere Yahwists were in all likelihood connected with the centers of prophetism (§ 422), if not their direct result. The political opposition was therefore strengthened by the religious, and thus there came the revolt.

407. A northerner of the tribe of Ephraim, Jeroboam by name, had been appointed by Solomon as the superintendent of the workers of the house of Joseph. A self-made man, the son of a widow, he had shown himself to be an intelligent worker when Solomon built Mello. The king singled him out for reward and made him his superintendent. His new authority plus his firsthand knowledge of the extent of the grievances, led him to pose as something between a Spartacus and a Masaniello. That his following included political opponents of the regime as well as members of the lower classes is not surprising, but it is remarkable that he also found followers who were inspired by religious motives. Ahia, an adherent of prophetism, one day revealed to him, accompanying his prediction with a symbolic action, that he would become in time the head of ten tribes of Israel.

Although the movement led by Jeroboam met with a widespread and profound sympathy, it could still be dealt with by a powerful monarch. "And Solomon sought to put Jeroboam to death, but Jeroboam fled and took refuge in Egypt with Sesac king of Egypt, and remained there until the death of Solomon" (1 Kings 11:40). The reasons why such gracious hospitality was extended to the enemy of Solomon have already been explained (§ 36).

408. After this episode, so indicative of the true state of affairs, little more of importance is known of the reign of Solomon. The fire smoldered under the ashes and grew ever more intense; if it did not blaze forth openly on more than one occasion it was either because of the effective power of the old monarch, or because his advanced age led to the hope that a speedy resolution of the crisis would be found after his disappearance from the scene.

Solomon died, according to the best indications, in 932 B.C., leaving the door open to fatal competition. No one better than he could appropriate to himself the saying of another ruler: *Après moi le déluge.* The deluge came indeed, and destroyed forever the unity of Israel.

❀   ❀   ❀

409. Roboam, the son of Solomon, ascended his father's throne by right of succession as Solomon had succeeded his father David. The

Israelite monarchy, however, was not so theocratic as to exclude in practice all democratic tendencies. It was an authoritarian regime of the father-of-the-family extended over the whole nation, a regime which could be sharply limited by his own subjects (§ 297).

The proclamation of Roboam must have been read without difficulty among the "southerners" (§ 366). On the other hand, the "northerners" had no hostile bias against the person of the new king, but they did have serious objections against his father's system of government, and wanted an assurance that it would cease. They were ready to recognize the new monarch, but under certain conditions, and after a clear understanding. The propitious moment for a long-awaited accounting had arrived.

410. Roboam, probably already proclaimed king by the southerners, went farther north to Sichem (§ 88) to assure himself of the loyalty of the north, about which he must have had a well-founded doubt. The negotiators conferred together in that city of ancient memories. The petitions of the plaintiffs would be more efficacious if re-enforced by a veiled threat; so Jeroboam was sent for from Egypt (§ 407) and this man accused of *lèse majesté* was made their spokesman before the new king. Their requests were not extravagant. In substance they said to the king: "Thy father laid a grievous yoke upon us; now therefore do thou take off a little of the grievous service of thy father, and of his most heavy yoke which he put upon us, and we will serve thee" (1 Kings 12:4). The king asked for three days in which to reply, and during this time took counsel first with the older men, who advised moderation, then with the younger men who advised him to be intransigent. As might be expected from one formed under the imperious absolutism of Solomon, he decided on firmness. To the messengers sent to receive his reply, he said: "My father made your yoke heavy, but I will add to your yoke; my father beat you with a whip, but I will beat you with a whip tipped with scorpions" (1 Kings 12:14).

411. The swaggering young king could not have directed a more telling or violent blow against his own throne than this. "Israel," that is, the northerners, reacted to his program by repudiating the dynasty of David. The refrain of Seba (§ 379), an expression of the ancient rivalry, was revived and sung with all the intensity of a vendetta:

> "What portion have we in David?
> No inheritance with the son of Jesse!
> To thy tents, O Israel!
> Now David, look to thine own house!"
> (1 Kings 12:16; cf. 2 Sam. 20:1)

In his arrogant ignorance Roboam still failed to realize the seriousness of the revolt and thought to suppress it by a gesture of authority, and here he made another mistake, so stupid as to border on the ludicrous.

Wadi el-Qelt near Jericho; boundary between Juda and Israel.

To reassert his royal authority over the rebels he sent Adoniram, the very man who had been in charge of the forced labor (§ 405). The sight of this cruel taskmaster so exasperated his former underprivileged subjects that the royal messenger was promptly stoned. Finally then, the king understood and began to be afraid. He hastened to his war chariot (he had come to Sichem, therefore, with a prudent escort) and took refuge in Jerusalem. A reconquest by force of arms, which had at first been planned, was abandoned.

412. The northerners elected as their king Jeroboam, a man entirely independent of the south. Thus the nation was divided into two kingdoms, northern and southern. The southern kingdom continued to recognize the dynasty of David, now reduced to the rule of only one tribe — Juda (1 Kings 11:13, 32, 36; 12:20; 2 Kings 17:18), which nevertheless had greatly increased, since it had practically incorporated the tribe of Simeon and various elements of Benjamin. Hence the southern kingdom continued to be called the Kingdom of Juda. The other ten tribes (1 Kings 11:31, 35) formed the northern kingdom, called also the kingdom of Ephraim (or of the House of Joseph) after the strongest tribe there, or kingdom of Israel because of the numerical preponderance of its members. In territory also the kingdom of Israel was larger than the kingdom of Juda. Juda was limited to the southern part of Canaan; its border began a little north of the outlet of the Jordan into the Dead Sea and crossed Palestine east and west, rising slightly northward in the vicinity of the Mediterranean. The kingdom of Israel had the rest of Canaan and all of conquered Transjordan.

ROBOAM—PROPHETISM—THE KINGDOM OF ISRAEL

413. With the nation split in two, the history of Israel naturally is divided into that of the kingdom of Israel and the kingdom of Juda.

The schism was a severe blow to the nation. It can in all truth be compared to a shipwreck. The two parts of the doomed ship did not immediately sink, yet they began at once to drift apart, and even though they seemed for a time to ride the sea bravely their doom was certain. The floating hulks both ended in the depths of the sea, one after the other.

Immediately after the division, the two kingdoms were in different circumstances. The kingdom of Israel, though greater in territory and more numerous in population, also had less compactness among its tribes, and less organization in its territory. Above all it was quite exposed to attack from the various Aramean states (§ 51), and beyond these by Assyria. The lack of a peacefully established monarchy and the lack of an indisputable general authority gave to its regime an ever vacillating character always ripe for revolution, and prevented the stable organization and unification of the state. The position of the national religion was also precarious. The schism had created an antagonism against Jerusalem, the center of Yahwism, but in its place had substituted no other of similar authority and importance. Animosity toward the old religion fostered a progressive syncretism (§ 313), especially under the influence of the Phoenicians to the northeast, and of the Arameans to the north.

Although greatly inferior in territory and population, the kingdom of Juda was in other respects in a much more favorable condition. There were no great states around it to menace it, except Egypt, and from her it was separated by the desert. There flourished within the kingdom a sufficiently strong spirit of unity, strengthened by the stability of the authoritative ruling dynasty and by the possession of the city, which once was the capital of the whole nation and around which there revolved a familiar organization. Because of its national prestige and its religious centralization, the possession of the national sanctuary such as the Temple of Jerusalem also redounded to the advantage of the realm.

Roughly speaking, the kingdom of Israel could be compared to a very muscular but flaccid body with too small a head; the kingdom of Juda, on the contrary, had a puny body with a gigantic head. Of the two organisms the first to die was the one with the little head.

414. It was up to Jeroboam, the first king of Israel, to give proof of the separation of his reign from that of Juda. He began by establishing a capital. In the beginning this was Sichem (§ 88), and later Penuel on the Jabbok in Transjordan (§ 147). The transfer of the capital to Penuel was more probably due to an armed threat on the part of the kingdom of Juda than to the invasion of Sesac (§ 416). Between the two kingdoms there was continual strife from the very first (1 Kings 14:30; 15:6, 16), although the details have not come down to us. Later on Jeroboam resided at Tirsah (1 Kings 14:17), perhaps the present Talluza, to the east of Samaria, which in the future was for a time the capital of the kingdom of Israel (15:21, 33; 16:6, etc.; cf. § 84 a).

To accentuate the separation still further, Jeroboam furnished his subjects with state sanctuaries as a substitute for the Temple at Jerusalem. Pilgrimages to Jerusalem were politically suspect and burdensome as well, so the king provided two sanctuaries in his kingdom, one at Dan for those in the north and one at Beth-el for those in the south. The religious pre-eminence of these two localities invested them with an aura of authoritativeness (§§ 143, 149, 335 ff.). To compensate for the lack of the Ark and other traditionally sacred objects of Yahwistic worship possessed by the Temple in Jerusalem, Jeroboam provided more attractive objects which in many respects also corresponded to ancient inclinations. He made two golden calves, one for each sanctuary, and instituted a staff of attendants and a liturgical cycle of feasts. It was not his intention to change the God of the nation who was Yahweh; the representation of Yahweh in the form of a calf suggested itself and was not new in Israel (§ 254). Probably also this was done in imitation of the neighboring Arameans, who delighted in representing the principal Baal Adad (§ 107) in the form of a bull or a calf. Needless to say, such officially sanctioned religious ideas were conducive to syncretism.

415. Even in this regard, however, Juda did not go unscathed. Side by side with and notwithstanding the Temple at Jerusalem, there existed not only syncretistic places of worship but some which were thoroughly idolatrous in the Canaanite manner. The example of the builder of the Temple (§ 403) was not without fruit. The subjects of Solomon's son "also constructed *bamoth* and *masseboth* (§ 104) and *asherim* (§ 105) on every hillock and under every flowering tree; and there were also [male] *quedhesh*[*im*] (§ 108) in the land" (1 Kings 14:23–24).

Pharaoh Sesac and the list of cities conquered by him in Palestine. (Karnak.)

Israelite types in the inscription of Sesac.

416. The fifth year of the reign of Roboam (927 B.C.; the seventeenth of Sesac, about 930) saw the incursion of the Pharaoh Sesac in Palestine (§ 36). Sesac's hatred for the friends of the Twenty-First Dynasty, which he had overthrown, was a more than probable cause of the invasion, but was doubtless not the only one. He also wanted to assert his prestige to the outer world and to gather booty. In his list of conquered cities, inscribed on the southern wall of the great temple of Amon at Karnak (§ 394), it is evident that Roboam, the dynastic enemy of the Pharaoh, was not the only one to suffer from the invasion, but also Jeroboam, his guest and friend (§ 407). More than a hundred of the localities enumerated there pertained to the kingdom of Juda; it is also distinctly confirmed by recent discoveries made at Megiddo (§ 79) that more than fifty pertained to the kingdom of Israel. It does not therefore seem justifiable to suppose that the incursion was occasioned by the invitation of Jeroboam for the purpose of hurting his rival Roboam.

Despite the dithyrambic tone of the list of Karnak, the incursion must have been for Sesac little more than a military march. The two Hebrew kingdoms, so divided and opposed to each other, were hardly a shadow of the nation which existed in the later days of David. However, the enterprise netted a fair amount of booty, chiefly at the expense of the kingdom of Juda. Jerusalem was captured; the riches of the Temple and the royal palace were carried away by the Pharaoh including, of course, the shields of gold which adorned the "House of the Forest of Libanus" (§ 396). The splendors of Solomon, therefore, remained intact little more than twenty years. Stripped of its veil of gold by the Egyptians, only the walls and woodwork of the buildings of Solomon remained, and perhaps not all of these intact. An occasional allusion suggests that in place of the shields of gold, Roboam had others made out of copper (1 Kings 14:27–28); this statement of fact would savor of bitter jest, were it not such a tangible measure of the decay which had taken place in the few years between father and son.

The Chronicler (2 Para. 11:5–10) has preserved the record of works of fortifications completed by Roboam in various localities of his reign (among which Lachish [§ 74] and Azeka [§ 75] have special archaeological importance). These works, despite the sequence given by the Chronicler, must have been completed after the incursion of Sesac, since the localities enumerated are all in the southern parts of the kingdom through which the invaders passed. That visit must have been a warning for the future. Roboam then placed his 28 sons (he had 60 daughters too) in command of these forts, fearing perhaps the animosity that might spring up between them and his favorite son Abia, whom he retained with him in Jerusalem and to whom he had planned to leave the throne.

The authors of the schism and first monarchs of the two separate kingdoms died, Roboam after 17 years of rule and Jeroboam after 22. Their enmity (§ 414) was handed down to their successors and remained alive and operative for some decades; then it gave way to friendly relations which, however, were always those of two entirely independent states (§ 436).

417. The chronology of the individual monarchs of the kingdoms of Israel and of Juda has been the object of lengthy, minute, and oftentimes useless studies in an effort to harmonize the various biblical dates among themselves or with those of extra-biblical monuments. Here, of course, the details cannot be gone into, but we may recall what was said above concerning biblical chronology (§ 226); the epoch now under consideration, however, is subject to much less elasticity in the matter of dates than the others already considered, precisely because the chronological contact may occasionally be made with extra-biblical sources. Some of these dates, known through Assyrian monuments and which are almost unanimously accepted by modern scholars, are as follows:

853 B.C. – Battle of Qarqar (§§ 19, 435).
841 B.C. – Tribute of Jehu of Israel to Salmanassar III (§§ 19, 445).
738 B.C. – Tribute of Menahem of Israel to Tiglath-pileser III (§§ 48, 450).

733 B.C. — The league of the kingdoms of Damascus and Israel defeated by Tiglath-pileser III (§ 452).

722 B.C. — Fall of Samaria and the end of the kingdom of Israel.

The following synchronized table of the individual monarchs of Juda and Israel, taking account of the above-mentioned biblical and extra-biblical dates, is approximately accurate.

Juda		Israel	
Roboam	932–915	Jeroboam	932–911
Abia	915–913		
Asa	913–873	Nadab	911–910
		Baasa	910–887
		Ela	887–886
		Zimri	886
		Omri (Amri)	886–875
Josaphat	873–849	Achab	875–853
		Ochozias	853–852
Joram	849–842	Joram	852–842
Ochozias	842		
Athalia	842–836	Jehu	842–815
Joas	836–797	Joachaz	815–799
Amasias	797–769(?)	Joas	799–784
Azarias (Ozias)	(?)769–737(?)	Jeroboam II	784–744
		Zacharias	744
		Sellum	744
Joatham	(?)737–733	Menahem	744–735
		Peqahia (Phaceia)	735–733
Achaz	733–718(?)	Peqah (Phacee)	733–731
		Osee	731–

Fall of Samaria: End of the kingdom of Israel, 722

Ezechias	(?)718–689	Joachaz (Sallum)	609
Manasses	689–641	Joachim	608–597
Amon	641–639	Joachin	597
Josias	639–609	Sedecias	597–

Fall of Jerusalem: End of the kingdom of Juda, 586

Before proceeding to the separate histories of the two kingdoms, a permanent phenomenon in Israel, and one which from now on will have an even greater importance in the political and religious events of the Hebrews, must be examined.

❋ ❋ ❋

418. As the secret of the luxuriant life of an oasis surrounded by arid desert lies in the bubbling fountain which irrigates the palms and other plants there, so in the history of Israel the "fountain of living waters" (Jer. 2:13), through which Yahweh maintained his nation in an ever renewed verdure, was prophetism.

The *prophet* is designated by the Bible by three terms: *ro'eh, hozeh,* and *nabhi.*

The first two seem today to be absolutely synonymous: they are two active participles, which, according to their respective roots, signify "seeing," "perceiving," i.e., in the present case, one who was able to perceive things hidden from other mortals, as, for example, where the asses were which were lost (1 Sam. 9:6), the cause or outcome of an illness (1 Kings 14:2; 1 Kings 8:8), the method of curing it (2 Kings 5:3, 8). Foremost among such *arcana,* of course, were the will and the designs of God.

The third term, *nabhi,* is etymologically of uncertain meaning. There are in Hebrew verbal forms of this root (*nibba, hithnabbe,* "to act as a *nabhi*"), but there are denominative forms, i.e., formed from the noun and not the other way around. Philologists agree that the underlying root of the substantive *nabhi* is of foreign origin and not Hebrew, like the Italian verb *razziare* (raid), which is a substantive of Arabic, not Italian origin.

Most philologists seek the root of *nabhi* in the Assyrian *nabu,* "to call," "to announce"; from which comes the name Nebo, *Nabu,* god of speech and the interpreter of the gods. The Arabic has a similar verb *naba'a,* which in the second form has the sense of "to carry forward," "to adduce" (especially a discourse or a message), and in Ethiopian *nababa,* "to mutter," "to speak in a low voice." Some, however, favor rather the root *naba'a,* which is found not only in Hebrew but also in Assyrian, Syriac, and Ethiopic, with the usual meaning of "to be in effervescence," "to overflow," which applies especially to springs of water but which can readily be transferred to mean a person who, in a state of excitement, causes his words to rush out. Such a metaphorical application does occur in the Hebrew Bible. Others push this idea further, maintaining a strictly physical meaning of effervescence, perceiving here an allusion to the foam and froth which issued from the mouth of ancient diviners in their mantic or epileptic trances. From an exclusively philological viewpoint, each explanation has its probability and its difficulties; but history can furnish us with new light to help us form our judgment.

419. A precious bit of information is supplied by the editorial note on 1 Sam. 9:9, where the editor states that one now called a "prophet," *nabhi,* was called a "seer" (*ro'eh*) in days of old. Thus *nabhi* is a more

recent term than *ro'eh* or *hozeh*, but once it began to be used it practically replaced the other two. When was this substitution made? Certainly not all at once, nor absolutely, for while even the Chronicler, as
late as he is, uses the term "seer," a manifestation of group "prophetism"
(*nabhi*) is described (Num. 11:24) as occurring in the time of Moses
which seems in great part similar to the one mentioned in Samuel (1
Sam. 10), and was the occasion of the afore-mentioned editorial note. The
word, then, may allude to a prevalent but not an exclusive use. Taking
into consideration the inevitable substitutions of modern for archaic
terms in the most ancient documents, and of archaic terms in more
recent documents, there came a time when the term *nabhi*, "prophet,"
generally won out over "seer" or "perceiver."

At the time of the prophets whose writings are preserved in the Canon
(§ 109), the substitution of "prophet" for "seer" was complete, as is
clear from an examination of these writings. The time was about the
eighth century. A start had been made in this direction long before,
probably, as can be argued from the histories of pre-monarchical times,
in the time of the Judges. If this be so, the change of terminology is
not fortuitous, but is related to the profound social transformation
undergone by Israel once it was settled in Canaan, that is, when Israel
changed from a nomadic to a sedentary people, when the Yahwism of
the desert was all too often contaminated by syncretism with Canaanite
cults. Then they began to call the ancient "seer" by the name of "prophet."

On the other hand, modern discoveries have shown that "prophetism"
was widespread among the Canaanites before the Israelite monarchy.
Jeremias will later on vouch for it among Edom, Moab, Ammon, and
the Phoenicians (Jer. 27:9; cf. verse 3).

The report which the Egyptian Wenamon made of his own voyage
to the coasts of Palestine-Phoenicia about 1100 B.C. contains the following description of a scene which took place in a temple of Byblos
(§ 99):

"When the prince of Byblos finished a sacrifice to his gods, the god
took possession of one of his noble pages and put him in ecstasy and
said:[1] Bring him here![2] Bring the messenger who is carrying him! It is
Amon who has sent him; he has made him come! – While the ecstatic
was in his ecstasy that night, I found a ship bound for Egypt and loaded
all my effects on it. I awaited darkness then, because I reasoned: When
darkness falls, I will put the statue of the god on the ship, so that no
other eye might see it!" etc.[3]

---

[1] The god himself or the one in ecstasy. It amounts to the same thing, as the
god spoke through the mouth of the one possessed by him.

[2] An idol of the god Amon, which Wenamon had hidden.

[3] The journey of Wen-Amon to Phoenicia, in *ANET*, 25 ff.

420. It is noteworthy that Canaanitic prophetism ordinarily manifested itself, not in parallel Semitic manifestations, but by those habitual to the cults of Asia Minor, the cradle of the cult of Cybele. Ever since the time of Hammurabi, Babylonia had its *baru,* i.e., etymologically the "seer," of which hereditary corporations from father to son existed; ancient Arabia had its *kahin* who – quite unlike the *kohen* or Hebrew "priest" – was essentially a diviner who foretold the future and in general "saw" what was hidden. In these ancient Semitic institutions, however, ecstaticism was not the ordinary condition – still less so were the spectacular "seizures"; on the contrary the prophets exercised their professions in cold blood and in full control over their faculties, almost as the "prophetess" Debora can be imagined to have exercised her office under the famous palm tree (§ 308). Around 1100, however, the first explicit testimony of an ecstatic mantic among the Phoenicians of Byblos appears. More to the north the orgiastic cults of Cybele were in full swing. In view of these conditions, it is natural to think Asiatic cults exerted some influence on Canaanitico-Phoenician "prophetism."

The incident of group prophetism during the time of Moses (§ 256) presents no grave difficulty, but may help rather to clarify the issue. The episode is considered by most moderns as an historical projection back to the Mosaic era of an ordinary phenomenon of a much later date. This position is open to debate. It is not known when the first manifestations of ecstaticism among the Semites actually occurred, and all conclusions should be limited to what the available sources tell us. Furthermore, the influence of Asia Minor or Canaanitico-Phoenician prophetism can always be conveniently explained by supposing that it did not really create *ex novo,* but rather developed more fully a germ which pre-existed also in Semitic divination, and of which there were perhaps at first uncertain and sporadic manifestations. In fact it seems difficult to deny that wherever divination is practiced, there is a natural propensity to that special psychic state which lies at the root of ecstaticism. The manner in which the diviner Balaam acts (§ 268) is a rather typical case of it.

421. Shortly after the admixture of Asiatic mysticism with Canaanitico-Phoenician divination, the above-mentioned substitution of "prophet" for "seer" is encountered. It was a repercussion within Israel of what was happening in the neighboring peoples, or better yet, a repercussion within Canaanitico-Israelite syncretism. Repercussion, of course, does not always mean assent or imitation; it can also signify opposition or rectification. The Council of Trent was undoubtedly a reaction within Catholicism to the Protestant Reformation, but it was surely neither an assent nor an imitation. About the time of the monarchy, when there was in Israel a principle of distinction between political and religious power (§ 349 ff.)

the "seer" of the desert began to assume an official mission in the sense that besides "seeing" he must now also "speak" to the nation. He became, therefore, "one speaking" in the name of Yahweh, i.e., the "prophet." The inspiration in the ultimate analysis is the same but the form it assumes is different. The "seer" is above all expositive, the "prophet" is especially polemical. The "seer" is circumscribed in his arguments, he limits himself to a single fact, he solves this or that case without expressly ascending to abstract principles applicable to similar cases: the "prophet" defends or attacks general principles; in the contingent fact he sees above all the idea, he carries his metaphysics into practical affairs. Debora is a type of "seer": Jeremias is a "prophet" of the later and more perfect type.

Rightly then has *nabhi* been translated by προφήτης because it is the ancient "seer" who has received the official mission of *speaking in the place of* (προ-φημί) Yahweh as his ambassador to the whole nation. He speaks as a herald of Yahweh and speaks in a loud voice — morally and physically — so that all can hear. "As often as I speak, I cry out; destruction and desolation do I proclaim!" Jeremias complains (Jer. 20:8), picturing in vivid colors the nature of the "prophet's" mission insofar as it is distinct from that of the "seer." It was the cry of the watchman who signals danger to the whole camp (§ 430). The danger could be strange cults, foreign alliances, scandals concerning the king and the elders, the snares of city life with its corruption and corrupting influence, everything in fact which was practically unknown to the life of the desert where the "seer" was master.

422. Insidious syncretism also played a part in the change from "seer" into "prophet." In fact the Bible, in speaking of a prophet, does not always intend to portray him as an authentic prophet; on the contrary, not even when it treats of an authentic prophet does it intend to present all the manifestations as consequences of his ministry; very often it limits itself to revealing the facts without attempting to judge them. In fact, during the time of Samuel, the last of the Judges, there appear in Israel groups of prophets who prophesy all together — just as in the time of Moses — but for the most part in a state of exaltation induced by music and singing; such a state of psychic exaltation was "contagious," i.e., was transmitted to spectators not at all disposed to participate in it. It led to unusual acts such as divesting oneself of clothing, and in the end led to a morbid state of exhaustion (1 Sam. 10:5; 19:20).

Later, in the time of Elias and Eliseus, there are corporations or schools of prophets, organizations set up on a permanent basis, and located for the most part near places of special religious veneration. Members were called "sons of the prophets," the word "son" being taken in the Semitic sense of member of a corporation, similar to the "sons of

The so-called "school of the prophets" at Mount Carmel.

the perfumers," "sons of goldsmiths," etc. (Neh. 3:8, 31). These corporations of prophets marked an important novelty in the development of
Israelite prophetism, and from the moment they appear in history they
are so powerful – the antiquity of the phenomenon cultivated by them
attests to their power – that they formed within the respective kingdoms
a kind of religious state, which was almost autonomous, and so influential
in politics as to decide even the fate of a dynasty (§ 443).

Among the Hebrew people there were other examples of prophetism
which had this corporate character. At the time of Jehu, king of Israel
(§ 445), Jonadab ben Rechab imposed on his followers, known as the
Rechabites, these special prescriptions: not to plant vines nor drink
wine, not to sow seed or plant, not to build houses but to dwell in
tents. Since the members of this clan were zealous Yahwists and
adversaries of every kind of syncretism (2 Kings 10:15), it is clear that
the ideal of desert life as more favorable to Yahwism lay at the base
of these special prescriptions. They professed a kind of Israelite Fran-
ciscanism, devoid of theory but pursued with enthusiasm (cf. Jer.
35:2 ff.). It is noteworthy that, according to 1 Para. 2:55, the Rechabites
were a group of Qenites (§ 291).

423. The power attained by the prophetical corporations brought with
it the usual consequences. The number of entrants grew ever greater,
and being a "prophet" became something of a career or profession,
further enhanced by the social prestige enjoyed by a "prophet." If one
lacked the requirements necessary for such a state, these could be

supplied by various types of deception and fraud. The Spirit indeed breathed where he willed and often rested upon men who had never dreamed of becoming "prophets" nor of being enrolled among the "sons of the prophets." Many of them were not interested in the reality but in the outward appearance of being a "prophet," for this brought with it both authority and profit. With this historical background in mind, the dispute between Amasias, the priest in Beth-el, and Amos, the prophet, is easily understood. The dispute was animated because economic interests were involved, and Amasias recommended that Amos exercise his profession of "prophet" in the kingdom of Juda where he belonged, and to stop his competition in the kingdom of Israel, where he was alienating the clients of Beth-el. Amos rejected the implicit accusation of cupidity when he replied: "I am not a *prophet* nor the *son of a prophet*" (Amos 7:14), and went on to say that he had become the herald of Yahweh unexpectedly; he was only a shepherd and he had tended his fig trees without ever having dreamed of entering into the corporations of the prophets or of exercising that profession. Yet Yahweh had chosen him as his herald from amid the herds of cattle and the fig trees.

It would, of course, be unjust to conclude that all the members of these guilds were grasping charlatans, especially since in more ancient times men like Elias and Eliseus were connected with such bodies. Even more cautious should be the judgment passed upon the "frenzied" manifestations which occurred among them, or upon the artificial means (chiefly music) by which they were induced. The matter is frequently met with in the history of other religions ranging from primitive forms to Christianity, and the difficulty of a proper evaluation is augmented by the fact that *that* spiritual world was so different from the one in which we live. A condemnation *en bloc* of such manifestations and of artificial means would certainly be wrong. It is enough to recall that while in those times an authentic prophet like Eliseus had recourse to music to enter the "prophetic state" (2 Kings 3:15). On the other hand, charismatic phenomena such as the glossolalia, prophecy, etc., were likewise met with in the first two or three centuries of Christianity; they were undoubtedly genuine and accompanied by extraordinary psycho-physical manifestations which are quite incomprehensible to us.

424. In better times the "sons of the prophets" lived together, holding themselves in readiness to become subjects of that phenomenon, so widespread at that time, which was the prophetic vocation. In the meantime they prepared and practiced, putting themselves under the guidance of a recognized prophet. The personal call might not indeed come, in which case the honest would resign themselves to see how the Spirit made use of, for example, a peeler of fig trees; on the contrary ambitious and avaricious men chose themselves to be prophets, thus

creating that caste of pseudo-
prophets who formed the
greatest obstacle to the mission of authentic prophets,
especially of Jeremias. Auto-
suggestion must have played
an important part in the mentality of these pseudo-prophets; imitation of the ecstatic
and frenetic practices of
Canaanite cults supplied the
rest. What better way to impress minds hungry for emo-
tionalism and wonderment
than to display those neuro-
pathic phenomena which go
by the name of "dervishism"?
Few things drew Israel more
powerfully toward syncretism.

These historical gleanings,
therefore, seem to confirm the
theory that underlying the
substantive *nabhi* is a foreign
root (§ 418), meaning in substance "to speak." As for the

Modern dervish.

root *naba'a*, "to overflow," it seems philologically less suitable because of
its strong guttural; at any rate, if it is understood in the moral sense of
"overflowing [words]," it would be the same as one of the preceding
meanings. If, however, it is taken in its physical sense of "overflowing
with [foam], etc.," there arises the historical difficulty of considering as
primary and essential what in reality was a later and imported element.

425. Prophetism in Israel is divided into an early and a late period.
This division has some basis, since we have a vague and generic idea of
ancient prophetism, formed from very meager information about it,
and from the eighth century on we possess the writings of prophets.
For the later prophets we have not merely a summary of their deeds, as
for the others, but also their words, their thoughts, and intimate feelings,
all set down by them in writing. Not a few passages are strictly autobiographical. The great Jeremias has recorded for posterity not only his
external life but something more precious still, his internal biography,
how he felt toward his prophetic mission, his inner struggles, the bitterness, and his unfulfilled aspirations. What Jeremias relates of himself
can with due proportion be applied to other prophets, and from indica-

tions scattered throughout these writings one can attempt a rough sketch of a "prophet."

So much for the generalities. Naturally individual characteristics vary from one prophet to the next. All are equally prophets, but Jeremias is not an Amos, nor Isaias, nor Ezechiel, just as later on Paul is not Apollo, nor is John, Peter. The Spirit used them and sublimated them, but without suppressing their individuality. With greater reason, then, will the variation be apparent between a representative of early prophetism and one of later date, for it will be based upon a different maturity of religious concepts, customs, civilization, etc. But the moral *virtus* — one may also say "charism" — which animates both, is substantially the same. The earlier prophets, like Nathan who alone dared to reprove David for his adultery (§ 377), and Micheas ben Jemla who alone deterred Achab from the expedition against Ramoth Galaad (§ 436), are in this respect not at all different from Jeremias who alone, centuries later, will advise Sedecias against resisting the Chaldeans (§ 532 ff.).

426. The "prophet" was therefore a herald, the "mouthpiece" of Yahweh. From this office, recognized by society, he derived his authority. In the midst of the society which rested on a theocratic foundation he made his appearance suddenly as an extraordinary messenger of Yahweh; all, therefore, held or should have held him in reverence and often he was so treated. In virtue of his mission the prophet presented himself either to the king or to the priests; he voiced his reproof in a sanctuary or in the Temple of Jerusalem, and from there passed on to utter threats on the threshold of the royal palace. He inveighed against political alliances; turning from this he deplored syncretistic cults. It was he who publicized the scandals of the court cliques. He cursed entire dynasties. He held up to popular scorn greedy ministers of the sanctuary, and reproached his astonished listeners for their corrupt morals. His right to do this was recognized by all from the moment he spoke in the name of Yahweh. An ambassador so stamped could play the part of political dictator, papal legate, or commissioner of police.

He was in truth the "man of God" (*'ish ha'elohim*) *par excellence*. In view of his mission, his utterances were the word of God who sent him and spoke through his mouth; one substituted for the other, and both sender and sent were for all practical purposes one and the same. Even as an individual the prophet lived in so intimate a relation with God that he almost seemed to divest himself of his own personality. God and his mission so conquered him that he even acted in a way which the common man, or at least his contemporaries considered indecorous and unseemly. It was never considered good form to marry a harlot, yet the prophet Osee did so because this was a part of his mission.

Celibacy was looked upon as next to sinful by the ancient Hebrews, always so proud of a numerous offspring; yet Jeremias never married because, as one scholar puts it, "he willingly made even this most onerous sacrifice; his earthly pilgrimage had to be solitary and without joys so that it might be wholly given over to God and to his commands."[4] It is not surprising, then, that the prophets often impressed their contemporaries as being eccentric. The prophet who anointed Jehu king (§ 443) was called "mad" by the courtiers (2 Kings 9:11), but they promptly recognized the anointed Jehu as king. Centuries later Jeremias was also described as mad in a letter of one of his contemporaries which dealt with that prophetic activity of his which was anything but irrational (Jer. 29:26–27).

427. The enthusiastic exaltation of the early prophets died out gradually. Except for a few passages in Ezechiel, concerning whose real or symbolical nature some doubt has been raised, the writings of the later prophets indicate that they shunned the example of the pseudo-prophets and others who with an eye on material gain deliberately set out to imitate the orgiastic and corybantic activities of neighboring peoples. As a matter of fact they restored prophetism to its original Semitic form, to a mission exercised in full possession of one's senses (§ 420), with a full consciousness of action in virtue of daily reflection and under the promptings of a clear conscience. The chief reason adduced to justify their conduct was always the same: *Yahweh has spoken!* or *Word of Yahweh!* or *Oracle of Yahweh!* That reason was repeated with an insistence which, while it may oftentimes pall on the more literate reader, finds its explanation in the psychological condition of the speaker, and is historically of the greatest importance. The consequence of this *Word of Yahweh* they saw in all its clearness:

> "If the lion roars, who will not fear?
> If the Lord Yahweh *speaks,* who will not prophesy?"
>
> (Amos 3:8)

In other words, no one could withdraw himself from the driving force of this *Word of Yahweh;* the man who was filled with it was conquered by it and ended up willy-nilly by *prophesying.*

It is highly important to note that when faced with the *Word of Yahweh,* the prophets were not overanxious to assume the burden of its proclamation. They not infrequently manifested a positive reluctance, and sought to escape it. Isaias (Isa. 6:8), it is true, responded to the call to the prophetic office with alacrity; but Amos could not explain why Yahweh singled him out to be his prophet from amid his cattle and fig trees (§ 423), and Jeremias from the very beginning tried

---

[4] Quoted from C. Cornill, *Das Buch Jeremia erklärt,* Leipzig, 1905, 202.

to evade his mission (Jer. 1:4 ff.; § 509); when he did accept it and discharged it for awhile, he groaned under the heavy burden, wavered, and would have liked to shake the yoke from his shoulders. He tried not to announce the *Word of Yahweh,* and with sublime impetuosity called Yahweh his "seducer." The seduction whereby Yahweh had conquered him was, precisely, the prophetic mission; the wavering and doubts of the man reveal the weakness of a nature overwhelmed by the charismatic impulse.

"Thou hast seduced me, O Yahweh, and I allow myself to
be seduced,
Thou hast been stronger than I and hast prevailed!
I have become a laughing-stock all day long,
everyone makes sport of me!

"Whenever I speak, I cry out,
I proclaim 'Ruin and desolation'!
The *Word of Yahweh* has become for me
an insult and a reproach every day!

"I exclaimed: 'I will not think of him,
or *speak* anymore in his name!'
Then in my heart there was as it were a burning fire
shut up in my bones: I am worn out from holding it in,
I cannot endure it!"[5]

(Jer. 20:7–9)

The vocation of authentic prophets had about it a truly compulsive character. As prophets, they did things they would never have done as ordinary men, going under the charismatic impulse where they would never have gone otherwise. This rigorously historical fact is admitted by both independent scholars and those who tend to be systematically radical. They write: "It is precisely in the compulsive character of the prophetic vocation that we are to seek the proof of its divine origin."[6]

428. Nothing is known nor will ever be known, of course, about the intimate nature of this charismatic action. So eminently mystical a reality cannot be analyzed and described except by one who has experienced it. Such men were the prophets, and although they communicated the divine decrees which resulted from their communings with the Divinity they have said nothing about the way they became so certain of their direct communication with the Lord, or how the charism acted upon their minds, or how their minds and the charism

---

[5] *Holding it in* should be added to the Hebrew according to the Greek, Itala and Vulgate.

[6] Cf. *Encyclopedia Biblica* (Cheyne), III, 3868.

are related. A mystical modesty seems to prevent them from divulging such information. At most they refer to their visions, but these are rather vague and often symbolical. More than this is needed for analysis, especially since writers of every nation and epoch have had recourse in various measure to visions and symbols. To distinguish with certainty what is simply literary device from what is a direct consequence of the charism would call for a direct experience of it.

Yet in the midst of this mysterious darkness there is a ray of light. The permanent relation of the prophets with the Divinity did not always terminate in a divine communication to man. There were times when although it was most urgent for the prophet to know the divine decree, the Divinity was "silent" and the *Word of Yahweh* was not forthcoming. It was, therefore, something analogous to what John of the Cross would call the *dark night of the soul*.

A typical case of these divine "silences" occurred in the life of Jeremias. Clues provided by the history of prophetism, however, justify the conclusion that the "silence" Jeremias experienced was known also by other prophets. When Jerusalem was destroyed, the Chaldeans installed Godolias as governor of the country, but he was murdered shortly thereafter by fanatics. Chaldean reprisals were sure to follow, so the survivors decided to flee to Egypt (§ 543 ff.). Before starting on their journey, they wanted to know the *Word of Yahweh* from Jeremias. "Let Yahweh thy God show us," they said, "the way by which we should go, and what we ought to do . . . whether it be good or evil, we will hearken to the voice of Yahweh our God, to whom we send thee" (Jer. 42:3–6). There was need of haste; to know the *Word of Yahweh* at once was extremely urgent as the Chaldeans might at any moment descend upon the survivors. Jeremias agreed to consult Yahweh; but only "after ten days did the *Word of Yahweh* come to Jeremias" (42:7). Ten days, not before; ten hours could have been fatal, and every apparent interest both of the people and the prophet demanded an immediate answer. Yet the divine "silence" lasted for ten days, nor could the conscientious prophet announce as the *Word of Yahweh* that which was not such. He spoke when Yahweh spoke to him.[7]

429. Another consequence of the prophetic charism in a man was the stamp it put on his moral and religious life. The prophet was the "man of God" both because of his mission and because of the heroism of his religious conduct. In other words, he was a saint.

Dedication of oneself to a genuine prophetic mission was a dedication to trouble. It is true that the prophet was generally recognized as a messenger of Yahweh but very often, if not always, his admonitions

---

[7] Cornill, 420, considers this verse to be one of the most important for an understanding of the notion of prophecy.

grew tiresome, reason enough for his opponents to stone him. Death by violence was the ordinary and usual prospect of a prophet; anything else was an exception. The invective of Jesus is well known: "Woe to you, scribes and pharisees, hypocrites! Because you build the sepulchres of the prophets and adorn the tombs of the just, and say: 'If we had lived in the days of our fathers, we would not have been partakers with them in the blood of the prophets!' Thus you are witnesses against yourselves that you are the sons of them who killed the prophets!" (Mt. 23:29 ff.; cf. Acts 7:52.) This blast is a bit of historical testimony and not mere rhetoric; its historicity is confirmed by the famous description of the sufferings of the prophets who "had experience of mockeries and stripes, chains and prisons; they were stoned, sawed in two, put to death by the sword," etc. (Heb. 11:36 ff.). In general, therefore, the prophets were deliberate martyrs who for long years contemplated the end which awaited them. Some of them did not meet with a violent death, but that daily possibility was equivalent to martyrdom.

The trouble to which the prophets vowed themselves came not only in death but also in life, wherein perhaps more than in death their sanctity shone forth. They were always going against public opinion and were opposed to the vast majority of their fellow countrymen. What Yahweh said to Jeremias at the beginning of his career can be applied substantially to all the prophets: "Behold I have made thee this day as a fortified city . . . and as a wall of bronze against the whole nation, kings . . . priests . . . people" (Jer. 1:18). Within that fortified city and behind those walls of bronze was preserved what was most noble in Israel: its Yahwism. When the people would lean toward syncretistic cults, the prophet would unexpectedly appear at their orgiastic festivities and would announce the imminent thunderbolts of Yahweh. The people attributed a *quasi*-magical power to the Ark, the Temple, to the sacrifices and the other ritual practices; they were sure these sufficed to prevent any misfortune, even if they continued to practice immorality and injustice. At the door of the Temple the prophet cried out publicly that before they offered sacrifice it was necessary to wash their hands of the blood which stained them, to render justice to the orphan and the widow, to circumcise their heart and ears more than their flesh. He would go on to describe, with terrible vividness, the future destruction of that idolized material temple (§§ 499, 523). The people and kings might put their faith in Egypt and Assyria, but the prophets never. Time and again the prophet reminded them that the sole faith of the nation ought to be Yahweh, and he likened those who put their trust in political alliances to one who leaned on a hollow reed, whose thorns pierced the hand (§ 476). The people might become more and more infected with moral corruption, and adultery, usury, extortion, and all kinds of wickedness might flourish everywhere, but in the streets, the squares, in the palace of the mighty and in the hovel of the poor, in the atrium of the Temple and in the shop of the potter, the prophet reproved the guilty for their crimes in language so harsh that, read even today, their words raise goose pimples on the reader.

Such conduct naturally made the prophet an unwelcome figure. From annoyance to hatred and persecution is a short step, and that kind of annoyance was appeased only by stones. But the prophets did not yield or swerve a hair's breadth from their line of action. It would have been easy and sometimes even opportune to yield on some point or other. It would have been so easy to flatter the people a little, win the good will of the powerful by pleasant words, bow low at the right time before the priests, not see some action of the king, and in the end exercise a more complete domination over those who would finally recognize that the prophet was sent by Yahweh. This was a trick well known to the pseudo-prophets, and one which gave them much authority and money. But the authentic prophets never stooped to such artifices, because they had what the pseudo-prophets lacked, a profoundly religious conscience and a conviction of their mission. Remissness on their part would have been an adulteration of the *Word of Yahweh;* that word had to be kept pure at all costs.

430. The attitude of the people toward the prophets was the usual attitude of moral pygmies toward giants in their midst. It was an illogical, changeable attitude, veering in turn from veneration to abomination, from faith to incomprehension which in a moment of bestial exasperation would stone the giant, and immediately afterward use the same bloody stones to raise up a monument to him. Even in the violence shown toward the prophets, the people were vaguely aware of the tremendous importance of their mission in the national life. The prophets were many times compared to sentinels, stationed in high towers to signal the approach of the enemy; to sentries, who watch over the security of the camp; to night-watchmen who peer out into the mysterious darkness. Even when they were annoyed by the cries of these sentinels, the people sensed the superiority of their mission in life.

Indeed, Israel had become accustomed to these vigilant cries, and to the sight of a prophet arising in its midst in times of crisis. When periodically through the years the whirlwind built up by their crimes ravaged the people, they knew that Yahweh would send medicine along with the storm, and that with the catastrophe there would come also a spiritual dictator who would rebuild. How bewildering, then, it was later on to be when adversities multiplied, and yet the ancient standards recalling them to salvation were no longer seen to arise aloft. What heartbreak is contained in the lament of a contemporary, which, after describing the profanation of Jerusalem and the Temple, reaches the climax of misfortune:

> "Our *standards* are no longer seen,
> there is no longer any *prophet*,
> there is no one among us who knows anything!"
>
> (Ps. 74 [73]:9)

The star of prophetism was setting. It had fulfilled its mission of dissolving the darkness of the night (Rom. 13:12). The light of morning was approaching.

431. Jeroboam's immediate successor on the throne of Israel was his son, Nadab, a phantom king. He reigned two years and was killed by Baasa, of the tribe of Issachar, who had conspired against him (for the probable reason, cf. § 459) while he was besieging Ghibbeton, a city of the tribe of Dan north of Gezer which had fallen into the hands of the Philistines. The conspiracy of Baasa against his own king proved that the example of Jeroboam was not forgotten in the kingdom of Israel; the reappearance of the Philistines (§ 370) revealed the prevailing weakness of the Hebrews. Nadab and his whole family were slain, and the dynasty of Jeroboam thus came to an end.

Baasa the regicide succeeded to the throne. He seems to have been courageous and enterprising. The enmity against the kingdom of Juda was continued by him (1 Kings 15:16), and led him to ally himself with Ben-Hadad I, king of Damascus to the north. Strengthened by this alliance he turned southward, where he captured and fortified Rama (§ 344) in order to close the approach to the kingdom of Juda. Asa of Juda, however (§ 460 ff.), won Ben-Hadad over to his own cause by plying him with gifts, and the latter invaded the north of Israel, occupying various localities north of the lake of Tiberias. Baasa then ceased to fortify Rama, and the materials of the construction were used by Asa of Juda to fortify Gabaa (§ 85) and Mispah (§ 89) against Israel. After about 24 years of rule Baasa died a natural death — a rare thing among the monarchs of Israel — and was buried at Tirsah (§ 414).

His son Ela succeeded him but reigned only two years before being murdered at Tirsah by conspirators who were led by Zimri. On taking possession of the throne, Zimri put to death all the members of the ruling dynasty, following Baasa's lead in this. Zimri did not reign more than seven days. At that time, a new war had broken out at Ghibbeton, and Omri, captain of the army, came with his troops to besiege the new king at Tirsah. Seeing that his plight was hopeless, Zimri set fire to the royal palace and died thus, as had other oriental monarchs (§§ 11, 13) before him.

432. The new dynasty (the fourth) inaugurated by Omri (Vulgate, *Amri*) ruled for about a half century and gave proof of ability and energy.

Once Tirsah was captured, Omri was proclaimed king by his soldiers. But the individualism of the tribes again made its voice heard; his opponent was a certain Thibni, the son of Ginath, possibly the candidate of Ephraim and others, while Omri, like Baasa, probably was of the tribe of Issachar. After about four years, Thibni disappeared and Omri remained on the throne undisturbed.

At first Omri lived at Tirsah, as his predecessors had done. In the sixth year of his reign, i.e., when he was freed of his competitor, he took an important step which speaks well of his military and political perspicacity; for two talents of gold he bought a little hill upon which he built his new capital. It was named Samaria (§ 84) from the name of the seller. The place was excellently chosen. The hill was admirably equipped to resist attacks on the city, as the long sieges later suffered under the Syrians and even the Assyrians demonstrated. Certainly Omri's move was not the only instance of his initiative, but must have been linked up with many others of a political and military character which are passed over by the biblical account, but which are supplied in part by extra-biblical sources.

Omri enjoyed a good reputation abroad. The Assyrian inscriptions of Adad-nirari III (§ 20), of Tiglath-pileser III, and of Sargon (§ 8) name the kingdom of Israel the "land of Omri," or "the land of the house of Omri." The "Black Obelisk" of Salmanassar III (§§ 19, 445) applies the expression of the "house of Omri" to Jehu; actually Jehu (§ 433 ff.) had founded a new dynasty by destroying that of Omri, but the latter's name had remained among the Assyrians both because he was the founder of Samaria and, more probably, because of his military enterprises. It is altogether likely that Omri paid tribute, spontaneously and with due prudence, to Ashur-nasir-pal II and that this latter, driving through to the Mediterranean, received it from Tyre (§ 19), of which Omri was a cordial friend.

The stele of Mesha (§ 439) also states that Omri ruled over the land of Moab (lines 4–5) and occupied the district of Madeba (lines 7–8). It can also be deduced from another source that he levied tribute on King Mesha (2 Kings 3:4). Omri maintained the same friendly relations with Ethbaal king of Tyre which had existed with that people in the time of David and Solomon. Paralleling the relations of Solomon with the court of the Pharaoh, a political marriage was arranged between Achab, son of Omri (§ 433), and Jezabel, the daughter of Ethbaal. With the Arameans it was another story. From an occasional mention (1 Kings 20:34), it is clear that after an unfortunate war, Omri had to yield certain cities to Ben-Hadad I of Damascus (§ 431) and one of them was probably Ramoth Galaad (cf. 1 Kings 22:3). Besides this he had to allow the conqueror to construct within Samaria special quarters something like "open ports" for the Arameans engaged in trade, advantageous of course to the people of Damascus for their traffic with the Mediterranean coast, but disadvantageous and humiliating for Samaria. Relations were very much improved with the kingdom of Juda. The Bible not only contains no mention of hostilities in this period but under his successor Achab there blossomed, with the help of the marriage of Athalia, a true friendship. The groundwork for this must have been laid in the time of Omri. At any rate, in his twelve years of rule, Omri was one of the most active and successful monarchs of Israel.

Not surprising is the reproof which the Bible levels against Omri for having, in religious matters, faithfully followed the footsteps of Jeroboam (1 Kings 16:26). The broadening of relations with foreigners and the prevalence of an ever more secular policy favored the syncretism already begun by Jeroboam (§ 414).

433. Omri's son Achab succeeded him. An astute politician and a courageous warrior, he was under another aspect weak in character. His wife was the Phoenician Jezabel, a bold, resolute woman who wielded great influence over her husband, and who was responsible for many of his decisions.

With a woman like Jezabel in command it was to be expected that the customs and even the religion of her country would be spread throughout the kingdom. The cult of the Baal of Tyre, Melkart ("king of the city": § 107), was made official, and boasted a temple at Samaria complete with a liturgical personnel maintained by the crown. The progress of the cult was not confined to the limits of an accommodating syncretism, but became almost absolute, and logically led to a persecution of the more or less pure Yahwism. Yet the rising flood did not succeed in submerging the summits upon which the Yahwism of the realm took refuge. The loftiest of these was Elias, whose story the Bible relates at this point as if by way of contrast.

434. Elias is the typical figure of ancient prophetism. His activity and the very tenor of his life were vigorous protests against the prevailing syncretism, and called for a clear distinction between Yahweh and Baal, with of course a complete repudiation of the latter. His campaign was, as his name proclaimed, *'Eliyyah*[*u*], "Yahweh is God."

Concerning his origin there is only the indication in 1 Kings 17:1, in which he is called "the Thesbite" and a native of Galaad; about his native city called Thesbeh nothing is known. Dressed in rough, shaggy garments (2 Kings 1:8), accustomed to the life of the desert and a regimen of privations and fasts (1 Kings 17:5; 18:46; 19:3 ff.), he had

Mount Carmel overlooking the sea.

a profound conviction of being guided by Yahweh (18:15 ff.; 19:10; cf. 2 Kings 2:16), and chose as his dwelling place Mount Carmel, as if to face the region to the north whence idolatry issued. The prophets of Yahweh were persecuted and dispersed by the crown until they numbered only about a hundred (1 Kings 18:4), but those of Baal and Astarte "eating at the table of Jezabel" numbered 450 and 300 respectively (18:19). Elias courageously and publicly predicted that as punishment for such a state of affairs, Yahweh would send a terrible drought, and one such actually occurred, c. 857 B.C. He then withdrew and hid near the torrent Carith, probably in Transjordan. When this also dried up, he took refuge in Sareptha near Sidon, in the house of a widow whose victuals he miraculously multiplied and whose son he raised from the dead. As the drought lasted at least until the end of 856 (18:1; cf. Lk. 4:25), King Achab was impressed by the truth of Elias' prediction and was willing to meet him, and to permit a public trial which would demonstrate clearly which of the two religions, that of Yahweh or Baal, was the right one.

When the hundreds of idolatrous prophets were gathered on Carmel, Elias, the last remaining prophet of Yahweh, stood before them (1 Kings 18:22; but cf. verse 4). To the people who were gathered there from all parts of the kingdom, he addressed a reproach which summarized his activity: "How long are you going to dance [root, *pasah*, § 216] on the two *se'ippim*?[8] If Yahweh is God, follow him; if Baal, follow him!"

---

[8] This word (used only this once in the whole Bible) is significantly of doubtful meaning. Ordinarily it is translated as *sides*, but it probably alludes to that liturgical ceremony in which one "danced" before the altar.

(18:21). The trial was disastrous for the idolaters. Two altars were built and two bullocks were placed thereon as victims; the victim for Baal remained intact despite bloody and frenzied rites on the part of the idolatrous prophets to bring about the intervention of the god. After the prayer of Elias, however, the fire of Yahweh fell on the victim for Yahweh and entirely consumed it. Seeing this, the people shouted "Yahweh is God! Yahweh is God!" (18:39.) The prophets of Baal were put to death, and shortly afterward the welcome rain fell upon the land.

Elias, persecuted by Queen Jezabel because of these events, retired to Beersheba (§ 59) and beyond that into the desert. Next he betook himself to Damascus with the intention of anointing Hazael as king of Damascus (§ 441), Jehu as king of Israel, and Eliseus (§ 442) as a prophet.

Yahwistic prophetism was marked by its deep-seated passion for human justice, as is illustrated in the story of Naboth. This man owned a vineyard which bordered on King Achab's park, and the king wanted to obtain possession of it. Naboth refused to part with his property, whereupon Jezabel, a woman devoid of scruples, took a hand. She arranged to have false testimony given against Naboth, who was therefore condemned and slain, his vineyard automatically then becoming the property of the king. When Achab went to take over the property he was confronted by the formidable figure of Elias, the only man among the many who disapproved the deed to take him to task for what he had done, and this publicly. Let Achab know, in the name of Yahweh, that he would suffer the same fate as his victim. Again but briefly the prophet appeared during the short reign of Ochozias, Achab's son (§ 437), to reproach him for having consulted Beelzebub when ill. A fleeting reference to his relations with Joram, king of Juda, is made by the Chronicler (2 Para. 21:12 ff.).

The end of Elias is described in the Bible as the crowning point of his activity. A man like Elias did not deserve to die; ancient (2 Kings 2:1 ff.) as well as modern tradition in Israel (Ecclus. 48:1–3) mentions his being swept up to heaven on a fiery chariot, drawn by horses of fire and with a roar like a whirlwind.

435. Achab's foreign policy was quite unsettled during the last years of his reign. At first relations with the Arameans must have continued as they were in the time of Omri, i.e., Samaria was clearly inferior to Damascus, and little love was lost between them. Later years brought war, probably fought for economic reasons. In 858 Ben-Hadad II of Damascus with his army and 32 allied kings (cf. the 31 kings in the time of Josue, § 280) laid siege to Samaria, but the city resisted and in one encounter inflicted notable losses upon the attacking Ara-

Damascus. The city and the Antilibanus.

means. The next year (857) Ben-Hadad tried again, with a new organization of the army. He succeeded in drawing the enemy into a
plain, where his tactics promised great advantages. The battle took
place at Apheq (probably the present Fiq, to the east of Lake Tiberias),
but Achab soundly defeated him and succeeded in taking him prisoner.
The victor was extremely generous; he spared the life of the prisoner
and limited his demands to the restoration of the cities ceded by Omri
to the Arameans. Then it was his turn to demand special quarters in
Damascus for the Israelites engaged in commerce (§ 432). Such generosity on the part of Achab was denounced by a prophet of Yahweh.
Achab had a good political reason for so acting, however, as the
Assyrian threat was visibly taking shape. The peace with the Arameans
was an uneasy one, and poorly kept; at the first opportunity war broke
out again.

Achab was also successful in his dealings with Moab. The stele of
Mesha (§ 439) states that "Omri occupied the region of Madeba, and
(*Israel*) dwelt in it in his days and half the days of his son [or: of his
sons]; forty years" (lines 7–8). If one reads "of his son," the revolt of
Moab against the yoke imposed by Omri would have taken place in
the eleventh year of Achab (who reigned 22 years); if, however, as
seems better, one reads: "of his sons," the words refer to the three
monarchs who succeeded Omri as well as to his own dynasty; i.e.,

Achab-Ochozias-Joram (all of them spanning the years 875–842).
Even so 40 years given by the stele $(12 \ [\text{Omri}] + \dfrac{875-842}{2} = 28\frac{1}{2})$
are not obtained; the revolt, moreover, would fall in the reign of Achab, although according to 2 Kings 1:1; 3:5, it took place after his death. The more reasonable solution is to follow this last bit of information which the Bible gives so clearly. The 40 years mentioned in the stele, already explained as a typical figure (§ 255), and "half of his days," should be interpreted as an approximation only. Doubtless Achab ruled over Moab at least during the first half of his reign; if Madeba was lost in his time, it was because the Moabites strove to profit by the difficulties in which Achab found himself because of his wars with Syria.

The reasons which impelled Achab to strike a generous peace with Ben-Hadad are passed over in silence by the Bible, which gives no indication of the important events in which Achab took part after the above-mentioned peace. However, we know something of both events from Assyrian sources. As for the motives of the generous peace, it can be maintained that the king of Samaria wanted to keep Damascus as a cushion to absorb the blows of Assyria. In the very year of the peace, 857, Salmanassar III conquered Carchemish (§ 19), with the avowed intention of extending his conquests toward Syria and Palestine. Against that threat from the north Achab took good care not to weaken the natural defense he had in Damascus. As the attacks of Assyria were continuing, a league of twelve kings was formed in which the enemies of yesterday were the leaders, i.e., Ben-Hadad (called *Adad-idri* in Assyrian monuments) and Achab (*Ahabbu Shirlai*). Achab eventually took part in the battle of Qarqar (in the year 853), with the circumstances and results already noted (§ 19).

Es-salt (Ramoth Galaad?).

436. Achab survived this battle by only a few months. In the same year he received with pomp Josaphat, king of Juda, who had come to visit him in Samaria (1 Kings 22:2 ff.); this visit sealed the peace now existing between the two nations (22:45).

The palace of Omri and Achab in Samaria.

Once again a marriage helped confirm the pact; Joram, son of Josaphat, married Athalia, daughter of Achab (2 Kings 8:18, 26). At the time of Josaphat's visit the anti-Assyrian league had practically lost any value it had ever had, and the antagonism between Samaria and Damascus had begun again. It was intensified by the fact that Damascus had not returned the city of Ramoth Galaad, as it should have done according to the treaties (§ 435). Achab invited his visitor Josaphat to take part in the armed conquest of that city. Yahweh was consulted about the proposal; 400 prophets of those who were affiliated with the official syncretistic cults gave an affirmative answer which presaged success; one alone, Micheas ben Jemla, predicted failure. The expedition was undertaken. Although Achab fought in disguise, he was found out by an arrow. He remained courageously in his war chariot facing the enemy, but died that same day.

His reign had marked a period of flowering and power. Besides his successes over peoples of another stock, the friendship between Israel and Juda brought out Juda's "subordination"; it would continue for some time. During the reign of Achab Jericho was rebuilt by Hiel (§ 80), no doubt as an outpost against treacherous Moab (§ 439). Resuming the tradition of Solomon, Achab did a good deal of building, mostly for purposes of fortification or comfort. In Samaria he built a "house of ivory," probably a complete renovation of the royal palace built there by Omri (§ 84) with ample coverings of ivory.

He made his great error in the field of religion. Here the influence of his foreign wives and his flair for imitating foreigners led him to take a series of steps which tended to cancel out the Yahwism which was so characteristic of the nation he governed. His friendly advances to Juda were a fine opportunity to strengthen himself with the southern kingdom not only politically but also spiritually. Harmoniously united, the two kingdoms could have accomplished great things, but Achab let the opportunity slip away, and perverted his people by importations from the Phoenician spiritual world.

437. The revolt of Mesha (§ 439 ff.) seems to have occurred under the brief reign of Ochozias, son and successor of Achab. Mesha must have tried to take advantage of Achab's death or of Ochozias' unfortunate fall from a balcony of the royal palace in Samaria; he was gravely injured and after uselessly consulting Beelzebub, the god of Accaron (§ 107), died after a few months of enforced inactivity. During this time Mesha progressively asserted and strengthened his independence.

438. Next there ruled the other son of Achab, Joram, the last king of the dynasty of Omri. His attitude toward religious questions was in line with the syncretism officially inaugurated by Jeroboam, but he favored Yahwism, and went so far as to overturn "the *massebah* (§ 104)

Stele of Mesha.

of the Baal his father had made" (2 Kings 3:2). Evidently the action of Elias had produced some effect.

Relations with the kingdom of Juda were consistently friendly, although Israel enjoyed a certain superiority. Family connections had been formed by the marriage of Athalia, sister of Joram of Israel, with Joram of Juda (§ 436). Against Assyria, the position held by Achab was maintained; the anti-Assyrian league (§ 435) having been revived, principally through the efforts of Damascus, the allies from Samaria intervened to put a stop to the incursions of Salmanassar III (in the years 849, 845; cf. § 19) without, however, a clear victory resulting for either party.

Joram went all out against

Moab and sought to bring about the reconquest which the ailing Ochozias had not been able to accomplish. It is of this campaign of Joram (2 Kings 3:4–27) that the famous stele of Mesha speaks.

439. This stele was found in 1868 by Bedouins at Diban (the *Dibon* of the Bible and *Daibon* [ita] of the stele [lines 1–2, 21] about four miles north of the Arnon: § 66). "Squeezes"[9] were made of it at once and negotiations begun for its purchase. This sharpened the cupidity of the natives, who thought to obtain more money for the stele by breaking it into many pieces. When most of the fragments had been purchased and fitted together, the missing parts were restored with the help of the impressions which had been made. The stele thus restored is at Paris (Louvre) and measures about 3 feet by 4. The doubts often expressed against its authenticity have proved to be groundless. The following is a linear translation:[10]

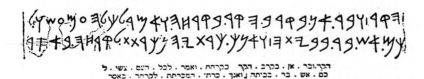

דהקר.ובר . אן . בקרב . הקר . בקרחת   ואמר . לכל . הים . גשי . ל
כם . אש . בר . בביתה.נואנך . כרח . המברתת . לקרחד . באסר

The 24th and 25th lines of the Stele of Mesha with Hebraic transcription.
(Benzinger, *Hebr. Archäol.*)

1. I am Mesha', son of Chemosh[kan?] king of Moab, the Dai-
2. bonite. My father ruled over Moab thirty years, and I reigned
3. after my father; and I made this *bamah* (§ 104) at Chemosh in Qarhoh, *bam*[ah of sal-]
4. vation; because he saved me from all my assailants (?) and caused me to prevail over all my enemies. Omr-
5. i was king of Israel and oppressed Moab for many days, since Chemosh had been angry with his
6. land. And his son succeeded him; and he also said: "I will oppress Moab!" — In my days he spoke [thus],
7. but I have prevailed over him and his house, and Israel has utterly perished forever! Omri had occupied the [re-]
8. gion of Madeba, and (*Israel*) had lived in it in his time and the half the time of his son [*or*: his sons]; forty years; but there [dwelt?]
9. in it Chemosh in my time. And I built Baal-meon, and in it made the reservoir; and I e[rected]
10. Qaryaten. And the people of Gad dwelt in the land of 'Ataroth from ancient times, and for himself built the king

---

[9] A technical term meaning that a wet layer of pulpy paper was worked into the inscription, then pulled off in one piece when dry.
[10] The complete text of the Moabite Stone, in *ANET*, 320 f.

11. Of Israel 'Ataroth; but I warred against the city, and I took it, and slew all the people

12. of the city: a spectacle for Chemosh and Moab! And I took away from there the altar of its Dodh (§ 355) and car-

13. ried it to Chemosh in Kerioth; and made the people of Sharon live in it and the people

14. of Maharith. And Chemosh said to me: Go, take Nebo (*by fighting*) against Israel! And I

15. went by night and fought against it from daybreak to midday. And I

16. took it; I slew all in it, seven thousand, [men and boys] and women and [young]

17. girls and slaves; since I made *herem* (§ 271) of them to Astarte-Chemosh. And I took from there the [ob-]

18. jects of Yahweh and carried them to the presence of Chemosh. And the king of Israel built

19. Jahaz, and dwelt in it during his war with me, and Chemosh cast him out before me.

20. I took from Moab two hundred men, all his chiefs (?) and led them against Jahaz and I took it

21. in order to annex it to Daibon. I built Qarhoh, the wall of the forest and the wall of

22. Ophel (§ 96), etc.

Chemosh plays such a large part in this inscription because he was the god of Moab and had been adored in Jerusalem during the idolatrous reign of Solomon (§ 403). From the expressions used in line 7 it would seem that the stele was written after the destruction of the dynasty of Omri and the coming of Jehu.

440. Mesha, however, does not tell the full story in this piece of self-glorification; naturally he omits any part unfavorable to himself, but this is supplied by the biblical account.

Mesha was paying a heavy tribute of smaller animals to Israel, but refused to continue it after Achab died (§ 435). Joram, realizing that it would be poor strategy to attack Moab from the north (where the enemy was well defended by fortifications and by the deep ravine of the Arnon, and where there was also the danger of being surprised from the rear by rival Damascus), saw the necessity of attacking from the south, along the southern extremity of the Dead Sea. He came to an agreement with Josaphat of Juda and the king of Edom on this plan, and the march through these territories was undertaken. They planned to penetrate Moab from the southeast.

The march was long and toward the end was aggravated by a lack of water. The prophet Eliseus, who was present, suggested that they dig some trenches and so obtain water. Even today the inhabitants of this region often obtain water by digging thus into the earth. The water thus obtained has a reddish hue and apparently filtrates in from the surrounding plateaus.

In the meantime the news of the difficulties in which the aggressors found themselves spread through Moab; Moabite scouts, judging from their exuberance, seemed to interpret the reddish color glimpsed from the enemy's camp as blood, and reasoned that one of those unforeseen struggles which oriental opportunism oftentimes caused between allies (§ 463) had taken place. They therefore proceeded to attack the camp of the allies.

The unorganized attack was easily broken up. Giving chase, the allies literally devastated the territory and besieged the capital Qir-Haresheth (the present Kerak: Vulgate, *muri fictiles*) situated in the center of Moab. The siege was a savage one. The King of Moab attempted a sortie in order to open a way to the king of Aram,[11] but it did not succeed. He then had recourse to a deed which recalls the Canaanite usages and the example of Jephte (§ 325). "He took his first-born son, who was to have reigned after him, and offered him as a holocaust upon the wall" (2 Kings 3:27). This sacrifice was undoubtedly intended to propitiate Chemosh, the god so highly praised in the stele, and to turn his anger against the besiegers. In fact, "great indignation arose against Israel, and [the allies] departed from him and returned to [their] country" (*ibid.*). "Great indignation" is a typically biblical way of describing the divine anger, especially that of Yahweh. What actually happened was that, after Moab's king had offered this human sacrifice, the allies either retired in horror, or better, were defeated by the Moabites, in whom this horrible spectacle had aroused the courage of desperation.

In conclusion, the campaign, which for the most part had been a success, turned out to be a failure for Joram and his allies. From that time on Moab was independent, at least until the time of Jeroboam II (§ 448). It is noteworthy that both the Bible and the stele report the final failure of Joram. For the rest the Bible dwells upon his initial success; the stele passes it over in silence, for that theme did not lend itself to the self-laudatory style of the inscription.

441. The attitude of Joram toward Damascus was pretty much the same as Achab's had been, and resulted in a series of alliances alternating with hostilities. When the Syrian menace became too threatening, the two kingdoms drew closer together; when they felt secure, the aggressions of Damascus against Samaria recommenced (2 Kings 6:8–23). The Syrians laid siege to Samaria during the reign of an unnamed king

---

[11] The Hebrew text has Edom but the usual exchange must have occurred (§§ 306, 351, 451 note) between 'DM (*Edom*) and 'RM (*Aram*). Since the king of Edom was one of the besieging allies, certainly Mesha could not have been thinking of seeking refuge with him, but he could well have hoped to find help from the king of Damascus (*Aram*), the inveterate enemy of the kingdom of Israel.

of Israel (2 Kings 6:24–7:20). This occurred under Joram, perhaps after the last incursion of Salmanassar III (in the year 845) and as a result of the failure of the campaign against Moab. Others, however, are of the opinion that the unnamed king was Joachaz, the successor of Jehu (§ 446). The siege was severe, and hunger in the city reached such a point that some mothers cooked and ate their own children, as was to happen later on during the siege of Jerusalem (§ 540). The city was unexpectedly delivered when panic seized the besiegers by night and caused them to flee.

Shortly thereafter Hazael, one of Ben-Hadad's generals, seized the throne of Damascus after smothering the king as he lay sick in bed. Joram took advantage of the occasion to liquidate the old question of Ramoth Galaad (§ 436), and moved against the city with his nephew and ally, Ochozias, king of Juda. In the course of the operations Joram was wounded. Leaving Jehu in charge of the army he retired to Jezrael in the valley of Esdraelon, and here Ochozias of Juda came to visit him. At this point prophetism, whose greatest exponent Eliseus had become, made itself felt directly in the sphere of politics.

442. Eliseus, son of Saphat, was originally from Abel-meholah, in the valley of the Jordan south of Beisan (§ 86). He must have been a well-to-do farmer, since he was able to plow with twelve pair of oxen. Elias surprised him at his plowing and chose him to be his colleague in the prophetical office, symbolically throwing his own mantle upon his back. Eliseus followed him promptly, and was a devoted disciple throughout the last years of Elias' life.

The disciple, however, was of somewhat different character from the master. Eliseus, it seems, did not imitate the austerity of Elias in his clothing, nor in his preference for solitude. He preferred to exercise his ministry in the crowded centers; he frequented the prophetical corporations (§ 422 ff.) and also had a servant Giezi (Gehazi), who usually accompanied him. Like Elias, he dwelt for a time on Carmel. Elias sought to commune with God especially in the stillness of mountains or valleys, but Eliseus had recourse to musical instruments (§ 423). His whole career, finally, is interspersed with more miraculous deeds than that of Elias.

For example, after the ascension of Elias, Eliseus touched the waters of the Jordan with the mantle of the master and they opened to let him pass over, a sign which brought him recognition as the successor of the former prophet by the "sons of the prophets," who chanted: "The spirit of Elias has settled upon Eliseus!" (2 Kings 2:15.) When mocked for his baldness by some of the urchins at Beth-el, he cursed them in the name of Yahweh, and at once two bears emerged from a nearby wood and tore forty-two of them to pieces. This incident contrasts harshly with the one mentioned in 2 Kings 6:20–22, when he multiplied a widow's supply of oil so that she could pay her creditors. He implored God that a son should be granted to a sterile woman of Shunem and some years later brought that same son back to life. His fame as a wonder-worker spread even to Aram, and Naaman, the general of the army of the king of Damascus, came to him to be healed of his leprosy. Eliseus cured him, but the leprosy was transferred to the servant Giezi, who had tried to capitalize on the miracle. Many other wonders were worked.

Apparently he enjoyed a large measure of authority not only in Israel, whose king he accompanied in his expedition against Moab (§ 440), but also in the kingdoms of Juda and Damascus. In his last illness Ben-Hadad sent Hazael to consult Eliseus and the prophet told Hazael that he would be king of Damascus. Moved by the prediction, he seized the throne upon his return by killing the king (§ 441). The intervention of Eliseus was more direct and decisive in the reigning dynasty of Israel.

443. The dynasty of Omri could not have been pleasing to the prophets. Although Joram had attenuated the syncretism traditional in his dynasty (§ 438), its continuance led to an unyielding antagonism between the two rivals. This is not surprising, as Joram's father was Achab, Elias' personal enemy, and his mother was the Phoenician patroness of the prophets of Baal, Jezabel. The memory of their systematic anti-Yahwism lingered on. On the other hand Eliseus had not been a special disciple of Elias in vain. Joram and Eliseus were symbols of two contrasting spiritual worlds, between which there could be only opposition. "What [connection] have I with thee? Go to the prophets of thy father and to the prophets of thy mother!" These words of Eliseus to Joram (2 Kings 3:13) paint a picture of their mutual relations and respective positions; they also explain the scene which followed.

While the convalescent Joram rested in Jezrael with Ochozias of Juda, and Jehu was at Ramoth (§ 441), Eliseus sent a prophet who was his disciple to Ramoth, secretly to anoint Jehu king of Israel. Prophetism thus took up a political stand also against the dynasty of Omri. When the news spread through the camp, the captains promptly aligned themselves with the new king (2 Kings 9:13). Jehu desired that the affair remain secret and hastened off in the direction of Jezrael. Being warned there by the sentinels, the two kings, surprised at his coming, went out to meet him in their chariots. As Joram drew near he asked, "Is everything all right, Jehu?" but he replied: "How all right, so long as the fornications (§ 318 ff.) of thy mother and her many sorceries [continue]!" (9:22.) The reply of the new king revealed an anti-idolatrous sentiment, coupled for political reasons to his election by a Yahwistic prophet.

Joram was killed on the spot. Ochozias of Juda, wounded as he fled, died at Megiddo (2 Kings 9:27; or Samaria, cf. 2 Para. 22:9). These two out of the way, Jehu entered Jezrael, where Jezabel awaited him, resolved to die as a queen. Adorned and arrayed in splendor, she appeared on the balcony and spoke to the successful conspirator as he entered the gate. He had her thrown down into the street where she was trampled on by his horses. After that he massacred forty-two princes of the dynasty of Jerusalem who had come to visit Ochozias (cf. § 465), and seventy princes of the house of Achab residing in Samaria. The dynasty of Omri being thus wiped out, Jehu took possession of the capital.

✿   ✿   ✿

444. The dynasty (the fifth) inaugurated by Jehu ruled for a century. The outstanding fact of this period is the predominance of Assyria over the kingdom of Israel. The intervention of an enemy who had already been fought against at the side of Damascus was provoked by the ancient rivalry between Damascus and Samaria. Allayed only when the Assyrian peril was imminent, it flared up anew when the danger was removed. There came a day when Samaria, tired of this state of affairs and, being situated farther south than Damascus, decided to change its policy, thus placing her vacillating ally between two fires. Once Samaria became the friend of Assyria, that nation could strike Damascus from the north, and thus free Samaria from its troublesome neighbor.

The "Black Obelisk" of Salmanassar. (About 6½ feet high.) (British Museum.)

So it came about, but the remedy was worse than the disease. Assyria was not a power which dispensed favors freely, and for smaller states to become her ally meant their becoming her vassal and tributary. Thus to the rivalry with Damascus there was now added subjection to Assyria, because Damascus was to last a long time yet, and made her ex-ally to the south feel the bite of her ill-will. Under the dynasty of Jehu, then, the situation deteriorated.

445. Jehu began his reign with an act which was radically opposed to idolatry, and was aided in this by a zealous Yahwist named

Jonadab ben Rechab (§ 422). By means of a clever stratagem he wiped out the cult of Baal, killing all its followers gathered for that purpose in their temple, and then demolished the temple. It was new proof of his opposition to the policy of the preceding dynasty, yet the Yahwism of which Jehu made himself the champion was that held by Jeroboam, one which adored Yahweh in the form of a golden calf at Beth-el and Dan (§ 414).

Jehu and his tribute. (From the "Black Obelisk" of Salmanassar.) (British Museum.)

Foreign relations were generally bad. Both Tyre and Jerusalem, related by marriage to the two murdered kings whose deaths had enabled Jehu to obtain the throne, now turned against Samaria. At Damascus, the new king Hazael (§ 442) was attacked in 841 by Salmanassar III (§ 19), and on that occasion Jehu not only inaugurated his new policy of not sending the usual help against Assyria, but arrayed his forces on her side and sent tribute to the invader. Hazael was defeated on Antilibanus, yet Damascus was not captured and the Assyrians withdrew. They returned once more in 839 but without any better results against Damascus, and were satisfied to renew the levy of tribute on the peoples already subjugated; nor did they reappear in Syria for another ten years. Salmanassar III mentions these tributes in his "Black Obelisk," which boasts of his victories, and on which Jehu "of the house of Omri" (§ 432) is depicted in the act of adoration before the Assyrian monarch.[12]

In reality Jehu paid the heaviest price, for when the Assyrians had departed, the vengeance of Hazael was unleashed against him. In a series of campaigns, not specified clearly in the Bible (2 Kings 10:32–33), Hazael seized all Israelite territory beyond the Jordan. With Moab (§ 440) and the rest of Transjordan lost, the kingdom of Israel was diminished by about a third. This conquest was moreover accompanied

---

[12] ANET, 208 f.

by atrocities of war which the Assyrians in particular had made habitual in the ancient world and the memory of which was long and bitter (2 Kings 8:13; Amos 1:3). Jehu died in these circumstances after a reign of twenty-eight years.

446. During the seventeen-year reign of his son Joachaz who succeeded him, a catastrophe occurred which led to Israel's complete subjection to Damascus. Israel's army was literally destroyed, and it was only with the permission of Damascus that Joachaz was allowed to maintain a garrison; it amounted to 50 horsemen, 10 war chariots, and 10,000 infantry (2 Kings 13:7), no more than would be allowed a vassal. Another opinion is that the terrible siege of Samaria was the catastrophe in question, taking place in the time of Joram (§ 441). Further proof of the triumph of Damascus over Israel is that Hazael could push on to the south, conquer the city of Gath (§ 75), attack also the kingdom of Juda and threaten Jerusalem itself. The city was only relieved from this threat when Joas, king of Juda, spontaneously sent the Temple and palace treasures to the invader (2 Kings 12:17–18).

How long the oppression of Aram lasted is uncertain. Treating of the reign of Joachaz the Bible says that when he implored Yahweh, "Yahweh gave Israel a liberator so that they escaped from the hand of Aram" (13:5). Who this "liberator" was cannot be definitely stated. Perhaps this is a simple chronological anticipation, possibly referring to Jeroboam II, the second successor of Joachaz (2 Kings 14:26–27); but even admitting that the renascence of the kingdom of Israel reached its zenith under Jeroboam II, the impulse had likely been given from the time of Joachaz, and grew steadily stronger under Joas and Jeroboam II.

Some hint of this is given by extra-biblical documents. The inscriptions of Adad-nirari III[13] (§ 20) not only record generally among his other conquests his subjugation of all the Occident from the Euphrates to Tyre, to Sidon, "to the land of Omri," to Edom, to Philistia, and to the "great sea" (the Mediterranean), but, referring especially to his campaigns in Syria (during the years 805–802), they record that the Assyrian monarch besieged king *Mari* in Damascus and 'forced him to surrender and to pay an enormous tribute. That there ever was a king *Mari* of Damascus cannot be established by any other document; it is here probably a question of a simple regal title ("[my] lord," as it is used in Syria today), by which the Assyrian inscription designates Ben-Hadad III, who had, shortly before, succeeded his father Hazael on the throne.

Undoubtedly this humiliation of Damascus by Adad-nirari brought relief to the oppressed kingdom of Israel and it is not impossible that

---

[13] Adad-nirari III, expedition to Palestine, in *ANET*, 281.

the victorious Assyrian monarch appeared as its "liberator" (by a curious coincidence *Adad-nirari* means "Adad is of help"). It is certain not only from the policy inaugurated by Jehu (§ 445), but also from the inscription of King Kilamu, king of Ya'di (found at Zenjirli in 1902) that the ever-bickering kinglets of northern Syria were accustomed "to hire the King of Assyria" (cf. Isa. 7:20), that is, call to him for help against their adversary. The inscription of Zakir, king of Hamath and Lu'ush on the Orontes (discovered near Aleppo in 1903), relates how, not much before 800, several small Aramean states had formed a league against this king. At its head was "Ben-Hadad son of Hazael," but it was Zakir who emerged the victor. This precious information becomes clearer in its details if one supposes that (1) The league against Zakir was inspired by hatred for Assyria, whose partisan Zakir was; (2) Zakir, less well-prepared for war than the league, won out, thanks to the intervention of Adad-nirari III; (3) Joachaz of Israel, aided as it were by a "liberator," gained much by the double defeat which Zakir and Adad-nirari inflicted on Damascus. However, so uncertain is the chronology that this attempt at synchronization has of necessity no more than a relative probability.

447. At any rate, it is certain that during the sixteen years of the reign of Joas, son and successor of Joachaz, the kingdom of Israel recovered rapidly. During this era Eliseus died; when King Joas visited him he gave him the title already given by Eliseus to Elias (2 Kings 2:12), "the chariot of Israel and its driver" (13:14), not without a veiled allusion to the lack of chariots and horsemen imposed by Damascus (§ 446) and to the nationalistic activity of the prophet which substituted for it. At death's door, the old man urged the king once more to act resolutely against the inveterate enemy of Israel and of Yahweh, promising him repeated victories. After this prediction the dauntless champion of Yahweh died. Taking advantage of the state of decline in which Damascus found itself because of the defeats inflicted on it by Assyria, Joas attacked Ben-Hadad III, was thrice victorious, and recovered the cities lost by his father Joachaz (13:25), that is, a good part of Transjordan at least (§ 445).

The kingdom of Israel thus once more came to wear that aura of superiority which it had enjoyed in the past over the kingdom of Juda. The contemporary king of Juda, Amasias, found this annoying, the more so as his successful campaign against Edom (§ 471) had inspired in him great confidence in his own strength. He dreamed of humiliating Samaria, and thus becoming the leader of the whole Israelite race. He accordingly attacked the northern kingdom. After vainly trying to avoid war, Joas fought against and defeated Amasias, making him prisoner at Beth-shemesh, conquered Jerusalem, despoiled the Temple and palace, and destroyed a long section of the wall. He then left the humiliated Amasias on the throne of David.

448. The reign of Jeroboam II, son and successor of Joas, can without fear of exaggeration be compared to that of Solomon, on a reduced scale of course, and in quite different circumstances. The biblical narrative tells very little of his forty-one years of reign, concerned as it is chiefly with the vicissitudes of the kingdom of Juda (a preoccupation which is carried to extremes by the Chronicler who shows practically no interest in the schismatic kingdom of Israel): yet, these few items are highly significant. "He restored the borders of Israel from the entrance of Hamath [§ 60] to the sea of the 'Araba [§ 61]" (2 Kings 14:25), and moreover reasserted ancient rights over Damascus and Hamath (14:28; ?). The limits of his kingdom therefore extended to practically all of Palestine except the territory of Juda, but including Moab which had again been subdued after the revolt of Mesha (§ 440).

This restoration had to be brought about by the kingdom's own efforts. Assyria was in a period of decadence and much embroiled in Babylonia and Urartu, so that — except for the expedition in 773–772 against Damascus — it did not appear in the West. Damascus was reduced to fending for itself, defending itself as best it could from the attacks of Israel. From the north Jeroboam had no threat to contend with, and very little resistance. To the south there was much less danger, for after the rout of Amasias the kingdom of Juda lay in a state of absolute subjection.

These victories afford a glimpse of a reawakened military and civil organization in the kingdom, one which brought to mind the better days of David and Solomon. The unified internal command, unchanged for forty-one years, found a happy counterpart in an uninterrupted series of favorable circumstances outside the kingdom, and thus created an era of true prosperity and greatness. A clear proof of the material well-being of this period is the license and dissoluteness which usually accompanies it and which are described by contemporaries (Amos 2:6 ff.; 3:9 ff.; 4:1 ff.; 6:3 ff.; etc.). The literary activity of this period, putting into writing and re-editing ancient translations, or in composing works entirely new (§ 484) must also have been considerable.

＊　　＊　　＊

449. This flowering was, however, the result of exceptionally favorable circumstances, rather than of a solid national strength. Once the circumstances changed, the flower was in danger of shriveling up for want of deep roots.

The personal authority of Jeroboam II evidently commanded respect. When he died and his son Zacharias succeeded him, what had happened to the other successors of Solomon was repeated, except that now conspiracy had become a tradition in the kingdom of Israel. After six months on the throne Zacharias was murdered. The conspirators were led by Sellum, who thus brought to an end the dynasty of Jehu and seized the throne.

Sellum himself, however, fell victim to a conspiracy after only a month in office. Menahem came from Tirsah (§ 414), seized Samaria, and, having killed Sellum there, took over his kingdom. The bare facts are noted by the Bible, but it is easy to see that the period from the death of Jeroboam II to the first days of Menahem was one of semi-anarchy, and probably that period described in Osee 7:1 ff.; 8:4. Although the throne had passed in the regular way to Zacharias, other factions were continually being organized, and their hopes of success were in proportion to the strength of their arms. Sellum was the first one to succeed. Menahem, coming later, was better prepared, and used the fortress of Tirsah as a base of operations. He was therefore able to dispose of Sellum and perhaps of other rivals as well. The text of Osee 7:11 suggests that the various contending parties were divided into two general factions, one seeking the support of Egypt, the other that of Assyria (cf. § 522). The overthrow of Sellum by Menahem — who during his reign was in a state of absolute vassalage to Assyria, then at the height of its glory — seems to indicate that Sellum had placed his hopes on Egypt, which was at that time (the end of the Twenty-Third Dynasty; § 37) in a state of collapse.

The method used by Menahem to obtain possession of the throne and to preserve it afterward was typically Assyrian, recognized no limits to cruelty, and relied on the moral effects of fear. "At that time Menahem destroyed *Tiphsah* and all that was in it and all the environs thereof from Tirsah [down], because they did not open [their gates to him]; and he ripped open women who were with child [who were found] there" (2 Kings 15:16). *Tiphsah*, the reading of the Hebrew text, is certainly erroneous since it could not in any way refer to Thapsacus of the Euphrates (§ 216). In its stead one should read, with Lucian, the name *Tappuah*, a city to the south of Sichem (cf. Jos. 16:8; 17:7–8).

450. Despite his regime of terror at home Menahem must have felt the shakiness of his throne, and relations abroad did not serve to steady it. He had recourse to Assyrian arms. "In his days Pul, king of the Assyrians, came into the land; and Menahem gave Pul one thousand talents of silver so that he would help him keep the kingdom in his grasp. And Menahem levied the money from Israel, from those who were rich in property, fifty sicles of silver each, for the king of Assyria. Thus the king of Assyria turned back and did not stay in the land" (2 Kings 15

[18]:19–20). Since one talent of silver was equivalent to 3000 sicles, 3 million sicles were handed over to the king of Assyria. On this basis there must have been 60,000 persons "wealthy in property" in the kingdom of Israel. Because this sum was so promptly paid, the Assyrian king retired from the land at once, without leaving garrisons of troops behind to guarantee collection. At any rate, this was the first time that an Assyrian army had penetrated Israelite soil.

The king of Assyria was Tiglath-pileser III, called also Pulu (§ 8). After attacking Urartu (in 743), he besieged Arpad and conquered the Arameans of northern Mesopotamia. Shortly afterwards he was to confront an anti-Assyrian league headed by Azriyau of Yaudi (§ 472), but here too he was victorious (in the year 738). Taking the city of Kullani (cf. Isa. 10:9; Amos 6:2), he reduced the region to an Assyrian province and levied tribute on the surrounding states. In the annals of Tiglath-pileser III, among the many kings who paid tribute on this occasion, mention is made of Rasin of Damascus, Hiram of Tyre, and Menahem of Israel. There is no doubt, therefore, that the tribute described in the Assyrian document as a sign of vassalage is the one described in the Bible as an offering from Menahem. Menahem welcomed the coming of Tiglath-pileser III, because it cooled the anti-Assyrian fervor of Rasin, king of Damascus, who, knowing that Menahem leaned toward Assyria, must have already threatened him. Thus it is explained how Tiglath-pileser III "lent his aid" to Menahem to hold on to his kingdom.[14]

451. This heavy tribute, however, must certainly have caused profound discontent among the people, and served to strengthen the anti-Assyrian faction. Menahem's son, Peqahia (Phaceia) succeeded him and had reigned scarcely two years when the now usual conspiracy put an end to him and his (the seventh) dynasty. The leader of the conspirators was Peqah (Phacee), son of Remaliah, general of Peqahia who, as was to be expected, was unfriendly toward Assyria. In fact once Tiglath-pileser III penetrated into the kingdom of Israel, the domestic and foreign policy of Israel was dominated by its attitude toward Assyria. Israel was left the choice of subjection with tribute in its hands, or rebellion, with weapons in them.

In view of the character of the faction which had brought him to the throne, Peqah naturally enough chose to rebel. It would have been suicidal, however, for a state as weak as Israel to defy the Assyrian giant singlehanded, and if Peqah pursued an anti-Assyrian policy, it was because he knew he was not alone. The Damascus-plan was favored by the anti-Assyrian faction, and it had perhaps already been proposed with threats by Rasin to Menahem. The old league of Aramean states

---

[14] Inscriptions of Tiglath-pileser III, in *ANET*, 282 ff.

against Assyria under the direction of Damascus was resurrected, and Phoenicia and Palestine were obliged to take part in it.

Rasin of Damascus, an unwilling tributary of Tiglath-pileser III, was the first to rebel. To strengthen the league and protect its flank Juda had to be induced to enter it. This was especially important, for it would put the league into direct communication with Egypt, from whom they could always expect some help, for Egypt was always at opposite poles from Assyria. Rasin's threatening invitation to Mena-hem must also have been made to Joatham, king of Juda, but this latter considered Assyria a remote danger, and refused to enter the dangerous league. His refusal was interpreted as a threat to the league, and both Rasin and Peqah began hostilities against him (2 Kings 15:37), intending to divide between themselves his kingdom of Juda (Isa. 7:6). Joatham died a little later and was succeeded by his son, who was placed by the ensuing hostilities in a difficult position.

While the two allies broke through from the north, other enemies arose against Juda from the south. Elath, the port on the tip of the Elanitic Gulf, was lost to Edom.[15] To the west the Philistines awakened and invaded the southwestern section of the territory of Juda (2 Para. 28:18).

452. Beaten in the open, Achaz shut himself up in fortified Jerusalem, and there resisted the attack of the besiegers. It was probably during some crisis of defense that this idolatrous descendant of David offered up his own son as a holocaust (2 Kings 16:3), according to the Canaanite custom observed by Mesha (§ 440). The child must have been a very young one, as Achaz was only twenty years old when he ascended the throne. But this time the burning of the child did not frighten the besiegers. Achaz sent to ask help of Tiglath-pileser III, and bolstered his appeal by sending the treasures of the Temple of Yahweh and of the palace of the dynasty of David. The prophet Isaias was one of those in the beleaguered city, and with Yahwistic zeal counseled a remedy entirely different from the sacrifice of a child or an appeal to the Assyrian monarch (Isa. 7; §§ 476, 488).

The embassy and the treasures of Achaz found the Assyrian monarch, if not actually on the march, at any rate ready to intervene against the enterprising league. According to Assyrian sources, his campaign began in 734 and lasted until 732; the many particulars given prove that it was conducted with brilliant strategy and aimed at reducing these regions to submission. The attack did not begin from the north where the Syrians were better prepared, but from the south, for Tiglath-pileser

---

[15] Thus should be corrected the passage in 2 Kings 16, 6, where by means of the usual change (§§ 306, 351, 440 note) the Hebrew text has *Aram*, which has caused some to consider the name of Rasin as a gloss. The Syrians, that is, *Aram*, never pushed so far southward, much less did they settle there.

skirted the territories of the league, descended along the Mediterranean coast, rapidly conquered the Phoenician cities and placed his lieutenants over them. Bringing pressure to bear against Philistia, he made an assault on Gaza, thus bringing immediate relief to Achaz at Jerusalem. Hannon king of Gaza — the instigator certainly of the Philistine invasion of Juda, § 451 — took flight, Tiglath-pileser relates, to *Musri* (*Egypt;* § 22), leaving everything in the hands of the victor. After cutting the communications of the league with the south, the Assyrian returned to deal with its two principals, who had at his approach retired from the siege of Jerusalem and fled precipitously to their strongholds, where they barricaded themselves in. The Assyrian invaded Syria from the south and the west in 733; Damascus was besieged and fell in 732. According to 2 Kings 16:9, King Rasin was killed, his territory devastated, hundreds of villages and towns were razed to the ground, and a large part of the population was deported, according to Assyrian war policy, to far-distant lands toward Elam. Thereafter Syria was nothing but an Assyrian province.

453. The fall of the league's pivot spelled its ruin. Some of the smaller members hastened to make their act of homage; others were quickly subdued. Soon after the fall of Damascus, if not at the same time, Assyrian troops invaded the kingdom of Israel, meeting no serious resistance. All of Galilee and Transjordan were lost (2 Kings 15:29); the tribes of Nephtali and those of Transjordan were deported to Assyria (cf. 1 Para. 5:26) and only the mountainous territory around Samaria, a mutilated trunk, remained of the ancient kingdom. Internal sedition was not slow to raise its head among these ruins. King Peqah was thenceforward only a shadow, surviving as a witness to the catastrophe; a certain Osee, son of Elah, conspired against him, killed him, and took his crown (2 Kings 15:30).[16]

Tiglath-pileser also makes mention of the fact: "I have deported the house of Omri, all its people together with its possessions to Assyria. When they overthrew (*iskipuma*) Peqah their king, I placed Osee to govern them." These words are not necessarily an autobiographical boast; the conspiracy against Peqah referred to in the biblical narrative may have been instigated by the same Tiglath-pileser, who used Osee to execute his plans. The murderer was rewarded with the crown, but was recognized only as a vassal king, and — according to the same Assyrian document — he had to give as tribute to Tiglath-pileser ten talents of gold and an unspecified amount of silver.

454. Osee's political position was clearly defined by the circumstances. As a survivor of the Assyrian flood, he was left on the Samaritan

---

[16] Text of Tiglath-pileser III relative to Osee (Hoshea), king of Israel, in *ANET*, 284.

island, sandwiched in by an Assyrian province on the north and on the south by a vassal kingdom of Assyria; he himself had become king through an Assyrian faction and with the consent of Assyria. The essential condition of his existence was, definitely, Assyria. There could be no possible doubt about this. And Osee, during the first year of his reign was a humble vassal of Nineve, and paid his tribute punctually.

Meanwhile, another factor was at work within the mutilated kingdom. Perhaps among no other race of antiquity were there such persistent and tenacious factions as among the Semites and particularly the Israelites (§§ 458, 528 ff.). Beaten down and broken, a faction among them never died out entirely; although a leveling scythe would pass through it, it would send forth new buds and spring up again with inexhaustible vitality from the soil. Thus it happened under Osee. The anti-Assyrian faction which had been in power under Peqah had not died in the catastrophe of 732, and scarcely had it found a breathing spell when it began again the threats and intrigues which it had temporarily suspended.

In Syria, which had become an Assyrian province, something similar must have occurred. The heavy yoke of Nineve did not prevent the formation here and there of nuclei in which hopes for revolt were nourished. Egypt must have had a part in all this crafty planning. The various contenders for the throne of the Pharaohs in this period (§ 37 ff.) had everything to gain by the uprisings in Syria-Palestine, and received with benevolence the princes deposed by Nineve (§ 452).

However, as long as Tiglath-pileser III was alive there were no sudden changes. With the coming of Salmanassar V in 727, the province of Syria began to stir almost immediately, for in the brief reign of Salmanassar there were, besides the long siege of Samaria, other warlike events.

455. The Babylonian Chronicle states that Salmanassar destroyed the city of Shabara'in (probably the Sibraim of Ezech. 47:16, which apparently was in northern Palestine). Menandrus of Ephesus (in the *Antiquities*, IX, 14, 2 of Josephus) reports that he effected a long blockade against Luli (Eluleo) of Tyre when he also rebelled; and from 2 Kings 17:3–6 it appears that the insurrection had in the meantime made progress and reached the kingdom of Samaria.

The fires of revolt, now blazing all through the north, inflamed the hopes of the anti-Assyrian faction in Samaria, and in the prospect of an imminent victory it won the support of the king. Osee refused the annual tribute to Assyria, and Salmanassar, being perhaps near Tyre at the time (725?), made a feint in his direction. At this threat Osee, with a volubility which attests to his lack of a fixed policy, sent the tribute (2 Kings 17:13). Salmanassar, wishing to concentrate his attention against Tyre, was for the moment satisfied. As the campaign progressed, he learned more and more of the secrets of the anti-Assyrian league, among other things that Osee was also in secret contact with So' (Sua) of Egypt (§ 37). Here was clear proof that the vassal king who owed everything to Assyria (§ 453) was a traitor to his master, and was serving as a mediator for the enemies farther to the south. What happened after this discovery is not too clear. The biblical account refers to a new refusal of tribute on the part of Osee (2 Kings 17:4), but, strictly speaking, this could be the same one as in 725. What is certain is that after the discovery, Salmanassar decided to settle affairs with his rebellious vassal and his kingdom. Osee was bound and imprisoned (724); if war had broken out right away, it may be that he was taken prisoner in battle; if, however, he was taken peacefully, it may be that he had presented himself to Salmanassar in order to explain his relations with Egypt. From this moment the last monarch of the kingdom of Israel disappeared from history.

The anti-Assyrian faction of Samaria did not, however, lose courage. Placing their hope in the resistance of Tyre to the blockade and in the help of Egypt, but inspired still more by their own fanaticism, they prepared for a desperate defense of the well-fortified capital (§ 432). The siege was begun immediately (724) and indeed called for the full strength of Assyrian organization. Although it did not yield, Tyre had to fight alone, for not a single soldier came from Egypt to help the allies. Thus the two sieges were prolonged for years. In the month of Tebeth of the year 722 Salmanassar V died in rather mysterious circumstances, leaving no children. Sargon, one of his officials (§ 8), succeeded him both in the command of the army and in the government of the empire. In the first year of his reign (722–721), after three years of siege, Samaria fell; hence, while Sargon in his Annals gives himself credit for taking the city, the Bible narrative attributes it to Salmanassar (2 Kings 18:9–10: if that name is not a gloss), following perhaps a convention of attributing to the preceding king the entire year in which he died and all the events which took place during it.[17]

456. Although the biblical report of the fall of Samaria and the kingdom of Israel is briefer than that of the fall of Jerusalem and the kingdom of Juda, it must not be thought that the event is less important or less crucial. The ferocious methods of Assyrian warfare were then applied in the usual cold-blooded fashion. There followed the systematic destruction of the countryside, the demolition of buildings, victims were impaled or flayed as if they were sheep, and mass deportation to far-distant regions of a good part of the survivors of the better class was carried out. It had happened to Damascus (§ 452) and other places, and so it was done to Samaria.

Sargon himself supplies special information about the deportation in

---

[17] The fall of Samaria, *ibid.*, 284 ff.

Aftermath of an Assyrian victory. (Left, booty being carted away; center, prisoners impaled; right, trees being destroyed.)

his Annals. "At the beginning of my rule and in my first year of government [. . .] I conquered Samaria [. . .] my triumph. I deported 27,290 persons who dwelt there. I restored 50 chariots for my royal army from them [. . .] and restored better than before. I made the people of the villages, the booty of my hands, dwell there; I placed my officers as governors over them. I imposed tribute upon them as is customary for Assyrians."[18]

These facts agree with what happened in the time of Menahem (§ 450). At that time there were 60,000 persons "who were wealthy in property"; in this case about half that number are deported. The other half and more was certainly made up of those deported in the time of Peqah (§ 453), those who died in the war, and those isolated persons who remained in the country and intermingled with the poor and the peasants, who were generally exempted from deportation (§ 542).

457. The biblical account supplies the details of what befell the two groups into which the people were divided. Some of the deportees

Tiglath-pileser besieges a fortress. (Left-hand corner, impaled prisoners.)

---

[18] The "Sargon Chronicle," *ibid.*, 284 ff.; cf. 266 ff.

Assyrian prisoners (possibly Israelites) playing on harps. (Nineve: time of Sennacherib.)

were taken to Halah — bitterly ironical, since it was the region near Harran from which Abraham went out (§ 123) — and some were taken more to the east, into Gozan and toward the borders of Media. Those left behind in the conquered kingdom were not alone, for the Assyrians transported populations of other conquered territories there. Thus it came about that little by little the Samaritan region was populated by, first, the Arabian tribes of Tamud, Ibadid, Marsimani, Hayapa, overthrown by Sargon ("Cylinder of Sargon"), and then by various races of Babylonia, Cutha, Hamath, Avva, etc. (2 Kings 17:24; cf. Esdras 4:9–10) subjugated by Sargon's successors.[19]

Among this hybrid mixture of races something occurred which was, according to ancient oriental mentality, quite normal. The principle that every region had its local god, or *numen loci*, was admitted by all, and so the foreign populations transported to Samaria would venerate the god of Samaria, i.e., Yahweh. Moreover the king of Assyria sent to them one of the priests who had been deported "in order to teach them the cult of the god of the region" (2 Kings 17:27). Naturally there resulted a religious as well as an ethnical mixture. The cult of Yahweh in the vanished kingdom of Israel had hinged on the idolatrous sanctuaries of Beth-el and Dan (§§ 414, 445), but the new Samaritan cult was a veritable pantheon, since the immigrant races, while making room for the local god, preserved their ancient divinities (17:30–31). It is to be noted that the priest who came to teach the cult of Yahweh established himself at Beth-el (17:28), of the two ancient sanctuaries the one closer to Jerusalem.

This race, so racially and religiously deformed, was the *Samaritan* race, for the Jews of the last centuries before Christ the object of the profoundest ethnical and religious abomination.

458. Even after the final catastrophe and the deportation, this troubled land must not immediately have found peace. The anti-Assyrian faction was so tenacious (§ 454) that it attempted a revolt by associating itself with a foreign uprising; of this the only information comes not from

---

[19] Resettling of deportees in Samaria, *ibid.*, 284.

the Bible but from documents of Sargon. In 720 occurred what is reported in his Annals: "In my second year of reign Ilubi'di of Hamath [. . .] gathered a powerful army in Qarqar, and violated the oath of the great gods. He encouraged Arpad, Simirra, Damascus and Samaria to revolt against me [. . .]. He made Sib'e, his *turtan* (§§ 37, 8), enter into a league with him and set out against me to deliver a decisive battle. In the name of Assur, my Lord, I defeated them. Sib'e fled away alone, as a shepherd whose flock is stolen, and ran away. I took Hanunu (*Hannon:* § 452) prisoner and led him in fetters to my city of Assur. I destroyed, devastated, and burned the city of Rapihu (*Raphia:* § 8); I deported 9033 persons with their possessions." In the inscription of the palace of Khorsabad, Sargon relates substantially the same thing with added details.[20]

Thus, the greater of the two hulks into which the ship of Israel had been divided after shipwreck (§ 413), disappeared beneath the waves. The smaller hulk continued to float for a time, but before very long it too would sink.

---

[20] Text of Annals of Sargon relative to the campaign of 720, *ibid.*, 285.

THE KINGDOM OF JUDA

459. Abia, Roboam's favorite son (§ 416), succeeded his father on the throne of David, but reigned only three years. A tangible effect of his father's hostility toward the kingdom of Israel was his friendship with Tab-Rimmon (1 Kings 15:18–19), king of Damascus and father of Ben-Hadad I (§ 431). This friendship had placed the hated kingdom between two fires, but it was also the beginning of the interference of Syria in the affairs of Israel and Juda, from whose quarrels Damascus was sure to profit.

With Damascus' support, hostility was translated into action. In characteristic style the Chronicler (2 Para. 13:3 ff.) speaks of a serious defeat inflicted by Abia on Jeroboam near Mount Semarayim (probably to the east of Beth-el), conquering also Beth-el, Jeshanah (the present 'Ain Sinya?), and 'Ephron (et-Tayibe?). The military reverses suffered by Israel not only fit in well with the contemporary game of alliances and political rivalries, but could have been the underlying reason for the discontent which later led on to the conspiracy of Bassa, through whom the dynasty of Jeroboam was destroyed (§ 431).

460. Abia was succeeded by Asa, his son (or brother?; cf. 1 Kings 15:2, 10), who reigned forty-one years. He is portrayed not only as a promoter of pure Yahwism, but also as a reformer in the sense that he intended to annul that which had come to be received with favor by the court. "He took away the [male] *qedheshim* (§ 415) from the land, and removed all the idols which his fathers had made" (15:12). The idolatry had reached such proportions largely because of the assent of the reigning descendants of David. Maacha, the mother of Asa, in particular "had made a *miphleseth* for the *asherah* [§ 105]" (1 Kings 15:13); the *miphleseth*, etymologically "abomination," is translated by the Vulgate in its full historical meaning of *Priapus* (§ 104), and was certainly a statue of such a kind as to be the feminine counterpart of Yahweh in His Temple of Jerusalem. Asa had the statue thrown out of the Temple into the nearby valley of Cedron, and there he burned it. He also deposed Maacha from her position as *ghebhirah*, "queen [mother]." That she had

been a promoter of the unusual cult was the more surprising because
it was applied to Yahweh.

Asa also brought to the Temple of Jerusalem the various precious
votive objects consecrated to Yahweh by his fathers or by himself.
While this served to favor the centralization of the Yahwistic cult in
Jerusalem, as opposed to the decentralization in the kingdom of Israel
(§ 414), it indicates that such centralization had not been accomplished up to that time. Indeed, it was not accomplished then either, for
even in the time of Asa "the *bamoth* had not been removed" (1 Kings
15:14), that is, those sacred places (§§ 104, 337) scattered throughout
the land in which a more or less syncretistic cult was practiced in honor
of Yahweh on private initiative.

The sincere Yahwism of Asa did not prevent him at the end of
his reign from having the prophet Hanani imprisoned, because, in
conformity with those political directives which had always guided
prophetism (§§ 429, 452, 476, 522), Hanani had openly rebuked him
for his alliance with Syria (2 Para. 16:7 ff.). Evidently for Asa, just as
for some of his successors, an apparently advantageous political decision
was not to be influenced by Yahwistic ideology.

461. From the beginning Asa continued in foreign affairs a policy
of hostility toward Israel. He purchased the friendship of Ben-Hadad,
alienating him from the friendship of Baasa with the results already seen
(§ 431); yet at the end of his reign relations with Israel must have
improved much.

The invasion of Zerah the Ethiopian (§ 36) had occurred even before
the alliance with Ben-Hadad. Abstracting from the figures given by the
Chronicler, the invader, pushing on to near Maresa (§ 75), was routed
by Asa, who pursued him as far south as Gerar (§ 92), with heavy losses
of men and material (2 Para. 14:9 ff.).

That Zerah is the Pharaoh Osorkon is not certain. To equate the two
names *Zerah* = O[serak]hon is a working hypothesis, but not a very good
one; the Twenty-Second Dynasty of Osorkon was of Libyan, not Ethiopian, origin. On the other hand, ethnic groups to the south of Palestine
who were of Arabian stock, especially the Madianites (2 Para. 21:16,
cf. § 465; Hab. 3:7), were also called "Ethiopians" in the Bible. It is
possible that the invaders were not Egyptians but booty-hungry Bedouins
who came this time from the south, rather than from the east, as in the
time of Gedeon (§ 314).

462. The long reign of Asa was followed by that of his son Josaphat,
also a long one, and inspired with the same Yahwistic spirit. It is well
to bring out by way of contrast that during the reign of Asa and
Josaphat eight monarchs of four different dynasties occupied the throne
of Israel. The consequences of this diversity of government could not
but be felt in the two kingdoms (§ 413).

The reign of Josaphat is portrayed differently by the two accounts in *Kings* and *Paralipomenon*. A fervent Yahwist like his father, Josaphat had to drive out of the country the *qedheshim* "remaining from the time of Asa his father" (1 Kings 22:47; § 460); it is also stated, however, that despite his zeal "the *bamoth* were not removed, the people still offered sacrifice and burned incense on the *bamoth*" (22:44), so little had been the progress made toward the centralization of the cult since the time of Asa (§ 460).

Despite his Yahwistic zeal the reign of Josaphat is reckoned an unfortunate one in the book of *Kings*. Peace had been made with the kingdom of Israel and confirmed by the marriage of Athalia with Joram, Josaphat's son (§ 436), with the result that Josaphat was little more than a satellite prince. Humbly following the ruler of Israel, he took part in the disastrous expedition against Ramoth of Galaad (§ 436); and again because of his position, co-operated in the expedition against Mesha which had also resulted in defeat (§ 440). It is probable that he had previously entered the league of the twelve kings against Assyria at the side of the king of Israel, but that league too was overthrown at Qarqar (§ 435). A final misfortune narrated in *Kings* has to do with a maritime enterprise: "Josaphat made ships of Tarshish to go to Ophir and [obtain] gold; but he did not go, for the ships were wrecked at Ezion-geber" (1 Kings 22:49). The "Tarshish ships" were long voyage ships and could well have been constructed at Ezion-geber, at the tip of the Elanitic Gulf. It was impossible to go from there to Tarshish (if this was really situated in the West, somewhere on the Spanish coast). The term had lost its primitive geographic meaning (somewhat as our word "Transatlantic" may not involve the Atlantic at all). The enterprise attempted by Josaphat reveals a desire to reach one of his grandfather Solomon's sources of wealth (§ 385); his failure may perhaps have been due to a violent storm, but also, no doubt, to the lack of the Phoenician sailors who had once managed Solomon's prosperous fleet and whose maritime skill was conspicuously lacking in the untrained and inexperienced Hebrew sailors.

463. The Chronicler, on the other hand, not only gives many details about the Yahwistic activity of Josaphat, but portrays him as a prosperous and fortunate king (2 Para. 17–20). His military success against a sizable invasion of Moabites, Ammonites, and tribes inhabiting the mountains of Seir, which broke into his kingdom from the southeast, was due especially to a falling-out among the enemy troops; as so often happens, they had quarrelled among themselves (2 Para. 20:22–23; cf. § 440). It is quite probable that the invasion itself, however, was a consequence of the defeat inflicted on the two Hebrew kings by the Moabites (§ 440) who sought to reap the fruits of their victory by attacking in their turn the nearest of the defeated. That Mesha makes no mention of this incursion into the kingdom of Juda is explained by the outcome; nor is it elsewhere stated that the incursion did not take place under one of the Mesha's successors. The Chronicler also records that Josaphat collected tribute from the Philistines and the Arabs (2 Para. 17:11), and that inside his country he established a commission, made up of officials and levites, which would visit various centers of his territory, and they "taught in Juda having with them the book of the *torah* of Yahweh, and they went about all the cities of Juda and instructed the people" (2 Para. 17:9). It was, therefore, an itinerant missionary venture, the purpose of which was to bring the minds of the people into direct contact with that codex which was to be their religious and civil guide; a written *torah* (§§ 109, 273, 294). Josaphat built much with a view to war (2 Para. 17:12–13), set up a military recruiting system and also a judiciary administration which, abstracting from numbers, was substantially like the one used in Juda in postexilic times (17:14 ff.; 19:5 ff.).

To sum up, the two reports of *Kings* and *Paralipomenon* are different but not contradictory, and they can be harmonized. If Josaphat was unfortunate in his war efforts when he followed the king of Israel, he achieved success when he acted on his own initiative. It is noteworthy that his failures were always related to his servile friendship for the king of Israel, sealed as it were by his son's marriage to Athalia. The introduction into the dynasty of David of this daughter of Achab and Jezabel (§ 432) was Josaphat's most serious error, and it was to have fatal political and religious consequences. However, this blunder does not cancel out the sincere and zealous Yahwism of this king. The writer of *Kings* prefers to expound the events of Josaphat's reign very succinctly; the Chronicler deliberately stresses his Yahwism, making it the criterion of the judgment he passes on his reign.

* * *

464. The father was succeeded by a son quite different in character, Joram the husband of Athalia. The lineage and character of Athalia explains in great part the conduct of Joram. The totally different direction of his policy manifested itself from the very beginning of his reign, at which time (according to 2 Para. 21:4), he, the first-born and heir apparent to the throne, not only slaughtered his brothers, but also some of the elders of the kingdom. This massacre must have been dictated by fear of what the future would bring, for Joram must have foreseen the opposition his new anti-Yahwistic policy would arouse among the other sons of Josaphat. The same reason prompted the slaughter of the elders, who were evidently the most authoritative representatives of the policy followed until then. It is easy to blame the inspiration for the new policy on the new queen, half Phoenician by blood and a daughter of Baal worshipers (§ 433); it may even be that the idea of the fratricide should also be charged to her, because when she alone will have full power in her hands, she will act in the same way (§ 467).

In his eight years of reign it is probable that Joram sent troops to help his brother-in-law check the invasions of Salmanassar III (§ 438). The peoples on the southern borders who had made their presence felt during the reign of Josaphat took advantage of the absence of these troops. The Edomites of the mountains of Seir (§ 463) rebelled against the sovereignty of Juda, doubtless encouraged in this by the example of Mesha. Joram set out with an army to suppress the rebellion, and although one night he was surrounded by the enemy, he succeeded in fighting his way through. In general, however, the campaign resulted in failure, and from that time on the Edomites enjoyed permanent independence under their own king (2 Kings 8:20–22), which clearly points to a serious defeat for Joram. It was then the turn of the city of Libna (Lobna) situated to the southwest in the Shephelah (§ 63). Behind this revolt it is not hard to detect the hand of the Philistines.

465. The Chronicler paints an even more somber picture, but one which might possibly refer to a prolongation of the preceding wars in which the Philistines and the Arabian tribes of Edom had figured. The "Philistines and the Arabians who live beside the Ethiopians [*Cushites;* § 461], came up to Juda and invaded it, taking as booty all the riches which were found in the house of the king, and also his sons and his wives, so that no son was left to him except Joachaz [= *Ochozias*] his youngest" (2 Para. 21:16–17). Some have maintained, but without foundation, that the "house of the king" does not refer to the palace of Jerusalem. Beyond all reasonable doubt the Chronicler refers to a pillaging of Jerusalem and the royal palace, and the deportation of the royal family living there. It was therefore a real disaster, a large scale raid completely successful owing to the weakness of the invaded kingdoms and to the hasty retreat of the raiders to the lands from which they came.

However, this incident presents difficulties when compared with other massacres such as the one perpetrated by Jehu on the forty-two princes of the dynasty of Jerusalem (§ 443), and the massacre by Athalia at about the same time of the members of the same dynasty (§ 467). Not only were the victims of these two massacres closely related to Ochozias ("brothers," half brothers, etc.), but also the victims of the present invasion were sons of Joram, and hence brothers of Ochozias. On the other hand, Ochozias was not the only descendant of Joram to escape the effects of the invasion, for later on a woman of the same descent, "Josaba daughter of king Joram, sister of Ochozias" (§ 467), is to play a decisive role in the happenings of the court. The victims of the three episodes were of an impressive number even taking into account the large numbers of persons in royal harems (§§ 400, 416); as a result the deportation consequent to the invasion, and the slaughter carried out at Athalia's and Jehu's orders, could not have been very great. Geographical difficulties arise especially concerning the slaughter of the forty-two princes, i.e., concerning the place where the princes, met by Jehu, were killed; it was apparently to the north of Samaria, whereas one would expect it to be to the south. These difficulties are similar to the geographical difficulty concerning the exact place of Ochozias' death (Meggido or Samaria: § 443), and lead to the suspicion that two reports of the various facts existed, one being preserved in the redaction of *Kings* and the other by the Chronicler; each presented the facts from a particular viewpoint, emphasizing certain aspects in preference to others.

The Chronicler alone (2 Para. 21:18 ff.) states that Joram died after a long and loathsome illness, which fits in well with his death at about forty years of age (2 Kings 8:17), and with the fact that he was not buried in the royal sepulcher.

466. His successor and son Ochozias (Ahaziahu) escaped the deportation of the royal family, but reigned only one year. With his uncle Joram of Israel he took part in the expedition against Ramoth Galaad. He was slain at about the same time as his uncle (§ 441) at Jehu's command (§ 443).

That Ochozias showed himself to be anti-Yahwistic during even this brief reign is not surprising. The reason given by the Chronicler is that "he walked in the ways of the house of Achab, because his mother was his counselor in doing evil" (2 Para. 22:3).

467. His mother Athalia indeed was an extraordinary woman. Along with her Phoenician blood and an attachment to the cult of the native Baal, she had inherited from Jezabel an imperiousness of character which her royal husband was the first to experience. Joram's premature death did not diminish but rather strengthened her sphere of influence. In many oriental courts the queen mother (§ 460) had greater power for all practical purposes than the queen consort. Athalia, queen mother in the court of Ochozias, gave every indication of surpassing herself in the court of Joram. The death of her son Ochozias undid her plans.

Athalia, however, did not give up. Rather than yield her power, she assured herself of it by those measures which she had doubtless suggested to her husband (§ 464), and which were not new in Juda and even less so in Israel. Athalia, "seeing that her son was dead, arose and slew all the royal seed. But Josaba, the daughter of King Joram, sister of Ochozias, took Joas, son of Ochozias and stole him from among the king's sons that were to be slain and [sent] him and his nurse to a bedchamber, hiding him from the presence of Athalia so that he was not slain" (2 Kings 11:1-2). The child was then about a year old; the aunt who saved him from his grandmother's massacre — and who was certainly a half sister of Ochozias and not a daughter of Athalia — succeeded in her plan because of her social position, being, according to the Chronicler (2 Para. 22:11), the wife of the high priest Joiada. This detail also explains what followed.

The bloody purge instituted by this woman ceased only when she saw no longer around her any descendant of that dynasty whose throne she now occupied alone. About her was a silence which she interpreted as surrender and subjection; it meant, however, something else. The Phoenician stranger, the propagandist of Baal, the murderer of her own children and nephews, was triply offensive to the throne of David. Despite her cold-blooded scheming she made the mistake of thinking that nationalism, Yahwism, and justice were so dead in Jerusalem and throughout the kingdom of Juda that a queen like herself could be tolerated.

468. These three sentiments were not dead. They revived in times of stress and, as always, grew stronger. In the Temple at Jerusalem the youthful survivor of the slaughter grew up, hidden in some guarded location accessible only to the high priest Joiada or to persons in his confidence. Six years passed thus, during which time the unsuspecting child was for others the symbol of an idea and the pledge of the future. It is not difficult to identify these others, or their idea and their hopes. These were the various Joiadas who were lower than the high priest in the social scale, but who shared his love for Yahwism and his hopes for a Davidic restoration. The husband of the aunt who saved the boy was the prime mover of a nationalistico-religious faction. He capitalized to the full on the advantages of his privileged condition, staking everything on his plan, and covering what must have been an intense activity with a veil of prudent dissimulation. The faction must have recruited members from all classes; that special groups, like the Rechabite solitaries who at that time worked so actively for Yahwism in the kingdom of Israel (§ 445), were engaged in it is not explicitly brought out, but is a probable assumption, given the secret character of the activity.

In the meantime Athalia continued her religious propaganda. Her native Baal had a temple in Jerusalem, with many idols and altars and with a priest by the name of Mattan (2 Kings 11:18). The temple of Yahweh was scornfully tolerated and allowed to continue. The Chronicler (2 Para. 24:7) reports that Athalia had damaged the Temple, perhaps to the advantage of the temple of Baal which may have been adjoining, and that she had turned objects consecrated to Yahweh to the service of Baal.

469. When the boy Joas was seven years old, Joiada came out into the open. Force was necessary and readily obtained. Joiada knew that he could depend on the military leaders who commanded the Temple and the palace guard; these had already been won over to his cause. A Sabbath day was chosen for the coup. On this day the three groups into which the guard was divided were assembled, one to take over its duties, another going off duty, and the third marching from one building to the other. Gathering the leaders of the three groups in the Temple, Joiada made them swear an oath, and then presented to them the surviving descendant of David, whom he entrusted to their arms. A great clamor greeted the boy who came forth after six years in hiding. He was acclaimed with long pent up jubilation in the Temple as Yahweh's king. The uproar was heard by Athalia in the adjoining palace, now bereft of its guards. Suspecting something sinister, she ran to the Temple, for her masculine temperament made up for the disappearance of her guards. The spectacle that there greeted her eyes was enough to dash her hopes. She was allowed to withdraw, cursing, from the sacred place, but once outside, was struck down.

The regime of Yahweh now restored, the temple of Baal was demolished, and its priest Mattan slain.

* * *

470. Joas became king at the age of seven and reigned for forty years. Of his long reign very little is known. It was to be expected that in his early years, under the guidance of Joiada, he was entirely dedicated to the cause of Yahweh, but it is significant even in his case that the refrain is repeated: "The *bamoth* were not taken away, and the people still offered sacrifices and burned incense on the *bamoth*" (2 Kings 12:4), as they had in the times of the Yahwistic kings Asa and Josaphat (§§ 460, 462). Although the regime of Yahweh had returned, the centralization of cult was not achieved, nor was the cult of Yahweh pure and exclusive. It dominated the others, it is true, but many remnants of the cult of Baal lingered on, and sought to live side by side with Yahwism in a sort of tolerant syncretism.

In matters of religion Joas had his heart set on restoring the Temple, a necessary project after the damage done to it by Athalia (§ 468). For this purpose he had determined that the various money offerings for the Temple be handed over to the priests, who were to assume the burden of restoration. But in the twenty-third year of his reign, the priests had not yet begun their labors, but had kept the money. The king intervened. Joiada was told to place in the Temple a chest with an opening in the top to receive offerings of the people (of course there is no question here of minted money, but of bracelets, rings, and the like).

From time to time the royal accountant came and consigned the contents of the chest to the contractors in charge of the work of restoration. The matter of the expenses of the cult thus settled, the Temple of Jerusalem was restored.

In the political field Joas had to buy off Hazael, king of Damascus, to keep him out of Jerusalem (§ 446). Joas was murdered by two of his scheming courtiers (2 Kings 12:20); this deed grew out of the popular discontent over the economic hardships the people suffered as a result of the humiliating peace purchased from Damascus. Also, as the Chronicler tells us, after the death of Joiada Joas gave himself up to idolatry. He had the son of Joiada, Zacharias, who had reproved him, killed; the conspiracy which led to the king's death was motivated by this murder. The two accounts are mutually complementary.

471. Joas' son Amasias succeeded him, and from the start his reign showed marks of vigor and firmness, at least in comparison to preceding reigns. When he felt himself firmly established on the throne, he had the murderers of his father put to death. It is noteworthy that he meted out this punishment according to individual responsibility, and did not extend the penalty to their descendants and families. This detail is expressly brought out in the biblical narrative (2 Kings 14:6), an indication that the idea of collective responsibility was, at least in practice, still in vogue (this notion survived in the law of many Christian states up to the dawn of modern times) and the punishment of grave crimes was felt by those who were in any way connected with the culprit.

In foreign policy also there was from the outset a marked improvement. The loss of Edom under Joram (§ 464) had been a very serious blow to the kingdom of Juda, as it severed direct communication with the commercial centers of Arabia and with the Red Sea. Amasias sent an expedition into Edom (§ 92; *Gerar*), struck the Edomites to the south of the Dead Sea and permanently conquered Sela', which may be the city of Petra or some place farther south (probably Khirbet Sil'). His success went to his head; he conceived such an exaggerated idea of his forces that he provoked Joas of Israel to a fratricidal war with resulting disaster for Juda (§ 447). Worse, according to the Chronicler (2 Para. 25:14 ff.), Amasias returned from his victory over Edom bringing with him the idols of the conquered foe, and set up their cult in his own land, a not uncommon practice among Semitic peoples (§§ 343, 476). In other respects Amasias is portrayed as a pious Yahwist, although the refrain (§ 470) concerning the permanence of the *bamoth* in the land is repeated (2 Kings 14:3–4).

Amasias was permitted to remain on the throne of Juda by grace of Joas of Israel. It is not certain whether he reigned in Lachish or in Jerusalem, but a conspiracy did break out against him in Jerusalem and he fled to Lachish. One possible explanation is that his son Azarias, who succeeded him at sixteen years of age, was proclaimed king by the conspirators while the father still occupied the throne. After some time, the conspirators succeeded in killing Amasias in Lachish (cf. 2 Kings 14:17–21; 2 Para. 25:25–27).

472. The reign of Azarias (Ozias) was fortunate in its external relations and notably prosperous internally. He pursued with intelligence and tenacity the course begun by his father in the early days of his reign.

With regard to the relations with other kingdoms, it seems that Azarias is not the Azriyau of Yaudi defeated by Tiglath-pileser III (§ 450). Apart from the chronological difficulties of such an identification, the list of the localities conquered by Tiglath-pileser III, carefully enumerated in his inscription and found in the inscriptions of Zenjirli (§ 446), rather points to the conclusion that Yaudi is not Juda, but a kingdom situated in northwestern Syria, near Mount Amano. The similarity of the names, Azarias and Azriyau, Yaudi and Yuda (Juda), is a wholly fortuitous coincidence not without historical precedent.

Azarias maintained friendly relations with the kingdom of Israel. He solidified and perhaps amplified his father's reconquest of Edom, and re-enforced the port of Elath, the commercial center of the Red Sea (2 Kings 14:22). The Chronicler gives further details about external relations (2 Para. 26): Azarias gained military successes against the Philistines, on the west, against various Arabian tribes to the south, and levied tribute on the Ammonites. Besides having a large and perfectly organized army, he employed the latest available technique to fortify the walls of Jerusalem.

473. Internally the kingdom must at length have enjoyed excellent economic prosperity, as appears from the writings of contemporary prophets (Isa. 2:7, 16; Mich. 2:2 ff.). This was in part due to the revival of commerce with the Red Sea, but perhaps even more to the many projects for the improvement of agriculture and grazing set on foot by Azarias; they are listed by the Chronicler. Azarias "loved the soil" (2 Para. 26:10).

From the religious viewpoint, Azarias received nothing but praise from the writer of *Kings* (2 Kings 15:3–4), although with the usual refrain (§ 471) about the *bamoth,* which still tenaciously survived. Next it is recorded that he became a leper, but when this occurred is not stated. At any rate, he segregated himself from the court and from affairs and left the government to his son Joatham. The Chronicler explains in some detail (2 Para. 26:16 ff.) that Azarias' leprosy was a direct and immediate punishment visited upon him in the Temple, where he had gone with the intention of usurping the strictly sacerdotal function of burning incense on the altar. Keeping in mind the great influence exercised by the Yahwistic priesthood in the person of Joiada during the reign of Athalia and Joas, it might well be that the end of Azarias' reign was marred by a deeper and more abiding rivalry between the sacerdotal and monarchical powers.

474. Little is known about Joatham, who reigned after the death of his father for about five years. In 2 Kings 15:35, it is recorded that he built the "upper gate" of the Temple; other works of his are mentioned by the Chronicler (2 Para. 27:3 ff.). Joatham's victory over the Ammonites was apparently connected with his father's victory over the same people. He is portrayed in every respect as a Yahwistic king; but the usual complaint is made against the people, that they worshiped on the *bamoth,* and "still acted perversely" (2 Para. 27:2).

An attempt to force Juda into the anti-Assyrian league headed by Rasin of Damascus and Peqah of Israel occurred in his reign. When the attempt failed, the two allies opened the hostilities against Joatham (§ 451) which were to have very serious consequences in the reign of his son and successor Achaz.

      ❖   ❖   ❖

475. The salient fact of the reign of Achaz was the war waged against him from the beginning of his rule by the anti-Assyrian league. It drove him to turn to Tiglath-pileser III (§ 452).

The immediate purpose of his appeal to the Assyrian king was achieved when the league was defeated, but in the final analysis conditions in the reign of Achaz were worse than before, and the Chronicler was right in saying that "Tiglath-pileser, king of Assur, came to him, but he was more of a burden to him than a help" (2 Para. 28:20). Not only had he to suffer the damage inflicted on him by the league before the intervention of the Assyrian king, but the treasures of the Temple and the palace passed into the hands of Tiglath-pileser. The port of Elath, which fell into the power of the Edomites who had revolted at the first signs of war (§ 451, note), was not recovered (2 Kings 16:6). The regions of Juda were invaded on the same occasion by the Philistines and were lost when Tiglath-pileser marched his armies into Philistine territory (§ 452), conquering it for his empire, not for Achaz'. Worst of all was the resulting absolute dependence of Juda on Assyria. From that time on the kingdom of Achaz was but one of the many little states of the west over which the colossus of Nineve played the master. No longer protected on the north by the kingdom of Damascus, now destroyed, nor by that of Israel, now reduced to a shadow (§ 453), Achaz' kingdom became the target of Assyria. Among the smaller Palestinian rulers — Sanipu of Ammon, Salamanu of Moab, Qaushmalaka of Edom, etc. — who paid regular tribute to Tiglath-pileser, mention is made in his inscriptions of "Yauhazi [*Achaz*] of Juda."[1] The annual tribute must have been grievously oppressive, for the strongboxes of the Temple and palace had already been emptied and their contents sent to the monarch. Achaz was obliged to melt down the heaviest liturgical objects of the Temple in order to send the precious metals to the Assyrian monarch (2 Kings 16:17–18).

When Tiglath-pileser held court in Damascus immediately after its fall (2 Kings 16:10), Achaz was presented to him as a humble vassal paying homage — and this he certainly dared not do with empty hands.

476. Pre-eminence in political matters had as its usual corollary imitation in cultural and religious matters. This was one of the principal reasons behind the hostility of prophetism to alliances with idolatrous nations (§§ 429, 460, 522); witness on this occasion Isaias' opposition to the alliance with Assyria (§§ 452, 488). In ancient times a victory was the best possible propaganda for the civilization of a nation, and gods who were victorious in the struggle with other gods, i.e., in the struggle between two nations representing their respective gods, were recognized as being the more strong and powerful. They were thought to deserve the worship of the defeated nation, which, if not an exclusive one, was at least on a par with that paid to the regular gods. On the other hand, the victorious nation willingly worshiped, though to a lesser degree, the vanquished gods (§ 471), a practice which redounded to their own greater glory. It was, once again, a syncretism which was not devoid of political wisdom, for to turn to four gods, whether victorious or vanquished ones, would be more advantageous than turning to two only, even if these two were the national gods and the victors.

Achaz' mentality was syncretistic to an extraordinary degree. He had no intention of either persecuting or putting Yahweh aside; he merely affirmed his intention of paying his respects and of "not tempting Yahweh" (Isa. 7:12). But side by side with Yahweh he allowed place, in one way or another, to any gods he happened to come across. At Damascus he paid homage to the Assyrian monarch, and there saw an altar he liked. It is hardly likely that the altar was a Syrian one, since the city and especially the temple (as happened later on at Jerusalem) must have been almost totally destroyed on the occasion of the conquest; it must have been an Assyrian altar, erected by the victors in honor of their own gods in the conquered city. The new type of altar amid the incense of victory and the masculine voices of exultant warriors seemed to the wretched vassal to be a good-luck charm, and he desired one like it in his capital. "King Achaz sent to Urias the priest [in Jerusalem] a pattern of the altar and a model according to all the work thereof. And Urias the priest built the altar according to all that

---

[1] Cf. *ANET*, 284.

King Achaz had sent him. Urias the priest made it before King Achaz came from Damascus. When the king had come from Damascus and had seen the altar, he approached the altar and made an offering on it; and he burned his holocaust and his oblation and poured out his libation, and dashed the blood of his peace offerings over the altar. And he removed the altar of bronze which was in the presence of Yahweh from before the Temple, between the altar and the Temple of Yahweh [?], and placed it on the north side of the altar" (2 Kings 16:10–14). This text is not clear toward the end, but it tells of a substitution of altars (it is significant that the Chronicler makes no reference to the fact); the old one, perhaps Solomon's, was piously put to one side and its place taken by one modeled on the Assyrian. Probably, together with the altar, other things also found entrance. Judging from Ezechias' large-scale cleansing of idolatrous objects from the Temple (§ 481), it may be presumed that on this present occasion images of the victorious Assyrian gods were also installed. It is a matter of record that thenceforward liturgical sacrifice in the Temple of Yahweh was carried out on the new altar.

In the syncretism of Achaz there was also room for other gods side by side with Yahweh and the Assyrian gods. His holocaust of his own son (§ 452) was probably in honor of Moloch (§ 107), the god of the Ammonites, whose cult prescribed human holocausts. The Chronicler's statement (2 Para. 28:23), that he also honored the gods of Damascus in order to receive help, refers in all likelihood to the time of his defeat by the king of Damascus and before his liberation by Tiglath-pileser; as if by partaking of all these cults he would deprive the victorious king of divine help.

It need hardly be mentioned that under such a ruler, the *bamoth*, which never had wholly disappeared, multiplied exceedingly (2 Kings 16:4).

477. It was along these lines and as a complete vassal of Assyria — from which vassalage neither the fall of Samaria nor the uprising of Ilubi'di (§ 458) shook him free — that Achaz ruled until the end of his days. It is impossible to say precisely when he died or when his son Ezechias succeeded him. The ever fluctuating biblical chronology (§226) is here more uncertain than ever, resulting in many different and disputed dates (cf. 2 Kings 16:2; 18:1, 10, 13; Isa. 36:1; also 2 Kings 18:2). Following 2 Kings 16:2, according to which Achaz reigned sixteen years, it can be maintained that he died around 718, certainly after the collapse of Samaria (contrary to 18:1, 10). Since the invasion of Sennacherib occurred about 700 (§§ 9, 489 ff.) and in the fourteenth year of Ezechias (18:13; Isa. 36:1), 715–716 would mark the beginning of Ezechias. It seems impossible to eliminate the discrepancy of the few years between the two dates, 718 and 715–716. This may trace back to inexact transcription of the dates (perhaps in the places cited one should read "the seventeenth year" of Ezechias instead of the "fourteenth year"?). The other dates (2 Kings 18:1, 10) are today generally considered as later attempts at synchronization.

❀ ❀ ❀

478. Ezechias' position as he ascended the throne was an extremely delicate one. Under his father, the foreign and domestic policy had been one of total, unconditional surrender to Assyria so as to save the throne. Such a policy cannot really be called a mistake, nor yet a success. Although deprived of all its luster, the throne had been saved, but not the nation. Once the last and weakest bulwark raised against Assyria had fallen, an Assyrian governor had taken up his abode in Samaria, undoubtedly so as to be able to keep an eye on the vassal king of Jerusalem. This latter had been allowed to keep the throne simply as a token which could be taken from him at a nod from the monarch of Nineve. Moreover, at the fall of Samaria (§ 455) or on the occasion of the campaign against Ilubi'di (§ 458), the armies of Sargon may have inflicted serious damage on the territory of Juda, and the words of Ezechias in 2 Para. 29:8–9 seem to allude to something of this sort. If it is shown that, when Sargon is called "the subjugator of the distant country of Yaudu," reference is made to the kingdom of Yuda (Juda) rather than to Yaudi in northwestern Syria (§ 472), then there would be proof that the troops of Sargon actually entered the territory of the vassal king.[2]

479. In any case, total surrender to Assyria meant a change of the essential characteristics of the nation, i.e., the nation was lost. The throne of Juda may not have been shattered, but its foundations were badly twisted. The effects of the tenacious, inexorable penetration of the Assyrian world into Israel appeared in all their tragic seriousness after the fall of Samaria and after the Assyrian organization of the territory. In its policy of surrender, the court of Jerusalem had probably foreseen and prepared for this blow, but the catastrophe of the brother kingdom must have made a great impression on the common people. Despite the centuries-old religious and political rivalry between the two kingdoms, in the hearts of the people there had always remained a consciousness of the ethnical, social, and religious ties which bound Juda and Israel together. As everyone knew, they were like two brothers who because of incompatibility of character had had a falling out, and had taken to living in adjoining but separate rooms. That way they were at least in the same house and were sons of the same father. The older brother's room had

---

[2] Inscription of Sargon relative to Yaudu, *ibid.*, 287.

been demolished; Israel had disappeared, and the ruins of the room
had become — as ruins always do in the Orient — a dung hill, i.e.,
of the "Samaritans" (§ 457). Was it possible that the surviving younger
brother should refuse to weep over him, as over someone dead in the
family? And what was even worse, could he not perceive in the end of
his brother a prediction of his own, as long as he continued the policy
of surrender to Assyria?

It was understood then, in Juda, that the enemy was Assyria, the de-
stroyer of nationalities among peoples. It was understood that safety
lay in shutting themselves up slowly and persistently in the spirituality
of the nation by living close to Yahweh. This was the thesis of contemporary prophetism, from Isaias who disdainfully rejected every foreign alliance to save the nation (§ 476), to Micheas who foresaw the flood
of the misfortune unleashed over Samaria sweep also over Jerusalem.

480. Prophetic activity had never died out, even when Achaz was,
apparently, triumphant (§ 476). It must have been even more pronounced at the end of his reign, when the failure of his policies had become evident. Because of the tragic circumstances, Yahwistic thinking,
until then confined to the circles of the adept, began to gain a wider
acceptance and make fresh converts. Politico-religious reaction against
the past regime was maturing.

Ezechias ascended the throne as the exponent of that reaction, and
so unswervingly did he follow this course that he is praised above all
the monarchs of Juda for his Yahwism: "He did that which was right
in the sight of Yahweh, according to all that David his father had done
. . . and after him there was none equal to him among all the kings of
Juda, nor before him" (2 Kings 18:3–5). He acted along the lines of this
policy both at home and abroad.

To rebel openly against Nineve at the very beginning of his reign
would have been a childish mistake, there being no opportunity abroad
nor readiness at home for such a task. He could, however, immediately
start the internal reforms which were a preparation for a changed foreign policy. Thus, when on the occasion of the campaign against Ashdod
(in 711; cf. § 488), Sargon still enumerates the kingdom of Juda among
his tributaries, Ezechias had for several years been pursuing his internal
reforms, where the influence wielded by men like Isaias, Micheas, and
other Yahwists of their caliber is evident.[3]

481. Ezechias began with the Temple and places of cult, where he
undid the work of his father: "He removed the *bamoth,* broke up the
masseboth [§ 104], cut down the *asherah* [§§ 105, 460] and broke
the bronze serpent which Moses had made, for until that time the Israelites burned incense to it, and it was called Nehustan" (2 Kings 18:4).

---

[3] Sargon and the campaign against Ashdod, with mention of Juda, *ibid.*, 287.

The serpent idol deserves closer inspection. Although it was mentioned in the episode of Moses (§ 264), it was given practically the same worship as was paid to similar Canaanite idols (§ 106). Possibly it had been set up in the Temple itself, as had been the *asherah* (ancient versions have the plural) and some *masseboth*. Other such objects were to be found in the numerous *bamoth* scattered about throughout the kingdom. Although not expressly mentioned, it is very likely that on this occasion Ezechias also rid the Temple of the Assyrian altar his father had placed there (§ 476). The centralization of the cult of Yahweh, which had remained practically only a pious desire of the Yahwistic kings until then (§ 462), began to be realized with the removal of the *bamoth* dedicated to Yahweh alone. Even outside the kingdom the news spread concerning the energy with which Ezechias acted, and the practical effects of his centralizing reform of the national cult attracted the attention also of the Assyrians (2 Kings 18:22; cf. 21:3; 23:5, 8).

482. In carrying out his plans, Ezechias sensed a feeling of compassion among the people over the catastrophe of Samaria, and at the same time he strengthened his rule more and more in view of the desired change in foreign policy. In the disaster of the brother kingdom much had been irremediably lost, but not a little yet remained. There were many groups which still had not amalgamated with the Samaritan foreigners and had preserved a great part of their ethnic patrimony. The fate of these remnants may be likened to bits of a shipwreck; either they would sink beneath the waves of other nationalities or be saved on the banks of their own nation. Ezechias strove to draw them morally and materially toward his kingdom, now the sole survivor of a common nationality. The task was not particularly difficult. When the victorious Assyrian settled the boundaries, he gave to his vassal in Jerusalem as a reward and pledge of his fidelity a section of the southern territory which once formed a part of the now-defunct kingdom of Samaria, especially that part near Jericho which had belonged to the tribe of Benjamin; the remainder was reduced to the status of an Assyrian province, but even there a certain influence was exercised by the king of Jerusalem over his fellow countrymen, especially in the matter of religion (§ 457). The Assyrian governor stationed in Samaria was responsible for the political and military peace in the province, but apart from this there must have been that benevolent toleration which often permitted a kind of autonomy among the subject populations, and of which typical cases are known in the Orient before the coming of the Arabs and Turks.

483. Ezechias, prompted by religious motives, launched a truly national appeal among the survivors of the fallen kingdom, recalling them

Ashurbanipal and his wife dining in their garden.

morally and in part also physically to the ancient Yahwistic center of
the nation, the Temple of Jerusalem. The appeal was not everywhere favorably received. Many, however, had enough Israelite blood
and Yahwistic spirit in them to heed the voice of Jerusalem and to gather
there for the solemn celebration of the Pasch. Nothing more significant
had happened since before the division of the two kingdoms (2 Para.
30). Something also needed to be done to purify the Yahwistic cult in
the Assyrian province of Samaria (2 Para. 31:1).

This appeal produced results. In a general way, so too did Ezechias'
insistence on salvaging as much as possible of the wreck of Israel. The
tragic catastrophe had mended the schism of the nation, and the man
who still felt the call of blood could not but gaze with longing at the
monarch reigning in Jerusalem. The kingdom of Israel had disappeared,
and he remained the one ruler over the nation of Israel. From various
passages of a contemporary, Micheas — in which he apostrophizes the
remnant of the entire nation after 722 by calling it *Jacob* or *Israel* —
it is reasonable to suppose that at that time the practice of referring
to the king of Jerusalem as "King of Israel," i.e., of the entire nation,
had been established. Perhaps Ezechias really bore this title, and if so,
history knows no other instance where a change of meaning was more
tragic.

484. The reform of Ezechias included the gathering, co-ordinating,
and editing of the traditions and documents of Israel. In the disaster that

kingdom had suffered, part
of its patrimony of traditions
had surely been lost. Those
oral (§ 189 ff.) or written
(§§ 273, 463) traditions, as
they passed from mind to
mind or from hand to hand,
had formed a precious and
well-diffused heritage, and
could in part at least have
coincided with similar traditions preserved in Juda —
coming as they did from a
national source common to
both kingdoms — and bore in
part the peculiar characteristics of the northern tribes or
the mark of their later origin.
A moral patrimony so prized
in the Orient (§ 180) had the
more value in the eyes of

Hebrew priests.

Ezechias because it was of a religious nature, or was intimately connected with the vicissitudes of the nation to which Yahweh had manifested His wonders. The zealous king must have spared no effort to
salvage that precious patrimony.

There is nothing more historically justified than the casual remark of
Prov. 25:1, referring to the "men of Ezechias," a commission entrusted
with the task of gathering and editing such documents. Criticism of
biblical sources can, moreover, single out texts and accounts incorporated
in the versions which have come down to us, whose characteristics
hint at a northern origin. It is then not arbitrary to suppose that most
of these documents made their way into Juda, and hence into our
versions, through redactions dating from the time of Ezechias. These
in turn may have had some connection through written sources with
northern recensions probably made during the reign of Jeroboam II
(§ 448). This Israelite custom has other and more famous parallels
in oriental history. During Ezechias' reign Sargon collected many ancient
texts at Nineve. Later still the great Ashurbanipal (§ 11) became as
famous for the great library upon which he lavished his personal care
as he was for his military deeds. Into this library he gathered all the
ancient documents he could find, and it remains today the great mine
of Babylonian-Assyrian literature (§ 184).

485. The practical exigencies of the reform led in all probability to a great deal of literary activity in legal circles also. Collections, harmonization, modernizations, and revisions of ancient laws certainly occupied much of the energies of the Yahwistic circles inspired by the king's reform. It was to these men that he committed the practical realization of his plans. Their very magnitude precluded any rigorous application in his own time, unless one supposes the existence of a code sufficiently ample to sum up the ancient norms which were already to some extent codified (§§ 273, 294, 463) and to serve as the legal basis for the work of the reformers. The appeal to antiquity which issued from the reform was justified by the antiquity of the norms entered into the codex; the new severity which activated the reform was justified by the new sanction given to the norms by their codification.

486. During the progress of his reform Ezechias proceeded even more directly in his preparation for a public change in foreign policy and a withdrawal from the sovereignty of Assyria. That such a change could not be accomplished without a clash with Assyria was obvious. Biding his time for a favorable moment, he had to prepare with craft and as opportunity offered. He applied himself to the task with farseeing tenacity, and succeeded in filling up his treasuries and strongboxes (2 Kings 20:13), for even in his day it took money to wage war. He was also able to build up his stocks so well that if war were to break out suddenly he would be well enough armed to inspire the highest confidence (Isa. 22:8; 2 Para. 32:5).

He concentrated his efforts then in fortifying Jerusalem so that it could resist the siege that would certainly come. The ancient circle of walls, many times breached, was rebuilt and re-enforced with towers. A second wall was thrown up on the outside in order the better to protect the city on the northern side, always its most vulnerable point (§ 97), and for this reason he tore down the houses which had been built in that suburb (Isa. 22:9 ff.; 2 Para. 32:5). Most essential to resistance in any attack upon the city was the water supply. Sometime before 701 (§ 489 ff.) Ezechias also took care of this. The city was supplied by Gihon, a spring which, being outside the walls (§ 96 ff.), could in case of siege, be cut off by, and be of great help to the enemy. Ezechias took care of these two possibilities. To the various ancient works built around the precious spring he added an entirely new construction, assuring the water supply by a tunnel through which water from the spring of Gihon was conducted to the interior of the city (§ 98). The construction is described with archaeological exactness by the Chronicler: "Ezechias stopped up the upper source of the waters of Gihon and turned the waters underneath toward the west of the city of David" (2 Para. 32:30; cf. Isa. 22:9, 11; 2 Kings 20:20; Ecclus. 48:17 [Vulgate 19]). To the *west* of the spring of Gihon is the hillock of Ophel (§ 96), and the tunnel which empties into the *city of David* passes *underneath* this hill.

487. In 1880, a few yards from the outlet of the tunnel into the pool of Siloe, a six-line inscription written in ancient Hebrew characters was discovered. Now in the museum of Constantinople, it is dated around 700 B.C. It was not a public inscription, but seems rather to have been done by the engineers and workmen who did the work and were desirous of leaving behind them some record of their efforts. The complete text reads: "[. . .] the boring. And this is the story of the boring through. While the pickers [worked] one against the other[4] and

רגקבה . חה . היה . רבר . רגקבה . בעור
רגרון . אש . אל . רעי . ובעור . שלש . אמת . להב קל . אש ק
רא . אל . רעי . כי . חת . זרה . בצר . מימן ' יבים . ר
נקבה . הבו . החצבם . אש . לקרח . רעו . נרמן . סל . נרון . וילכו
המים . מן . המוצא . אל . הברכה . במאתים . ואלף . אמה . ומאון
ת . אמה . היה . נבה . הצר . על . ראש . החצבום]

Text of the inscription of Siloe and Hebrew transcription.
(Benzinger, *Hebr. Archäol.*)

while there still [remained] 3 cubits to be [*bored through, there was heard*] the voice of one crying to another, that there was a *zedah* (= "deviation"? "overlap"?) in the rock to the right [. . .]. And on the day of the perforation the diggers struck in the direction of each other, pick against pick. And the water was guided from the source to the pool for 1200 cubits: and the height of the rock above the heads of the diggers was 100 cubits."[5]

488. While Ezechias pursued his material and moral projects within his kingdom, important events had taken place outside. After a few years the memory of the battle of Raphia (§§ 8, 458) no longer sufficed to hold the small Syro-Palestinian states and their restless political factions in check (§ 454), especially as Egypt was behind every plot and it was to her interest to fan the flames. In Philistia the hegemony of Asdod had succeeded that of Gaza, subdued under its king Hannon (§§ 452, 458). It was at Asdod that Sargon had deposed King Azuri,

---

[4] The tunnel was dug from both ends simultaneously and the two squads of pickers sought to meet as they advanced toward each other.

[5] The Siloam Inscription, *ibid.*, 321.

whose brother Ahimiti he placed on the throne, and who was to be a faithful vassal of Assyria. For this reason he was, naturally, detested by the anti-Assyrian factions of his own and the surrounding kingdoms, and one day was murdered. The leader of the hostile party, Yamani, stepped into his place. The new king immediately plunged into action and succeeded in organizing a league against the speedy and inevitable retaliation of Assyria. Among other smaller states "Pir'u, king of Musuri" had a part in this league, as the same Sargon says; he is commonly thought to be the "Pharaoh, king of Egypt" (§ 22), Bokenranef (Bocchoris; § 38), although this is not certain. The formation of the league must have seemed to Ezechias a splendid occasion openly to initiate the anti-Assyrian foreign policy for which he had been preparing for years. The temptation was certainly very great, so much so that it aroused the characteristic opposition of Isaias (Isa. 20), who was definitely opposed to placing any reliance on Egypt (§§ 452, 476, 522). Ezechias, bombarded by the two opposing factions, probably pursued an ambiguous course; he did not enter officially into the league, but privately and secretly furnished help and showed his complete sympathy to it. But the league was of short duration. Sargon's army, under the command of his generalissimo (called *turtan* in Isa. 20:1; cf. § 37), captured and destroyed Ashdod; no other battles seem to have occurred, because at the advance of the Assyrians the colleagues lost all taste for war. The ambiguous position Ezechias had taken, however, had openly compromised him in the eyes of Nineve, and in fact the kingdom of Juda — together with Philistia, Edom, and Moab — is mentioned in an inscription of Sargon as "a plotting enemy, wickedness without limit." If the Assyrian army did not march against Ezechias, it was certainly because he and the other compromised princes made haste to send the usual tribute to Sargon, which they perhaps increased when Ashdod was taken. The date was c. 711.[6]

489. This first abortive attempt demonstrated clearly to Ezechias that the time was not yet ripe for breaking openly with Assyria, and above all it must have convinced him how fallacious were those political alliances with the surrounding peoples, including even Egypt, so deprecated by Isaias. After a few years Sargon died, and in 705 Sennacherib succeeded him on the throne of Nineve. The change revived Palestinian hopes; perhaps the new Assyrian monarch lacked his predecessor's political sagacity, and especially his expertness in war. The beginning of his reign was fraught with special difficulties. Besides the more or less widespread unrest among all the peoples under the Assyrian yoke, that implacable enemy of Nineve, Merodach-baladan, commenced immediately another of those attempts which until then

---

[6] Sargon, campaign of 711, against Ashdod, *ANET,* 287.

had always failed (§ 9). Everything seemed to indicate that the day of liberation was about to dawn for Juda.

In the midst of this political ferment, seemingly so full of promise, the activity of Ezechias was halted somewhere around 704 by a serious illness. For some time he was in danger of death and was cut off from feverish international activity. The critical condition of the king who in Palestine could be a most valuable participant in an anti-Assyrian league was quickly noised abroad, followed by the news of danger past. The king, cured, returned to his duties, becoming once again the object of widespread hopes. From afar Merodach-baladan, with faultless courtesy, sent ambassadors to Ezechias to congratulate him on regaining his health. The ambassadors, with a diplomacy equally faultless, certainly discussed the constitution of a league which would be very advantageous to the irrepressible Chaldean agitator.

During these conversations concrete details were discussed, and covered even the contribution each ally should furnish. Ezechias showed the ambassadors his well-stocked treasuries and storehouses, a sight which evidently made his adherence to the pact all the more desirable (Isa. 39:1 ff.). Others hold that the ambassadors of Merodach-baladan visited Ezechias around 712, shortly before Sargon set out against Babylonia (§ 8) and Ashdod (§ 488). In any case exchanges of ambassadors and negotiations with every possible ally must have been intensified after 704, especially with Egypt; even if the Ethiopian mission (Isa. 18:1 ff.) is assigned to a later period, that of Taharqa (§ 38) for instance, something similar to it may be reasonably supposed to have occurred in this period also (Isa. 30:1 ff.).

This undercover diplomacy continued as long as Merodach-baladan kept Sennacherib (§ 9) busy in Babylonia. In 702 Sennacherib was again master of Babel, but the fire which was extinguished, or which — more accurately — had subsided in the Orient, had already spread to the West, where the league had been formed.

490. The league became both strong and large (§9). From Libanus to Philistia it included all of the more important political units, with Luli of Sidon and Ezechias as its exponents; only some smaller states remained, at least apparently, undecided. Only Padi of Accaron is mentioned as being faithful to Assyria, and after being bound and sent to Ezechias as a prisoner by the anti-Assyrian faction of his kingdom he was held in custody in Jerusalem. There was good reason for the intransigent attitude of the allies toward the king of Accaron; his kingdom bordered on the road to Egypt, and that road had to be free and secure, as the whole league practically hinged upon the kingdom of the Pharaohs. Whether on this occasion the conquest of the Philistine city of Gaza was undertaken and completed by Ezechias (2 Kings 18:8), and for the same reason, it is not possible to determine, but it is probable, seeing that Ezechias was the *quasi* superintendent of the league in the south, and, at war's end, Sil-Bel the king of Gaza was compensated by Sennacherib with special territorial concessions taken from the kingdom of Juda (§ 492). When the various governors imposed by Assyria were driven out, and tribute withheld from Assyria, the allies began to prepare themselves for an expected attack by Nineve, at the same time counting on the help of the Pharaoh. Meanwhile Ezechias must have accelerated and completed his fortification of Jerusalem, especially around the spring of Gihon (§ 486 ff.).

491. As soon as he felt secure in the east, Sennacherib turned to the west. He understood very well that his true enemy was not the vanguard of the league, that is, the little Palestinian states, but Egypt. He therefore conducted his campaign with Egypt in mind. It was a model of dispatch and military ability. The little Palestinian states which were still at the beginning of their preparations were struck down one after another with such startling rapidity that the invader considered taking the Egyptian forces by surprise. First to fall was Sidon, whose king Luli fled to Cyprus (cf. Isa. 23); after this several of the lesser allies submitted without fighting, thus opening the way to the south. Ascalon and Jerusalem showed resistance and a little farther north Accaron remained to be liberated; but Sennacherib bypassed these fortresses, leaving a contingent before Ascalon. He advanced southward toward Egypt, conquering the lesser fortresses and devastating the country as he advanced to confront the Egyptians. Ascalon soon fell and its king Sidqa ended his days in Nineve. The Assyrian army turned back toward Accaron, and only then did an Egyptian army enter upon the scene. Battle was joined at Elteqeh near Accaron, and the Egyptians were routed (§§ 9, 38), but not pursued because Sennacherib — besides not feeling secure about affairs at Babylonia (§ 9) — still had to subjugate the remaining Palestinian rebels. Accaron was quickly conquered; the rebels who had put King Padi (§ 490) in chains were impaled, and Padi — released meanwhile by Sennacherib — was again placed on the throne. Timnah and other cities to the west of Jerusalem fell a little later while Sennacherib pushed on farther to the south to direct in person the siege of Lachish (§ 74) and then of Libna; a general was placed in charge of these two places. Jerusalem, where Ezechias had shut himself up, still remained untaken.

492. What occurred between Ezechias and Sennacherib is related by the latter in the following manner: "... As for Ezechias of Juda, who had not placed himself under my yoke, I lay siege to 46 of his cities fortified by walls, and to countless small villages in their environs, by assaulting from ramps and by attacking with engines of siege, by means of infantry

battles, breaches, sapper-work and axes [?][7] and I conquered them. 200,150 persons, young and old, men and women, horses, mules, asses, camels, oxen and smaller animals without number I led out of them and considered as booty. He himself [Ezechias] I shut up like a caged bird in Jerusalem, his dwelling-place; I constructed earthworks against him and I repaid the iniquity (?) of anyone who went out from his gates. His towns which I had plundered, I cut off from his territory and gave them to Mitinti, king of Ashdod, to Padi, king of Accaron, to Sillibel, king of Gaza (§ 490), and thus I reduced his land. In addition to the former tribute, to be delivered annually, I added another tax as an offering to my majesty and I laid it upon them. As for Ezechias, the splendor of my majesty prostrated him and his irregulars, i.e. the *Urbi* and his choice soldiers — whom he had brought in and adopted as auxiliary troops to guard his dwelling place in Jerusalem — he sent after me to Nineve, the city of my dwelling, 30 talents of gold, 800 talents of silver, precious stones, antimony, crayons (?), large lapis lazuli, beds of ivory, thrones of ivory, elephant-hides, ivory, ebony, boxwood (?), as much as is possible [to find in] a large treasury; likewise his daughters, his young ladies, male and female singers; both to pay his tax and to render me homage he sent his messengers." So reads the famous prism of Sennacherib (Taylor Cylinder).

Another inscription discovered at Nebi-Junus near Nineve reads: "... I took away from Luli, king of Sidon, his royal dignity: I put Tuba'lu on his throne, with tribute for my majesty. I laid waste the remote country of Juda; I imposed my yoke upon its king Ezechias."[8]

493. From these two inscriptions it follows that most of the territory of Juda was conquered and was distributed to neighboring kings who had been faithful to Assyria; that Jerusalem, hard-pressed by the rigorous siege, was reduced to a desperate plight by the defection of chosen troops and of the foreign *Urbi* (perhaps the *Arabs* or more probably semi-nomadic Aramean tribes who in time of war took refuge in cities, as did the Rechabites during the last siege of Jerusalem: Jer. 35:11; § 537). Under the circumstances, Ezechias capitulated and offered an enormous tribute. It does not, however, follow that Jerusalem was taken by storm nor that personal violence was done to Ezechias nor that he was stripped of his kingly dignity.

In fact the failure to mention these last items is highly significant. If they had really happened, Sennacherib, who so carefully records the fall of the kings and kingdoms of Sidon, Ascalon, Accaron, and the rest, would not have failed to mention the same of the king and kingdom of

---

[7] "*Instrumentis bellicis adhibitis*," Pohl, *Historia Populi Israel* (Roma, 1933), p. 23.

[8] Sennacherib's campaign against the league, with mention of Ezechias, *ANET*, 287 f. The Nebi Yunus Slab, *ibid.*, 288.

The city of Lachish besieged by Sennacherib. (Layard,
Monuments of Nineveh.)

Jerusalem, for that would have been for him the most glorious victory
of all. What actually was the real result of the war? If it did not wipe
out the rebel state, did it at least lead to a greater intensification of the
preceding vassalage? Considering the language of the two inscriptions,
not even this can be safely asserted. The first inscription expatiates on
the description of the tribute, but it is the exceptional tribute offered
because of the capitulation. The second speaks of a "yoke imposed," but
in a bombastic style such an expression may refer either to the tribute
of capitulation, or to the conquest and partition of the territory. (Some
scholars look upon 200,150, the number of persons given in the first
inscription, as too high and probably an exaggeration common to a
bombastic style; the same may perhaps also be said of the 800 talents of
silver.) Such omissions give rise to the suspicion that something has
been held back. These two inscriptions, in fact, suggest vaguely that the
mighty warrior does not tell all that he could, and also that — even
though he does not alter the facts — like Mesha (§ 440), he has a
motive for hiding something.

494. The biblical account not only substantially confirms the inscriptions but at the same time supplements them, and while it does not
clarify them entirely, contains some information which they omit.
What happened at that time can be likened to a drama in two acts;
the first act reads substantially the same in the inscriptions and in the
Bible, but the second act is missing from the inscriptions and is recounted only by the Bible.

The first act as found in the Bible (2 Kings 18:13–16) ends with
Ezechias sending tribute to Sennacherib. This is the capitulation de-

scribed in the first inscription; preceding it was the conquest of almost all the territory mentioned in the second inscription (cf. 18:13).

The second act is contained only in the Bible (2 Kings 18:17–19:37), and describes what happened after the sending of the tribute. In this act — abstracting from 19:21–34 which is of poetic construction — are two distinct historical scenes each treating of an attempt made by Sennacherib to obtain the surrender of Jerusalem. In the first scene (18:17–19:9a) the Assyrian sent three of his high officials from Lachish to demand the surrender of the city. Standing before the walls, the officials sought to win over the assembled citizens; in order to make their message perfectly clear they refused the request of Ezechias' ministers that they speak Aramaic (§ 51) and spoke instead in Hebrew, hoping thus to induce the people to imitate the example of the *Urbi* (§ 492 ff.). The people were not moved and the counsels of the prophet Isaias, who urged resistance, prevailed. The discussions thus came to naught and the officials returned not to Lachish but to Libna, where in the meantime Sennacherib had moved his headquarters. Meanwhile information had arrived that "Tirhaqah, king of Ethiopia" (§ 38), had come out of Egypt to attack the Assyrian army.

In the second scene (chapter 19, verses 9b — [21–34]–37) Sennacherib sent letters to Ezechias asking him to surrender the city. Again Isaias intervened, assuring the king that the Assyrians would be routed. That same night the angel of Yahweh killed 185,000 men in the enemy's camp, so Sennacherib returned to Nineve, where, while praying in the temple of the god Nisrok (?), he was killed by his sons Adrammelich and Sarezer.

495. Several questions could be posed concerning these two scenes of the second act of the drama, which are passed over in silence by the inscriptions. The net result of the two scenes is such that — granting for the sake of argument that they really occurred — it is not at all surprising if the self-laudatory Assyrian inscriptions omit them. Moreover, these scenes confirm what the inscriptions indicate, namely, that Jerusalem was not taken.

A further point: were they two different scenes or is it a question of only one account transmitted by two different traditions? The second alternative — preferred by some scholars — seems to have little in its favor, since Sennacherib had many reasons to persist in his attempt to obtain the spontaneous and speedy surrender of Jerusalem: he was unable to pursue the Egyptian army which he had defeated at Elteqeh (§§ 9, 38), and from one moment to the next he could expect a counter-attack from them; besides, turbulent conditions at home urgently called for his presence there. As a result, seeking to save his army and at the same time to make haste, his first oral attempt was followed by a written one.

That the Egyptians returned to the attack after a short time offers no difficulty. The territory of the Nile was split up into different governing units, and "Egyptian" was more a geographical than a political term. The army defeated at Elteqeh was that of Shabaka; the one that came up the second time was that of Taharqa. He was called "king of Ethiopia," and in fact acted as Pharaoh of Egypt and commanded its army, but a sufficient explanation of this can be traced to the elasticity of military and court terminology (§ 38). On the other hand, it is quite certain that in the last days of the Pharaoh Shabaka, and especially under his insignificant successor, Shabataka, Taharqa managed the affairs of the empire and was Pharaoh in fact if not in name, a fact which is confirmed by his later assumption of the title of Pharaoh (§ 38). It is therefore not surprising that he was the leader of the Egyptian army. For this reason also the hypothesis of two campaigns made by Sennacherib in Palestine (§ 38) seems unnecessary;[9] it is known that around 690 he conducted an expedition against the Arabs but there is no trace in any document of one against Palestine.

496. More complicated, however, is the exact connection of the endings of the two scenes. The first terminates by saying that Sennacherib received notice of the approach of Taharqa; it does not say what he did about it (2 Kings 19:9a; that the document ended in ancient times with 19:36, has been claimed but not demonstrated). The information could have induced him either to withdraw or to await the enemy, but the biblical account does not affirm explicitly either of these alternatives. It is nevertheless implied that he awaited the enemy; in fact he desired with his second attempt to come to speedy terms with Ezechias, so as to secure his rear and his left flank against the coming encounter. If he withdrew, he could afford to disregard Jerusalem, which would then remain in the enemy's sector. In the meantime and for the same reason, he straightened his lines by bringing up his troops from Lachish to Libna (§ 491), which lay somewhat to the northeast. In this way, the second scene, joined as it is so immediately to the first, helps ascertain what was left undetermined in the first.

Confirmation of this comes from the conclusion of the second scene. Abstracting from the detail of the death of Sennacherib (2 Kings 19:37), it affirms in substance that a disaster overtook his army and that he returned to Nineve (19:35–36). The ending of the whole drama is related in strictly biblico-Yahwistic language. The disaster which struck the army of the enemy of Yahweh is portrayed from the religious point of view of the nation, and so it is directly attributed — as in other, similar cases — to Yahweh and his angel. Translated into ordinary language the report says that an immense number of persons in Sennacherib's

---

[9] W. F. Albright, *Stone Age*, p. 240, holds for two campaigns (transl.).

army died in a very short time, and that they were not killed in battle but in exceptional circumstances.

497. Here too a parallel to the biblical account is found among another people directly interested in the event. Three peoples were interested in it: on the one hand were the Assyrians, who suffered the disaster; on the other, the Hebrews and Egyptians for whom the disaster was a liberation. It is very significant to discover that while the Assyrian documents maintain a profound and understandable silence about the disaster (§ 493 ff.), its memory is preserved not only by the Hebrews but also by the Egyptians. In the fifth century B.C. the "Egyptians and priests" spoke to Herodotus about it (Herodotus, II, 141) and this is what they told him: "After him [*a King Anysis who was blind, successor to the Ethiopian Sabakon*], I was told, the priest of Hephaestus, Sethos by name, ruled, and he despised and neglected the Egyptian soldiers as though he had no need of them. Besides various injuries which he inflicted on them, he took from them the lands which had been given them by the preceding kings, consisting of 12 acres to each one. Later on Sanacharib, king of the Arabians and the Assyrians, marched a large army against Egypt. Then the soldiers of Egypt would not help the priest. At the end of his resources, he went to the temple to the image and lamented the many misfortunes he had to endure. As he wept sleep overtook him and he seemed to see in a vision the god standing near him to console him, assuring him that no harm would befall him in facing the army of the Arabians because he himself would send him allies.

"Encouraged by such dreams, he gathered about him those Egyptians who were willing to follow him and encamped at Pelusium, which commands the entrance [to his country]. None of the warriors, but traders, artisans and market-people followed him. During the night there came a multitude of field-mice which devoured all the quivers and bow-strings of the enemy, and ate the thongs of their shields. Thus the next morning they fled away, and as they had no arms, many of them fell. There stands to this day in the temple of Hephaestus a stone statue of Sethos with a mouse in his hand, and an inscription which reads: Look on me, and learn to reverence the gods" (Herodotus, II, 141). Divested of its legendary and Egyptian covering, this story is at bottom substantially the same as that of the biblical narrative. The period in which the fact took place also fits, namely, after the time of Shabaka (Sabakon); and it is notable that the name of the invader is "Sanacharib, king of the Arabians and the Assyrians." Even the locality is more or less the same, for Pelusium was in reality "the entrance to the country" (§§ 24, 33), and in a fluctuating tradition could be a generic indication of the region which extended northeast toward Palestine; Egyptian tradition located the event in this rather indeterminate sector. The nature of the fact also is more identical than appears at first glance. The mice of the Egyptian account are parallel to the angel of Yahweh in the Hebrew account; both terms however — mice and angel — have to do with the same phenomenon, a pestilence. The Egyptian account emphasizes the visible and etiological cause of the pestilence, the Hebrew account brings out the invisible theological cause (§§ 211, 256, 379). As far as that goes, rats are directly related in the Bible to pestilence (§ 343).

Hence the nucleus of this account, as well as that of the Bible, is this: Sennacherib's army was decimated by a violent plague near the border of Egypt and Palestine, and because of it was compelled to withdraw and leave the two countries free. It is most natural then that the two nations which benefited by the event and which alone preserve its happy memory should each interpret it according to its own religious viewpoint. Finally, to evaluate correctly this agreement of the two traditions, it is sufficient to remember that it is entirely impossible for Herodotus to have depended on the Bible, or vice versa; the agreement in this case can only be an echo of the truth.

498. The dramatic Assyrian invasion was ended. The Bible adds that Sennacherib, on his return to Nineve, was the victim of parricide (§ 494). As elsewhere the Bible may give the impression that nothing else intervened, but, as a matter of fact, Sennacherib ruled actively and victoriously for another twenty years or so. The disastrous termination of the Palestine incident was only an isolated incident from which he quickly recovered. Soon afterward he was in a position to recommence the large-scale offensive against Babylonia which terminated in that city's destruction (§ 10). On the twentieth of the month of Tebeth (January) of 681, he was actually killed by his son, according to the Babylonian Chronicle. Whether the parricide was perpetrated by one or two sons, and whether it happened in Babel in the temple of Marduk (the biblical *Nisrok?*; cf. § 2), rather than at Nineve, is uncertain.[10]

499. Of the ten or more years during which Ezechias continued to rule little is known in detail, but the years immediately following the invasion must have been especially troublesome. The hurricane had not uprooted the tree, but it had snapped off almost all its branches. In the midst of a "desolate country" and a "city burned by fire," the capital had remained "as a tower in a vineyard, as a hut in a cucumber field, as a besieged city" (Isa. 1:7–8). Even so, Ezechias must have recovered quickly from the grievous trial thanks to the feeling of

---

[10] The death of Sennacherib, in *ANET*, 288; cf. also R. C. Thompson, *The Prisms of Esarhaddon and of Ashurbanipal found at Niniveh, 1927–1928*, London, 1931, where the murder is attributed to Assarhaddon's brothers and not to Assarhaddon.

pride which swept over the kingdom. Yahweh had effectively conquered the gods of Nineve, and his prophet Isaias, the soul of the resistance, had counseled and predicted it accurately. As long as they could exult in true Semitic style: "There is no god equal to Yahweh and Isaias is the prophet of Yahweh!" no misfortune was serious. From one point of view, the universality of ruin facilitated the renascence of the state; in the return to normalcy in various Palestine states, the prestige of Jerusalem was greater than before, because the hill of the Temple had been the only peak not covered by the Assyrian flood. The lands taken from Ezechias were in all probability again united to the kingdom, spontaneously or otherwise. It was also to be expected that after a few years the reign of Ezechias was the strongest and most prosperous in Palestine.

Inside the kingdom, Yahwism triumphed. Who would have dared oppose another god to Yahweh after such a great sign? The triumph, however, hid an insidious formalism. Several passages of Isaias, assigned with good reason to this period, seem to reflect a growing laxity of conscience which extended to religious — or better, ritualistic — practices as well as to morals. There were sacrifices of animals to Yahweh, in any desired quantity, incense, feasts, crowds in the Temple so gloriously preserved from the Assyrians (Isa. 1:15 ff.); but in practical life, orphans were defrauded, widows oppressed, justice was sold, and hands were stained with blood (Isa. 1:15 ff.). In a word, Yahwism was corrupted by a magical confidence in the rites and in the Temple, as formerly in the Ark (§ 342). Meanwhile the people lived as they chose, like the people of Sodom and Gomorrha (Isa. 1:10). The Temple had proved to be a charm against any misfortune, and the rites celebrated there with punctuality and full observance would avert any ruin.

*　　*　　*

500. In this state of affairs, ripening and spreading all too quickly, a return to the old wantonness was inevitable, and Yahwism, reduced to an exterior shell of ritual, was sure to crumble once again.

It crumbled under Manasses, son and successor of Ezechias. Never in the history of the Jewish people was there so glaring a contrast between two successive monarchs as between Ezechias and Manasses. When the latter became king, he was only a boy of twelve, more preoccupied with his toys and games than with Yahwism or anti-Yahwism.

If his reign was inspired by a rabid anti-Yahwism and an unbridled syncretism, the initial responsibility for that fact lies with the associates, teachers, and ministers whose product Manasses was. In like manner, the Yahwist Joas had been in former days the spiritual son of his teachers (§ 470). One need not picture these educators of the boy-king as anti-Yahwist or syncretists; it was sufficient that they be formalistic

Yahwists, as was the fashion in the last years of Ezechias. What followed, though certainly fostered also by the personal character of the monarch, was pretty much a foregone conclusion. Formalistic licentious Yahwism gradually metamorphosed into a credulous syncretism to which the people had always been quite susceptible. After some time, the memory of the great miracle wrought by Yahweh during the reign of Ezechias grew dim, and once more the people began to think of the gay, exciting cults of Baal and Astarte. Things went from bad to worse until they reached the stage of a real and formal hostility toward Yahwism. This spiritual metamorphosis of Juda was not, apparently, accomplished in a short time; probably it stretched over years as human affairs go. At any rate there was ample time for it, as Manasses reigned about a half century (55 years, according to 2 Kings 21:1, but the figure is doubtful).

501. The political condition of Juda also contributed to the fostering of foreign cults. The greater part of Manasses' long reign was contemporaneous with that of the Assyrians Sennacherib, Assarhaddon, and Ashurbanipal (§ 10 ff.), and Manasses was no doubt a faithful vassal of Assyria (§ 503). Perhaps Ezechias had himself resumed the payment of tribute to Nineve despite the failure of the expedition of Sennacherib. He may have thought that in the final analysis a permanent pecuniary sacrifice would help to prevent a repetition of invasions which were always destructive, and that it would be well not to provoke anew the colossus of Nineve. But Manasses entered into the spiritual orbit of Nineve, bewitched, like Achaz (§ 476), by the power of this dominant nation. The gods of Assyria, and of other nations, made their appearance in Juda, and were given places of honor there.

Side by side with the *bamoth*, the idols of Baal and Astarte, of ancient memory, reappeared. The astral cult, in which worship was paid to the god Shemesh, "sun" (2 Kings 23:11 [5]; § 333), and to the Assyrian goddess Ishtar (§ 107), was however something new. Altars were set up in the Temple of Jerusalem for these divinities; Assyrian cult was copied with such exactness that, either within the Temple or adjacent to it, pavilions were built for the sacred prostitution of both men and women (2 Kings 23:7; § 108). The Canaanite gods were likewise welcomed, including hungry Moloch (§ 476), to whom, it seems, Manasses offered his own son as a holocaust (21:6), not on the occasion of some impending misfortune (§§ 440, 452), but solely out of devotion. In fact, in the Valley of Hinnom (§ 95), Topheth was set aside in his honor, and ritual burning of children was carried out there (23:10; cf. Jer. 7:31). Magic, necromancy, and related forms of popular divination (2 Kings 21:3 ff.) also flourished at this time.

502. While the tide of idolatry rose ever higher, however, there was much opposition to it. Yahwism had been too dominant and prophetism too powerful under Ezechias to capitulate under Manasses without a struggle. The defense was as tenacious as the attack was determined; nothing much is said on this point, but the general report given in the Bible is impressive. "Moreover Manasses shed also very much innocent blood, so that he filled Jerusalem up to the brim" (2 Kings 21:16). This illuminating remark affords us a glimpse of a long series of brutalities, oppressions, and violence directed against the old Yahwists and the centers of prophetism; the latter especially, in accordance with their sublime mission (§ 429), must have contributed their share in filling the symbolic chalice "up to the brim." The report gathered from the Talmud (Babli: *Yebamoth,* 49 b; *Sanhedrin,* 103 b) and also from apocryphal and Christian writers, according to which Isaias was killed at Manasses' command, does not constitute historical proof, but it may represent a rather old tradition. In any case, the fact is altogether likely.

It is easy to imagine the moral consequences of this state of affairs. Formalistic Yahwism had led to corruption (§ 499); official idolatry served to extend, deepen, and multiply it. The picture sketched by Micheas (Mich. 7:1 ff.) in all probability applies to this era, and contains no artistic hyperbole; it is the harvest of the seed sowed by Manasses.

503. Of special interest regarding Manasses,[11] and an event related only by the Chronicler, is the following: "Yahweh caused the captains of the army of the king of Assyria to come against them [*Manasses and the people of Juda*] and they took Manasses with hooks, bound him with a double chain of copper, and led him to Babel" (2 Para. 33:11). This seems to be a description of abject imprisonment: the prisoner was bound with chains, and hooks were fixed in his lips in order to lead him without resistance wherever his captors wished. The son of Taharqa and King Baal of Tyre are

Stele of Assarhaddon. (The kneeling prisoner is the son of Taharqa.) (Berlin Museum.)

---

[11] Manasses, king of Juda, is mentioned in Assarhaddon's campaign record, in *ANET,* 291; in Ashurbanipal's, *ibid.,* 294.

shown in like condition on an Assyrian stele and the cord that goes from the hooks in their lips terminates in the hands of Assarhaddon, their conqueror (§ 39). The question, however, of the when and why of this imprisonment of Manasses, remains.

This incident was formerly regarded as very questionable and was attributed to the inventive mind of the Chronicler, who used it to bolster up his thesis. Today it is almost unanimously held to be most probable and — although still based on the authority of the Chronicler alone — to correspond exactly to the contemporary historical background. It is certain that Manasses was the vassal of Assyria for a long time; Assarhaddon, among other rulers of Phoenicia and Palestine who were his tributaries, mentions also "Menase, king of Juda." Ashurbanipal likewise mentions "Minse, king of Juda" among other vassal kings who furnished auxiliary troops for his campaign of 667 against Egypt (§ 40). There is documentary evidence also that hooks and chains and deportation into Mesopotamia were also employed on other vassal princes of Assyria; thus when the prince of Sais, Nechao, and his colleague Sharruludari of Pelusium, who had joined Taharqa in a plot against Assyria, were discovered, they too were sent bound to Nineve. Nechao's prerogatives were later restored to him and he was sent back to govern the Delta under Assyria (§ 39 ff).

Manasses must have had to endure the same fate as Nechao. The Chronicler adds that the prisoner afterward was sent back to Jerusalem where he reigned for some time, completing works of fortification and building a wall for the enlargement of the city. Having been converted to Yahwism during his imprisonment he gave himself to the task of destroying as much as he could of his idolatrous innovations and worked to restore the cult of Yahweh to its pristine purity (2 Para. 33:12–16).

504. It is a precious bit of information to learn, thanks to the Chronicler, that Manasses was led prisoner to "Babel." One would have expected him to be led to Nineve, the capital of Assyria, but this unexpected destination enhances the value of the detail. Manasses' deportation, in fact, must have occurred under Ashurbanipal instead of under Assarhaddon, on the occasion of the revolt of Ashurbanipal's brother, Shamash-shum-ukin, king of Babel. When Babel, around 653, broke out into open revolt against Nineve, all anterior Asia up to Egypt was in ferment, and many states entered into the anti-Assyrian league (§ 11). For forty years a tributary of Nineve, Manasses may have aspired to independence and supported the league. One by one, however, the allies were eliminated and Ashurbanipal took possession of Babel in 648. From that time on he, like Assarhaddon before him, lived there at frequent intervals, no doubt to supervise in person the pacification of that conquered but unruly city. Manasses and Nechao may

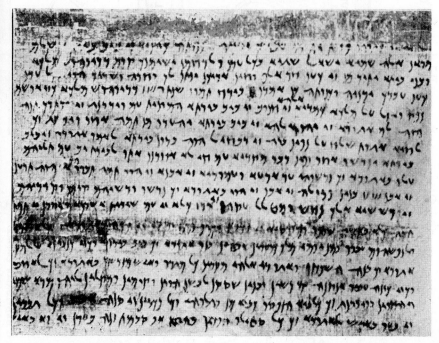

A papyrus of Elephantine. (Letter to Bagoas, governor of
Judea — 408 B.C.)

have been captured, as the Chronicler says, by some Assyrian general
who was patrolling Palestine while Ashurbanipal was investing Babel.
After the fall of that city, the prisoner was led to Ashurbanipal, not in
Nineve but "in Babel."

How long his imprisonment lasted is not stated, but it was probably
brief. The Assyrian monarch, sure now of Babylonia and counting on
the lesson given to the whole world, a lesson which smaller princes
would take to heart, allowed Manasses to return to his own territory,
as he had formerly allowed Nechao to do.

505. The strict surveillance exercised by Assyria over the ancient
territory of Israel is confirmed by the fact that, under Manasses, the
Assyrians twice more imported great numbers of foreign peoples into
the district occupied by the Samaritans (§ 457). The reason for this
was, no doubt, that among the Samaritans of that time the predominantly
Hebrew element had grown too vividly aware of its own nationality,
a result probably of the measures Ezechias took for that purpose
(§ 483 ff.). This nationalism, a danger for Assyria either because of the
times or because of its proximity to the ethnic center of Jerusalem, led
to a new importation of foreigners by Assarhaddon (Esdras 4:2), and

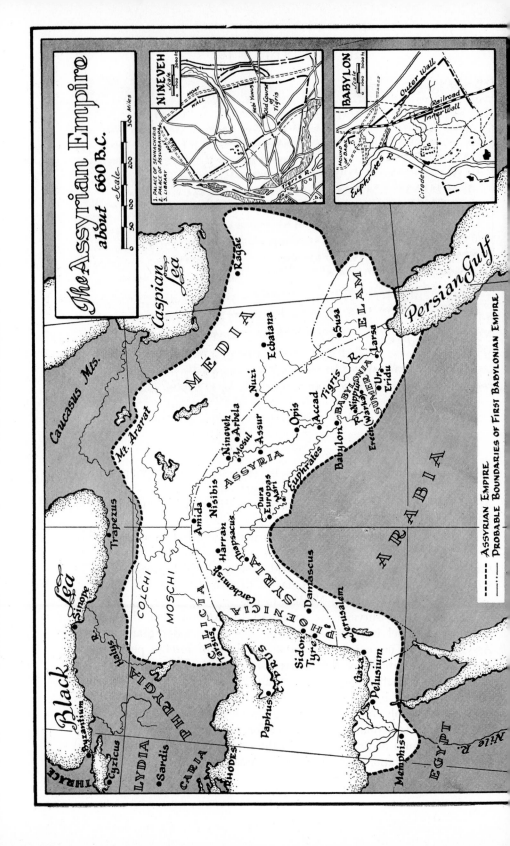

The Assyrian Empire about 660 B.C.

Scale
0 50 100 200 300 Miles

NINEVEH
Scale
0 1000 3000 ft
1. PALACE OF SENNACHERIB
2. PALACE OF ASSURBANIPAL
3. LIBRARY
MOAT
WALL
Nebi Yunus
Old Course of Tigris
Tigris R.

BABYLON
Scale
0 1000 3000 ft
Outer Wall
Railroad
Inner Wall
Mound of Babil
Citadel
Euphrates R.

Black Sea
Caspian Sea
Persian Gulf

Caucasus Mts.
Trapezus
Mt. Ararat

MEDIA
Ragae
Ecbatana
Susa
ELAM
Tigris R.

Nineveh
Mosul
Arbela
Assur
Nuzi
Opis
Accad
ASSYRIA
Babylon
BABYLONIA
Nippur
SUMER
Warka
(Erech)
Larsa
Ur
Eridu

Amida
Nisibis
Harran
Thapsacus
Dura Europas
Nari
Euphrates

Carchemish
CILICIA
Tarsus
Damascus
SYRIA
PHOENICIA
Sidon
Tyre
Jerusalem

COLCHI
MOSCHI

Byzantium
Cyzicus
Halys R.
PHRYGIA
LYDIA
Sardis
CARIA
RHODES
CYPRUS
Paphus

ARABIA

Gaza
Pelusium
Memphis
EGYPT
Nile R.

THRACE

––––––– ASSYRIAN EMPIRE
- - - - - PROBABLE BOUNDARIES OF FIRST BABYLONIAN EMPIRE

still another shortly afterward by Ashurbanipal (called *'Asnappar* in Esdras 4:10: Aramaic text).

Internally too the reign of Manasses marked the decline of the national character. For this his religious and foreign policies are responsible, as well as the intensification of private contacts with the outside world and the notable economic well-being produced by the long peace and the increased commerce. Without going so far as to say that the Jewish military colony of Elephantine, which flourished in upper Egypt in the fifth century B.C. (§ 208), originated in Manasses' time, it seems certain that there was much emigration from Juda at this time. Many Jews, partly for commercial reasons, partly for better living conditions elsewhere, responded to the urge to leave the kingdom. Egypt especially attracted them, and there Jeremias found a goodly number of them (Jer. 44:1) at the beginning of the sixth century.

Never before as during the time of Manasses had the international wind blown so fiercely within the closed receptacle of the nation and the religion of Yahweh.

506. Manasses' son, the twenty-two-year-old Amon, succeeded him but reigned only two years. He followed the bad example his father had set before his conversion to Yahwism, a fact which indicates how effective the Yahwistic renascence under Manasses had been. Amon was killed as a result of a palace conspiracy, but the reasons for this, and the identity of the plotters have not been preserved. It is certain that the "people of the land" did not approve the murder of the king; the murderers were slain and the king's son, Josias, a lad of only eight years, was placed upon the throne (2 Kings 21:24). The "people of the land" are to be understood as the people in general, and not only those who lived in country districts, as opposed to those living at court. The "people" took these drastic steps also because of their attachment to the reigning dynasty, but other reasons may have played a part. Was it perhaps fear that the conspirators might change the foreign policy? Was it perhaps their dislike of some religious reform which would have caused Amon, the syncretist, to weep? Or was it perhaps a violent popular protest against the powerful cliques at court? It is impossible to say.

* * *

507. With the ascent of young Josias to the throne, the regency was once again influential as in the times of his grandfather Manasses. Only this time the regency — servants, teachers, ministers — was of a different character, and demonstrated its Yahwistic spirit by instilling Yahwistic principles in the eight-year-old monarch.

When the young king grew up and began to reason things out for himself according to the principles impressed on his conscience — that is, when he was about sixteen years old — "he began to seek out the God of David his father"; when he was about twenty years old and felt the urge to act according to his conscience, "he began to cleanse Juda and Jerusalem" of the idolatrous trappings his father and grandfather had brought in (2 Para. 34:3 ff.). It was a general Yahwistic reaction to the preceding period, but was not very different from previous reactions; quite naturally it assumed the character of a religio-national movement similar to that of Ezechias' reign (§ 479 ff.) which was its source of inspiration.

An important coincidence deserves mention here. Josias began his reform when he was about 20 years old (627), and intensified it from year to year. But around his kingdom and in all anterior Asia, political events of a permanent and radical nature were taking place: a veritable revolution, accomplished within the short span of twenty years or so, but one which completely changed the political aspect of these regions.

508. Under Ashurbanipal Assyria reached the summit of her power. But it was too steep and slippery a peak to be occupied for long, and even in the closing years of his reign the first cracks in the immense empire already presaged its fall. To the southwest the farthest provinces no longer responded with minute exactitude to the commands of the capital; to the northeast large displacements of Indo-European peoples had created the fresh and vigorous kingdom of the Medes, which hovered over its mountains like a cloud threatening the adjacent empire of Nineve (§ 13). From these mountains the thunderbolt was soon to come hurtling down. Countless hordes of Scyths (cf. Herodotus, I, 103–106) spewed forth from the upper reaches of the Caucasus,[12] crossed Media like a flood inundating Assyria and spreading as far as Palestine, stopping only at the frontiers of the Nile (§ 41). Thanks to its famous walls, Nineve was not overwhelmed by the invasion, but the rest of the empire was submerged. Doubtless the barbarians passed into Palestine (cf. the double name Beisan-Scythopolis; § 86), yet either because of their haste to reach Egypt, or because of the poverty of the country, did no serious damage there. Herodotus (I, 106; IV, 1) ascribes twenty-eight years to the Scythian domination, a figure which is probably exaggerated, for later historical data indicate that it should be reduced to about ten years, from about 632–622. In the end the barbarian flood was partially absorbed by fixed permanent settlements, or was repelled to its place of origin by the nations it had submerged.

During the flood tide of the Scythian invasion Ashurbanipal died (626). From this moment the slow decline of Assyria changed into open disintegration (§ 12). The situation was far from clear at first,

---

[12] J. Pazyluski, "Nouveau aspects de l'histoire des Scythes," in *Rev. de l'Univ. de Bruxelles*, 1937.

owing to the abnormal situation caused by the presence of the Scyths. But when anterior Asia, freed from the barbarians, began once more to breathe, the universal passion for liberty awakened by the death of Ashurbanipal could no longer be denied, but burst into action and led to the definitive fall of Nineve (612; § 13 ff.).

509. The same passion for liberty was felt at Jerusalem, where Josias was pressing the first measures of his reform. The sixteen-year-old youth had begun to "seek out the God of David his father" (§ 507), but instead had found in the Temple of Yahweh astral idols of Assyrian origin (§ 501), gods strange to his nation and unknown to David, but of political significance, inasmuch as they were reminders of the sovereignty of the nation from which they were imported (§ 476). Josias' first impulse to a reform was a religious one, but it was quickly fused with and re-enforced by nationalistic motives. To this Yahwistic king Nineve and Jerusalem were contradictory terms, mutually exclusive in the same manner and for the same reason as were Yahweh and Ishtar. As a beginning, then, he cleansed the Temple of the Assyrian Ishtar and all her astral court.

The first place to be cleansed of idolatry was the Temple of Jerusalem, where the latest Assyrian cults, least solidly rooted in the people and the most hated politically, had taken up their nest. The attack was next directed against the Canaanite cults and syncretistic Yahwism, more ancient but less significant from a nationalistic viewpoint (2 Kings 23:4–24; a résumé, and anachronistic). Along with the destruction of idolatry went Josias' efforts to restore authentic Yahwism. Both programs must have meant a tremendous amount of work extending over several years. To evaluate it correctly one must remember that it came after more than a half century of intense, methodical activity in the opposite direction. Despite the ineffectual efforts of Manasses' declining years, Yahwism had been left a spiritual desert. More than fifty years of fanatical and unceasing persecution had interrupted the old usages, dispersed many organizations, abolished rights, and led to barbaric practices. From an institution which was governed principally by traditional norms and the habits of centuries it had wrested landmarks and guides. Now, therefore, even after the abolition of all idolatrous and syncretistic practices there remained the task of searching, of retracing, restoring, rebuilding, and revivifying everything which for more than half a century had lain in ruins.

This enormous task was prosecuted by groups which were inspired by prophetism and labored under the royal protection of the crown. Because of the favor of the court, and the reawakening of the nationalistico-religious conscience within the nation, and also because the profound confusion of the world outside seemed to further the designs of Yahweh, prophetism recovered rapidly. The first days of Josias witnessed the coming of Nahum and probably also of Sophonias. It was in the thirteenth year of the same reign (626) that Jeremias was called to be a prophet and began his mission (§ 427). How direct a part these three prophets, whose writings we possess, took in the first phase of the reform of Josias has been discussed at length. Jeremias has received special attention. His oldest oracles were directed against both Canaanite cults and syncretism, which suggests that the astral cults of Assyria had been already removed.

510. During this reform something happened which was to intensify its spirit and at the same time stamp it with a very definite character. The Temple of Jerusalem was in need of repair after the removal of the many idolatrous innovations, or because of the usual ravages of time; a similar situation had faced Joas (§ 470). It was the eighteenth year of the reign of Josias and the fifth of the ministry of Jeremias (621). One day the High Priest Helcias, administrator of the restoration, announced to the secretary of the king his discovery in the Temple of the "book of the *torah*" (§§ 109, 273, 285, 294, 463); it was immediately brought to the king and read in his presence (2 Kings 22:8–10). The reading made a profound impression on the king because of the serious maledictions which Yahweh pronounced against the transgressors of the *torah*. As its prescriptions were not in fact being observed, the king sent to consult a prophetess, Hulda, wife of Salbum, who was living in Jerusalem and enjoyed much authority in prophetic circles. The prophetess confirmed the threatened sanctions of the discovered *torah*, but predicted that as a reward for his good will (2 Kings 22:11–20) these would not be applied to Josias.

After this reply, the king intensified the work of reform. No longer, however, according to oral norms which often were vague and indefinite, and which could be culled from prophetic circles or from some respectable Yahwist; now he could proceed according to the clear written prescriptions of the newly discovered Law. This new period of reform intensified the struggle against the traces of the Canaanite cults still remaining in the kingdom, and against the still numerous syncretistic practices which had infiltrated into Yahwism, and gave great impetus to the constructive part of the reform, the fixing of various rules of worship according to the new written code. The official promulgation of the new document which was henceforth to be the foundation of religious and civil life was accomplished with great solemnity. The people, king, priests, and prophets gathered in the Temple of Yahweh, and the newly found *torah* was read. All present solemnly swore to Yahweh to observe its statutes, and entered into a formal pact or alliance with Yahweh, according to ancient custom (§§ 243, 285, 294). In fact, at this point the account calls the discovered document the "book of the Pact" (2 Kings 23:2–3); the Chronicler consistently refers to it as the "book of the *torah* of Yahweh, by the hand of Moses" (2 Para. 34:14; § 273).

511. What was the book found on this occasion, and what is the historical value of the biblical account of its finding? The importance of these questions can hardly be exaggerated, being so intimately connected with the process of formation through which the writings constituting the Bible, our chief source for the history of Israel, has passed (§ 113 ff.).

Analyzing the biblical account (as was too often done in the past century) and taking care to place it in the historical background in which it was presented (this perhaps has been done all too rarely), it is unmistakably clear that the biblical account is such that it should be accepted or rejected in its entirety.

Many have supposed that there was no true discovery here at all. To say that a book was "found" in a temple was, in Egypt, the usual manner of presenting a book, written recently within the temple itself, in such a way as to win authority for it. Something not unlike this occasionally took place in Christianity in regard to the apocryphal writings. True, "new" sacred books were often passed off as "found," and this is a possibility which must be reckoned with, but it is not the only possibility. There is another possibility, equally factual and actually of more frequent occurrence: namely, that temples were favorite places for the safeguarding of important writings, and that often all trace of the writings placed therein for the purpose of their preservation was lost. Later these forgotten writings would, during works of repair or restoration, be unexpectedly "found." The ancient Orient yields classic examples of this old practice for profane as well as religious writings (§§ 253, 274). So tenacious indeed was the practice that it lasted until the Middle Ages both in the Christian West and in the Arabic Orient, and has resulted in the occasional but genuine modern "discoveries" of writings hidden for centuries in sacred places. Apart from some curious incidents in the West, mention may here be made of a letter written in Latin by Gerard Ridefort, seneschal of the Templars (twelfth century), discovered at Jerusalem in 1926, under a pillar of the mosque el-ʿAqsa (for the Haram esh-Sherif cf. § 390) during the course of repairs. It is more interesting still to point out that hiding-places in ancient Egyptian temples contained not only religious or legal documents of extraordinary importance, but also, because of their value as annals, reports of military expeditions and the lists of the officials who took part in them; the same lists today would be entrusted to the quartermaster. The following excerpt from the Annals of Thutmose III, in which he speaks of his campaign against Megiddo (§ 34), is illuminating: ". . . Everything which his Majesty did against this city and against that wretched prince and

his wretched army, is marked for its respective day under the name of
the expedition and under the names of the officers. It is set down on
a leather roll in the Temple of Amon [at *Karnak;* § 394] to the present
day."[13]

Thus the custom of a pretended "discovery" cannot be the only
explanation of the biblical account. The possibility of a genuine "discovery" must be entertained as being as least equally plausible, although
it remains uncertain and must be decided by other considerations.

512. The general tone of the account suggests that the discovery was
of something already known, although only by hearsay and in a rather
vague way, just as one might know the title and general subject matter
of a book which he has never read or held in his hands. It should be
remarked that the discovered writing was immediately called the "book
of the *torah*," and no one asked or offered any information as to its
nature, authenticity, or presence in the Temple. This lack of any argument about the document is most naturally and obviously explained if
the writing, already known in a vague sort of way, was clearly identified
by a simple reading and by reason of the place where it was discovered.

If *per impossibile* someone were today to discover, amid the ruins of
Caesarea of Palestine, a quantity of parchment rolls whose paleography
was that of the third century A.D., and if they contained the text of
the Bible in parallel columns of Hebrew and Greek, a single reading
would suffice to identify them at once as the "Hexapla." Nor would
there be need of any discussion of their nature, authenticity, or the
reason why they were deposited in Caesarea. The contents alone and
the fact that they were found in the city where Origen left them would
suffice to identify them clearly, presupposing the vague knowledge that
is had of them today. Thus, *mutatis mutandis,* the recognition of the
discovered "book of the *torah*" must have taken place.

If the "discovery" was a real one and not fictitious, the historical
circumstances in which it came about provide its complete and adequate
explanation. The fact that the discovery took place during the work
of restoration (§ 510) explains the accidental character of the discovery.
The consequences of its discovery clearly show that the document was
essentially Yahwistic, which explains why it was deposited in the
Temple and why it was lost sight of. As a collection of Yahwistic
laws it was placed in the Temple for the same reason that the
tables of the Law (§ 252) were put into the Ark, or the collection
of juridic norms interpreting and applying the tables were placed near
the Ark (§ 274). Since the moment was one of recovery from the

---

[13] The *RB,* 1926, 288–295, relates the details of the discovery of Gerard's letter;
and records similar incidents in both Eastern and Western history. The passage from
the Annals of Thutmose is reproduced in *ANET,* 237.

more than fifty years of rabid anti-Yahwism which had raged especially within the Temple (§ 509) it was quite understandable that the
document deposited there had dropped from view and been lost. It is
not necessary to suppose that it was walled up in some recess; more
probably it was hidden away at the bottom of a closet in one of the
small rooms annexed to the Temple (§ 392), having been thrown there
during the time of Manasses as something uninteresting and out of date.

513. Going back to the origin of the discovered document, beyond
the epoch of Manasses to that of his predecessor Ezechias, not only do
we enter a Yahwistic period, but one of specifically literary and legal activity. The magnitude and rigor of the reform set in motion by Ezechias
readily suggest that some special codification of ancient laws was
completed in his time (§ 485). Thus the period of Ezechias, Yahwist
reformer and codifier, was followed by the period of Manasses, a long
period of laxity and immorality; finally came the period of Josias, who
was inspired in his reform by Ezechias (§ 507), and who took as the
norm for the second period of his reform the newly discovered Yahwistic
"book of the *torah*." Unless all these things conspire to deceive us, the
newly found book must date from the time of Ezechias, and was the
codex which had directed his reform.

514. Judging the discovery in the light of modern circumstances, one
marvels that the copy which was brought to light again should have
caused such surprise. Indeed one might suppose that other copies should
have survived outside the Temple and that, during the period of
Manasses, they remained hidden, to be freely circulated again in the
time of Josias as something desirable and venerated. The supposition, however, does not take into account the respective importance
which "memory" and "writing" had among the Semites, which has been
discussed above (§§ 189 ff., 242). The newly found codex of Ezechias
had been put into "writing" so as to give it public and official binding
force, and it had to be a document of testimony and protestation. But
everything seems to indicate that the greater portion of its directives
were already known by "memory" through tradition, and were likewise handed down by "memory" even after its codification. During
the time of Ezechias there may have been only one copy of the
codex, or at most very few: one to be deposited in the Temple "for
a testimony" (§ 274), perhaps another for the king, the royal chan-
cellor, etc. Under Manasses, the copy in the Temple alone remained
unharmed, but all the others were destroyed. Among steadily
dwindling Yahwistic circles and amid the difficulties of the times,
that small portion of the contents of the codex which was transmitted
by "memory" sufficed to identify it clearly when the complete "written"
text could be compared with the fragmentary "memory" text.

515. That the discovered codex was *Deuteronomy* was the opinion of some of the older writers (Jerome, *Adv. Jovin.*, 1, 5, in Migne, *P.L.*, 23, 225–227; *in Ezech.* 1, 1, in Migne, *P.L.*, 25, 17; Athanasius, *Epist. ad Marcellinum*, 32, in Migne, *P.G.*, 27, 44; John Chrysostom, *Homil. 9 in Matt.*, 4, in Migne, *P.G.*, 57, 181; *Hom. 7 in I Cor.*, in Migne, *P.G.*, 61, 58; Procopius of Gaza, *In Deuter.*, 17, 18, in Migne, *P.G.*, 87, 916), and they are followed by many moderns (§ 114) who, however, are not unanimous in deciding how many and which parts of *Deuteronomy* correspond to the discovered codex. It is certain that the codex must not have been very extensive, as it was not only read twice in succession, and probably on the same day (2 Kings 22:8, 10), but in the ceremony of official promulgation "all the words" of it were read to the people (23:2); this would have been a practical impossibility if it had been of notable length.

As the prosecution of the reform of Josias was based on the newly found codex, it is possible that not only new copies of it were made, but new editions as well, so as to introduce into it other ancient *normae extravagantes*, modernizations, adaptations, etc., as in the times of Ezechias (§ 485).

516. From a famous but not altogether clear passage of Jeremias, it appears that the new codex gave impetus to a literary activity which was insidiously syncretistic. Jeremias, a contemporary of the discovery and entirely dedicated to a mission which was in perfect harmony (however much this may be disputed) with the fundamental principles of the discovered codex, cried out in a dispute with his syncretistic adversaries as follows:

"How is it that you say: 'We are wise,
   and the *torah* of Yahweh is with us'?
Behold the lying pen of the scribes
   has changed it to a lie!"

(Jer. 8:8)

That the first two lines refer to the discovered "book of the *torah*" cannot be reasonably denied, considering the circumstances in which the prophet wrote. The last two lines, however, certainly do not allude to the same *torah* as before, for this would be a direct denial of his own mission; hence, he seems to allude to the products fabricated by private "scribes" for the purpose of "lying." In fact syncretism did not yield to the reform of Josias without a struggle, and even after the discovery of the codex it must have tried to justify syncretistic usages by various depositions of the codex itself. Thus, for example, the law concerning the consecration of the first-born to Yahweh (Deut. 15:19; cf. Exod. 13:2; 22:28) could with but a slight modification be used to justify human sacrifices to Moloch (§ 476). By taking particular prescriptions out of their context, syncretistic "scribes" could alter them "to a lie" and disseminate them widely for their own purposes. Jeremias seems here to allude to this type of literary activity which probably prompted the Temple and palace authorities to hasten their own publication of new and de luxe editions of the codex.[14]

517. The religious reform was not restricted to the kingdom of Juda but extended northward to the districts of Samaria, among the denser ethnographic Israelite groups, and to centers greatly venerated in the nation's history (2 Kings 23:19–20; 2 Para. 34:6–7). This fact has a special significance. The historical circumstance which made it possible was this, that after 626 Assyrian authority over the territory of the Samaritans was practically nonexistent (§§ 12, 508); on the other hand, this interest of Josias for co-nationals religiously and politically different from himself, once more brings out the religious and national motives behind his reform. It shows also that he drew his inspirations from the analogous reform of his grandfather Ezechias (§ 482 ff.).

The representatives of prophetism could expect, then, a return to happier times in which the whole nation of Yahweh would be united around Yahweh, under one Yahwistic monarch, with one Yahwistic temple. They could foresee a time in which Yahweh would restore the desolate kingdom of Israel to all its ancient glory (Nahum 2:3), when the mountains of Samaria would again be adorned by fruitful vineyards and from whose peaks the sentries would call out their reminders to all the peoples:

> "Arise! Let us go up to Sion,
> to Yahweh our God!"
>
> (Jer. 31:6)

518. Yet the grandiose nationalistico-political design conceived by Josias was destined to fail. At the time when the internal reform was going well, political events outside were rushing to a climax. In 612 Nineve fell and the Assyrian empire began a death-agony which was protracted until 609 (§ 134 ff.). The Pharaoh Nechao II, friend of Assyria, made an attempt to save the straitened nation. He marched from Egypt with a powerful army, crossed Palestine in forced marches and pushed on toward Harran hoping to arrive in time to bring effective aid to the last Assyrian king, who, having been dislodged from Harran (609), was attempting to reconquer it. At this point the cuneiform report ("Babylonian Chronicle" of Gadd, cf. J. Flavius, *Antiquities*, X, 5, 1) joins the biblical report (2 Kings 23:29–30; 2 Para. 35:20 ff.).[15]

---

[14] Cf. Ricciotti, *Il libro di Geremia*, Turin, 1923, 120 f.

[15] Cf. *ANET*, 294, and Dhorme, "La fin de l'empire assyrien d'après un nouveau document" in *RB*, 1924, 218–234.

The state of mind of the ardent nationalistico-Yahwistic monarch after the fall of Nineve and during the agony of Assyria can easily be imagined. It was an anxious period of waiting, vibrant with hope. He stood ready to intervene with any action which might help cast out once and for all the hated tyranny. Everything augured well. The agony was somewhat prolonged, but it was hardly to be expected that the Assyrian giant would die from one blow; the end however appeared not too far off. What a glorious day when Assur would be done! Of the two opposing cities Nineve and Jerusalem (§ 509), the first would disappear forever, and the nation of Yahweh, reunited and strong (§ 517), would, with its God, remain to triumph.

519. An unforeseen danger threatened to spoil these wonderful hopes. Nechao hastened to the aid of Assyria and would perhaps arrive in time to save the moribund nation. That danger had to be averted; no help should be allowed to reach Assyria, whose destiny was running out. Should he oppose the Pharaoh by force? Why not? The generosity of the nationalistic king and his faith in Yahweh led him to his decision, there being no other way to prevent the joining of Egypt with Assyria. The decision was certainly paradoxical: the insignificant king of Juda seeking out the Pharaoh of Egypt for battle. It was a paradox of heroism, prompted by the profound sentiments which animated this heroic little king.

Josias arrayed his army at Megiddo, a strategic center (§ 64; cf. Herodotus, II, 159?). Seeing that the road was blocked before him, Nechao tried persuasion. Either because of the haste with which he marched or because he did not understand the reason for such an obstacle, he discussed the matter with Josias to explain to him that he had no hostile intention toward him, that he was aiming at other enemies. Josias would not be moved: the way was barred to the Pharaoh (2 Para. 35:21-22). The battle which followed was surely a brief one (cf. the last words of 2 Kings 23:29). Juda was routed, and Josias, who took part in the fray personally, was seriously wounded and died not long after. His body was brought to Jerusalem and given an honorable burial amid the sincere laments of the people. This catastrophe for Yahwistic nationalism occurred between March and August of 609 (§ 14).

*   *   *

520. The consequences of the catastrophe in the political field were immediate. Josias had left three children, Eliaqim, Joachaz, and Mattanias. The throne should have gone to the eldest, Eliaqim, but, as had happened after the murder of Amon (§ 506), the people intervened and, discarding the unpopular Eliaqim, put Joachaz on the throne (he is also called Sallum, in Jer. 22:11). His reign was very

brief. After the victory of Megiddo, Nechao had hastened toward the
north, at the same time keeping an eye on Palestine, over which, in
virtue of his victory, he now exercised supreme dominion. Meanwhile
he had established his general quarters at Ribla on the Orontes, and
there learned of the election of Joachaz. He may have considered
this autonomous action a blow struck at his supreme sovereignty, or
perhaps Joachaz was known to be hostile to Egypt, or perhaps he
thought the rejected eldest son might work unostentatiously in Egypt's
favor. At any rate, after three months of rule Joachaz was deposed and
sent as a prisoner to Egypt, where he died.

The rejected Eliaqim was then placed on the vacant throne. So
that he would appreciate his dependence on Egypt, the Pharaoh
changed his name to Joachim, and imposed on the realm, as a fine,
one talent of gold and one hundred of silver (2 Kings 23:31–34;
Jer. 22:11–12).

521. Megiddo was a very severe test for Yahwism. In the eyes
of the people, Yahwism and Josias were the same thing; what had
happened at Megiddo was for the faithful Yahwists disconcerting and
mystifying. The partisans of syncretism looked upon it as a perfect
vindication of their views: the king, so fervent a Yahwist, was now dead,
cut down in the flower of manhood by an enemy hand, and precisely at
the moment that he was fighting for a nationalist-Yahwistic cause! For
the Yahwists, these facts were an inexplicable mystery; others interpreted them an evident punishment traceable to the idolatrous divinities
persecuted by the reform, and also to Yahweh himself, whose various
local sanctuaries Josias had suppressed in favor of the one in Jerusalem.

Such a satisfactory and spontaneous interpretation of events must
have cost Yahwism many followers. The austerity of the reform ended
with Josias, and syncretism must have immediately begun to sprout
under Joachim.

From a picture of Joachim's moral character which Jeremias has
preserved, it appears that this king was a presumptuous despot,
coarse in disposition, superficial in his attitudes, quite superstitious,
and at the same time a skeptic. He was not indeed the fiery anti-Yahwist
his grandfather Manasses had been, but he in no way favored the
reform his father Josias had begun. Yet he does not seem to have been
a syncretist who would exert himself to couple Baal with Yahweh.
To his cynical mind the one was as the other, and as far as he was
concerned he could dispense equally with them both. The others he
let alone and followed in practice a course of toleration, which of
course led to syncretism.

Nevertheless, especially from the beginning, Yahwism remained very
powerful, so efficacious had been the reform of Josias. A curious proof

of this can be seen in the name imposed by the Pharaoh on his vassal king, *Yehoyaqim,* "Yahweh establishes"; this substitution of a theophoric name of the God of the nation in place of the preceding *'Elyaqim,* "God establishes," could be a clever act of homage by which the Pharaoh sought to allay the hostile apprehensions of the Yahwist faction. It was Yahweh himself who *established* the new monarch.

522. The political question, however, almost immediately assumed prime importance. In the early days of Joachim, when Assyria had disappeared and its place of predominance in anterior Asia was still unoccupied, the smaller states were badly disorganized and for that reason were destined to become satellites. In Juda one faction sought the simplest and most promising way of settling the difficulty, through dependence on Egypt, the land of their forefathers. Israel had many nostalgic memories of that land of fertility and happiness with which it had almost always had social relations, and at times even alliances of one kind or another. At present the Pharaoh was in Syria with his army in order to proclaim his rights over anterior Asia (§ 15), and all things pointed to the possibility of his becoming the master of all the regions extending from the Delta to the Euphrates. The idea of a cordial surrender to Egypt seemed to be perfect.

For others, however, such considerations were deceptive, and in practice doomed to failure. Others held out not from political, but from religious reasons. The nation of Yahweh must steer clear of alliances and political surrenders; political expediency was an act of distrust in Yahweh, and an apostasy from the God of the nation.

This last was evidently the thesis of prophetism (§ 476). As once it had consistently opposed the policy of surrender to Assyria, now, appealing to that failure, it opposed surrender to Egypt. In this regard the warning of Jeremias to the nation is most emphatic:

> "Thou shalt be put to shame through Egypt also,
>   as thou wert through Assur!"
>
>   (Jer. 2:36)

Prophetism therefore and with it the pure Yahwists, although not advocating hostility toward Egypt, disapproved of any commitment made to her. The syncretists, however, expected great things from a secret agreement with her. Upon these, the religious ideals of the Yahwists made little impression, and in order to secure a greater theologico-political security, they were ready to make room by the side of Yahweh for the whole Egyptian pantheon, as they had done for the Assyrian and were again doing for the Canaanite pantheon.

523. The mentality of the syncretists of this period reflected more or less accurately that of former syncretists. The cult of Yahweh was far from being set aside and was perhaps intensified, but besides being coupled with that of Baal and being reduced to a pure formalism as in the time of Ezechias (§ 499), it now for the most part took on the aspect of a magic ceremonial. The very material elements of the rite, mechanically fulfilled, would not fail to obtain their effect; by itself the rite had an infallible power because it "obligated" Yahweh. For example, the Temple of Yahweh was in its very materiality an infallible safeguard which had preserved Jerusalem from misfortune; what, if not the presence of that sacred dwelling place of Yahweh, had preserved the city from Sennacherib (§ 497)? This was fetishism with a thin veneer of Yahwism, but a fetishism not entirely new in Israel (§§ 342, 499). This complex mentality, made up of syncretism, formalism, and fetishism, is clearly reflected in the invective which Jeremias hurled at his co-nationals in the time of Joachim: "Thus saith Yahweh . . . Do not put your trust in lying words, such as 'The Temple of Yahweh! The Temple of Yahweh!' . . . What? to steal, murder, commit adultery, swear falsely, burn incense to Baal, run after strange gods which you know not, and then present yourselves before me in this house [the Temple] which is called by my name, and exclaim 'We are saved!' meaning to continue all these abominations! Is then this house which is called by my name become a den of robbers in your eyes? . . . Go then to my dwelling which was in Silo . . . and see what I did to it [§ 343] because of the wickedness of my people Israel! . . . and I will do to the house which is called by my name, in which you put your trust, and to the place which I gave to you and your fathers, as I have done to Silo" (Jer. 7:3–14; cf. 26:1 ff.).

524. Such was the politico-religious situation of the kingdom during the first years of Joachim's reign. In 605, however, things changed. The battle of Carchemish (§ 15) eliminated Nechao forever from the Palestinian scene, for he was never again to leave his frontiers (2 Kings 24:7); it also distinctly delineated the renovated empire of Babylonia which would succeed Assyria as supreme ruler over anterior Asia. The syncretistic faction of Jerusalem, which had based all its hopes on Egypt (§ 522), suddenly found itself bereft of any foundation. The Chaldean victors had become the supreme sovereigns of Palestine, and might arrive from one moment to the next. Some understanding had to be reached with the new masters.

What happened in the kingdom of Juda after Carchemish is not entirely clear: some of the facts are difficult, and the chronology varies in some cases.

The following are certain chronological points of reference, computed from the certain date of the battle of Carchemish (605 B.C.).

605 — First year of the reign of (Jer. 25:1)
      Nabuchodonosor
605 — Fourth year of the reign of (Jer. 46:2)
      Joachim
597 — Eighth year of the reign of (2 Kings 24:12, 8, 17)
      Nabuchodonosor, three months
      of the reign of Joachin, and
      the beginning of the reign of
      Sedecias
587 — Eighteenth year of the reign of (Jer. 32:1)
      Nabuchodonosor, and the tenth
      year of Sedecias
586 — Nineteenth year of the reign (Jer. 39:2; 52:5, 12;
      of Nabuchodonosor, and the   2 Kings 25:1–3, 8)
      eleventh of the reign of Sedecias

The preceding dates are gathered from different sources; all agree and so confirm each other. One dissenting date is found in Dan. 1:1–2 which states that Nabuchodonosor besieged Jerusalem in the third year of the reign of Joachim, captured the king, and took as his booty some of the furnishings of the Temple. The Chronicler also reports that Nabuchodonosor put Joachim in chains and despoiled the Temple, but furnishes no chronological date (2 Para. 36:6–7).

It is evident that Nabuchodonosor could not have besieged and captured King Joachim in the third year of his reign, because at that time the Pharaoh Nechao was still the master of Syria-Palestine, and only in the fourth year of Joachim's reign did he lose that control in the battle of Carchemish; hence the text of Dan. 1:1–2 has either suffered one of the usual corruptions at the hands of a copyist (§ 526), or follows some other system of computation.

525. From the very beginning things in Palestine failed to go according to expectations. Nabuchodonosor was unable to reap the full fruits of his victory at Carchemish because, although he pursued the fleeing Pharaoh to the borders of Egypt, he had to hurry back to Babylonia at the unexpected death of his father (§ 15; cf. Berossus, reported by Josephus, C. Apion., I, 19; Antiquities, X, 11, 1).

The supreme sovereignty of Babylonia under which Palestine automatically passed as a result of Carchemish remained for some years only nominal, and did not make itself felt effectively. This is the gist of 2 Kings 24:1 which states that the vassalage of Joachim under Nabuchodonosor lasted three years, i.e., from about 601 to 597, when Joachim died. From 605 (Carchemish) to 601, Palestine was practically nobody's possession, and the kingdom of Juda enjoyed almost complete independence. Held in Babylonia by the uncertainty of the new situa-

tion in western Asia, and by a desire to consolidate his own position at
home, Nabuchodonosor was unable to intervene in Palestine and garner
the fruits of his victory at Carchemish, or there to translate his nominal
sovereignty into reality. However, toward 601 he did intervene, it
seems (cf. Josephus, *Antiquities*, X, 6, 1–2), and on that occasion, when
the princes of Syria and Palestine hastened to present their tribute to
him, Joachim was certainly among their number.

526. The above-mentioned item of the Chronicler states that Nabuchodonosor put Joachim in chains and despoiled the Temple, and this
may refer to the events of 601. Knowing the inclination of Joachim and
his faction for Egypt, Nabuchodonosor, in accepting his act of vassalage,
treated him as Ashurbanipal had treated Manasses of Juda, Nechao of
Sais, and his colleague (§ 503); however, upon receiving renewed
promises of fidelity and relying on the effectiveness of fear, he freed
him and allowed him to occupy the throne of Juda, now actually little
more than a footstool of Babylonia. On that same occasion the Chaldean monarch took as booty a good part of the furnishings of the
Temple and perhaps also deported some hostages to Babylonia.
This last detail would fit in with Dan. 1:1 (§ 524), although in that
case the troublesome reading of the "third" year of Joachim would
have to be corrected, on the supposition that the original text had
the "eighth" and not the "third" year. As a matter of fact the "eighth"
year of Joachim was the year 601. To eliminate the chronological discrepancy, some suppose that Nabuchodonosor laid siege to Jerusalem
immediately after Carchemish, which is difficult to harmonize with
Nabuchodonosor's haste as he marched first southwards in pursuit of
the fleeing Pharaoh, and later toward the north as he repaired to
Babylonia.

527. The vassalage of 601, and it was a reality, was accepted by
Joachim as an inevitable necessity, but secretly he still favored Egypt.
Up to that year the syncretistic faction which favored Egypt (§ 522) had
had a free hand, although there was always the vague fear that after
Carchemish the Chaldeans might arrive at any moment. Their delay
served to strengthen this faction and helped it become more and more
influential in Jerusalem and throughout the kingdom, thanks to the favor
of the court. This was the most laborious, the most bitter, and the most
heroic period of Jeremias' activity, for that genuine Yahwist, the opponent of the Egyptian policy, was persecuted uninterruptedly as a
prophet and as a defeatist. He was arrested and threatened with death
more than once (Jer. 26:8 ff.); dark conspiracies were formed against
him (18:18 ff.); humiliating blows, the stocks, and insults of the
rabble were his unhappy lot (Jer. 20 ff.). He was also singled out
for persecution by Joachim. In the fifth year of his reign (36:9 ff.) the

king had all the prophecies of Jeremias, which had been recently written on a scroll, read to him. As the reading progressed, the king, with a penknife, contemptuously cut off the parts read and threw them into a brazier full of coals. What little effect the knife and brazier of this royal buffoon had on the prophet can be seen from the fact that Jeremias again dictated to his secretary Baruch the same prophecies which were burned (he knew them therefore "by memory"; § 189 ff.) and to them he added others, among which the following concerned the cynical king:

> "He shall be buried with the burial of an ass:
> Dragged along and cast forth
> outside the gates of Jerusalem!"
>
> (Jer. 22:19)

528. Jeremias was a person of consequence even to his enemies. The great prestige he had enjoyed at court in the time of Josias made him a Yahwist with exceptional authority; even Joachim's courtiers considered him their master, and tried to protect him (Jer. 36:19). It is easy, therefore, to imagine the fate of those other less-publicized Yahwists who did not have the protection his exceptional prestige gave him. There are no details here as there were none for the times of Manasses; one phrase of the biblical account, however, pierces the obscurity like a flash of lightning and, using the very same words (§ 502), lifts the veil on what happened. Joachim was responsible "also for the innocent blood which he shed, and he filled Jerusalem with innocent blood" (2 Kings 24:4). In a word, there was a methodical persecution of those guilty of not adoring Baal and refusing to place their hope in Egypt.

The real vassalage of 601 was a poor remedy or none at all for this state of affairs. The Yahwists were seen to have been politically wise, although the pro-Egyptians were not entirely disposed to admit the fact. Unwilling to accommodate themselves to the new political situation, they devoted their efforts, with the tenacity characteristic of Semitic factions (§§ 454, 458, 469), to schemes of recovery. They prudently kept their plans secret, for Babylonia was not only watching, but was minutely informed about everything that happened inside Jerusalem, even to the point of knowing whether a certain person was hostile or favorable to Egypt (Jer. 39:14; 40:1 ff.).

529. These hidden activities, constantly watered by "innocent blood," culminated in 597, i.e., three years later (2 Kings 24:2), in open rebellion against Babylonia. Nabuchodonosor was perhaps then too busy in Babylonia, or the rebellion, limited to the kingdom of Juda, may not have merited a special expedition; at any rate, it seems certain that the Chaldean king did not intervene immediately, but restricted himself to sending against the rebel Joachim armed bands of people who were near him — Arameans, Moabites, Ammonites, mixed with Chaldean regulars. These auxiliaries executed the orders from Babel all the more willingly, because all had old grievances to settle with the Israelites, and their raids would inflict heavy damage on Juda.

Some months later Nabuchodonosor, fearing lest the revolt get out of hand, intervened in person and decided to rid himself of the rebel vassal. And Egypt, dashing the hopes of the faction then in power in Jerusalem, did not lift a finger to help! The revolt did not spread, and when Nabuchodonosor arrived at Jerusalem he found that King Joachim had died shortly before. The fact that he died at the age of thirty-six might lead to the suspicion that he died a violent death, that he was either killed in combat against the armed raiding bands or through some conspiracy. His very sepulcher (2 Kings 24:6; 2 Para. 26:8, Greek text) and his corpse seem to have been profaned and dishonored not much later (Jer. 22:19; 36:30). Nabuchodonosor found Joachin, the son of the dead king, on the throne.

530. When the city was besieged, Joachin immediately surrendered, thus ending his reign of only three months. By going out to the Chaldean king of his own accord he managed to save his life, but he was sent to Babylonia along with the queen mother and the court. There the unhappy youth remained a prisoner for thirty-seven years, a symbol among his fellow countrymen of the misfortune which was soon to strike the whole nation. On the same occasion Nabuchodonosor completed the first deportation of the people of Juda, exiling to Babylonia 7000 adults and property holders of the realm, 1000 skilled workers to be used in his great building projects in Babylonia, and an undetermined number of other persons (cf. 2 Kings 24:16 with 24:14); he also despoiled the Temple of its most precious furnishings. This was the same system of forced colonization employed by the Assyrians (§ 452 ff.). The first group settled near the river Kebar, which is not the Chaboras of northwestern Mesopotamia but *Nar Kabari*, "great canal," which crossed the city of Nippur which lay to the southwest of Babel (§ 2). The prophet Ezechiel was deported there with the others (Ezech. 1:1–3).

To replace the imprisoned king Nabuchodonosor lifted to the throne of Juda one of the king's uncles, Mattanias, the son of Josias (§ 520). The Chaldean king also, as the Pharaoh Nechao had done with Joachim (§ 520) and for the same reason, changed the name of the new vassal to that of Sedecias.

✿   ✿   ✿

531. If the last king of Juda were not intimately connected with the final catastrophe of the kingdom and the entire nation, he would be an almost comical figure. There is no doubt that Sedecias, the king in these circumstances, was a tragic buffoon. As a man he was of mediocre intelligence and average in character, without special talents or grave defects. It seems that up to his twenty-first year, when he found himself placed on the throne, he had been prudently kept far from public life. When upon the throne he relied on the intelligence of others, made his decisions according to the dictates of others, and through the mistakes of others brought about his own and the kingdom's ruin. The majority, or at least those who cried out the loudest, were always successful in winning him over to their side; these he would follow while looking backward for fear of taking the wrong road, and looking for a different one.

Such a man was quickly surrounded by the leaders of the faction favorable to Egypt, i.e., the anti-Babylonians. He became as putty in their hands. The happenings of 597 had taught these politicians nothing, but had only increased and intensified their hatred for Babylonia, while fanning the fires of their desire for revenge and recovery. The well-being of the nation for them meant revenge on Babylonia, and of this Egypt was the indispensable means. Such a course was the height of folly, and the means were horribly fallacious, nor did they ask if both did not inevitably lead to national catastrophe. It had to be *their* way, despite all reason to the contrary. They would not have been fanatical Semitic politicians had they not shown themselves at once so immovable in their stubbornness (§§ 454, 458) and so lacking in practical intelligence.

532. Working underground and prudently concealing their activity, they could hardly wait to take over after the departure of the Chaldeans. But they met with resistance from the Yahwistic faction, the outgrowth of prophetism, which had its own politico-religious reasons for propaganda. In short, the situation of Joachim's time was more or less prolonged during the period of this new vassalage to Babylonia (§ 528). The king cut a sorry figure as he tried to balance himself on the two waves whose crests and troughs are described so vividly by Jeremias. The king had a sincere veneration for the prophet (Jer. 21:1–2; 37:3), but did not wish to show it publicly for fear of the Egyptian faction. He even permitted them to imprison Jeremias, but secretly sent to consult him while he was in prison (37:15 ff.). He permitted his courtiers, against whom "the king could do nothing" (38:5), to throw the prophet into a cistern to die of hunger, but soon afterward, at the request of a mere employee in the palace, had him extricated, anxiously consulted him anew, and at the same time commanded under penalty of death that he tell no one that he consulted him (38:5–26). Despite all this, Jeremias continued as before, and to the questions of the king he returned the unswerving answer: "Rebel not against the Chaldeans."

533. The pro-Egyptians also continued to go their way, but as long as Nechao lived their plans made no headway, for the Pharaoh was much wiser than the fanatics of Jerusalem, and adhered closely to the principle established after Carchemish of having nothing to do with Palestinian affairs (§ 524). When he died in 593 and was succeeded by Psammetichus II (§ 42), the fire of their smoldering hopes burst into flame. They expected a great deal of the new Pharaoh, and the various little Palestinian states contacted each other to decide upon a common program of action. A mysterious gathering was also held with much caution in Jerusalem in the same year 593, and messengers from Edom, Moab, Ammon, Tyre, and Sidon were present (Jer. 27:3). The mystery, however, was quite transparent, and despite the precautions taken by the fearful gathering, it was an open secret that the plot was against suspicious Babylonia. Jeremias, of course, understood it full well, and on this occasion publicly reaffirmed that the yoke of the Chaldeans was inevitable (27:4 ff.). Babylonia understood this also, and must have shown her suspicions openly.

Psammetichus, faithful to the foreign policy of Nechao, was unwilling to embroil himself, and proffered no help of any kind to the projected league. About 590 this Psammetichus repaired to Phoenicia, most probably by sea, to venerate there an ancient Egyptian sanctuary of Byblos (§ 99), but certainly his voyage — contrary to what was believed until very recently, and according to what has been demonstrated by documents which have later come to light — was not a political plot against Babylonia.[16] Thus, the projected league, deprived of its most important member, miscarried. Sedecias, the host of the revolting ambassadors, was thereby compromised in the eyes of Babylonia, and in the same year 593 made a voyage to Babel (Jer. 51:59). The reason for this voyage is quite obvious: if the vassal king was not called by the authorities *ad audiendum verbum* because of the gathering held at Jerusalem, he himself must have felt the necessity of presenting himself voluntarily to his master to explain what had happened so as to allay those suspicions.

534. The visit must have made an impression on the fickle Sedecias. The amazing display of magnificence and power in the capital of his master aroused the admiration of the twenty-five-year-old vassal, and must have given him much food for thought, causing him to reflect on the madness of the proposals and plots against such a power in little, far-off Jerusalem. It was his fate, however, that any such impression could be quickly canceled out of his memory, and he would yield to others exactly opposite. When he returned to tiny Jerusalem he

---

[16] For Psammetichus' real reason for a trip to Phoenicia, cf. *Cambridge Ancient History*, III, 300 f.

became an easy prey of the anti-Babylonian faction; pseudo-prophets became ever more numerous and aggressive and aroused the people with
impassioned exhortations and symbolic actions, prefiguring the imminent self-rule of the kingdom (Jer. 28:37, 19), while the Temple at Jerusalem was becoming the center of various idolatrous cults (Ezech. 8).
For a year or so things remained at a standstill, and everything seemed
calm, but it was a deceptive calm — the quiet which precedes a storm.
The momentary equilibrium was due to three factors: in the center
was the fanaticism of the anti-Babylonian faction of Jerusalem; on one
side was the armed and ready vigilance of Babylonia, counterbalanced
on the other by the neutrality of Egypt. Once the counterbalance was
removed, Babylonia would cast itself upon Jerusalem.

535. The last factor was removed in 588 with the death of the Pharaoh
Psammetichus. His successor Hophra (§ 42) abandoned the principle of
non-intervention in Asia followed up to that time, and looked favorably
upon the troubled strivings of the anti-Babylonian faction beyond
the Delta. The Egyptian faction of the kingdom of Juda was then
no longer controllable. The longed-for moment for action had arrived.
Every measure of prudence with respect to Babylonia was abandoned, and the unwarlike Sedecias, with his doubts and fears, was carried
along by the current of enthusiasm which flooded Jerusalem and the kingdom. The old undercover relations existing among the various Palestinian
states resulted in the immediate formation of a league, composed, as
in the time of Ezechias (§ 490 ff.), of a vanguard of Palestinian states
with Egypt as the principal member. Hophra without further ado joined
the league. Not only did Juda and Ammon (Ezech. 21:25 [Vulgate, 20])
form part of the vanguard but probably also others of those nations
which had sent their messengers to the convention of 593 at Jerusalem
(§ 533), and certainly maritime Phoenicia with Tyre at its head. Starting
from the sea, military operations were begun in 588. With Tyre the
base of his maritime operations, the Pharaoh brought the Phoenician
hinterland also under his sway. The Chaldeans had to pass him in
order to attack the rebels, and the Pharaoh, probably not yet outfitted
with land forces, intended to raise as many obstacles as possible in the
way of their advance, at the same time utilizing his naval forces, the
support of Tyre, and the local Phoenician resources.

536. Nabuchodonosor, suspicious and armed for a long time, did not
delay his reply. Departing from Babylonia with a strong army, he made
a sudden appearance on the scene in the same year, 588. He established
his headquarters at Ribla on the Orontes (as Nechao had done before him; § 520), so as to dominate the entire theater from the north.
Thence he directed the entire campaign with a sure eye and rare skill.
The heart of the league, Egypt, was at that time out of reach, operating

indirectly by way of the sea. The vanguard of the league which was to be immediately attacked presented a chainlike front: Phoenicia along the Mediterranean, Ammon in Transjordan, Juda in the center. Phoenicia was to be attacked after the other two sectors because it could with Egyptian sea support prolong its resistance indefinitely, and would allow the Pharaoh time to bring up re-enforcements. Ammon and Juda were the remaining choices and Nabuchodonosor, hesitating for a moment over which of the two to attack first (Ezech. 21:26-27 [Vulgate, 21-22]), decided on Juda, center of the vanguard. It was a classical example of frontal attack.

The Chaldean divisions beat down all resistance and wedged themselves between Phoenicia and Transjordan. They invaded all of Juda and soon there remained unconquered of the fortresses of the kingdom only Lachish (§ 74), Azeka (§ 75), and Jerusalem (Jer. 34:7). On the tenth day of the tenth month (December–January) of the ninth year of the reign of Sedecias (the year 588), the Chaldean army began the siege of Jerusalem (2 Kings 25:1). When this city fell the vanguard of the league would be split in two, and Nabuchodonosor would have a clear road to Egypt. While the siege was in progress, he also guarded against attack from the Mediterranean, the only flank on which he could be threatened. Part of his army he sent against Phoenicia, and rapidly subjugated it except for Tyre, inaccessible on its rock. He left a division there to begin a siege which lasted thirteen years, according to Menander, and the queen of the seas finally fell in 573.

537. The defense of besieged Jerusalem was protracted for eighteen months and was truly heroic. Its natural position (§ 96 ff.) re-enforced by the improvements of centuries, the confident courage of its defenders in the first phase, and the desperation begotten by the realization that there was no escape in the second phase, contributed to this heroism.

As usual, during times of siege, many people poured into the city from the countryside, and among these were the Rechabites (Jer. 35; cf. § 493). There was no lack of combatants. From the beginning even the slaves, who were given a freedom later unfairly revoked (Jer. 34:8 ff.), were armed; at the beginning too, they must have been well provided with arms and foodstuffs. For the rest, no one dreamed of defeating the Chaldeans or chasing them away; the essential thing was to resist in Jerusalem, to give the Pharaoh time to finish his preparations and enter the war with his troops. How welcome the Egyptians would be when they arrived to defeat and chase out the Chaldeans! It was essential not to give up before their arrival, for Egypt stood for definite victory.

The morale of the besieged during this confident wait was high. In the besieged city, however, was one man — at least there is explicit

information of only one man — who did not share in the general
confidence, and who furthermore demoralized the combatants by publicly crying out in a loud voice that they should yield to the Chaldeans.
His name was Jeremias. Such a defeatist of course wound up in
prison, and then was thrown like a dog into a muddy cistern. He later
returned to prison, but under this tempest of persecution he "did not
move his neck nor bend his side," with sublime obstinacy replying
publicly to the people and to the trembling Sedecias who consulted him
in secret that it would be to the advantage of all to yield to the Chaldeans (Jer. 37:38). He had confidence, better still, he had certainty.
While he was in prison affirming the imminent fall of the city and
the destruction of the kingdom, he bought a field located in the attractive
district of Anathoth (§ 382) from one of his cousins. He had a regular
contract drawn up, and took steps to have the document preserved with
care for future generations, although the field was in the sector already
occupied by the enemy. Jeremias wished by this transaction to express
his own certainty of the consolation which, after the imminent desolation,
Yahweh would bestow upon his country (Jer. 32).

A modern historian is in a better position to judge these events,
after the lapse of twenty-six centuries. If he were to look in that
epoch for the genuine Israel, he would find it in that obstinate, imprisoned defeatist, rather than in the courageous defenders of Jerusalem.

538. The dawn of victory finally appeared. The siege of Jerusalem
had lasted exactly one year (cf. Ezech. 29:1, which reckons from 597),
when information arrived that the Pharaoh Hophra was coming from
Egypt with his army. He was doubtless heading for Phoenicia, which
at that time was falling bit by bit into the hands of Nabuchodonosor,
and he probably also had hopes of liberating Jerusalem from its siege.
The Chaldeans, to prevent being taken in the rear, turned about and
headed south to meet the Pharaoh, a move which obliged them to
interrupt the siege of Jerusalem and leave that city to their rear. But
they had nothing to fear from a city so exhausted by the siege.

What a day of exultation it was for the besieged when they saw the
Chaldeans withdraw from the walls of the city! After such great tribula-
tion, they saw their hopes almost fulfilled. At any moment now news of
the destruction of the Chaldeans would arrive and the augury of the
times of Ezechias (§ 497) would, thanks to Yahweh, be repeated with the
help of the other gods newly introduced into the Temple (§ 534). Only
Jeremias took no part in the exultation. Over and over he repeated: "Behold, the army of the Pharaoh which is come forth to help you, shall
return into its own land, Egypt. The Chaldeans shall also come again
and shall fight against this city, and shall take it and shall burn it with
fire! Thus saith Yahweh: Deceive not yourselves, saying: 'The Chal-

deans have surely departed from us!' for they shall not go away. Even
if you should beat all the army of the Chaldeans who fight against you,
and only wounded men should be left of them, each one would arise in
his tent and they would burn this city with fire" (Jer. 37:6–10). The
intransigence of the prophet was based therefore on a theological vision
of history: it was the will of Yahweh which ordered events.

539. Proportioned to the anxiety of awaiting for the Egyptians was
the exultant joy at the interruption of the siege. The disillusionment
was therefore tragic. A veil as it were of national pride conceals at this
point the record of events. Even Jeremias, so generous in his patriotism,
does not dwell on the humiliation of his fellow countrymen, although he
might well have reproached them with his own facile triumph. But we
know from Ezechiel (Ezech. 30:20 ff.) that Yahweh had "broken the
arm of the pharaoh." In ordinary language, the Pharaoh had suffered a
grave and decisive defeat. This defeat could not have been that of
Carchemish, for that had happened twenty years before (§ 524); it
was the contemporary defeat suffered by Hophra. At any rate,
whether he was defeated or withdrew of his own will, shortly after
his exit the Pharaoh definitely returned to the Delta without having given
any help to his allies, the Palestinian states, but left them to their fate.
The Chaldeans, relieved so soon of the Egyptians, resumed the siege
of Jerusalem.

Their real situation in all its tragic horror then dawned upon the
besieged. Nabuchodonosor, furious because of repeated rebellions and
obstinate resistance, would surely mete out the usual punishments,
slaughter and mass deportations when the city was taken; and no help
could now be expected from others. To continue the defense in the
circumstances to which the city was reduced was to court death both
from within and without. In these circumstances, too, Jeremias counseled
yielding to the Chaldeans so as to avoid ultimate ruin. Twice after
the siege was resumed, the vacillating Sedecias secretly consulted the
imprisoned prophet (Jer. 37:17 ff.; 37:14 ff.), to ascertain whether "there
was any word on the part of Yahweh" and to learn what was to be
done, but he was not strong-willed enough to break away from the
influence of the anti-Babylonian ringleaders and follow the advice of
the prophet. The "word of Yahweh" (§ 427) he hoped for was perhaps that Yahweh would never permit the profanation of his Temple
and his city by the Chaldeans under Nabuchodonosor, as he had not
permitted it to the Assyrians under Sennacherib (cf. Lam. 4:12; Jer.
7:4). Instead he heard the reply: "You will fall into the hands of the
king of Babel!" (Jer. 37:17), and so it was that, with the angry courage
born of despair, they went ahead.

540. The second siege did not last long, as the besieged were in such straitened circumstances. The *Lamentations* furnish some particulars on this point and although they are presented in poetic dress, they are strictly historical facts. Outside the walls the sword threatened slaughter; inside hunger with its ally, disease (Lam. 1:20), decimated the inhabitants. Those who were killed by the sword were considered fortunate, compared to those who suffered the agonies of hunger (4:9). The countenances of all were transformed by suffering (4:8); the wealthiest were seen to stagger along the streets and fall, spent, on dung-heaps; and hunger so brutalized them that mothers cooked and ate their own children (Lam. 4:10; 2:20), as they had during the siege of Samaria (§ 441), and would do later during the siege of Jerusalem under Titus (Josephus, *War of the Jews,* VI, 3, 3).

541. On the ninth day of the fourth month (June–July) of the eleventh year of King Sedecias, the Chaldeans succeeded in breaching the walls of the city (Jer. 39:2; 52:5–7; 2 Kings 25:2–4). In the confusion of the invasion and under cover of the night, the king and the chief Jewish captains succeeded in fleeing, through a secret path in the royal gardens on Ophel (§ 96), to the southeast of the city. Once outside they fled toward Jericho, perhaps intending to cross the tip of the Dea Sea and escape by that road to Egypt, where they would be safe from the Chaldeans. They may also have intended to seek refuge in the kingdom of Ammon (§§ 536, 544). When the Chaldeans learned of the flight, however, they pursued and caught up with the group on the plains of Jericho, where the captains abandoned their king; he was taken prisoner, and led before Nabuchodonosor at his headquarters in Ribla (§ 536).

Sargon II blinding his prisoners.

The Babylonians pronounced the customary sentence: Sedecias' children were killed before his eyes, and then the eyes of the wretched father were put out, their last sight that of the death of his own children. Finally he was sent in chains to Babylonia, where he died in prison. He was the last monarch of the dynasty of David.

542. The capital and the conquered kingdom remained. After these repeated rebellions Nabuchodonosor was no longer to be satisfied with a simple substitution of rulers, new confiscations or heavier tribute. He decreed that the capital and the kingdom be destroyed. One month after the capture of Jerusalem (2 Kings 25:8; Jer. 52:12), during which the city was thoroughly sacked and its inhabitants made sport of by the

Chaldean soldiers (Lam. 5:11 ff.), the Chaldean leaders, acting on orders from headquarters, stripped the Temple and the palace of anything precious that remained and sent it to Babel (2 Kings 25:13–17; Jer. 52:17–23). Next they proceeded to burn the house of Yahweh, the house of the king, and private homes. Lastly the walls and fortifications of Israel were demolished. With this the "city of David," the pride of Israel and dwelling place of Yahweh, became a heap of ruins and charred timbers, a place where the foxes and jackals soon came to prowl (Lam. 5:18; Jer. 9:10).

Mass deportation was again the order of the day for the people of the realm. The more notorious ringleaders of the anti-Babylonian faction, some eighty persons in all, were led to Ribla and there slain before Nabuchodonosor (2 Kings 25:18–21; Jer. 52:24–27). This second deportation — the first was in 597 (§ 530) — included the deserters who went over to the Chaldeans during the war, the citizens of the more important centers of the kingdom, the rich, and other persons more in the public eye. In general, however, the citizenry (§ 456), especially the vinedressers and peasants (2 Kings 25:11–12; Jer. 39:10; 40:7), were left behind; they were needed to cultivate the fields, and were less likely to embroil themselves in politics or incite further revolts. The number of those deported cannot be given even approximately, as the only number given in the biblical account, 832 persons for Jerusalem, in Jer. 52:29, does not certainly refer to all the culprits in this deportation nor even to all of those from Jerusalem, but to a definite social category or to a district, according to criteria which today it is impossible to check. The deportees were settled in various localities of Babylonia according to the exigencies of colonization, but they were good locations and pleasant enough, especially those close to Babel, which Nabuchodonosor was then enlarging and rebuilding (cf. Berossus, in Josephus, *Antiquities,* X, 11, 1).

543. Godolias, a Jew friendly to the Chaldeans and a Yahwist, was made governor over the people left in the country. Jerusalem being no longer fit for habitation, he set up residence in Mispah (§ 89) where he immediately began work as reorganizer of the people and pacifier of their Chaldean overlord, who seemed to be rather well-disposed toward them. In this work he had the invaluable assistance of Jeremias. When Jerusalem fell, the Chaldeans who knew his attitude full well treated the prophet with respect. Liberated from prison (Jer. 38:11–14), he had remained in the city a free and protected man. Later on, however, in the confusion attendant upon the deportation, he was mistakenly chained and sent to Rama where the deportees were held. The error was discovered and he was loosed from his bonds and given his choice of following the deportees into Babylonia as a free man, or of remaining

in his own country. He chose to remain, and returned to Mispah with Godolias (Jer. 40:1–6). By co-operating with Godolias he hoped at least to initiate the moral resurrection of his own nation, in which he had always hoped (§ 537).

544. The desolate land, however, was not destined to have peace yet, for the same reason that it had lost it. The delicate work of reconstruction undertaken by Godolias and Jeremias was set at naught by the stubbornness of the anti-Babylonians, for not all the fanatics had fallen into the hands of the Chaldeans and been taken to Babylonia. Some of them had fled to the country where they led a life of violence and brigandage. Once the Chaldean army had withdrawn they began to gather in groups which grew larger and larger with the return of other refugees returning from nearby Moab, Ammon, and Edom. They too had their own plans for the reconstruction of the prostrate nation, and they at once opposed Godolias, the representative of the Chaldeans. The kingdom of Ammon, which had taken part in the unfortunate league (§ 536), directed the conspirators, and the Ammonite king, Baalis, a scant two months after Godolias had assumed the burden of government, secretly dispatched a cutthroat named Ismael to kill him. Godolias, warned, generously refused to believe the story. A few days later at Mispah, along with other Chaldean officials of his court, Ismael's hand struck him down.

545. The more moderate groups of Judeans were terrified at this assassination, knowing what vengeance the Chaldeans would exact for it. They sought Ismael and the conspirators in order to punish them, thereby demonstrating their disapproval and disavowing all participation in it, but Ismael succeeded in getting away and found refuge in Ammon. Then, seeing that they were compromised in the eyes of the Chaldeans, the others decided to flee to Egypt. Desirous of knowing the word of Yahweh concerning their departure, they first consulted Jeremias. After a long "silence" (§ 428) the prophet received the reply from Yahweh: the miserable remnants of the destroyed nation should not go down to the prosperous, alluring region of the Nile, but should rather stay in their own land to be seed for the rebirth of the nation. When the prophet communicated this oracle to them he was not believed; instead he was accused of adulterating the "word of Yahweh" for political reasons. Still, when the journey toward Egypt actually started, they were afraid to be separated from the venerable old man, and took him with them, against his will, into Egypt (Jer. 40:7–43:7).

There is the simple mention (Jer. 52:30) of a third deportation carried out by a high Chaldean official in the twenty-third year of the reign of Nabuchodonosor (the year 582); it is likely that this was occasioned by other local disorders, stirred up among the survivors by fanatical adventurers like Ismael.

Finally, it is most important to note that neither during these deportations nor afterward did the Chaldeans ever bring in other peoples in any great number to repopulate the depopulated region. The territory of the kingdom of Israel was contaminated by the Samaritans (§ 457) and fared differently than the territory of the kingdom of Juda, which was preserved from foreign immigration, and was host only to the few survivors of the catastrophe.

With the departure of Jeremias the real Israel was uprooted from the soil of Juda. Idle winter had now to descend upon this soil; next would come the turn of the renovating plow, while the pure seed destined for this soil was being readied elsewhere, far, far away.

Index

References are to paragraphs, *not* pages.